K. 7635 IGNITION.

FIAT X1/9 Owners Workshop Manual

J H Haynes
Member of the Guild of Motoring Writers
and B Gilmour

Models covered
All FIAT and Bertone X1/9 models,
including special and limited editions
1290 cc & 1498 cc

(273-8T7)   ABCDF
FGH

2

Haynes THE BOOK ®

Haynes Publishing Group
Sparkford Nr Yeovil
Somerset BA22 7JJ England

Haynes Publications, Inc
861 Lawrence Drive
Newbury Park
California 91320 USA

Restoring and Preserving our Motoring Heritage

Few people can have had the luck to realise their dreams to quite the same extent and in such a remarkable fashion as John Haynes, Founder and Chairman of the Haynes Publishing Group.

Since 1965 his unique approach to workshop manual publishing has proved so successful that millions of Haynes Manuals are now sold every year throughout the world, covering literally thousands of different makes and models of cars, vans and motorcycles.

A continuing passion for cars and motoring led to the founding in 1985 of a Charitable Trust dedicated to the restoration and preservation of our motoring heritage. To inaugurate the new Museum, John Haynes donated virtually his entire private collection of 52 cars.

Now with an unrivalled international collection of over 210 veteran, vintage and classic cars and motorcycles, the Haynes Motor Museum in Somerset is well on the way to becoming one of the most interesting Motor Museums in the world.

A 70 seat video cinema, a cafe and an extensive motoring bookshop, together with a specially constructed one kilometre motor circuit, make a visit to the Haynes Motor Museum a truly unforgettable experience.

Every vehicle in the museum is preserved in as near as possible mint condition and each car is run every six months on the motor circuit.

Enjoy the picnic area set amongst the rolling Somerset hills. Peer through the William Morris workshop windows at cars being restored, and browse through the extensive displays of fascinating motoring memorabilia.

From the 1903 Oldsmobile through such classics as an MG Midget to the mighty 'E' type Jaguar, Lamborghini, Ferrari Berlinetta Boxer, and Graham Hill's Lola Cosworth, there is something for everyone, young and old alike, at this Somerset Museum.

Haynes Motor Museum

Situated mid-way between London and Penzance, the Haynes Motor Museum is located just off the A303 at Sparkford, Somerset (home of the Haynes Manual) and is open to the public 7 days a week all year round, except Christmas Day and Boxing Day.

Telephone 01963 440804.

Acknowledgements

Thanks are due to the Champion Sparking Plug Company Limited, who supplied the illustrations showing spark plug conditions, and to Holt Lloyd Limited who supplied the illustrations showing bodywork repair. Thanks are also due to FIAT for their assistance with technical information and the supply of certain illustrations. Sykes-Pickavant provided some of the workshop tools. Lastly, thanks are due to all those people at Sparkford who assisted in the production of this manual.

© **Haynes Publishing Group 1991**

A book in the **Haynes Owners Workshop Manual Series**

Printed by J. H. Haynes & Co. Ltd., Sparkford, Nr Yeovil, Somerset BA22 7JJ, England

ISBN 1 85010 634 7

Whilst every care is taken to ensure that the information in this manual is correct, no liability can be accepted by the authors or publishers for loss, damage or injury caused by any errors in, or omissions from, the information given.

Contents

Fiat XI/9 - 1977 European specification model

About this manual

Its aim

The aim of this manual is to help you get the best value from your car. It can do so in several ways. It can help you decide what work must be done (even should you choose to get it done by a garage), provide information on routine maintenance and servicing, and give a logical course of action and diagnosis when random faults occur. However, it is hoped that you will use the manual by tackling the work yourself. On simpler jobs it may even be quicker than booking the car into a garage and going there twice to leave and collect it. Perhaps most important, a lot of money can be saved by avoiding the costs the garage must charge to cover its labour and overheads.

The manual has drawings and descriptions to show the function of the various components so that their layout can be understood. Then the tasks are described and photographed in a step-by-step sequence so that even a novice can do the work.

Its arrangement

The manual is divided into thirteen Chapters, each covering a logical sub-division of the vehicle. The Chapters are each divided into Sections, numbered with single figures, eg 5; and the Sections into paragraphs (or sub-sections), with decimal numbers following on from the Section they are in, eg 5.1, 5.2, 5.3 etc.

It is freely illustrated, especially in those parts where there is a detailed sequence of operations to be carried out. There are two forms of illustration: figures and photographs. The figures are numbered in sequence with decimal numbers, according to their position in the Chapter — eg Fig. 6.4 is the fourth drawing/illustration in Chapter 6. Photographs carry the same number (either individually or in related groups) as the Section or sub-section to which they relate.

There is an alphabetical index at the back of the manual as well as a contents list at the front. Each Chapter is also preceded by its own individual contents list.

References to the 'left' or 'right' of the vehicle are in the sense of a person in the driver's seat facing forwards.

Unless otherwise stated, nuts and bolts are removed by turning anti-clockwise, and tightened by turning clockwise.

Vehicle manufacturers continually make changes to specifications and recommendations, and these when notified are incorporated into our manuals at the earliest opportunity.

Whilst every care is taken to ensure that the information in this manual is correct, no liability can be accepted by the authors or publishers for loss, damage or injury caused by any errors in, or omissions from, the information given.

Introduction to the Fiat X1/9

With the introduction of the X1/9, FIAT have produced a small sports car that is very different from its competitors. They have departed from the conventional front-engine rear-drive production sports cars and adopted the mid-engined arrangement used on most competition cars.

To meet safety standards, the bodyframe and doors are specially reinforced to offset the loss of rigidity resulting from the 'Targa-Top'

body style. A roll-over bar is built into the body structure behind the cockpit.

The fibreglass roof section can easily be removed by one person and stored in the front luggage compartment.

The X1/9's 'wedge' shape not only looks good, but is very functional, providing 7 cu ft of luggage space, and having very good aerodynamics.

Buying spare parts and vehicle identification numbers

Buying spare parts

Spare parts are available from many sources, for example: FIAT garages, other garages and accessory shops, and motor factors. Our advice regarding spare part sources is as follows:

Officially appointed FIAT garages - This is the best source of parts which are peculiar to your car and are otherwise not generally available (eg; complete cylinder heads, internal gearbox components, badges, interior trim etc). It is also the only place at which you should buy parts if your car is still under warranty - non-FIAT components may invalidate the warranty. To be sure of obtaining the correct parts it will always be necessary to give the partsman your car's engine number, chassis number and number for spares, and if possible, to take the 'old' part along for positive identification. Remember that many parts are available on a factory exchange scheme - any parts returned should always be clean! It obviously makes good sense to go straight to the specialists on your car for this type of part for they are best equipped to supply you. They will also be able to provide their own Fiat service manual for your car should you require one.

Other garages and accessory shops - These are often very good places to buy materials and components needed for the maintenance of your car (eg; oil filters, spark plugs, bulbs, fan belts, oils and greases, touch-up paint, filler paste etc). They also sell general accessories, usually have convenient opening hours, charge lower prices and can often be found not far from home.

Motor factors - Good factors will stock all of the more important components which wear out relatively quickly (eg; clutch components, pistons, valves, exhaust systems, brake cylinders/pipes/hoses/seals and pads etc). Motor factors will often provide new or reconditioned

components on a part exchange basis - this can save a considerable amount of money.

Vehicle identification numbers

It is important the appropriate identity number for the model or sub-assembly is quoted when a spare part is ordered. The identification data plates may vary depending on the market.

USA

Vehicle plate. This is located on the right-hand side in the front luggage compartment.

Engine type and number. This is stamped on the crankcase at the flywheel end.

Chassis type and number. This is stamped on the front luggage compartment cross-rail, right-hand side.

Tyre data and capacity. This is located on the right-hand door pillar.

Emission control details. This is on a plate located on the underside of the engine compartment bonnet.

UK

Chassis type and number. This is stamped on the front luggage compartment cross-rail, right-hand side.

Engine type and number. This is stamped on the crankcase at the flywheel end.

Data plate, including type approval reference, chassis type and number, engine type, number for spares and paintwork colour reference. This is located on the right-hand side in the front luggage compartment.

The vehicle identification plate is located on the right-hand side in the front luggage compartment and gives the following information:

Chassis type
Order number for spares (preceded by the letter 'A' which identifies the North American version)
Engine type
Paint colour number

The engine number is stamped on the crankcase at the flywheel end

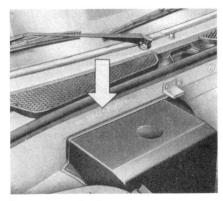

The chassis number is on the crossrail in the front luggage compartment

Tyre data and car capacity plate is on the right-hand door pillar

Air pollution control specifications for engine tuning and adjustment are on a plate on the underside of the engine bonnet

Location of spare wheel behind front seat

Location of jack in rear luggage boot

Using car jack

Routine maintenance

For modifications see Supplement at end of manual

1 Introduction

In the Sections that follow are detailed the routine servicing that should be done on the car. This work has the prime aim of doing adjustments and lubrication to ensure the least wear and most efficient function. But there is another important gain. By looking the car over, on top and underneath, you have the opportunity to check that all is in order.

Every component should be looked at, your gaze working systematically over the whole car. Dirt cracking near a nut or a flange can indicate something loose. Leaks will show. Electric cables rubbing, or rust appearing through the underneath paint will all be found before they bring on a failure on the road, or if not tackled quickly, a more expensive repair. Also it prevents the car becoming a danger to yourself or others because of an undetected defect.

The tasks to be done are in general those recommended by the maker. But we have also put in some additional ones which will help to keep your car in good order. For someone getting his service done at a garage it may be more cost effective to accept component replacement after a somewhat short life in order to avoid labour costs. For the home mechanic this tends not to be so.

When you are checking the car, and find something that looks wrong, look it up in the appropriate Chapter. If something seems to be working badly, look in the fault-finding section.

Always drive the car on a road test after a repair, and then inspect the repair is holding up all right, and check nuts or hose connections for tightness. Check again after about another 150 miles (250 km).

Other aspects of routine maintenance

Jacking-up. Always chock a wheel on the opposite side, in front and behind. The car's own jack has to be able to work when the car is very low with a flat tyre, so it goes in a socket on the side, taking up both wheels on that side. Using a small jack at one wheel is more secure when work has to be done. There are jacking points reinforced in the centre of the car at front and rear for a trolley jack. Never put a jack under the bodywork or the thin sheet steel will buckle.

Wheel bolts. These should be cleaned and lightly smeared with grease as necessary during work, to keep them moving easily. If the bolts are stubborn to undo due to dirt and overtightening, it may be necessary to hold them by lowering the jack till the wheel rubs on the ground. Normally if the wheel brace is used across the hub centre, a foot held against the tyre will prevent the wheel from turning, and so save the wheels and bolts from the wear when they are slackened with weight on the wheel. After replacing a wheel make a point later of rechecking again for tightness.

Safety. Whenever working, even partially, under the car, supplement the workshop jack with axle stands placed one each side under the sill jacking points.

Cleanliness. Keep the mechanical parts of the car clean. It is much more pleasant to work on a clean car. Whenever doing any work, allow time for cleaning. When something is in pieces, components removed improve access to other areas and give an opportunity for a thorough clean. This cleanliness will allow you to cope with a crisis on the road without getting yourself dirty. During bigger jobs when you expect a bit of dirt it is less extreme. When something is taken to pieces there is less risk of ruinous grit getting inside. The act of cleaning focusses your attention on parts, and you are then more likely to spot trouble. Dirt on the ignition parts is a common cause of poor starting. Large areas such as the bulkheads of the engine compartment, should be brushed thoroughly with a detergent like GUNK, allowed to soak for about ¼ hour, then carefully hosed with water. Water in the wrong places, particularly the carburettor or electrical components will do more harm than dirt. Detailed cleaning can be done with paraffin (kerosene) and an old paint brush. Petrol cleans better, but remember the hazard of fire, and if used in a confined space, of fumes. Use a barrier cream on the hands.

Waste disposal. Old oil and cleaning paraffin must be destroyed. It makes a good base for a bonfire, but is dangerous. Never have an open container near a naked flame. Pour the old oil where it cannot run uncontrolled. *Before* you light it. Light it by making a 'fuse' of news-paper. By buying your oil in one gallon cans you have these for storage of the old oil. The old oil is not household rubbish, so should not be put in the dustbin (trash can). Take it to your local garage.

Long journeys. Before taking the car on a long journey, particularly a long holiday trip, do in advance many of the maintenance tasks that would not normally be due before going. In the first instance, do jobs that would be due soon anyway. Then also those that would not come up until well into the trip. Also do the other tasks that are just checks, as a form of insurance against trouble. For emergencies carry on the car some copper wire, plastic insulation tape, plastic petrol pipe, gasket compound, and repair material of the plastics resin type. Carry a spare 'V' belt, and some spare bulbs. About 3 ft (0.9 metres) of electric cable, and some odd metric nuts and bolts should complete your car's first aid kit. Also carry a human first aid kit; some plasters, antiseptic ointment, etc., in case you get minor cuts.

On purchase. If you have bought your car brand new, you will have the maker's instructions for the early special checks on a new car. If you have just bought a second hand car then our advice is to reckon it has not been looked after properly, and so do all the checks, lubrication and other tasks on that basis, assuming all mileages and time tasks are overdue.

2 Every 300 miles (500 km) or weekly

1 Check the engine oil level. This should be done with the car stand-ing on level ground. Never allow the oil level to fall below the low mark. Do not overfill. Only replenish with the same type of oil as is in the sump.
2 Check the coolant level in the expansion tank. The expansion tank cap should only be removed when the engine is cold. Should it be necessary to remove the cap when the engine is hot, it should be

allowed to cool a little, then the pressure should be released by gradually turning the cap, while holding it with some rag to protect the hand. Top-up with coolant. This should not be necessary very often. A need to top-up frequently indicates a fault in the cooling system, refer to Chapter 2.
3 Check the tyre pressures. This should be done when they are cold. After running a few miles the pressure rises due to the heat generated by their flexing. The tyre pressures cold should be:

Front	*26 psi (1.8 kg/sq cm)*
Rear	*28 psi (2 kg/sq cm)*

4 Check the level of the brake and clutch fluid reservoirs. This can be seen without removing the cap. There should be no need for regular topping-up: if it is needed check for leaks. Use only DOT 3 fluid to FMVSS No. 116 specification. Always use new fluid.
5 Top-up the battery, if necessary, to ½ inch (13 mm) above the plates with distilled water.
6 Check the engine compartment for leaks.
7 Check all lights are in order.

3 Every 6,000 miles (10,000 km) or 6 months, whichever comes first

1 Change the engine oil and filter. Drain the oil when warm. A 12 mm Allen key is needed to undo the drain plug in the sump. Refit the plug after draining. Remove the splash shield underneath the filter and place a container under the filter, to catch the oil, and unscrew the filter. If it is tight use a strap wrench. Smear oil on the new sealing ring and fit the new filter, screwing it on hand-tight only.
Note: For stop-start driving in town or in dusty areas, change the engine oil and filter every 3,000 miles (5,000 km). Change the oil every

Front lifting bracket for workshop jack

Rear lifting bracket for workshop jack

Engine oil filler and dipstick

Check the level in the brake fluid reservoirs

Check the level in the clutch fluid reservoir

Use a 12 mm Allen key to remove the engine sump drain plug

6 months if the specified mileage is not covered in this time.
2   Check engine idling speed.
3   Renew the fuel filter. When fitting a new filter, make sure it is fitted as indicated by the arrow on the body. Ensure connections are tightened.
4   Check that the spark plug electrode gap is as specified in Chapter 4, and adjust if necessary. If the plugs are in poor condition, renew them as a set.
5   Check and adjust the contact breaker gap and lubricate the distrub
distributor. Refer to Chapter 4, Sections 2 and 3.
6   Check and reset the ignition timing. Refer to Chapter 4, Section 4.
7   Check clutch adjustment. Refer to Chapter 5, Section 2.
8   Check the transmission oil level. Remove the level/filler plug using a 12 mm Allen key. Top-up if necessary, use oil in a plastic container so that the tube can be put straight into the filler hole.
9   Check brake pads for wear.
10 Check seat belts for condition and security.

4   Every 12,000 miles (20,000 km) or 12 months, whichever comes first

In addition to, or instead of, the 6000 mile service operations

1   Check timing belt condition and tension (Chapter 1, Section 5).
2   Check valve clearances. Refer to Chapter 1, Section 29.
3   Check cylinder compression.
4   Check coolant antifreeze concentration.
5   Check all coolant and fuel hoses for condition and security.
6   Check exhaust system for condition and security.
7   Renew air cleaner element.
8   Check emission control system components. Refer to Chapter 3, Sections 14 to 16 (if applicable).

9   Renew contact breaker points and spark plugs.
10 Check brake pipes and hoses for condition and security.
11 Check the operation of the handbrake. Adjust the tensioner, if necessary. Access to the tensioner is provided by an opening under the body.
12 Check brake calipers for leakage.
13 Check headlamp alignment.
14 Check tension of alternator drivebelt.
15 Clean battery terminals, and apply petroleum jelly.
16 Check battery output.
17 Check front wheel alignment.
18 Check steering components for condition and security.
19 Check tyres for uneven wear, tread depth, cuts etc.
20 Check front wheel bearings.

5   Every 24,000 miles (40,000 km) or 2 years, whichever comes first

In addition to, or instead of, the 12,000 mile service operations

1   Renew coolant.
2   Renew transmission oil.
3   Renew hydraulic fluid.

6   Every 36,000 miles (60,000 km) or 3 years, whichever comes first

In addition to the 12,000 mile service operations

1   Renew the toothed timing belt.

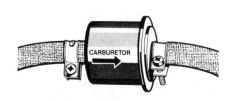

Fit the filter the right way round

Unscrew the wing nut, remove the cover and change the air pump filter cartridge

Change the transmission oil A - Drain plug B - Filler/level plug. Use a 12 mm Allen key when removing plugs

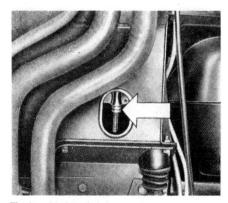

The handbrake adjusting nut is accessible from underneath the car

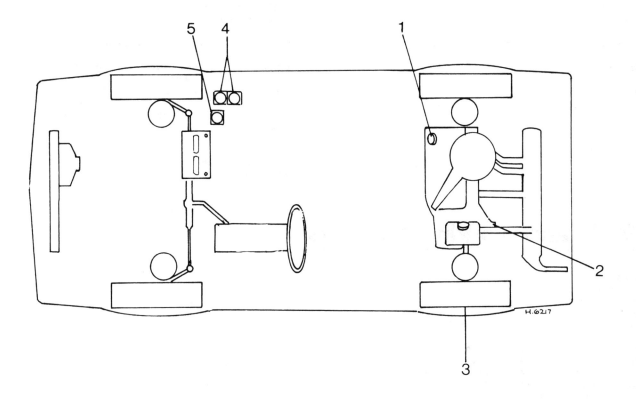

Recommended lubricants and fluids

Component or system	Lubricant type or specification
Engine (1)	Oliofiat VS+ Quattro Stagioni (SAE 15W/40 oil)
Gearbox and final drive (2)	Oliofiat ZC90 (SAE 80W/90 oil – not EP)
Constant velocity joints (outer) (3)	Grassofiat MRM2 (lithium based grease with molybdenum disulphide)
Braking system (4)	Liquido FIAT Etichetta Azzurra DOT 3 (FMVSS 116 DOT 3)
Clutch (5)	Liquido FIAT Etichetta Azzurra DOT 3 (FMVSS 116 DOT 3)

Note: *The above are general recommendations only. Lubrication requirements vary from territory to territory and depend on vehicle usage. If in doubt, consult the operator's handbook supplied with the vehicle, or your nearest dealer.*

General dimensions, weights and capacities

For information applicable to later models see Supplement at end of manual

Dimensions and weights*

Length	3830 mm (150.93 in)
Width	1570 mm (61.8 in)
Height	1170 mm (46.1 in)
Wheelbase	2202 mm (86.7 in)
Track (front)	1335 mm (52.5 in)
Track (rear)	1343 mm (52.9 in)
Kerb weight	880 kg (1940 lbs)

Due to differing specifications according to operating territory, the above dimensions and weights are given only as a guide.

Capacities

	Litres	Imp. units	US units
Engine sump and filter	4.25	7.4 pts	4 1/3 qts
Cooling system	6.5	11.5 pts	7 qts
Fuel tank	49	11 gals	12 gals
Transmission	3.15	5 3/4 pts	3 1/3 qts
Steering box	0.14	0.25 pts	1/3 pt

Tyre pressures

Front (cold)	26 psi (1.8 kg/sq cm)
Rear (cold)	28 psi (2 kg/sq cm)

Tools and working facilities

Introduction

A selection of good tools is a fundamental requirement for anyone contemplating the maintenance and repair of a motor vehicle. For the owner who does not possess any, their purchase will prove a considerable expense, offsetting some of the savings made by doing-it-yourself. However, provided that the tools purchased meet the relevant national safety standards and are of good quality, they will last for many years and prove an extremely worthwhile investment.

To help the average owner to decide which tools are needed to carry out the various tasks detailed in this manual, we have compiled three lists of tools under the following headings: Maintenance and minor repair, Repair and overhaul, and Special. The newcomer to practical mechanics should start off with the 'Maintenance and minor repair' tool kit and confine himself to the simpler jobs around the vehicle. Then, as his confidence grows, he can undertake more difficult tasks, buying extra tools as, and when, they are needed. In this way, a 'Maintenance and minor repair' tool kit can be built-up into a 'Repair and overhaul' tool kit over a considerable period of time without any major cash outlays. The experienced do-it-yourselfer will have a tool kit good enough for most repair and overhaul procedures and will add tools from the 'Special' category when he feels the expense is justified by the amount of use these tools will be put to.

It is obviously not possible to cover the subject of tools fully here. For those who wish to learn more about tools and their use there is a book entitled 'How to Choose and Use Car Tools' available from the publishers of this manual.

Maintenance and minor repair tool kit

The tools given in this list should be considered as a minimum requirement if routine maintenance, servicing and minor repair operations are to be undertaken. We recommend the purchase of combination spanners (ring one end, open-ended the other); although more expensive than open-ended ones, they do give the advantages of both types of spanner.

Combination spanners - 10, 11,13,14,17 mm
Adjustable spanner 9 inch
Engine sump/gearbox/rear axle drain key (where applicable)
Spark plug spanner (with rubber insert)
Spark plug gap adjustment tool
Set of feeler gauges

Brake bleed nipple spanner
Screwdriver - 4 in. long x ¼ in. dia. (plain)
Screwdriver - 4 in. long x ¼ in. dia. (crosshead)
Combination pliers - 6 inch
Hacksaw, junior
Tyre pump
Tyre pressure gauge
Grease gun (where applicable)
Oil can
Fine emery cloth (1 sheet)
Wire brush (small)
Funnel (medium size)

Repair and overhaul tool kit

These tools are virtually essential for anyone undertaking any major repairs to a motor vehicle, and are additional to those given in the Basic list. Included in this list is a comprehensive set of sockets. Although these are expensive they will be found invaluable as they are so versatile - particularly if varous drives are included in the set. We recommend the ½ in square-drive, as this can be used with most proprietary torque wrenches. If you cannot afford a socket set, even bought piecemeal, then inexpensive tubular box spanners are a useful alternative.

The tools in this list will occasionally need to be supplemented by tools from the Special list.

Sockets (or box spanners) to cover range 6 to 27 mm
Reversible ratchet drive (for use with sockets)
Extension piece, 10 inch (for use with sockets)
Universal joint (for use with sockets)
Torque wrench (for use with sockets)
'Mole' wrench - 8 inch
Ball pein hammer
Soft-faced hammer, plastic or rubber
Screwdriver - 6 in. long x 5/16 in. dia. (plain)
Screwdriver - 2 in. long x 5/16 in. square (plain)
Screwdriver - 1½ in. long x ¼ in. dia (crosshead)
Screwdriver - 3 in. long x 1/8 in. dia. (electricians)
Pliers - electricians side cutters
Pliers - needle nosed

Pliers - circlip (internal and external)
Cold chisel ½ inch
Scriber (this can be made by grinding the end of a broken hacksaw blade)
Scraper (this can be made by flattening and sharpening one end of a piece of copper pipe)
Centre punch
Pin punch
Hacksaw
Valve grinding tool
Steel rule/straight edge
Allen keys
Selection of files
Wire brush (large)
Axle stands
Jack (strong scissor or hydraulic type)

Special tools

The tools in this list are those which are not used regularly, are expensive to buy, or which need to be used in accordance with their manufacturers instructions. Unless relatively difficult mechanical jobs are undertaken frequently, it will not be economic to buy many of these tools. Where this is the case, you could consider clubbing together with friends (or a motorists club) to make a joint purchase, or borrowing the tools against a deposit from a local garage or tool hire specialist.

The following list contains only those tools and instruments freely available to the public, and not those special tools produced by the vehicle manufacturer specifically for its dealer network. You will find occasional references to these manufacturers special tools in the text of this manual. Generally, an alternative method of doing the job without the vehicle manufacturers special tool is given. However, sometimes, there is no alternative to using them. Where this is the case and the relevant tool cannot be bought or borrowed you will have to entrust the work to a franchised garage.

Valve spring compressor
Piston ring compressor
Ball joint separator
Universal hub/bearing puller
Impact screwdriver
Micrometer and/or vernier gauge
Carburettor flow balancing device (where applicable)
Dial gauge
Stroboscopic timing light
Dwell angle meter/tachometer
Universal electrical multi-meter
Cylinder compression gauge
Lifting tackle
Trolley jack
Light with extension lead

Buying tools

For practically all tools, a tool factor is the best source since he will have a very comprehensive range compared with the average garage or accessory shop. Having said that, accessory shops often offer excellent quality tools at discount prices, so it pays to shop around.

There are plenty of good tools around at reasonable prices, but always aim to purchase items which meet the relevant national safety standards. If in doubt, ask the proprietor or manager of the shop for advice before making a purchase.

Care and maintenance of tools

Having purchased a reasonable tool kit, it is necessary to keep the tools in a clean and serviceable condition. After use, always wipe off any dirt, grease and metal particles using a clean, dry cloth, before putting the tools away. Never leave them lying around after they have been used. A simple tool rack on the garage or workshop wall, for items such as screwdrivers and pliers is a good idea. Store all normal spanners and sockets in a metal box. Any measuring instruments, gauges, meters, etc., must be carefully stored where they cannot be damaged or become rusty.

Take a little care when the tools are used. Hammer heads inevitably become marked and screwdrivers lose the keen edge on their blades from time-to-time. A little timely attention with emery cloth or a file will soon restore items like this to a good serviceable finish.

Use of tools

Throughout this book various phrases describing techniques are used, such as:
"Drive out the bearing".
"Undo the flange bolts evenly and diagonally".

When two parts are held together by a number of bolts round their edge, these must be tightened to draw the parts down together flat. They must be slackened evenly to prevent the component warping. Initially the bolts should be put in finger-tight only. Then they should be tightened gradually, at first only a turn each; and diagonally, doing second the one opposite that tightened first, then one to a side, followed by another opposite that, and so on. The second time each bolt is tightened only half a turn should be given. The third time round, only quarter of a turn is given each, and this is kept up till tight. The reverse sequence is used to slacken them.

If any part has to be 'driven', such as a ball bearing out of its housing, without a proper press, it can be done with a hammer provided a few rules for use of a hammer are remembered. Always keep the component being driven straight so it will not jam. Shield whatever is being hit from damage by the hammer. Soft headed hammers are available. A drift can be used, or if the item being hit is soft, use wood. Aluminium is very easily damaged. Steel is a bit better. Hard steel, such as a bearing race, is very strong. Something threaded at the end must be protected by fitting a nut. But do not hammer the nut: the threads will tear.

If levering items with makeshift arrangement, such as screwdrivers, irretrievable damage can be done. Be sure the lever rests either on something that does not matter, or put in padding. Burrs can be filed off afterwards. But indentations are there for good, and can cause leaks.

When holding something in a vice, the jaws must go on a part that is strong. If the indentation from the jaw teeth will matter, then lead or fibre jaw protectors must be used. Hollow sections are liable to be crushed.

Nuts that will not undo will sometimes move if the spanner handle is extended with another. But only extend a ring spanner, not an open jaw one. A hammer blow either to the spanner, or the bolt, may jump it out of its contact: the bolt locally welds itself in place. In extreme cases the nut will undo if driven off with drift and hammer. When reassembling such bolts, tighten them normally, not by the method needed to undo them.

For pressing things, such as a sleeve bearing into its housing, a vice, or an electric drill stand, make good presses. Pressing tools to hold each component can be arranged by using such things as socket spanners, or short lengths of steel water pipe. Long bolts with washers can be used to draw things into place rather than pressing them.

There are often several ways of doing something. If stuck, stop and think. Special tools can readily be made out of odd bits of scrap. Accordingly, at the same time as building up a tool kit, collect useful bits of steel.

Normally all nuts or bolts have some locking arrangement. The most common is a spring washer. There are tab washers that are bent up. Castellated nuts have split pins. FIAT use special collared nuts on the suspension stub axles that are staked to the axle. Sometimes a second nut locks the first. Self-locking nuts have special crowns that resist shaking loose. Self-locking nuts should not be reused, as the self-locking action is weakened as soon as they have been loosened at all. Tab washers should only be re-used when they can be bent over in a new place. If you find a nut without any locking arrangement, check what it is meant to have.

Working facilities

Not to be forgotten when discussing tools, is the workshop itself. If anything more than routine maintenance is to be carried out, some form of suitable working area becomes essential.

It is appreciated that many an owner mechanic is forced by circumstance to remove an engine or similar item, without the benefit of a garage or workshop. Having done this, any repairs should always be done under the cover of a roof.

Whenever possible, any dismantling should be done on a clean flat workbench or table at a suitable working height.

Any workbench needs a vice: one with a jaw opening of 4 in (100 mm) is suitable for most jobs. As mentioned previously, some clean dry storage space is also required for tools, as well as the lubricants, cleaning fluids, touch-up paints and so on which soon become necessary.

    Another item which may be required, and which has a much more general usage, is an electric drill with a chuck capacity of at least 5/16 in (8 mm). This, together with a good range of twist drills, is virtually essential for fitting accessories such as wing mirrors and reversing lights.

    Last but not least, always keep a supply of old newspapers and clean, lint-free rags available, and try to keep any working area as clean as possible.

Spanner jaw gap comparison table

Jaw gap (in)	Spanner size
0.250	$\frac{1}{4}$ in AF
0.276	7 mm
0.313	$\frac{5}{16}$ in AF
0.315	8 mm
0.344	$\frac{11}{32}$ in AF; $\frac{1}{8}$ in Whitworth
0.354	9 mm
0.375	$\frac{3}{8}$ in AF
0.394	10 mm
0.433	11 mm
0.438	$\frac{7}{16}$ in AF
0.445	$\frac{3}{16}$ in Whitworth; $\frac{1}{4}$ in BSF
0.472	12 mm
0.500	$\frac{1}{2}$ in AF
0.512	13 mm
0.525	$\frac{1}{4}$ in Whitworth; $\frac{5}{16}$ in BSF
0.551	14 mm
0.562	$\frac{9}{16}$ in AF
0.591	15 mm
0.600	$\frac{5}{16}$ in Whitworth; $\frac{3}{8}$ in BSF
0.625	$\frac{5}{8}$ in AF
0.630	16 mm
0.669	17 mm
0.686	$\frac{11}{16}$ in AF
0.709	18 mm
0.710	$\frac{3}{8}$ in Whitworth, $\frac{7}{16}$ in BSF
0.748	19 mm
0.750	$\frac{3}{4}$ in AF
0.813	$\frac{13}{16}$ in AF
0.820	$\frac{7}{16}$ in Whitworth; $\frac{1}{2}$ in BSF
0.866	22 mm
0.875	$\frac{7}{8}$ in AF
0.920	$\frac{1}{2}$ in Whitworth; $\frac{9}{16}$ in BSF
0.937	$\frac{15}{16}$ in AF
0.945	24 mm
1.000	1 in AF
1.010	$\frac{9}{16}$ in Whitworth; $\frac{5}{8}$ in BSF
1.024	26 mm
1.063	$1\frac{1}{16}$ in AF; 27 mm
1.100	$\frac{5}{8}$ in Whitworth; $\frac{11}{16}$ in BSF
1.125	$1\frac{1}{8}$ in AF
1.181	30 mm
1.200	$\frac{11}{16}$ in Whitworth; $\frac{3}{4}$ in BSF
1.250	$1\frac{1}{4}$ in AF
1.260	32 mm
1.300	$\frac{3}{4}$ in Whitworth; $\frac{7}{8}$ in BSF
1.313	$1\frac{5}{16}$ in AF
1.390	$\frac{13}{16}$ in Whitworth; $\frac{15}{16}$ in BSF
1.417	36 mm
1.438	$1\frac{7}{16}$ in AF
1.480	$\frac{7}{8}$ in Whitworth; 1 in BSF
1.500	$1\frac{1}{2}$ in AF
1.575	40 mm; $\frac{15}{16}$ in Whitworth
1.614	41 mm
1.625	$1\frac{5}{8}$ in AF
1.670	1 in Whitworth; $1\frac{1}{8}$ in BSF
1.688	$1\frac{11}{16}$ in AF
1.811	46 mm
1.813	$1\frac{13}{16}$ in AF
1.860	$1\frac{1}{8}$ in Whitworth; $1\frac{1}{4}$ in BSF
1.875	$1\frac{7}{8}$ in AF
1.969	50 mm
2.000	2 in AF
2.050	$1\frac{1}{4}$ in Whitworth; $1\frac{3}{8}$ in BSF
2.165	55 mm
2.362	60 mm

Use of English

As this book has been written in England, it uses the appropriate English component names, phrases, and spelling. Some of these differ from those used in America. Normally, these cause no difficulty, but to make sure, a glossary is printed below. In ordering spare parts remember the parts list may use some of these words:

English	American	English	American
Accelerator	Gas pedal	Locks	Latches
Aerial	Antenna	Methylated spirit	Denatured alcohol
Anti-roll bar	Stabiliser or sway bar	Motorway	Freeway, turnpike etc
Big-end bearing	Rod bearing	Number plate	License plate
Bonnet (engine cover)	Hood	Paraffin	Kerosene
Boot (luggage compartment)	Trunk	Petrol	Gasoline (gas)
Bulkhead	Firewall	Petrol tank	Gas tank
Bush	Bushing	'Pinking'	'Pinging'
Cam follower or tappet	Valve lifter or tappet	Prise (force apart)	Pry
Carburettor	Carburetor	Propeller shaft	Driveshaft
Catch	Latch	Quarterlight	Quarter window
Choke/venturi	Barrel	Retread	Recap
Circlip	Snap-ring	Reverse	Back-up
Clearance	Lash	Rocker cover	Valve cover
Crownwheel	Ring gear (of differential)	Saloon	Sedan
Damper	Shock absorber, shock	Seized	Frozen
Disc (brake)	Rotor/disk	Sidelight	Parking light
Distance piece	Spacer	Silencer	Muffler
Drop arm	Pitman arm	Sill panel (beneath doors)	Rocker panel
Drop head coupe	Convertible	Small end, little end	Piston pin or wrist pin
Dynamo	Generator (DC)	Spanner	Wrench
Earth (electrical)	Ground	Split cotter (for valve spring cap)	Lock (for valve spring retainer)
Engineer's blue	Prussian blue	Split pin	Cotter pin
Estate car	Station wagon	Steering arm	Spindle arm
Exhaust manifold	Header	Sump	Oil pan
Fault finding/diagnosis	Troubleshooting	Swarf	Metal chips or debris
Float chamber	Float bowl	Tab washer	Tang or lock
Free-play	Lash	Tappet	Valve lifter
Freewheel	Coast	Thrust bearing	Throw-out bearing
Gearbox	Transmission	Top gear	High
Gearchange	Shift	Torch	Flashlight
Grub screw	Setscrew, Allen screw	Trackrod (of steering)	Tie-rod (or connecting rod)
Gudgeon pin	Piston pin or wrist pin	Trailing shoe (of brake)	Secondary shoe
Halfshaft	Axleshaft	Transmission	Whole drive line
Handbrake	Parking brake	Tyre	Tire
Hood	Soft top	Van	Panel wagon/van
Hot spot	Heat riser	Vice	Vise
Indicator	Turn signal	Wheel nut	Lug nut
Interior light	Dome lamp	Windscreen	Windshield
Layshaft (of gearbox)	Countershaft	Wing/mudguard	Fender
Leading shoe (of brake)	Primary shoe		

Chapter 1 Engine

For modifications, and information applicable to later models, see Supplement at end of manual

Contents

Specifications

Engine (general)

Type	128 AS.040.5
Bore	3.38 in (86 mm)
Stroke	2.19 in (55.5 mm)
Cubic capacity	78.7 cu in (1290 cc)
Compression ratio	9.2 : 1
Firing order	1 - 3 - 4 - 2 (No 1 at timing belt end)
Power (SAE net)	75 bhp (DIN)
Oil filter type	Champion C106

Cylinder block

	in	mm
Cylinder bore diameter (standard)	3.3858 to 3.3878	86.000 to 86.050
Cylinder bore diameter grading intervals	0.0004	0.01
Rebore sizes	0.008 - 0.016 - 0.024	0.2 - 0.4 - 0.6
Maximum rebore	0.024	0.6
Auxiliary shaft bushing seats:		
Drive end diameter	1.5236 to 1.5248	38.700 to 38.730
Inside end diameter	1.3794 to 1.3805	35.036 to 35.066
Length of rear main bearing seat between thrust ring seats	0.8716 to 0.8740	22.140 to 22.200

Connecting rods

	in	mm
Big-end bearing housing diameter	1.9146 to 1.9152	48.630 to 48.646
Small end bore diameter	0.9425 to 0.9438	23.939 to 23.972
Range of undersize big-end bearings for service	0.010 - 0.020 - 0.030 -0.040	0.254 - 0.508 - 0.762 - 1.016
Gudgeon pin clearance	0.0004 to 0.0006	0.010 to 0.016
Big-end bearings:		
Fit clearance	0.0014 to 0.0034	0.036 to 0.086
Maximum misalignment between C/Ls of connecting rod small-end and big-end -measured at 4.92 in (125 mm)		
from the shank	± 0.0039	± 0.10

Crankshaft and main bearings

	in	mm
Main bearing journal:		
Standard diameter	1.9994 to 2.0002	50.785 to 50.805
Main bearing seat bore	2.1459 to 2.1465	54.507 to 54.520
Main bearings, thickness (standard)	0.0718 to 0.0721	1.825 to 1.831
Main bearing undersizes for service	Std. - 0.01 - 0.02 - 0.03 - 0.04	Std. - 0.254 - 0.508 - 0.762 - 1.106
Crankpin standard diameter	1.7913 to 1.7920	45.498 to 45.518
Main bearing to journal fit:		
Clearance of new parts	0.0016 to 0.0033	0.040 to 0.085

	in	mm
Oversize thrust rings, thickness	0.0959 to 0.0979	2.437 to 2.487
Crankshaft endfloat:		
Thrust rings fitted (new parts)	0.0021 to 0.0104	0.055 to 0.265

Flywheel

	in	mm
Parallel relationship of driven plate face to crankshaft mounting face: maximum out of true	0.0039	0.10
Squareness of above faces to rotation axis: maximum out of true	0.0039	0.10

Pistons and gudgeon pins

	in	mm
Diameter of standard service pistons, measured at right-angles to C/L of gudgeon pin at 1.08 in (27.5 mm) from skirt edge:		
Class A	3.3827 to 3.3831	85.920 to 85.930
Class C	3.3835 to 3.3839	85.940 to 85.950
Class E	3.3842 to 3.3846	85.960 to 85.970
Oversize piston range	0.0079 - 0.0157 - 0.0236	0.2 - 0.4 - 0.6
Piston boss bore diameter:		
Grade 1	0.8660 to 0.8661	21.996 to 21.999
Grade 2	0.8661 to 0.8662	21.999 to 22.002
Piston ring groove width:		
Top groove	0.604 to 0.0612	1.535 to 1.555
Centre groove	0.0799 to 0.0807	2.030 to 2.050
Bottom groove	0.1562 to 0.1570	3.967 to 3.987
Standard gudgeon pin diameter:		
Grade 1	0.8658 to 0.8659	21.991 to 21.994
Grade 2	0.8659 to 0.8660	21.994 to 21.997
Oversize gudgeon pin	0.0079	0.2
Piston ring thickness:		
First: compression ring	0.0582 to 0.0587	1.478 to 1.490
Second: oil ring	0.0778 to 0.0783	1.978 to 1.990
Third: oil ring with oilways and expander	0.1544 to 0.1549	3.925 to 3.937
Piston fit in bore (at right-angles to gudgeon pin and 1.08 in (27.5 mm) from piston skirt edge). Clearance of new parts	0.0021 to 0.0028	0.050 to 0.070
Piston ring end gap (in bore):		
First: compression ring	0.0118 to 0.0177	0.30 to 0.45
Second: oil ring	0.0118 to 0.0177	0.30 to 0.45
Third: oil ring	0.0098 to 0.0157	0.25 to 0.40
Piston ring fit (side clearance):		
First: compression ring	0.0018 to 0.0030	0.045 to 0.077
Second: oil ring	0.0016 to 0.0028	0.040 to 0.072
Third: scraper ring	0.0008 to 0.0024	0.020 to 0.062
Oversize piston ring range:		
Compression and oilways	0.0079 - 0.0157 - 0.0236	0.2 - 0.4 - 0.6

Cylinder head

	in	mm
Valve guide bore	0.5886 to 0.5896	14.950 to 14.977
Outside diameter of valve guide	0.5921 to 0.5928	15.040 to 15.058
Inside diameter of valve guide fitted in cylinder head	0.3158 to 0.3165	8.022 to 8.040
Valve guide fit in cylinder head (interference)	0.0025 to 0.0043	0.063 to 0.108
Valve stem diameter	0.3139 to 0.3146	7.974 to 7.992
Valve stem fit in valve guide (new parts)	0.0012 to 0.0026	0.030 to 0.066
Valve seat angle	45º ± 5'	
Valve face angle	45º 30' ± 5'	
Valve head diameter:		
Inlet	1.4173 ± 0.0059	36 ± 0.15
Exhaust	1.2205 ± 0.0059	31 ± 0.15
Maximum run-out on a full turn at centre of contact face	0.0012	0.03
Width of valve seat (contact surface):		
Inlet and exhaust (approx.)	0.0787	2
Lift on C/L of valve (without play)	0.3839	9.75
Diameter of tappet bores in camshaft housing	1.4567 to 1.4577	37.000 to 37.025
Outside diameter of tappets	1.4557 to 1.4565	36.975 to 36.995
Clearance between tappet and bore	0.0002 to 0.0020	0.005 to 0.050
Valve clearance (cold):		
Inlet	0.018	0.45
Exhaust	0.024	0.60
Valve springs:		
Height under load of 85.5 lb (38.9 kg). Outer spring	1.417	36
Height under load of 32.71 lb (14.9 kg). Inner spring	1.220	31

Camshaft

	in	mm
Diameter of bores in housing:		
Drive end	1.1807 to 1.1817	29.989 to 30.014
Intermediate, drive end	1.8890 to 1.8900	47.908 to 48.005

	in	mm
Middle	1.8968 to 1.8978	48.180 to 48.205
Intermediate, flywheel end	1.9047 to 1.9057	48.380 to 48.405
Flywheel end	1.9126 to 1.9136	48.580 to 48.605
Diameter of camshaft journals:		
Drive end	1.1789 to 1.1795	29.944 to 29.960
Intermediate, drive end	1.8872 to 1.8878	47.935 to 47.950
Middle	1.8951 to 1.8957	48.135 to 48.150
Intermediate, flywheel end	1.9030 to 1.9035	48.335 to 48.350
Flywheel end	1.9108 to 1.9114	48.535 to 48.550
Clearance between bores and camshaft journals:		
Drive end	0.0011 to 0.0028	0.029 to 0.070
Intermediate, drive end	0.0012 to 0.0028	0.030 to 0.070
Middle	0.0012 to 0.0028	0.030 to 0.070
Intermediate, flywheel end	0.0012 to 0.0028	0.030 to 0.070
Flywheel end	0.0012 to 0.0028	0.030 to 0.070
Valve timing:		
Inlet	Opens 12° btdc, closes 52° abdc	
Exhaust	Opens 52° bbdc, closes 12° atdc	
For valve timing check set valve clearances to 0.020 in (0.50 mm)		

Auxiliary shaft

	in	mm
Inside diameter of bushings finished in bores:		
Drive end	1.4041 to 1.4049	35.664 to 35.684
Inside end	1.2598 to 1.2606	32.000 to 32.020
Diameter of shaft journals:		
Drive end	1.4013 to 1.4023	35.593 to 35.618
Inside end	1.2575 to 1.2583	31.940 to 31.960
Fit between bushings and bores in crankcase	Interference fit at all times	
Clearance between bushings and journals:		
Drive end	0.0018 to 0.0036	0.046 to 0.091
Inside end	0.0016 to 0.0031	0.040 to 0.080

Oil pump

	in	mm
Type	Gear	
End-clearance, gears to cover	0.0008 to 0.0041	0.020 to 0.105
Side-clearance, gear to housing	0.0043 to 0.0071	0.11 to 0.18
Length of new gear	1.101 to 1.102	27.967 to 28.0
Driven gear shaft to housing	Interference fit	
Driven gear fit on shaft	0.0006 to 0.0022	0.015 to 0.055
Clearance pump driveshaft to housing	0.0006 to 0.0023	0.015 to 0.058
Oil pressure at 185°F (85°C)	64 to 85.4 psi (4.5 to 6 kg/sq cm)	

Torque wrench settings:	lb f ft	kg f m
Bolt, flywheel to crankshaft	61	8.5
Nut, connecting-rod caps	36	5
Bolt, camshaft pulley	61	8.5
Cylinder head nuts and bolts (oiled threads):		
M12 (19 mm hexagon):		
Stage 1	29	4
Stage 2	47	6.5
Stage 3	69	9.5
M10 (17 mm hexagon, 1980 on):		
Stage 1	15	2
Stage 2	29	4
Stage 3	Tighten a further 90°	Tighten a further 90°
Stage 4	Tighten a further 90°	Tighten a further 90°
Nut, camshaft nousing	14.5	2
Bolt, main bearing caps	58	8
Nut, crankshaft drive pulley	101	14
Nut, belt tensioner bearing	32.5	4.5
Nut/bolt engine mounting, right end	25	3.5
Bolt, engine mounting bracket to body	18	2.5
Bolt, engine torque rod	11	1.5

1 General description

1 The FIAT X1/9 engine is transversely mounted just ahead of the rear wheels and inclined forward at an angle of 11°. It is a four cylinder, in-line, water cooled engine with an overhead camshaft which is driven by a rubber toothed drive belt from a gear on the crankshaft.

2 The cylinder block is cast iron and the head aluminium. The camshaft runs in bearings in a housing that is an extension of the cylinder head, with the cams operating directly on the tappets. There are five main bearings supporting the crankshaft. An auxiliary shaft, supported in bearings in the block, drives the distributor, the oil pump and, if fitted, the mechanical fuel pump. On some engines the distributor is mounted at the left-hand end of the engine and driven by the camshaft.

3 On cars for the North American market fitted with an air injection emission control system an air pump is mounted on the right-hand end of the engine and is belt driven from a pulley on the camshaft. The water pump and alternator are driven by a 'V' belt from a pulley on the crankshaft.

4 The transmission is fitted to the left end of the engine. Though it is integral with the engine, the transmission has separate lubrication.

5 Fitted under the engine are protective shields to keep off dirt. These must be removed for many jobs. The alternator is protected from the heat of the exhaust by a heat shield.

2 Major operations possible with engine in car

The following major operations can be carried out with the engine in place in the car:

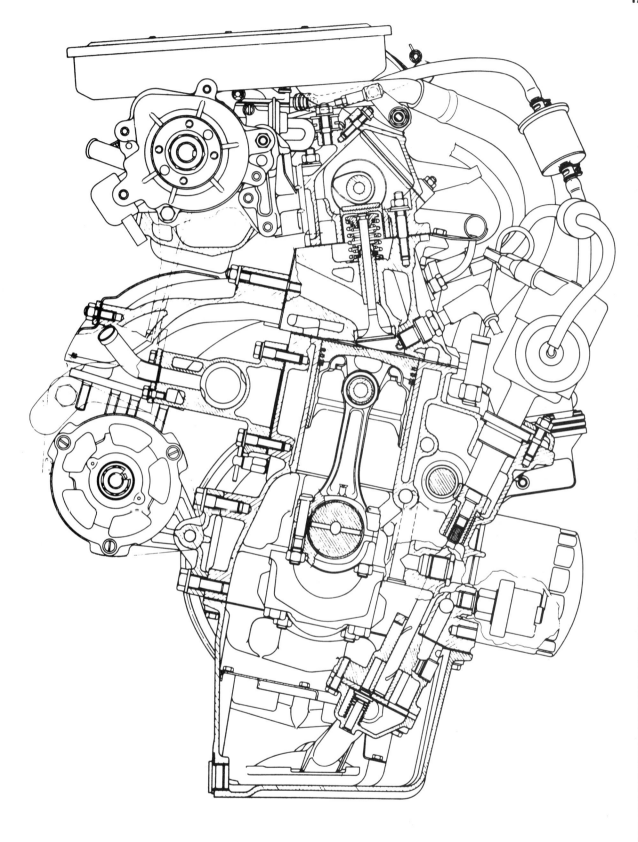

Fig. 1.1. Cross-section of engine for North-American market - fitted with air pump for exhaust emission control system

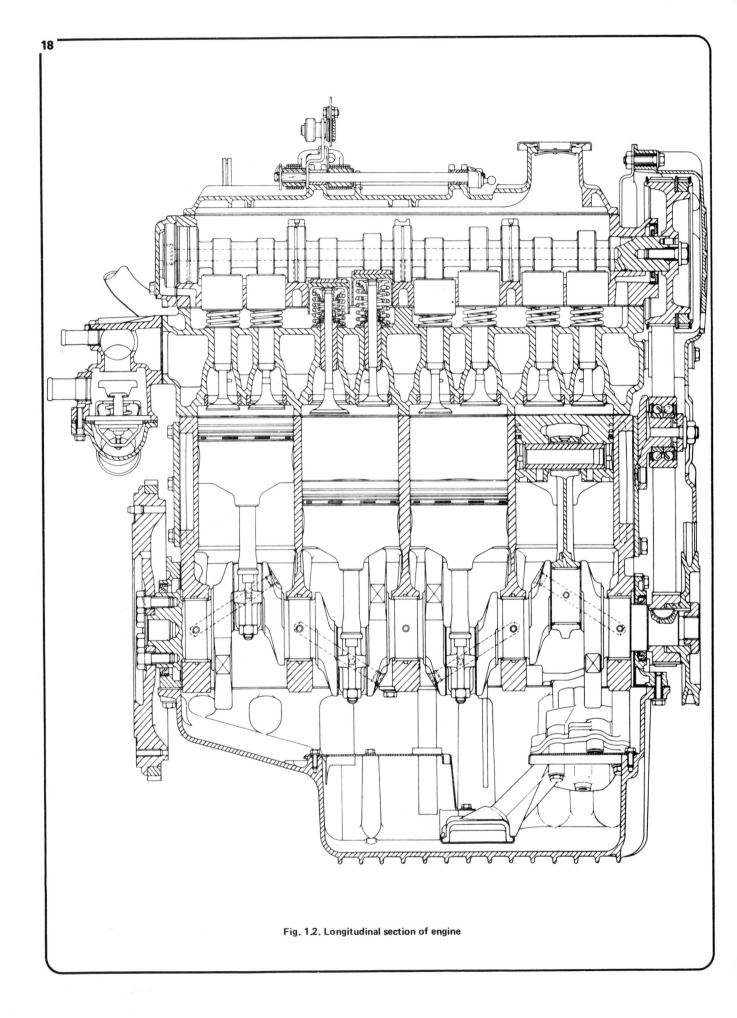

Fig. 1.2. Longitudinal section of engine

1 Removal and refitting of the camshaft housing.
2 Removal and refitting of the toothed drivebelt.
3 Removal and refitting of the cylinder head.
4 Removal and refitting of the sump, pistons and connecting rods
(not recommended).

3 Major operations requiring engine removal

The engine must be removed from the car to carry out the following
operations:
1 Removal and refitting of crankshaft.
2 Removal and refitting of main bearings.

4 Cylinder head - removal and refitting (engine in car)

1 Drain the cooling system and remove the air cleaner, as described
in Chapters 2 and 3.
2 Disconnect the two fuel hoses from the carburettor and pull the
hoses and grommets out of their support bracket.
3 Slide the spring clip down off the ball connector for the accelerator
rod and disconnect the rod from the ball connector. Disconnect the
choke cable.
4 Disconnect the spark plug cables. If the distributor is fitted at the
rear of the camshaft remove the distributor cap and leads.
5 Disconnect the vacuum hose for the distributor from the fitting
in the cylinder head.
6 Remove the stop bolt from the accelerator cable, slide the seal
off the cable and remove the clip holding the cable on the valve
cover. Remove the cable and tuck it out of the way.
7 Disconnect the water outlet and inlet hoses, the water pump to
thermostat housing hose and the expansion tank hose from the
thermostat housing.
8 On cars with fuel vapour and exhaust emission control systems,
note the run of the hoses and disconnect them from the carburettor
and air pump.
9 Remove the bolt holding the torque rod on its bracket on the
cylinder head and swing it out of the way.
10 Remove the bolts securing the right-hand protective shield from
under the car.
11 Remove the drivebelt cover. One bolt is reached from underneath
the car, accessible from where the protective shield was removed.
12 To remove the toothed drivebelt, take the tension off the belt by
slackening the nut in the centre of the tensioner pulley. Lever the
pulley against its spring, away from the belt, with a long screwdriver
and retighten the nut. Slip the belt off the camshaft pulley and leave
it round the crankshaft and auxiliary shaft sprockets.
13 Loosen the alternator bottom pivot bolt and the bolt attaching the
alternator to the adjusting bracket. Remove the alternator and water
pump drivebelt.
14 On engines with an air pump, loosen the pump pivot bolts, under
the bolts which mount the two brackets, swing the pump towards the
camshaft pulley and remove the pump drivebelt.
15 Remove the inside guard for the drivebelt, one bolt is just below
the tensioner pulley and the nuts are behind the camshaft pulley.
16 Remove the manifold shield by removing the four nuts securing
it to the manifold.
17 If 'crow's foot' type or other suitable spanners are available, the
cylinder head bolts can now be unscrewed, if they are not, proceed in
the following way.
18 Take off the two water pipes to the carburettor, at the thermostat,
and at the manifold. Remove the carburettor by undoing the two nuts
holding it to the manifold. Unclamp the drip tray pipe at the left end
of the exhaust manifold: take off the tray.
19 Remove the camshaft housing cover.
20 Remove the camshaft housing from the cylinder head. Slacken all
the nuts evenly and gradually. The valve springs will push the whole
assembly upwards. One row of nuts is on the outside of the housing, to
the rear, whilst the front ones are inside it.
21 Lift off the camshaft housing carefully, as the tappets and the tappet
adjustment shims will be loose. Keep each in its proper place: turn the
housing upside down as quickly as possible to keep them in, by tilting
the top towards the front of the car.
22 Slacken the cylinder head nuts and bolts gradually, and in reverse
order to the tightening sequence given in Fig. 1.23. Start at the outer
ends and slacken inwards.
23 Now break the joint between the cylinder head and the block. Do

not prise at the joint. Turning the engine on the starter might start it
off. Also rock it by pulling up on the manifolds.
24 Lift off the cylinder head. Put it where the carbon will not get wet
or knocked off, so that you can have a chance to look at it for signs
that will show the engine condition.
25 Peel off the old cylinder head gasket. Take care no carbon falls into
the cylinders.
26 If the 'crow's foot' spanners were available (see Paragraph 17) the
head should be removed with the camshaft still in place on the head,
and the carburettor on the manifold, and these removed more easily
later on the bench.
27 Remove the manifolds from the head, by removing the nuts and
large thick washers.
28 For the decarbonising of the engine, and work on the valves, refer
to Section 12.
29 Refitting is the reverse of the removal sequence. Tighten the cylinder
head holding down nuts and bolts in stages to the specified torque
(see Fig. 1.23). Refit and adjust the timing belt as described in Section 5.
30 Check the valve tappet clearance, as described in Section 29.

5 Toothed drivebelt - removal, refitting and adjusting

*If adjustment is required or the belt removed for any reason,
always replace the belt with a new one, never adjust using the old belt.*
1 The toothed drivebelt should be renewed at 36,000 miles (60,000
km). This can be done with the engine in the car.
2 Using a spanner on the crankshaft pulley nut turn the engine over
till the timing mark on the crankshaft pulley is aligned with the TDC
mark.
3 Check that the camshaft pulley timing mark is aligned with the
cast pointer of the engine mounting support, visible through the hole
in the timing cover.
4 Put the car in gear and apply the handbrake to prevent the engine
from being turned further. Note if the engine is turned over with the
drivebelt removed, the pistons may hit the valves and cause serious
damage.
5 Remove the drive belt cover, alternator/water pump drivebelt and,
if fitted, air pump drivebelt, as described in Section 4.
6 Slacken the nut in the centre of the tensioner pulley and push in
on the support to release the tension on the belt, then retighten the
nut. Slide the drivebelt off the pulleys.
7 Check that the crankshaft and camshaft pulleys have not moved from
their previously aligned marks. Also check that the distributor rotor
arm still points to the No. 4 contact in the cap. If not, turn the
auxiliary shaft sprocket as necessary (crankcase-mounted distributor
only). Fit the new belt, starting at the crankshaft sprocket, around the
auxiliary shaft and camshaft sprockets and under the tensioner pulley.
8 Slacken the tensioner pulley locknut to tension the belt, then
retighten the nut.
9 Take the car out of gear, and rotate the engine through half a turn.
Slacken the tensioner pulley nut, to remove any slack on the belt, and
then retighten the nut to 32.5 lb ft (4.5 kg f m). When tensioning the
belt, never turn the engine backwards or rock the crankshaft as slack
will develop in the belt and it may jump a tooth.
10 Refit and tension the alternator/water pump drivebelt as described
in Chapter 10, Section 7.
11 Refit the drivebelt for the air pump (if fitted).
12 Refit the drivebelt cover.

6 Engine - removal (general)

1 The engine and transmission are removed as a unit, it is not possible
to remove the engine separately although the transmission can be
removed without the engine.
2 The engine/transmission can be removed in about four hours. It
will be necessary to have a hoist, jack and two axle stands or a supply
of good solid wooden blocks as the rear of the car has to be supported
high enough to allow the engine to be removed from underneath the
rear of the car.
3 When the rear of the car is raised high enough to allow the engine
to be pulled from underneath, it is recommended that a weight be
placed in the front luggage compartment to provide stability.

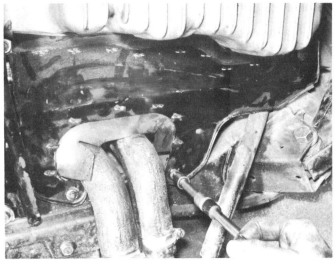

7.6a Remove the protection shields from under the engine

7.6b This one is under the alternator

7.6c The alternator heat shield (not fitted on engines having a heat shroud fitted on the exhaust manifold)

7 Engine - removal procedure

1   Disconnect the leads from the battery in the front luggage compartment.
2   Jack-up the rear of the car and support it on axle stands at the jacking points and remove the rear wheels.
3   Drain the cooling system, as described in Chapter 2, Section 2. If the coolant has recently been renewed, drain it into a clean container for possible re-use.
4   Remove the drain plug from the engine sump and drain the oil into a container. After draining, refit the plug to prevent residual oil from draining out as the engine is moved. If the transmission has to be dismantled drain it as well.
5   Remove the engine bonnet and the rear luggage compartment lid, as described in Chapter 12.
6   Remove the protective shields from under the car, three from the bottom of the engine compartment and one inboard of each rear wheel. Remove the alternator head shield.
7   Disconnect the engine breather hose from the air cleaner and remove the cleaner as described in Chapter 3, Section 6.
8   If an air injection exhaust control emission system is fitted, disconnect the hose from the air injection valve, the air pump and the hose between the air pump and filter.
9   Disconnect the heater hoses from the cylinder head and the water pump. Disconnect the radiator flow and return hoses and remove them.
10 Disconnect the plug from the alternator. Disconnect the leads from the starter motor.
11 Disconnect the ignition leads from the spark plugs, and the lead from the centre of the coil. Unclip the distributor cap and remove it, to prevent possible damage to it as the engine is removed, Disconnect the low tension lead at the distributor.
12 Unplug the lead from the temperature sender unit on the front of the cylinder head.
13 Unplug the leads from the oil pressure sender units on the front of the crankcase.
14 Disconnect the choke linkage from the carburettor.
15 Disconnect the throttle cables from the carburettor, free the cables from their support on top of the camshaft housing and tuck them out of the way.
16 Remove the screw from the clamp which holds the fuel lines to the front bulk head. Disconnect the fuel feed and return hoses, plug the ends to prevent the ingress of dirt, and tuck them to the side, out of the way.
17 Remove the bolts holding the expansion tank at the top and bottom. Lift the tank to allow any coolant to drain into the engine. Disconnect the hoses at the thermostat housing and remove the tank.
18 Remove the split pin holding the hydraulic clutch slave cylinder operating rod in the clutch shaft. Disconnect the return spring.
19 Slacken the bleed screw on the slave cylinder and push the rod

7.9a Disconnect the heater hoses from the water pump and cylinder head

7.9b Disconnect the engine to radiator hoses at the water manifold ...

7.9c ... and at the connection under the car

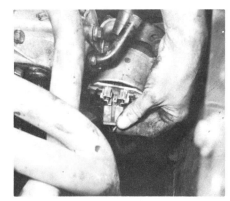

7.10a Disconnect the alternator ...

10b ... and the starter motor

7.12 Unplug the lead from the water temperature sender ...

7.13a ... and from the oil pressure warning sender

7.13b The oil pressure gauge sender has also to be disconnected

7.15 Disconnect the throttle cable. On some cars there is a catch for the hand throttle

7.16 The fuel lines have to be disconnected from the carburettor

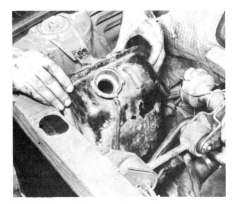

7.17 Lift out the expansion tank

7.19a Remove the clutch slave cylinder mounting bolts ...

7.19b ... and place the cylinder to the side out of the way

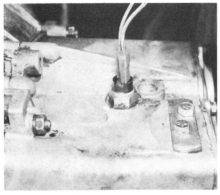

7.20 Disconnect the reversing light lead from the transmission

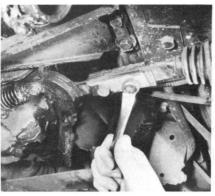

7.21 Remove the bolts from the gearchange linkage sandwich joint

7.24 Removing the exhaust silencer

7.25 The silencer mounting bracket is bolted to the transmission casing

7.26 The driveshafts are disconnected from the transmission

7.27 Remove the nuts attaching the handbrake cables to the control arms

7.28a Remove the control arms pivot bolts ...

7.28b ... and collect the shims. The shims must be refitted in the same positions

7.30 Remove the bolts attaching the engine support bracket to the body under the car

7.31 Disconnect the torque rod from the bracket at the flywheel end of the cylinder head

7.32 Remove the bolt from the left-hand engine mounting

7.34 Lower the engine out of the car

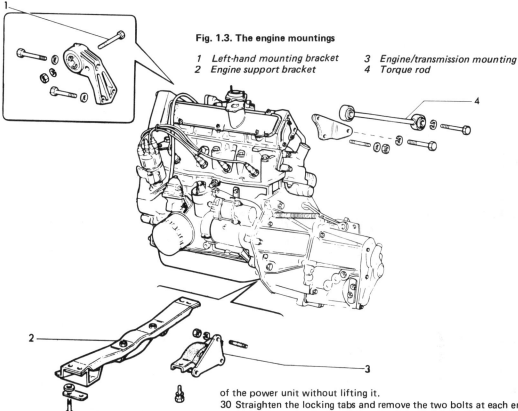

Fig. 1.3. The engine mountings

1   Left-hand mounting bracket   3   Engine/transmission mounting
2   Engine support bracket   4   Torque rod

back clear of the clutch arm. Remove the two mounting bolts, then
lift the slave cylinder and swing it to the side out of the way.
20 Disconnect the reversing light and seatbelt interlock leads
(if fitted) from the transmission. Unscrew the knurled collar on the
speedometer cable and pull the cable out. Tuck the leads and speedometer cable out of the way so that they will not foul the engine/
transmission unit as it is lowered out of the engine compartment.
21 Remove the bolts from the sandwich joint on the gearchange
linkage, loosen the bolt at the transmission end of the flexible link
and swing the link out of the way.
22 Disconnect the transmission to body earth strap.
23 On cars with a catalytic converter, remove the spring-loaded bolts
that connect the converter to the exhaust pipe. Remove the bolts
attaching the converter to the body and remove the unit.
24 Straighten the tabs on the exhaust manifold, then remove the four
securing nuts and the lockplates. Remove the two bolts attaching the
left end of the silencer to the upper mounting bracket and the two nuts
holding the centre support for the silencer to the crossmember. Remove
the silencer.
25 Remove the two nuts which attach the silencer mounting bracket
to the transmission casing and remove the bracket.
26 Place a container under the driveshaft rubber boots at the
differential and remove the three bolts from the left and right-hand
driveshaft boot retaining flanges. Slide the boots away from the
differential and allow any residual oil to drain into the container.
On models with 5-speed transmission, simply disconnect the driveshaft
flanges at the transmission.
27 Remove the nut securing the handbrake cable at the front end of
each suspension control arm.
28 Remove the four pivot bolts securing the control arms to the body,
collect and note the number of shims fitted at each mounting point,
so that they can be refitted in the same position. Pull the control arms
down out of their mounting brackets and away from the differential
until the driveshafts are free of the differential. Tie the driveshafts to
the control arms to keep them out of the way. **Note:** The complete
suspension and driveshaft assemblies may be removed from the car by
removing the brake calipers and the three nuts securing the shock
absorbers at their top mounting.
29 Connect the lifting sling to the engine. One eye is on the water
pump and the other is just in front of the thermostat housing. Arrange
the sling so that the power unit will hang horizontally. Take the weight

of the power unit without lifting it.
30 Straighten the locking tabs and remove the two bolts at each end
of the engine mounting bracket under the transmission which attach
the bracket to the body.
31 Remove the bolt attaching the torque rod to the bracket on the
engine at the rear.
32 Remove the bolt through the front engine mounting, adjust the
lifting tackle to ease the load on the bolt so that it can be pulled out.
33 Make a complete check to ensure that everything has been disconn
ected and that all cables, hoses and pipes are tucked out of the way
where they will not get caught up as the engine is removed.
34 Rock the engine to free it from the front mounting bracket and
lower it out of the car. A low trolley of the 'creeper' type placed
underneath the car, and the engine lowered on to it is the ideal way
to get the engine out from under the car. Make sure the trolley is
strong enough. If a trolley is not available lower the engine onto a
wooden platform and slide it out.
35 If, when pulling the engine out you find the car has not been
raised high enough, lift the car with the hoist to allow the engine to
be pulled clear.

7.35 It may be necessary to raise the rear of the car higher, to pull the
engine clear

8.2 Remove the starter motor

8.3 Withdrawing the engine support bracket

8 Engine and transmission - separating

1   Clean the outside of the engine and transmission.
2   Remove the three bolts securing the starter motor and lift out the starter motor.
3   Remove the three bolts holding the engine support bracket to the transmission that pass through the engine endplate.
4   Remove the shield below the engine to transmission joint.
5   Support the transmission so that its weight does not put any strain on the shaft through the clutch.
6   Remove the remaining nuts on the studs attaching the transmission to the engine.
7   Separate the transmission from the engine.

9 Engine - dismantling (general)

1   Keen d-i-y mechanics who dismantle a lot of engines will probably have a stand on which to put them but most will make do with a work bench which should be large enough to spread the inevitable bits and pieces and tools around on, and strong enough to support the engine. If the floor is the only possible place try and ensure that the engine rests on a hardwood platform or similar rather than concrete.
2   Spend some time on cleaning the unit. If you have been wise this will have been done before the engine was removed, at a service bay. Good solvents such as 'Gunk' will help to 'float' off caked dirt/grease under a water jet. Once the exterior is clean, dismantling may begin. As parts are removed clean them in petrol or paraffin (do not immerse parts with oilways in paraffin - clean them with a petrol soaked cloth and clear oilways with nylon pipe cleaners. If an air line is available so much the better for final cleaning off. (Paraffin, which could possibly remain in oilways would dilute the oil for initial lubrication after reassembly).
3   Where components are fitted with seals and gaskets it is always best to fit new ones - but **do not** throw the old ones away until you have the new ones to hand. A pattern is then available if they have to be made specially. Hang them on a convenient hook.
4   In general it is best to work from the top of the engine downwards. In any case support the engine firmly so that it does not topple over when you are undoing stubborn nuts and bolts.
5   Always place nuts and bolts back with their components or place of attachment if possible - it saves so much confusion later. Otherwise put them in small, separate pots or jars so that their groups are easily identified.
6   If you are lucky enough to have an area where parts can be laid out on sheets of paper do so - putting the nuts and bolts with them. If you are able to look at all the components in this way it helps to avoid missing something on reassembly because it is tucked away on a shelf or whatever.

8.4 Remove the shield below the engine to transmission joint

8.7 Separating the transmission from the engine

7 Even though you may be dismantling the engine only partly - possibly with it still in the car - the principles still apply. It is appreciated that most people prefer to do engine repairs if possible with the engine in position. Generally speaking the engine is easy enough to get at as far as repairs and renewals of the ancillaries are concerned. When it comes to repair of the major engine components, however, it is only fair to say that repairs with the engine in position are more difficult than with it out.

10 Engine ancillaries - removal

1 If you are stripping the engine completely or preparing to install a reconditioned unit, all the ancillaries must be removed first. If you are going to obtain a reconditioned 'short' engine (cylinder block, crank-shaft, pistons and connecting rods) then obviously the camshaft housing, cylinder head and associated parts will need to be removed and retained for fitting to the new engine. It is advisable to check just what you will get with a reconditioned unit as changes are made from time to time.

2 The removal and refitting of the following ancillaries is described in their respective Chapters.

> *Distributor*
> *Starter motor*
> *Alternator*
> *Fuel pump*
> *Carburettor*
> *Water pump*
> *Thermostat*

11 Engine - dismantling procedure

1 Remove and discard the oil filter. The filter should unscrew by hand, if it is too tight use a strap wrench to loosen it.
2 Remove the inlet and exhaust manifold securing nuts and lift off the manifolds. The inlet manifold complete with carburettor comes off first.
3 Remove the alternator, fuel pump and, if fitted, the air pump. Remove the distributor which may be fitted on the front of the engine if driven by the auxiliary shaft or fitted at the flywheel end of the engine if driven by the camshaft.
4 Remove the drivebelt cover.
5 Slacken the hose connection at the water manifold on the end of the pipe running from the water pump. Remove the pump retaining bolts and remove the pump and hose.
6 Remove the water manifold retaining nuts and pull the manifold off the studs.
7 Remove the crankcase breather fitting on the front of the engine.
8 Remove the engine mounting bracket from the right-hand end of the cylinder block, taking with it the spring-loaded plunger of the toothed drivebelt tensioner.
9 Remove the centre nut from the belt tensioner pulley and remove the drivebelt.
10 Remove the tensioner pulley mounting plate retaining bolts and lift off the tensioner pulley assembly.
11 Remove the oil pressure warning sender.
12 Remove the camshaft pulley retaining bolt, it is locked with a tabwasher, and take off the pulley.
13 Remove the drivebelt guard attached to the cylinder head and

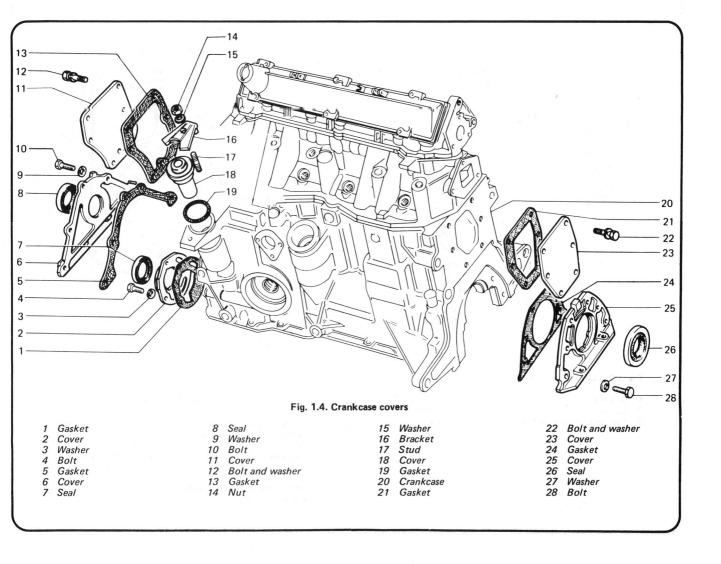

Fig. 1.4. Crankcase covers

1	Gasket	8	Seal	15	Washer	22	Bolt and washer
2	Cover	9	Washer	16	Bracket	23	Cover
3	Washer	10	Bolt	17	Stud	24	Gasket
4	Bolt	11	Cover	18	Cover	25	Cover
5	Gasket	12	Bolt and washer	19	Gasket	26	Seal
6	Cover	13	Gasket	20	Crankcase	27	Washer
7	Seal	14	Nut	21	Gasket	28	Bolt

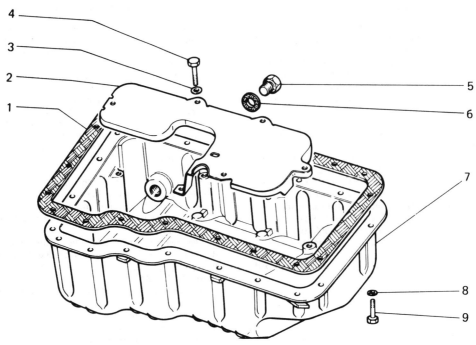

Fig. 1.5. Oil sump and gasket

1	Gasket	3	Washer	5	Drain plug	7	Oil sump
2	Cover	4	Bolt	6	Gasket	8	Washer
						9	Bolt

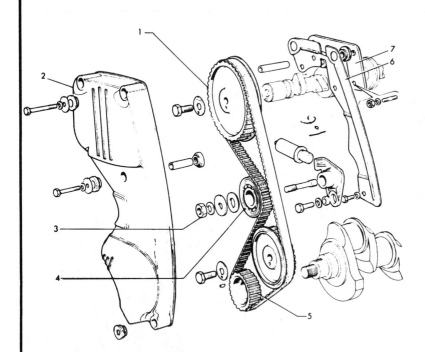

Fig. 1.6. Toothed drivebelt and cover

1	Drivebelt	4	Tensioner pulley
2	Belt cover	5	Crankshaft pulley
3	Tensioner pulley locknut	6	Beltguard
		7	Bracket

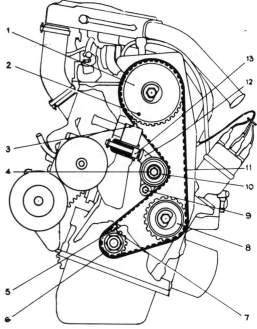

Fig. 1.7. Camshaft drivebelt installation

1	Camshaft pulley	8	Auxiliary shaft pulley
2	Camshaft pulley timing mark	9	Tensioner bracket bolt
3	Timing finger on engine support	10	Tensioner pulley
4	Tensioner pulley locknut	11	Toothed drivebelt
5	Timing mark on cylinder block	12	Lug on tensioner bracket
6	Crankshaft pulley	13	Tensioner spring
7	Timing mark on crankshaft drivebelt pulley		

crankcase.

14 Remove the camshaft housing cover.

15 Remove the nuts inside the camshaft housing, and those outside along the rear side, that secure the camshaft housing to the cylinder head. Slacken the nuts off evenly and gradually, to prevent any possible warping as the valve springs push the housing up. Later models use bolts instead of nuts and studs.

16 Lift off the camshaft housing, taking care that the tappets are kept in their correct bores. Lift the tappets out with their respective adjusting shim discs and place them so that they are kept in the right order. No. 1 cylinder is at the drivebelt end.

17 Slacken the cylinder head holding down bolts and nuts in the reverse order to the tightening sequence shown in Fig. 1.23. Remove the bolts and nuts and lift off the cylinder head. Tap the head with a soft-faced hammer to free the head, but do not use a lever to prise it off as the surface will be damaged. Remove the cylinder head gasket. If the cylinder head is sticking on the studs in the cylinder block put some releasing fluid on each stud and allow it to soak through.

18 Note that the pistons are fitted so that the cut-out section for the valves are on the rear side of the engine, away from the auxiliary shaft. Note the amount of carbon on each piston, as this will help to give an indication of the state of wear in the cylinders. Large amounts of carbon indicate that the engine has been burning oil.

19 Remove the clutch from the flywheel, as described in Chapter 5. Mark the relationship of flywheel to crankshaft flange.

20 Remove the flywheel retaining bolts and pull the flywheel off the crankshaft. Restrain the flywheel from turning while slackening the retaining bolts. A bolt fitted in one of the crankcase to transmission bolt holes and a wedge located in the flywheel ring gear makes a suitable lock to prevent the flywheel from turning. If the sump is removed a convenient way to restrain the crankshaft is to wedge a block of wood between a crank throw and the crankcase.

21 Turn the engine on its side, remove the sump securing bolts and lift off the sump.

22 Remove the oil drain pipe from No. 5 main bearing (flywheel end) (early models only). Remove the breather return drain from beside No. 3 main bearing.

23 Remove the three oil pump retaining bolts and lift off the pump.

24 Remove the three bolts securing the auxiliary shaft end plate to the cylinder block and withdraw the shaft from the block. If necessary, the pulley can be removed with the shaft, held in a vice.

25 Remove the 'V' belt and toothed drivebelt pulleys from the crankshaft. Wedge the crankshaft with a block of wood and using a 38 mm socket or box spanner remove the pulley retaining nut.

26 Remove the oil seal carrier plates from both ends of the crankshaft.

27 Remove the big-end bearing bolts, slackening each in turn slightly at first.

28 Remove the big-end bearing caps. The caps and the rods are both numbered on the side away from the auxiliary shaft. Keep each bearing shell with its own cap and rod.

29 Push the pistons and connecting rods out of the block.

30 If the pistons and connecting rods are being removed with the engine in the car, before removing the sump the weight of the engine must be taken by a support under the transmission to allow for removal of the engine bottom support bracket.

31 Mark the main bearing caps with a punch or chisel to identify the bearing number and which way round it is fitted.

32 Remove the main bearing cap bolts and lift off the caps. Keep each shell with its cap.

33 Lift out the crankshaft. Remove the other halves of the main bearings and keep them with their respective caps. Remove the thrust ring halves from No. 5 main bearing.

12 Cylinder head and valves - overhaul

1 It is assumed that the cylinder head has already been removed. Clean off all dirt and oil from the cylinder head.

2 Prepare a box for the valves and their retainers. The lid of a cardboard box can have eight holes punched in it to hold the valves. All the valves must be identified so that they can be refitted in the same location from which they are removed.

3 Using a valve spring compressor round the head, compress the valve spring enough to permit removal of the split collets. Remove the spring compressor. Take off the spring cap, the outer and inner valve

11.20 Fit a wedge to prevent the flywheel from turning

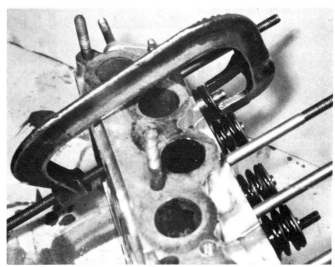
12.3a Compress the valve spring and remove the stem collets

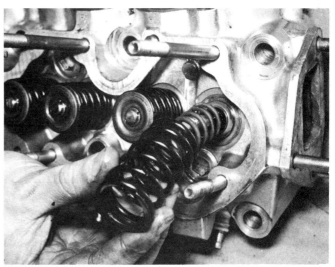
12.3b Remove the inner and outer valve springs ...

12.3c ... followed by the spring seats

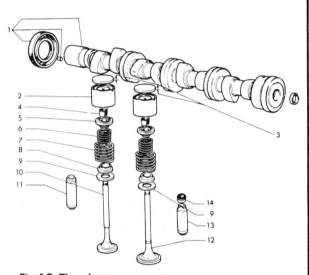

Fig. 1.8. The valve gear

1 Camshaft
2 Tappet
3 Tappet adjustment shims (in 30 thicknesses at 0.05 mm intervals)
4 Split cotters
5 Spring caps
6 Inner valve springs
7 Outer valve springs
8 Spring seats
9 Spring seats
10 Exhaust valve
11 Exhaust valve guide
12 Inlet valve
13 Inlet valve guide
14 Valve stem oil seal

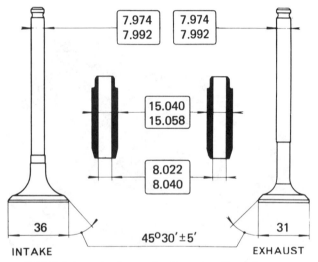

7.974
7.992

7.974
7.992

15.040
15.058

8.022
8.040

36

31

45°30′±5′

INTAKE

EXHAUST

Fig. 1.9. Inlet and exhaust valve dimensions (in mm)
Valve stem to valve guide clearance is 0.0012 to 0.0026 in
(0.030 to 0.066 mm)

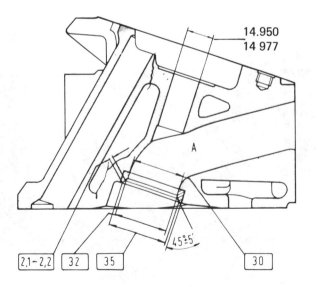

14.950
14 977

A

2,1 – 2,2   32   35   45°±5′   30

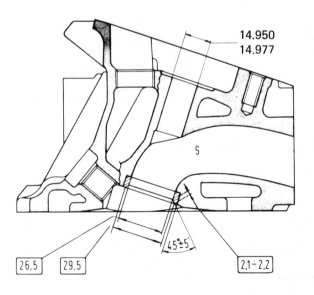

14.950
14.977

S

26,5   29,5   45°±5′   2,1 – 2,2

Fig. 1.10. Inlet valve seat (left). Exhaust valve seat (right)
Dimensions are in millimetres

springs, the two spring seats and the rubber sealing ring.

4   Examine the valve seats for bad fitting and in the case of the exhaust valve seats, burning. Check the mating surface of the head to the cylinder block for signs of gasket blowing. With the carbon still on the head the marks of leaks should be apparent. If the carbon deposit is thick, damp, and soft it indicates too much oil getting into the cylinders, either up past the piston rings or down through the inlet valve guides.

5   If the cylinder head gasket has been blowing then the head will need refacing. Either your FIAT agent or a local engineering works will get this done for you. The minimum amount necessary to get a clean flat surface should be removed.

6   If the valve seats are badly pitted or burned they will need refacing. Again your FIAT garage or any large repairer will have the cutters. If you try to do it by lengthy valve grinding then the valve will get badly worn, and the seating contact area will be too wide. The refacing operation includes narrowing of the seat with the cutters at 20° and 75°.

7   If the valve seats are being faced then the valves could be refaced too by the same firm at the same time. However, if the head is all right but the exhaust valves bad, then the most convenient and economical thing to do is to buy new exhaust valves. The inlet valves are usually in quite good condition.

8   The valve guides will be worn. It is very difficult to measure the wear. A useful yardstick is that if you need the crankshaft regrinding you will need new valve guides. It is tricky pressing the old ones out and the new in. It is recommended you get the FIAT agent to do it. He also will have the experience on which to judge the wear. The guides wear more than the valve stems so fitting new valves will not help this much.

9   Having decided what work must be done by a professional, now clean up the head. Scrape off all the carbon. Be careful not to scratch the valve seats. These are hard inserts, but a small scratch will be difficult to grind out. The head is made of aluminium, so soft, and easily cut when scraping. The combustion chambers, and inlet and exhaust ports, must be cleaned. A blunt screwdriver and flat paint scraper are useful. If using a wire brush on an electric drill wear goggles.

10   It is after this that the head should be taken for any machining. Also during the cleaning any cracks will be found. Should this unlikely event occur the only solution is another head.

11   Clean all carbon off the valves. It is convenient to do their head tops by putting them (unfixed) in their seat in the cylinder head. Scrape off all deposits under the head, and down the valve stem. The rubbing surface where the stem runs in the guide should be highly polished by wear; do not touch this, but the part of the stem nearer the head may have lacquered deposits that can be removed with fine emery paper. At this stage do not touch the valve's seating surface.

12   Now grind in the valves. Even new ones will need grinding in, to bed them to their actual seat. If the seats and valves or just the one, have been recut, the hand grinding must still be done.

13   The idea is to rub the valve to-and-fro, to mate valve and seat, and give a smooth flat perfectly circular sealing surface. The end product should be matt grey, without any rings or shine worn on it. The seating surface should be about midway up the valves 45° surface, not at the top, which happens if a valve is refaced so often it becomes small, and sits too deep in the seat.

14   The best tool is a rubber sucker on the end of a stick. Unless the sucker is good, and the valve absolutely oil free it keeps coming off. Handles that clamp to the stem overcome this, but they are clumsy to hold. On no account use an electric drill; a to-and-fro motion is essential.

15   If the valves and seats have been refaced you will only need fine grinding paste. If cleaning up worn seats start with coarse paste.

16   Smear a little of the paste all round the seat being very careful to get none on the valve stem. Insert the valve in its place. Put the valve grinding handle on the valve, and pushing it lightly down onto its seat rotate one way then the other. Every now and then lift the valve clear of the seat, turn it about half a turn, and then carry on. By altering the position the grinding paste is redistributed, and also the valve will work all round the seat and make it circular.

17   If coarse paste is used try and judge the change to fine just before all marks have disappeared so that they and the large grain of the coarse paste are ground out at the same time; the less metal rubbed off the better, otherwise the seat will get too broad.

18   The seat should be a uniform pale grey. Rings are a sign that the valve has not been lifted and turned enough. If a long grind is needed

the paste will get blunt, so wipe off the old and smear on some new. A spring under the valve head can help in the lifting, but it is difficult to find a suitable light one.

19   Clean off all traces of valve grinding paste very thoroughly. Wipe out the valve guides by pushing clean rag through a number of times. Engine oil makes a good detergent for this, particularly if squirted through hard with a good oil can. Leave everything oily to prevent rust.

20   The valve springs may need renewal. Measure their height as they stand free. If they have shortened by 1/16 in (1.5 mm) they should be renewed.

21   Reassemble the valves to the head. Make sure the valve goes into the correct seat, into which it was ground. Oil the guides, and the valves all over, before assembly.

22   Insert the valve in its seat, then fit the new oil seal, and push it down into place on the valve guide. Put the spring seats over the stem, followed by the springs. If the springs used have a varying spiral, put the end which has the spring coils closest together next to the head.

23   Put the cap on the spring.

24   Put the valve spring compressing clamp round the head and compress the spring. It needs to go just so far that the groove in the end of the stem is about half clear of the cap.

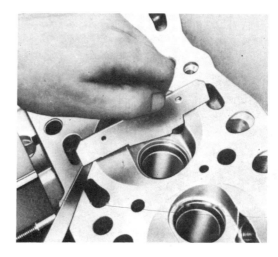

Fig. 1.11. Checking the depth of the combustion chamber with FIAT gauge A96216. Use a feeler gauge between gauge and head face. The gap must not exceed 0.01 in (0.25 mm)

12.16 Grind the valve with a to-and-fro movement, occasionally lifting and turning it to respread the grinding paste

12.25 Fit the split collets in position. A pair of long, thin-nosed pliers helps to get them located correctly

12.26a Valve tappet and adjusting shim

12.26b The valve tappets located on the valve springs

25 Put in the two split collets. Undo the clamp gradually, if necessary, moving the spring cap about to let it slide up the cotters to settle into position and clamp them properly.

26 When all the valves are assembled, fit the camshaft in its housing, with the tappets, to the head, whilst the latter is still on the bench, even though it will later have to be removed if the head is being fitted without the special spanners. Do not bother which shim goes to which tappet. Indeed use eight of the thinnest at this stage.

27 Now check the tappet clearances.

28 At the first try there may be no clearance on some valves, particularly if the seats or the valves have been refaced, and so allowed the valve to move a long way into its seat. If so, remove the camshaft housing again. If the thinnest made shim was already in use, the tip of the valve stem will have to be ground away. To do this, remove the valve from the head. On a fine grind stone, holding the valve very straight, grind a little metal off. Put the camshaft housing back on the head, and try the valve without springs, and using in the tappet a shim about a third of the way up the range from the thinnest. Keep trying the valve and grinding a little off at a time till it is a suitable length.

29 For other valves having some clearance at the trial assembly, write down the tappet clearances found. Then remove the camshaft, read off or measure the thickness of the shims in use, and change them for ones that will correct the tappet clearance. Put these shims with the tappets, ready for final assembly after the head is back on the engine. Note that the side with the number on it should be towards the tappet, away from the camshaft, so the correct side will take the wear.

30 After final assembly it may be necessary to alter some of the tappet clearance, so do not ignore later checks.

31 If the cylinder head face was remachined, it will bring the valves down nearer the pistons. If the machining was done by a FIAT agent he should have checked the height with the FIAT gauge A 96216. If the gap between the head and the measuring edge of this gauge is more than 0.01 in (0.25 mm) the head is too thin and must be replaced. If this gauge is not available then the head must be reassembled temporarily using tappet shims to reduce the clearance to 0.001 in (0.02 mm), and without a cylinder head gasket. Then turn the engine over very gently by hand to check there is no foul of piston and valve. If there is a foul, it is essential that the head is measured using the proper FIAT gauge. Though with normal tappet clearance and using a gasket, the valves might not foul when the engine is running slowly, at speed the pistons fly up to the top of their bearing clearance, and valves can deviate from close contact with the cam; so such a crude method of checking clearance as detailed earlier can only be used to a limited extent. See Fig. 1.11.

13 Cylinders, piston and connecting rods - overhaul

1   The oil consumption and exhaust oil smoke will have given some indication as to the wear of the bores and pistons. Once the cylinder head has been removed they can be measured properly.

2   Scrape the carbon off the unworn lip at the top of the bore so that its original size can be compared with the worn lip.

3   Measure the bore diameters. They will be worn more, near the top than the bottom, and more across than fore and aft. If the difference between the largest and smallest dimension exceeds 0.006 in (0.15 mm) then the ovality is excessive and a rebore is necessary. If the bores have any scores they should be rebored.

4   Even if the cylinders may not need reboring it is possible the pistons and rings will need replacing. They will have worn on their outer circumferential surfaces, and where the ring contacts the piston land in its groove.

5   Slide an appropriate feeler sideways into the piston groove to measure the clearance between each ring and its neighbouring land.

6   Carefully expand the rings and lift them off the piston. Insert the piston into the cylinder at its correct axis (valve cut outs away from the auxiliary shaft). Use the thickest feeler gauge that will pass between piston and bore with the piston halfway down its stroke, to get the widest part of the bore. Also measure opposite the ridge at the top. You have now got the actual clearance at the worn bit, and by comparing it with the clearance at the top, the cylinder wear. Take out the pistons. Insert a piston ring. Push it halfway down the cylinder with a piston, so that it is square. Measure the gap in the ring.

7   If the clearance between cylinder and piston or piston and ring is excessive then the pistons must be replaced, and new rings fitted to them. New rings can be fitted to old pistons by specialist firms who

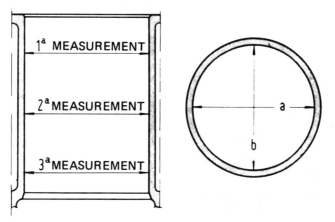

Fig. 1.12. Measuring the cylinder bore
Check the cylinder bores at three points both lengthwise and
crosswise

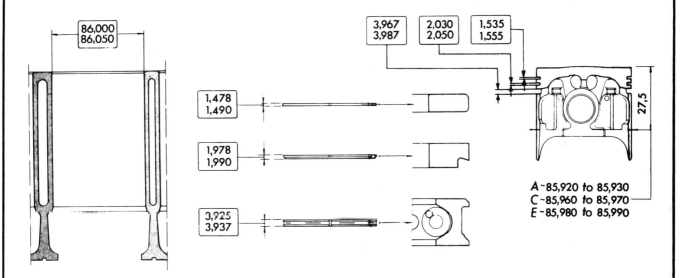

Fig. 1.13. Cylinder bore, piston and piston ring dimensions (dimensions in mm)

Fig. 1.14. Check clearance of rings in groove

| 1 Piston ring | 2 Piston | 3 Feeler gauge |

Fig. 1.15. Measuring the piston ring gap

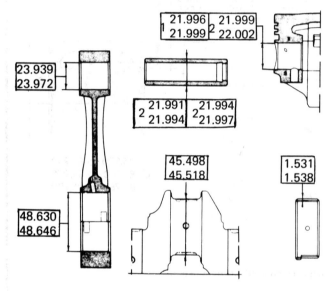

Fig. 1.16. Connecting rod big-end and small end dimensions

Fig. 1.17. Piston and connecting rod markings

1   *Piston boss bore class*   3   *Connecting rod and cap*
2   *Piston class letter*   *identification marking*

will machine out the grooves, which will be worn conical, and supply suitable rings. But this is not really economic. The wear limits are listed separately in the Specifications.

8   Note that it is most important if fitting new rings in the existing bores that the top ring has a step cut out of its top so that it will not hit the ridge left at the top of the bore. This will have been left by a worn piston ring. Should normal new rings be fitted, they will foul, which would anyway cause a knock, but probably also break the rings. Note also that the second and third rings have a special scraping bottom edge. The bores have three sizes, and the piston matching size is marked on it.

9   Fiat supply new pistons (and oversize ones) complete with rings and gudgeon pins; but not ones with the stepped top ring necessary if not reboring. This may persuade you to have the cylinder rebored, which would make a thorough job anyway.

10   The gudgeon pins are fully-floating and can be removed after taking out one of the circlips.

11   The small ends should last the life of the pistons. If new pistons are being fitted, then new gudgeon pins should also be fitted. This involves a replacement bush for the connecting rod. There should be no discernible free-movement in the small ends.

12   When renewing the gudgeon pins, first check the fit in the piston. It should be fitted by hand pressure, but be such a good fit that it will not drop out under its own weight. After fitting the gudgeon pin do not forget to fit the retaining circlip.

13   Before fitting the pistons to their connecting rods, weigh each piston and check their weights are all within the Specification. If not, see paragraph 17.

14   Before fitting the new rings to the pistons, check the size of the ring gap. Insert the ring into its cylinder, and push it halfway down the bore, using a piston so that it is square. Measure the gap with feeler gauges. If the gap is too small file it with a fine file, being careful, as the rings are brittle.

15   Check when fitting that all the rings are the right way up. They must be expanded only the minimum amount to get them over the piston lands. It is useful to cut a guide out of an old tin, and wrap this round the top of the piston.

16   The gaps in the three rings should all be equally spaced out, at 120° to each other.

17   The pistons' weights must all be within 2.5 grams, the same. If the spread is wider than this, the heavier ones must be lightened by milling metal off the underside of the small end bosses. If a proper milling machine is not available, then a disc of diameter 70 mm should be put on the sander of an electric drill. Use 'wet-or-dry' paper of grade 180. On no account reduce the piston height more than the minimum 2.055 in (52.2 mm), or the small end will be too weak (see Fig. 1.18).

14   Crankshaft and bearings - overhaul

1   The bearing surfaces of the crankshaft journals and pins should be bright and smooth. If there are scratches or scoring they will need regrinding. Measure the diameters of the bearings in a number of directions, looking for ovality. If the ovality exceeds 0.001 in (0.03 mm) then this is excessive purely as ovality, but also implies that overall wear will be too much. Take it to a FIAT agent, who can arrange the regrinding simultaneously with the supply of the main and big-end shells to the suitable undersize. Otherwise you must take it to a machine shop, who could regrind it for you to the journal sizes, less undersize, given in the Specifications. Then you order the new bearing shells from FIAT.

2   If the crankshaft ovality seems all right you may be able to measure the clearance to confirm overall wear is within the condemnation limit. It is difficult to measure, and difficult to measure the shaft accurately enough, to know how much of the wear is from the shaft, and how much off the shells. But ovality is easier to measure as it is only a comparison. No ovality means neglible shaft wear. It can be assumed the shells will have worn. One way to measure the clearance is to use 'Plastigage' a crushable plastic strip. The bearings are reassembled with the gauge inside, and the amount it is squashed is measured.

3   Unless the engine has done a very low mileage, and the shells appear of an even, matt colour, they should be replaced anyway, if events have made the engine require dismantling. Remove the shells from their caps. If they are stubborn, just slide them round by pressure at

the end. Confirm that the crankshaft is standard by looking at the markings on the backs of the shells. Because the shells are so easily fitted, are relatively cheap, it is false economy to try and make do with the old ones.

15 Flywheel and starter ring gear - overhaul

1   There are two things to check; the clutch pressure surface, and the starter ring.
2   If the clutch has been badly worn, or badly overheated by slipping, the surface on which the clutch presses may be scored or cracked. This would wear a new clutch plate rapidly. The flywheel should not be skimmed to remove these, but renewed.
3   Wear on the starter ring gear should not be bad, as the starter is the pre-engaged type. Check that there are no broken teeth, or burrs. Minor blemishes can be filed off. If there is a bad defect a new starter ring is required, though it may prove cheaper in the long run, and will certainly be easier, to buy a complete new flywheel.
4   To remove the old ring, it must be split by cutting with a cold chisel. Take care not to damage the flywheel, though again, minor burrs can be filed off.
5   To fit a new ring gear, it will be necessary to heat it gently and evenly with an oxy-acetylene flame until a temperature of approximately 350°C (662°F) is reached. (This is indicated by a grey/brown surface colour). With the ring gear at this temperature, fit it to the flywheel with the front of the teeth facing the clutch fitting end of the flywheel. The ring gear should be either pressed or lightly tapped onto its register and left to cool naturally when the contraction of the metal on cooling will ensure that it is a secure and permanent fit. Great care must be taken not to overheat the ring gear, for if this happens the temper of the ring gear will be lost.
6   An alternative method is to use a high temperature oven to heat the ring.
7   Because of the need of oxy-acetylene equipment or a special oven it is not practical for refitment to take place at home. Take the flywheel and new starter ring to an engineering works willing to do the job.

16 Oil pump - overhaul

1   Carefully clamp the pump housing in a vice, shaft downwards.
2   Take off the pump cover, with the suction pipe. This will release the oil pressure relief valve inside. Also inside is a filter.
3   Remove the internal cover plate.
4   Take out the driveshaft and the gears.
5   Clean and examine all the parts. Measure the clearances against the Specifications. The end clearance is measured by putting a straight edge across the cover face.
6   The oil pump should only need replacements after very long mileage, when the rest of the engine is showing great signs of wear.
7   The length of a new gear is given in the Specifications, so that the effect of just renewing that can be judged, to see if it will restore the end clearance to the Specifications. Otherwise the housing must be changed.
8   The driven gear shaft is mounted in the housing with an interference fit. If there is any slackness a new housing, which will come with shaft fitted, must be used.
9   The pump shares its drive with the distributor.

17 Camshaft and tappets - examination

1   The camshaft journals and cams should be smooth and shiny.
2   FIAT recommend that tappet shims should not be reused. Always obtain new ones. It is recommended the thicknesses are measured and tappet clearances adjusted using metric measure, as all the parts lists and orders are done by this.
3   Check the camshaft bearings and the tappets, and their corresponding parts in the housing are within tolerance.
4   Check the cam height. This is best done with a dial gauge.
5   Provided the cam height is satisfactory, the camshaft will probably be serviceable, and bearing wear be confined to the housing. If the

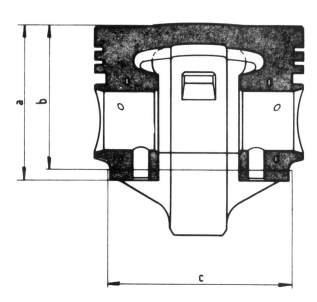

Fig. 1.18. Milling dimensions when balancing pistons
Maximum metal that can be removed is 0.177 in (4.5 mm)

a   *2.232 in (56.70 mm) nominal piston height*
b   *2.055 in (52.20 mm) minimum height after milling*
c   *2.775 in (70.50 mm) maximum milling diameter*

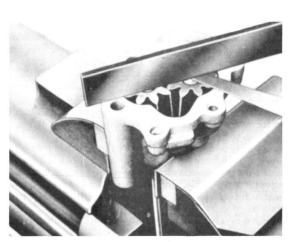

Fig. 1.19. Checking the oil pump end clearance - gears to cover

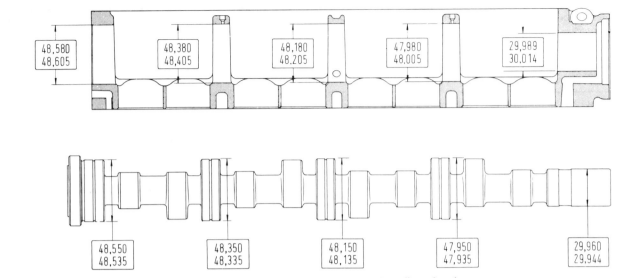

Fig. 1.20. Camshaft and bores in housing - dimensions in mm

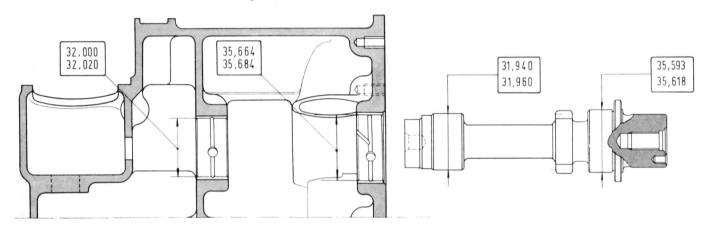

Fig. 1.21. Auxiliary shaft and bushes - dimensions in mm

housing is worn, either at the tappets or the camshaft bearings, it should be renewed. Worn bearings will allow too much oil to escape. Worn tappet bores allow the tappets to tilt, then wear becomes faster.

18 Auxiliary shaft - examination

1   The shaft journals, the fuel pump eccentric, and the drive gear for the distributor and oil pump should be smooth and shiny. If not, the shaft will have to be renewed.
2   The bushes should still be tight in the cylinder block, their oil holes lined up with those in the block.
3   Measure the bearing clearance. If excessive the bushes will have to be renewed. They are a press fit, and require reaming with a special reamer after fitting. This is a job best done by a FIAT agent with the special tools.
4   Ensure the new bushes are fitted with the oil holes lined up.
5   Also check the driven gear and its bush.
6   It is recommended a new oil seal is fitted in the endplate. Hold the shaft in a vice, and remove the pulley. Fit the new oil seal in the end-plate, lips inwards.

19 Drivebelt tensioner - examination and servicing

1   Check the bearing revolves smoothly and freely, and has no play. Do not immerse it in cleaning fluid, as it is partially sealed. But wipe the outside, and then smear in some new general purpose grease.
2   The action of the spring will have been felt when the belt was

taken off. It should be cleaned, and oiled, to prevent seizure through dirt and rust.

20 Engine mountings - examination

Check the rubber of the mountings. If they are deformed or soft through oil contamination, or badly perished, they should be renewed.

21 Lubrication system - general description

1   The oil pump is driven by the auxiliary shaft and is of the gear type. Incorporated in the pump is a pressure relief valve which opens when the oil pressure in the lubrication system is in excess of the normal operating pressure. The oil filter is of the disposable cartridge type and is located on the front of the engine. Incorporated in the filter mounting is a small spring-loaded bypass valve which opens if the flow of oil through the filter drops due to severe contamination of the filter element.
2   The oil pump drains oil from the sump via a pick up pipe and wire mesh filter, and it passes the oil, under pressure, through the filter element.
3   The crankshaft main bearings are supported under pressure from drillings in the crankcase from the main oil gallery whilst the connecting rod big-end bearings are lubricated from the main bearings by oil forced through the crankshaft oilways. The camshaft bearings are fed from a drilling from the main oil gallery. The cams and tappets are lubricated by oil mist from outlets in the camshaft bearings.

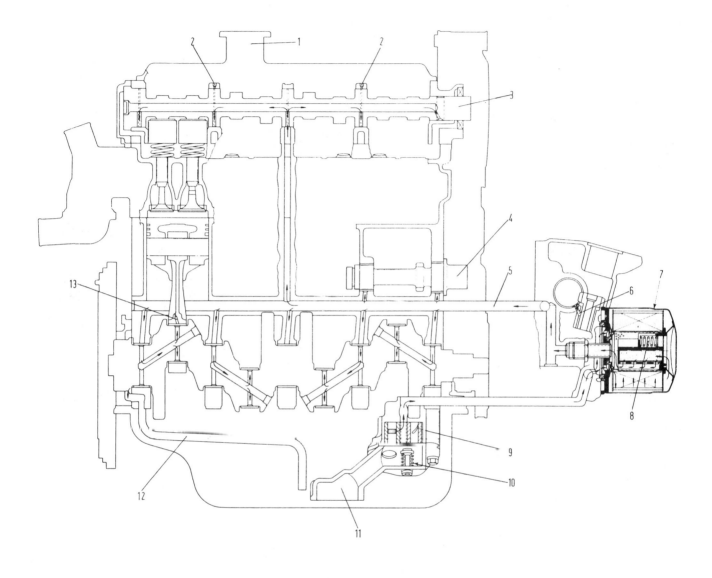

Fig. 1.22. Engine lubrication diagram

1	Oil filler pipe	4	Auxiliary units driveshaft	7	Full-flow oil filter
2	Oil mist outlets for camshaft lobes and tappets	5	Filter to engine components oil line	8	Bypass valve
3	Camshaft	6	Oil pump and distributor drive gear oil duct	9	Oil pump
				10	Oil pressure relief valve

11	Oil pump suction pipe
12	Oil return pipe
13	Oil mist outlet for cylinder walls

4   The cylinder walls, pistons and gudgeon pins are lubricated by oil splashed up by the crankshaft webs. An oil pressure gauge is fitted in the instrument panel to register the oil pressure in the main oil gallery. An oil pressure warning light is also fitted to indicate when the pressure is too low.

22 Engine reassembly - general

1   Cleanliness is vital. Particles of grit in components, particularly when starting up, will score them, the situation being aggravated by the good new tight fit, and the time taken for the oil pump to circulate oil to wash them clean.
2   All parts must be liberally oiled, with engine oil. This oil must serve the component till the oilways are all filled by the pump, after which proper circulation will start. The oiling is also a final protection against dirt, as it washes as well as lubricating.
3   All parts must be tightened evenly and gradually. New gaskets and oil seals must be used to ensure an oil-tight engine. and they must only be fitted to clean surfaces, with the remains of old gaskets removed.
4   Lay out the parts in order, checking you know where everything goes before starting. Sheets of clean newspaper should be laid out on the working surface. The garage should not be liable to wind blowing dust over the parts.

23 Crankshaft - refitting

1   Fit the main bearing shells to their seats in the crankcase and to

23.1 Make sure the bearing seats are clean before fitting the bearings in the crankcase

23.2 The thrust rings are fitted at No. 5 main bearing

23.3 Oil the bearings and crankshaft journals ...

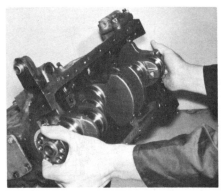

23.4 ... and then fit the crankshaft in the crankcase

23.5a The main bearing cap markings were noted during dismantling

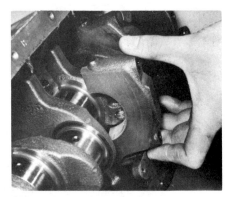

23.5b Make sure the main bearing caps are fitted the correct way round according to their identification marks ...

23.5c ... and fit the retaining bolts

23.6 Tighten the main bearing cap bolts with a torque wrench

23.8a Fit the oil seal carrier at the drivebelt end of the crankcase ...

the caps. The seatings and the rear of the shells must be spotlessly clean and dry or they will not seat properly.

2   Fit the thrust ring halves at No. 5 main bearing.

3   Oil the bearings in the crankcase, and the journals on the crankshaft.

4   Fit the crankshaft in the crankcase.

5   Fit the main bearing caps to the correct bearing positions and the right way round as indicated by the marks made at dismantling.

6   Tighten the caps evenly to a torque of 58 lb f ft (8 kg f m).

7   Check that the crankshaft rotates smoothly.

8   Fit the new oil seals in the carrier so that the lip of the seal will face inwards when fitted on the crankshaft. Using a new gasket, fit the carriers at each end of the crankshaft. Keep the bottom edge straight and level with that of the crankcase. Trim off any part of the gasket

that may show.

24 Pistons and connecting rod assemblies - refitting

1   Fit the new shells into the connecting rod and caps, ensuring the surfaces on which the shells seat, are clean and dry.

2   Check that the piston ring gaps are evenly spaced at 120° intervals. Oil them liberally.

3   Fit a piston ring clamp to compress the rings. If a piston ring clamp is not available a large hose clip of the Jubilee type can be used, but take care not to tighten it so much that it grips the piston.

4   Oil the cylinder bores. With the crankcase on its side insert the

23.8b ... and then the one at the flywheel end

24.1 The piston and connecting rod assembly ready for fitting in the block

24.4a The identification numbers stamped on the connecting rods are to the rear of the engine when fitted ...

24.4b ... and also the cut-outs on the piston crowns

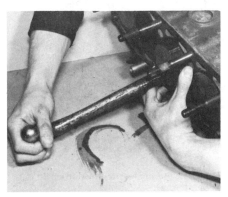

24.5 Tap the piston crown lightly to free it from the piston ring clamp

24.6 When fitting the connecting rod big-end cap make sure it is the right way round

24.7 The torque loading of the big-end nuts is important as they have no locking device

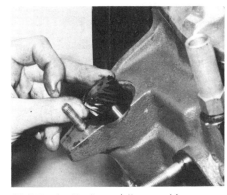

25.2 Fit the distributor/oil pump drive

25.3 Refitting the auxiliary shaft in the block with the endplate and pulley already fitted on the shaft

connecting rod and piston into the bore, checking that it is the right bore for the connecting rod. The number stamped on the big-end of the rod should be to the rear of the engine, away from the auxiliary shaft as should be the cut-outs for the valves in the piston crown.

5   Push the piston into the bore until the piston ring clamp is against the cylinder block and then tap the crown of the piston lightly to push it out of the ring clamp and into the bore.

6   Oil the crankshaft journal and fit the big-end of the connecting rod to the journal. Fit the big-end cap and nuts checking that the cap is the right way round.

7   Tighten the big-end nuts to a torque of 36 lb f ft (5 kg f m). The correct torque is important as the nuts have no locking arrangement. After tightening each big-end, check that the crankshaft rotates

smoothly.

25 Auxiliary shaft - refitting

1   Oil the auxiliary shaft and fit it into the crankcase.

2   Fit a new seal to the endplate and fit the plate to the crankcase. Fit the distributor/oil pump drive.

3   Fit the pulley, and its bolt, partially tighten the bolt for now and finally tighten it to a torque of 6 lb f ft (8.5 kg f m) after the drivebelt is fitted. The endplate and pulley can be fitted to the shaft before fitting the shaft in the crankcase, and the bolt tightened while holding the shaft in a vice.

26.1 Fit the oil drip pipe ...

26.3 ... and the oil pump

26.5 Stick the sump gasket on with grease ...

26.6 ... and then fit the sump on the crank-case

27.1a Bolt the engine/transmission shield in place

27.1b The flywheel can only go on the one way as the bolt holes are offset

27.2a Fit the lockplate and then the bolts

27.2b Wedge the flywheel to prevent it turning whilst tightening the bolts

27.3a Fit the drivebelt pulley and the alternator/water pump 'V' belt pulley

27.3b The crankshaft pulley retaining nut is tightened to 101 lb f ft (14 kg f m), using a 38 mm socket

28.3 The cylinder head gasket is fitted with the marking 'ALTO' upwards

28.4 Lower the cylinder head down over the studs

26 Oil pump and sump - refitting

1   Fit the oil drip pipe for the breather at No. 3 main bearing.
2   Fit the oil drain pipe to No. 5 main bearing.
3   Fit the oil pump. Use a new gasket between the pump and the crankcase, and tighten the three securing bolts.
4   Check that the auxiliary shaft turns without sticking. If there is any binding, release the oil pump securing bolts, shift the pump slightly and try again.
5   Place the sump gasket on the crankcase, stick it with grease to keep it in place.
6   Fit the sump and the retaining washers and bolts. Tighten the bolts evenly to prevent warping.

27 Flywheel, clutch and crankshaft pulleys - refitting

1   Bolt the engine/transmission shield to the crankcase and fit the flywheel on the end of the crankshaft. Make sure the mating surfaces of the crankshaft flange and the flywheel are clean, to ensure a good seating. The bolt holes are offset, but the flywheel can still be fitted in one of two positions, so align the marks made before dismantling.
2   Fit the bolt lockplate, then the retaining bolts, and tighten them to a torque of 61 lb f ft (8.5 kg f m). It will be necessary to restrain the flywheel from turning by wedging it, as described in Section 11.
3   Fit the drivebelt pulley, with the timing dot mark facing outwards, and the alternator/water pump 'V' belt pulley. Fit the retaining nut and, restraining the crankshaft from turning by wedging the flywheel, tighten the nut to 101 lb f ft (14 kg f m).
4   Fit the clutch assembly to the flywheel, as described in Chapter 5, Section 5, making sure that the driven plate is centred.

28 Cylinder head and camshaft housing - refitting

1   Make sure the top surface of the cylinder block is clean. Turn the engine until all the pistons are at mid-stroke with Nos 1 and 4 rising. This will avoid the risk of valves striking pistons when the camshaft is rotated prior to fitting the drivebelt.
2   Fit the two dowels in the cylinder block.
3   Fit the cylinder head gasket with the word 'ALTO' facing upwards.
4   Fit the cylinder head on the cylinder block.
5   Fit the large thick washers which spread the load on the aluminium head. Fit the cylinder head holding-down nuts and bolts. Using a torque wrench tighten them gradually and in the sequence shown in Fig. 1.23 to the specified torque.
6   Oil the camshaft and housing. Hold the housing on end and lower the camshaft into it. Fit a new gasket and then fit the endplate on the

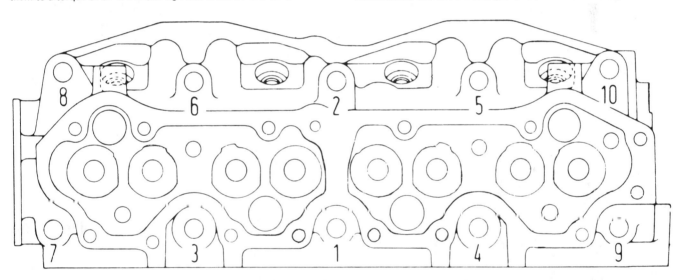

Fig. 1.23. Tightening sequence for cylinder head nuts and bolts

28.5 Fit the holding down bolts and nuts and tighten them to the specified torque

28.6 Lower the camshaft into its housing

28.8 Refit the camshaft housing on the cylinder head. Make sure the tappets locate correctly in their housings

28.10a Fit the backing plate first ...

28.10b ... and then the belt guard

28.11 The camshaft drive pulley retaining nut is tightened after the drivebelt is fitted

28.12 Using a feeler gauge to check the tappets clearance

28.13 Bolt the engine mounting support in position

28.14a Locate the belt tensioner on its dowel and fit the tensioner pulley...

28.14b ... followed by the spacer, stepped washer ...

28.14c ... support washer and nut

28.15 The camshaft pulley timing mark is aligned with the finger on the engine mounting support

28.16a Temporarily fit the drivebelt cover ...

28.16b ... and align the timing mark on the crankshaft 'V' belt pulley with the mark on the cover

left end of the housing (engine with the distributor fitted on the front of the engine only). Fit the drivebelt pulley on the camshaft after the belt guard is fitted.

7 Lubricate the tappet bores in the housing and refit the tappets in the same location from which they came. If any of the tappets fall out under gravity use a smear of grease to hold them in position.

8 Place a new gasket on the cylinder head and fit the housing. Before tightening down the camshaft housing, check that the pistons are still halfway down the cylinder bores. This is shown by the timing mark on the crankshaft 'V' belt pulley being in the 9 o'clock position, 90° before TDC. This avoids the risk of a valve striking a piston before the timing has been set.

9 Fit the washers and nuts to the camshaft housing studs, and tighten them gradually, so that the housing is pulled down level. Tighten the nuts to 14.5 lb f ft (2 kg f m).

10 Fit the two parts of the belt guard to the right-hand end of the engine.

11 Fit the camshaft drive pulley, leave the final tightening of the retaining bolt till the drivebelt is fitted.

12 Check the valve clearance. Make sure the pistons are still halfway in their bores and turn the camshaft by the pulley retaining bolt. Re-adjust any valve clearance, if necessary, as described in Section 29.

13 Fit the right-hand engine mounting support.

14 Fit the belt tensioner on its locating dowel and fit the belt tensioner pulley, spacer, washers and nut.

15 Turn the camshaft until the timing mark on the pulley is aligned with the finger on the engine mounting support.

16 Temporarily fit the drivebelt cover and turn the engine 90° to align the timing mark on the 'V' belt pulley with the right-hand line (TDC) on the cover.

17 If the above procedure is followed, there should be no piston-valve contact. If the crankshaft is turned through more than 90°, or if the camshaft is incorrectly set, the pistons may contact the valves at the top of their stroke. Be alert to this possibility and proceed with caution. *On no account turn the camshaft with the timing belt disconnected and any pistons at TDC.*

18 Remove the drivebelt cover. Fit and tension the drivebelt as described in Section 5.

19 Tighten the camshaft pulley and the auxiliary shaft drive pulley retaining bolts to 61 lb f ft (8.5 kg f m). Bend over the locking tabs to lock the bolts.

20 Fit the drivebelt cover.

---

29 Valve clearances - adjustment

1 The checking of the valve clearance is included in the 12,000 miles (20,000 km) routine maintenance. The clearance should also be checked if the camshaft housing has been removed from the cylinder head for any reason. It is important that the clearance is set correctly otherwise the timing will be wrong and the engine performance will be poor. If there is no clearance at all the valves and valve seats will soon burn. Set the clearance with the engine cold.

2 Remove the camshaft housing cover. Jack-up a rear wheel and engage top gear, so that the wheel can be used to turn the engine over.

3 Each tappet must be checked when its operating cam is pointing upwards, 180° away from the tappet. Check the clearances in the firing order, No. 1 cylinder first and then 3, 4 and 2. Do the exhaust of one cylinder and the inlet of the one after, at the same time to minimise the amount the engine has to be turned over. Counting from the timing cover end of the engine, the valve sequence is:

Inlet	*2-3-6-7*
Exhaust	*1-4-5-8*

4 Insert the feeler gauge for the appropriate valve. See Specifications for correct settings. The feeler should slide in readily, but with slight friction. Try one a size thicker and thinner. The thick one should not go in and the thinner one should be too loose.

5 If the clearance is wrong, measure the actual clearance and write it down. When all the clearances have been checked, calculate the required thickness of shim to obtain the correct clearance, and select a shim accordingly.

6 To change a shim, turn the engine till the cam is pointing upwards, then position the tappet in its housing so that the slot in the rim is towards you.

7 Depress the tappet with the special tool (No. A60421) which is

available from FIAT.

8 If you have not got a special tool, push the tappet down with one screwdriver placed centrally. Then wedge it down with another on edge at the side. This is very tricky. It might be quicker possibly to remove the camshaft housing. (See Section 4). Once the drivebelt is

28.18 The drivebelt fitted in position

28.20 Bolt the drivebelt cover in position

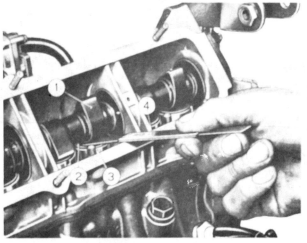

Fig. 1.24. Checking valve clearance

1 Cam lobe   2 Tappet shim   3 Tappet   4 Feeler gauge

Fig. 1.25. Using FIAT tool A60421 when changing a tappet shim

30.1 The oil filter is screwed on hand-tight

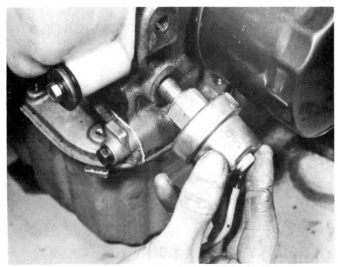

30.2a The oil pressure warning sender is fitted beside the oil filter ...

removed, however, it must be renewed. Best of all is to get the job done by the FIAT agent. As well as the tool, they will have a stock of shims from which to choose the necessary ones to correct the clearance. It is expensive to buy a stock.

9   Prise out the shim with a thin screwdriver in the tappet slot. The FIAT way is to blow them out with compressed air, which is effective if an air line is available. They are held in quite strongly by the oil film. They must lift up square, or else they jam.

10 Check the thickness of the shim removed, and substitute one of an appropriate thickness to correct the clearance. When new, shims have the thickness marked on the bottom, but this wears off, so they must be measured by micrometer. It is best to work in millimetres, as the new shims are marked, and listed in the parts list, under millimetre sizes.

11 Insert the new shim, numbered side down, towards the tappet and valve.

30 Minor components and ancillaries - refitting

1   Fit a new oil filter element. Oil the sealing ring and screw the filter on hand-tight.

2   Refit the oil pressure warning sender to the front of the cylinder block and the water temperature sender to the cylinder head.

3   Fit the fuel pump, as described in Chapter 3, Section 3.

4   Fit the water manifold on the cylinder head.

5   Fit the water pump and the hose to the water manifold.

6   Fit the crankcase breather and oil pressure gauge sender.

7   Fit the distributor, as described in Chapter 4, Section 5. On engines with the distributor fitted on the end of the camshaft housing, fit the blank and clamp plate in the distributor mounting on the front of the engine.

8   Fit the alternator and tension the 'V' belt as described in Chapter 10, Section 7.

9   Fit new manifold gaskets over the studs on the cylinder head. Fit the exhaust manifold, followed by the inlet manifolds with the carburettor fitted as described in Chapter 3.

31 Refitting the transmission to the engine

1   Refitting the transmission to the engine is the reverse of the removal sequence. Take care not to put any strain on the input shaft. An assistant to turn the engine by a spanner on the crankshaft pulley nut will help to align the splines and engage the input shaft in the clutch disc.

2   Tighten the nuts and bolts holding the transmission to the engine to 57 lb f ft (8 kg f m).

3   Fit the starter motor.

32 Engine - refitting in car

1   Refitting of the engine is the reversal of the removal procedure. Make sure the engine is properly slung for lifting into position . As the engine is raised check that it does not foul any projections, hoses or cables.

2   If new bearings and rings have been fitted it is likely that the engine will be stiff to turn, make sure the battery is well charged.

3   Carry out the following checks before attempting to start the engine:

  a) Fuel lines to pump and carburettor connected.
  b) Water hoses connected and clamps tight.
  c) Coolant drain tap closed.
  d) Coolant system filled.
  e) Sump drain-plug tight.
  f) Engine oil filled to correct level.
  g) Transmission oil filled to correct level and filler/level and drain plugs tight.
  h) LT leads connected to distributor and coil.
  j) HT leads connected to spark plugs, distributor and coil.
  k) Rotor arm fitted in distributor.
  l) Oil pressure and water temperature sender units screwed in tight and leads connected.
  m) Choke and throttle cables connected.
  n) Earth strap, transmission to frame connected.

30.2b ... and the water temperature sender is located on the cylinder head

30.4 Fit the water manifold to the cylinder head at the flywheel end of the engine ...

30.5 ... and then the water pump, and the hose to the water manifold

30.6 The crankcase breather is fitted on the front of the crankcase, next to the oil pressure gauge sender

30.7a On engines with the distributor driven from the end of the camshaft, the oil pump drive is retained in position by a blank spindle ...

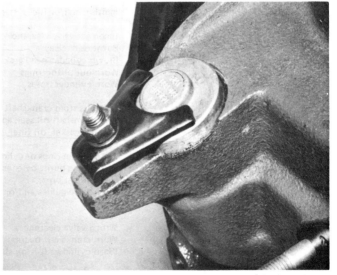

30.7b ... which is retained by a clamp

o) *Starter motor leads connected.*
p) *Alternator leads connected.*
q) *Fan motor lead connected.*
r) *Battery leads connected.*
s) *Make a final check of the engine compartment to ensure that no tools, rags, etc have been overlooked.*

33 Engine - initial start-up after overhaul

1   Switch on the ignition and check that appropriate warning lights come on.
2   On cars with electric fuel pump, check the fuel system for leaks.
3   Start up the engine.
4   Watch the oil pressure warning light and alternator charging indicator light. If there is no charge or if the oil pressure warning light does not go out after a second or two, having had time to fill the new oil filter,

switch off and recheck.
5   If the warning lights go out, set the engine to run on fast idle and check the engine for leaks.
6   Check the coolant level, it will probably go down as air locks are filled.
7   Keep the engine running at a fast idle and bring it up to normal working temperature. As the engine warms up, there will be some odd smells and smoke from parts getting hot and burning off oil deposits.
8   When the engine running temperature has been reached adjust the idling speed, as described in Chapter 3.
9   Stop the engine and wait a few minutes and check to see if there are any coolant or oil leaks.
10 Road test the car to check that the engine is running with the correct smoothness and power. Do not race the engine. If new bearings and/or pistons and rings have been fitted it should be treated as a new engine and run in at reduced speed for at least 500 miles (800 km).
11 After 500 miles (800 km) change the engine oil and filter.

34 Fault diagnosis - engine

When investigating starting and uneven running faults do not be tempted into snap diagnosis. Start from the beginning of the check procedure and follow it through. It will take less time in the long run. Poor performance from an engine in terms of power and economy is not normally diagnosed quickly. In any event the ignition and fuel systems must be checked first before assuming any further investigation needs to be made.

Symptom	Reason/s	Remedy
Engine will not turn over when starter switch is operated	Flat battery Bad battery connections Bad connections at solenoid switch and/or starter motor	Check that battery is fully charged and that all connections are clean and tight.
	Defective solenoid	Remove starter and check solenoid.
	Starter motor defective	Remove starter and overhaul.
Engine turns over normally but fails to fire and run	No spark at plugs	Check ignition system according to procedures given in Chapter 4.
	No fuel reaching engine	Check fuel system according to procedures given in Chapter 3.
	Too much fuel reaching the engine (flooding)	Check the fuel system as above.
Engine starts but runs unevenly and misfires	Ignition and/or fuel system faults	Check the ignition and fuel systems as though the engine had failed to start.
	Incorrect valve clearances	Check and reset clearances.
	Burnt out valves Blown cylinder head gasket	Remove cylinder head and examine and overhaul as necessary.
	Worn out piston rings Worn cylinder bores	Remove cylinder head and examine pistons and cylinder bores. Overhaul as necessary.
Lack of power	Ignition and/or fuel system faults	Check the ignition and fuel systems for correct ignition timing and carburettor settings.
	Incorrect valve clearance	Check and reset the clearances.
	Burnt out valves Blown cylinder head gasket	Remove cylinder head and examine and overhaul as necessary.
	Worn out piston rings Worn cylinder bores	Remove cylinder head and examine pistons and cylinder bores. Overhaul as necessary.
Excessive oil consumption	Oil leaks from crankshaft front and rear oil seals, camshaft oil seal, auxiliary shaft oil seal, cambox gasket, oil filter, sump gasket or drain plug	Identify source of leak and renew seal as appropriate.
	Worn piston rings or cylinder bores resulting in oil being burnt by engine, smoky exhaust is an indication	Fit new rings or rebore cylinders and fit new pistons, depending on degree of wear.
	Worn valve guides and/or defective valve stem seals	Remove cylinder heads and recondition valve stem bores and valves and seals as necessary.
Excessive mechanical noise from engine	Wrong valve clearances	Adjust valve clearances.
	Worn crankshaft bearings Worn cylinders (piston slap)	Inspect and overhaul where necessary.
Unusual vibration	Misfiring on one or more cylinders	Check ignition system.
	Loose mounting bolts	Check tightness of bolts and condition of flexible mountings.

Chapter 2 Cooling, heating and exhaust systems

For modifications, and information applicable to later models, see Supplement at end of manual

Contents

Specifications

Water pump

Type	Centrifugal, vane type
Pump drive	'V' belt
Clearance impeller/housing	0.031 to 0.051 in (0.8 to 1.3 mm)
Maximum bearing endplay	0.005 in (0.12 mm)

Cooling system capacity ... ... 11.5 Imp. pints (6.5 litres/14 US Pints)

Fan

Fan power	55 watts
Fan cut-in temperature	194°F (90°C)
Fan cut-out temperature	187°F (87°C)

Thermostat

Starts to open at	176 - 183°F (80 - 84°C)
Opening at 205°F (96°C)	Not less than 0.314 in (8 mm)

Expansion cap valve opening pressure ... ... 11 psi (0.8 kg/Sq. cm)

1 General description

1 The engine cooling system is of the sealed type and has a front-mounted radiator with an expansion tank located in the engine compartment at the rear. The radiator flow and return pipe are routed underneath the car to the engine. With the engine being mounted at the rear the fan cannot be driven in the usual way. Instead an electrically powered fan is mounted behind the radiator. It is controlled by a relay which in turn is controlled by a thermostatic switch in the left tank of the radiator. When the coolant temperature is 90°C (194°F) or above the switch closes, this starts the fan which continues to run until the temperature drops below 85°C (185°F).

2 The coolant is circulated in the system by the water pump which is mounted at the right-hand side of the engine and is driven by a rubber 'V' belt from the crankshaft pulley.

3 The heater is a hot water type which circulates the engine coolant through a small radiator. Air is drawn in through the cowl vent and

over the radiator by a small fan to heat the interior of the car. The heater cannot be fully drained to allow for this when flushing the cooling system.

4 The exhaust system consists of a short downpipe from the exhaust manifold to the silencer, which is secured to a mounting bracket attached to the power unit.

2 Cooling system - draining and filling

1 To drain the cooling system, open the heater control and remove the expansion tank cap. Take care if the engine is warm, allow it to cool before removing the cap as the system is pressurised and any sudden drop in pressure could cause the coolant to boil and result in a possible scalding. If the cap has to be removed when the engine is warm cover it with a thick rag and ease it open gradually to release the pressure.

2 Place a clean container under the hose connections under the car

2.2a Disconnect the radiator hose from the pipe to the engine

2.2b Open the drain tap on the engine block

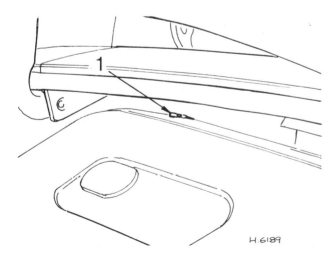

H.6189

Fig. 2.1. The air bleed valve is accessbile in the front luggage compartment

1　Air bleed valve

and disconnect the hoses where they join the pipes leading to the engine. Drain the coolant from the engine block by unscrewing the drain tap on the side of the block. Loosen the clamp on the expansion tank bottom hose and empty the tank.

3　Reconnect the hoses and close the drain tap. Open the air bleed valve on the top of the radiator, accessible from the front luggage compartment. Fill the system through the expansion tank cap till the level in the expansion tank is about 3 in (76.2 mm) above the 'MIN' mark on the outside of the tank. Tighten the bleed valve.

4　Fit the expansion tank cap and run the engine to its normal operating temperature. Check for leaks. Switch off the engine, allow the system to cool and top-up the expansion tank, if necessary.

3　Antifreeze and inhibitors - general

1　In cold climates antifreeze is needed for two reasons. In extreme cases if the coolant in the engine freezes solid it could crack the cylinder block or head. But also in cold weather, with the circulation restricted by the thermostat, and any warm water that is getting to the radiator being at the top, the bottom of the radiator could freeze, and so block circulation completely, making the coolant trapped in the engine boil.

2　The antifreeze should be mixed in the proportions advocated by the makers according to the climate. There are two levels of protection. The first cuts risk of damage, as the antifreeze goes mushy before freezing. But when mushy it does not circulate properly. It gives full protection allowing proper circulation to only a less cold temperature. The normal proportion in a temperate climate is 25% antifreeze by volume, with 33 1/3% for a colder one. This mix should be used for topping-up too, otherwise the mixture will gradually get weaker.

3　Antifreeze should be left in through the summer. It has an important secondary function, to act as an inhibitor against corrosion. In the cooling system are many different metals, in particular the aluminium of the cylinder head. In contact with the coolant this sets up electrolytic,corrosion, accentuated by any dirt in the system. This corrosion can be catastrophically fast. Reputable antifreeze of a suitable formula must be used.

4　After about two years the effectiveness of the antifreeze's inhibitor is used up. It must then be discarded, and the system flushed as described in Section 4, and then refitted with new coolant.

5　In warm climates free from frost, an inhibitor should be used. Again a reputable make giving full protection must be chosen and renewed every two years. Inhibitors with dyes are useful for finding leaks, and on some makes the dye shows when the inhibiting ability is finished.

4　Cooling system - flushing

1　Despite the use of inhibitors, the cooling system collects dirt and sludge. Whenever circumstances, such as renewing the antifreeze permit, or when it has been drained for removal of the cylinder head, the system should be flushed.

2　With the engine cold, open the tap on the engine block, located directly below the carburettor, and the drain plugs in the pipes running underneath the car. Put a hose in the expansion tank, and turn it on when the coolant is still flowing from the drain tap and plugs.

3　Disconnect the heater pipe at the cylinder head. Turn the heater full on. Transfer the hose from the expansion tank to the heater connection and fit the drain plugs so that more flow is available to flush the heater circuit, and ensure that water comes out of the disconnected heater hose.

4　Leave the heater hose disconnected whilst refilling the system, till the new coolant begins to come out of the connection as this helps to eliminate airlocks in the system.

5　On older cars, or ones used with very hard water in the cooling system, or without inhibitors, the water passages may become coated with hard deposits that will not come out with normal flushing. In this case, use a good proprietary cleaning agent, such as Holts Radflush or Holts Speedflush. It is important that the manufacturer's instructions are followed carefully. The regular renewal of antifreeze should prevent further scaling and contamination of the system.

6　When the engine has been stripped for a job such as decarbonising there will be dirt that has fallen into the water passage. So when refilling after such work put normal water in first, run the engine, and then flush out, before putting in the antifreeze or inhibitor.

7 After refilling, start up and allow the engine to warm up. Check the heater works, proving there is no airlock. Switch off. Check the level; it is likely to have fallen, as some air pockets will have now filled with coolant.

5 Cooling system - diagnosis and prevention of leaks

1 The fitting of hoses, and their freedom from leaks, will be better if whenever any of the simple clips originally fitted by FIAT are removed, they are replaced with screw worm ones such as 'Jubilee clips' or 'Cheney connections'.

2 New hose connections settle in, and the clips will need retightening 500 miles (800 km) and again at 2,000 miles (3,200 km) after fitting.

3 Clean antifreeze is 'searching' and will leak at weak spots. The system should be very carefully inspected after refilling with antifreeze.

4 Hoses should be examined regularly and renewed before failure. If the hoses become spongy or show signs of cracking it is unlikely that they will last long. Unless hoses are nearly new, they should be renewed when some job requires their removal.

5 Coolant leaks from the cylinder head gasket can give some strange symptoms. Water can get in the oil. This can give a rising oil level! Very quickly the oil becomes creamy coloured with the emulsified water. Oil can get into the water, though this is less common due to the pressurised cooling system. If the water is leaking into the combustion chambers, the water will show as excess vapour in the exhaust. Water vapour is always visible in the exhaust when cold, but a leaking head gasket can make it continue when hot. Unlike oil smoke it is white, and very wispy, blown more quickly by the wind.

6 Minor leaks from parts of the engine or the radiator can be successfully cured with proprietary sealants that are put in the coolant. Leaking hoses must be renewed. Bad leaks in metal parts must be properly mended.

6 Thermostat - removal and refitting

1 The thermostat is needed in all climates to give quick warm up, and in cold ones to prevent the engine running too cold all the time. It also ensures hot water for the heater.

2 The thermostat has a double acting valve to close off the bypass once the main passage is open. If there was no bypass system the coolant would be stagnant, so the top of the engine would heat too much compared with the bottom.

3 The thermostat is of the wax capsule type. If it fails it is most likely to do so in the closed position, and give immediate and bad overheating. Should it stick in the open position the engine will run cold, and take a long time to warm up. On cars without thermometers this will only show by poor output from the heater. Though the car will run well, it is harmful to it.

4 If the thermostat sticks in the closed position on the road it must be removed as trying to continue with the engine overheating can cause serious damage. If no replacement is available, then the engine can be run without the thermostat, but it must be replaced at the earliest opportunity.

5 To remove the thermostat, unscrew a drain plug from one of the pipes running under the car and drain about half of the coolant into a clean container so that it can be re-used. Draining this amount of coolant lowers the level of the coolant below the thermostat housing.

6 Remove the air cleaner. Disconnect the hose from the bottom of the housing. Remove the three bolts holding the cover to the housing and remove the thermostat and gasket.

7 The action of the thermostat can be checked by heating it in a container of water. The opening action can be seen as a definite movement well before the water boils. The operating temperatures can be checked accurately by using a thermometer.

8 Refitting of the thermostat is the reverse of the removal procedures. Make sure joint faces are clean and always use a new gasket.

7 Thermostatic switch - removal, checking and refitting

1 The thermostatic switch, fitted in the left-hand tank of the

radiator, controls the operation of the electric fan motor by sensing the coolant temperature.

2 The switch can be removed without draining the cooling system, provided the expansion tank cap is fitted and that there are no leaks in the system. When the switch is removed a small amount of coolant will drain out and the system must be topped-up after the switch is refitted.

3 If the thermostatic switch is being removed because the fan is not operating and the switch is suspect, check the fan fuse and the relay fuse first before removing the switch.

4 To remove the switch, disconnect the leads from the terminals and unscrew the switch.

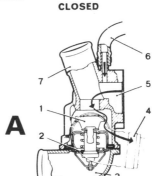

Fig. 2.2. Thermostat operation

1	Top valve	5 Inlet from cylinder head
2	Bottom valve	6 Pipe from carburettor
3	Union from radiator	7 Union to radiator
4	Outlet to pump	

7.4 The thermostatic switch

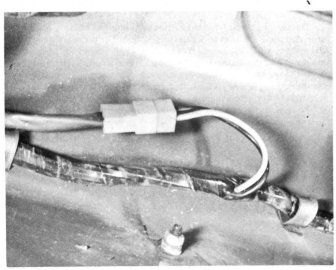

10.3 Disconnect the leads to the fan motor

10.5a Remove the bolts securing the cross-rail at each side ...

10.5b ... and remove the radiator and fan

5   Connect a test bulb across the switch terminals and immerse the sensing part of the switch in a container of water. Heat the water and, using a thermometer, check the temperature of the water when the bulb lights up, indicating the switch is functioning. The switch should operate at approximately 194°F (90°C). Allow the water to cool and check that the switch cuts out at 18°F (8°C). Renew a faulty switch.
6   Refitting of the switch is the reverse of the removal procedure. Always fit a new 'O' ring on the switch.

8   Fan motor and relay - checking

1   If the fan is not operating and the fuses and thermoswitch have been checked and found serviceable, check the fan motor and relay by connecting the two thick wires to the relay together. If the fan motor operates, the relay is at fault and must be renewed. If the fan motor does not operate then that is where the fault lies and the motor must be renewed.
2   If the cut-out, cut-in system fails this can be temporarily overcome as follows:

a) *Connect both thermoswitch leads to the same terminal. If it is the switch which is faulty the fan will operate and run all the time the ignition is switched on. If the fan does not operate reconnect the leads in the normal way.*
b) *Connect the two thick wires to the relay together, if the relay is at fault the fan will operate and run all the time even when the ignition is switched off.*

Note: Only the switch circuit at the relay is controlled by the ignition switch. The main feed through the relay is direct. If the relay leads are connected together, they must be disconnected when the engine is switched off or the battery will be discharged.

9   Cooling fan - removal and refitting

1   Disconnect the fan motor leads at the connector.
2   Remove the shroud retaining nuts and withdraw the fan and shroud.
3   Remove the nut securing the fan to the motor shaft. Remove the motor attaching nuts and separate the motor from the shroud.
4   Refitting is the reverse of the removal sequence.

10   Radiator - removal and refitting

Note: *If the reason for removing the radiator is concern over coolant loss, note that minor leaks may be repaired by using a radiator sealant, such as Holts Radweld, with the radiator in situ*

1   Drain the system, as described in Section 2.
2   Remove the three bottom screws holding the grille to the crossrail.
3   Disconnect the leads from the thermostatic switch and the connector from the fan motor.
4   Disconnect both hoses from the radiator.
5   Remove the bolts securing the crossrail at each side and carefully lower the radiator out of the car, taking care not to damage the fan.
6   Refitting is the reverse of the removal procedure. Refill the system, as described in Section 2.

11   Radiator - cleaning and repair

1   Clean the radiator inside and out. Clean the exterior of the radiator by hosing down the matrix with a strong jet of water to clean away road dirt, dead flies etc. Thoroughly flush out the inside of the radiator.
2   With the radiator out of the car, any leaks or damage can be repaired.
3   Inspect the radiator hose for cracks, internal or external deterioration and other damage. Renew hose clips which are rusted or distorted.

12   Water pump - removal and refitting

1   Remove the protective panels from the bottom right-hand side of the engine.

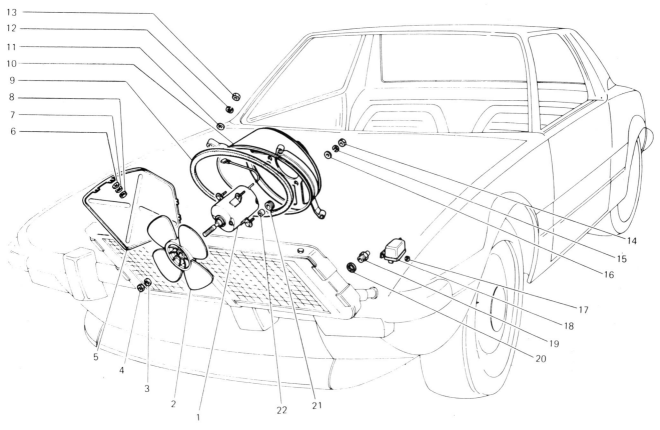

Fig. 2.3. Exploded view of fan installation

1	Fan motor	6	Washer	11	Washer	17	Nut
2	Fan	7	Lockwasher	12	Lockwasher	18	Relay
3	Washer	8	Nut	13	Nut	19	Thermostatic switch
4	Nut	9	Gasket	14	Nut	20	Gasket
5	Plate	10	Cowl	15	Lockwasher	21	Lockring
				16	Washer	22	Spacer

2 Remove the alternator, as described in Chapter 10, Section 7.

3 Drain the cooling system, as described in Section 2.

4 Disconnect the hoses from the water pump.

5 Remove the three nuts holding the pipe from the water manifold to the pump, and the bolt securing the support for the air pump (if fitted) to the water pump.

6 Remove the four bolts securing the water pump to the engine and remove the pump.

7 Refitting is the reverse of the removal procedure. Always fit a new gasket. Refill the cooling system as described in Section 2. Tension the 'V' belt as described in Chapter 10, Section 7.

13 Water pump - overhaul

1 The water pump is likely to need overhaul for worn or noisy bearings, or if the gland is leaking. There is a drain hole between the gland and the bearings so any leak can get out without contaminating the bearing grease, so ruining them. Gland leaks are usually worse when the engine is not running. Once started a leak is likely to get worse quickly, so should be dealt with soon. Worn bearings are likely to be noted first due to noise. To check them the pulley should be rocked firmly, when any free movement can be felt despite the belt. But if the bearings are noisy yet there is not apparently any free play, then the belt should be removed so that the pump can be rotated by hand to check the smoothness of the bearings.

2 Dismantling and assembly of the pump requires the use of a press.

3 Whenever the pump is dismantled, for whatever reason, always fit a new gland (or seal).

Fig. 2.4. Removing the water pump

1	Support	4	Nuts
2	Water pump	5	Pipe to water manifold
3	Alternator	6	Bolts

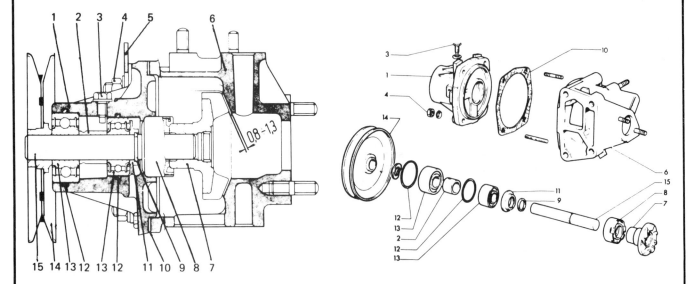

Fig. 2.5. Sectional view of water pump

1 Pump cover	8 Gland (seal)
2 Bearing spacer	9 Circlip
3 Bearing stop screw	10 Gasket
4 Cover nuts	11 Shouldered ring
5 Lifting bracket	12 Grommets
6 Housing	13 Bearing
7 Impeller	14 Pulley
	15 Shaft

Fig. 2.6. Exploded view of water pump

1 Pump cover	9 Circlip
2 Bearing spacer	10 Gasket
3 Bearing stop screw	11 Shouldered ring
4 Cover nuts	12 Grommets
6 Housing	13 Bearings
7 Impeller	14 Pulley
8 Gland (seal)	15 Shaft

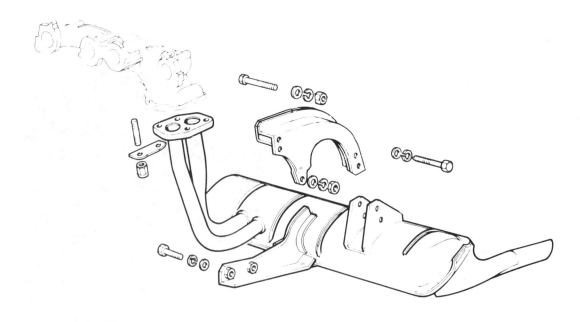

Fig. 2.7. The exhaust system (typical)

4   Remove the retaining nuts and separate the two halves of the pump.

5   The pump shaft is an interference fit in the impeller, bearings, and pulley boss. How the pump is dismantled depends on whether only the gland needs replacement, or the bearings as well, and what puller or press is available to get everything apart. (See Fig. 2.5).

6   Assuming complete dismantling is required, proceed as follows. Supporting it close in at the boss, press the shaft out of the pulley. Pull the impeller off the other end of the shaft.

7   Take out the bearing stop screw.

8   From the impeller end, press the shaft with the bearings out of the cover half of the housing.

9   Press the shaft out of the bearings, taking off the spacer, the circlip, and the shouldered ring.

10 Do not immerse the bearings in cleaning fluid. They are 'sealed'. Liquid will get in, but a thorough clean will be impracticable, and it will be impossible to get new grease in.

11 Check all the parts, Get a new gland, two new grommets, and a new gasket. Scrape all deposits out of the housing and off the impeller.

12 To reassemble start by inserting the new grommets in their grooves by each bearing. Fit the circlip to the shaft, then the shouldered ring, bearings and spacer. Fit the shaft and bearing assembly into the cover. Fit the stop screw. Press on the pulley.

13 Fit the new gland (seal), seating it in its location in the cover. Press the impeller onto the shaft. FIAT have special press tools to get everything in the right place. Without these the impeller must be put on part way, and then the housing held in place to see how far the impeller must go down the shaft to give the correct clearance. See again Fig. 2.5.

14 The impeller clearance can be checked through the water passage in the side of the pump.

14 Exhaust system - removal and refitting

1   Raise the rear of the car and support it on axle stands.

2   Remove the nuts securing the exhaust pipe to the manifold flange and collect the lockplates.

3   Remove the bolts securing the silencer to the mounting bracket and remove the silencer.

4   On some cars the exhaust manifold and down pipe are in one piece with a joint in the pipe close to the silencer. If the exhaust pipe and silencer cannot be separated at this point (because of rust and heat seizure) it is necessary to remove the manifold. To remove the manifold with the engine in the car first remove the centre retaining studs.

5   When a leak occurs in the exhaust system, it may be possible to use a good proprietary repair kit to seal it. Holts Flexiwrap and Holts Gun Gum exhaust repair systems can be used for effective repairs to exhaust pipes and silencer boxes, including ends and bends. Holts Flexiwrap is an MOT-approved permanent exhaust repair. However, if the leak is large, or if serious damage is evident, it may be better to renew the exhaust complete.

6   Refitting is the reverse of the removal procedure. Always fit a new gasket on the flanged joint, and do not forget the lockplates.

15 Heater - removal and refitting

1   Water flows from the water pump to the heater and returns to the water manifold.

2   The heater hoses are often disconnected for work on the engine and when working on other parts of the cooling system, the water valve of the heater should be left open, that is, the lever fully down, to allow flow for draining, flushing and filling.

3   To remove the heater, disconnect the heater hoses at the heater.

4   Disconnect the link to the air admission shutter in the intake. Undo the clips holding the air intake to the heater radiator. Tap out the screw in the centre of the intake and lift it out.

5   Disconnect the fan motor electrical leads and remove the housing.

6   Refitting is the reverse of the removal procedure.

16 Heater control valve - removal and refitting

1   The item most likely to fail is the water valve, not stopping all flow, so in hot weather there is unwanted heat. If this happens the valve should be renewed.

2   With the heater removed as described in Section 15, unscrew the two nuts attaching the valve to the radiator.

3   When fitting a new valve and gasket make sure the outer edge of the gasket is flush with the valve flange.

17 Fault diagnosis - cooling system

Symptom	Reason/s	Remedy
Overheating	Insufficient coolant in system	Top-up expansion tank.
	Water pump drivebelt too slack	Tighten belt to correct tension or renew.
	Thermostatic switch or cooling fan faulty	Check and renew as necessary.
	Radiator blocked or matrix dirty	Flush radiator and clean matrix.
	Kinked or collapsed hoses, restricting flow	Fit new hoses.
	Thermostat faulty (not opening properly)	Fit new thermostat.
	Fuel and ignition systems faulty	Check ignition and fuel system.
	Oil level in sump too low	Top-up as necessary.
	Blown cylinder head gasket (forcing coolant out of the system)	Fit new cylinder head gasket.
	Brakes binding	Adjust brakes.
Engine running too cool	Thermostat sticking in the open position	Fit new thermostat.
	Thermostatic switch faulty	Check and renew, if necessary.
Loss of coolant	Leak in system	Examine all hoses and clips, connections, drain tap and plugs, radiator and heater for leakage when cold, and when hot and under pressure. Tighten clips, renew hoses and repair radiator as necessary.
	Pressure cap spring worn or seal faulty	Fit new pressure cap.
	Cylinder head gasket blown forcing coolant out of the system	
	Cylinder head or block cracked	Dismantle engine for repair or renewal of cylinder head or block.

Chapter 3
Carburation;fuel and emission control systems

For modifications, and information applicable to later models, see Supplement at end of manual

Contents

Specifications

Carburettor type ... ...   Weber 32 DMTR Series

Air cleaner ... ...   Paper element

Fuel filter ... ...   Champion L101

Fuel pump ... ...   Electrical or mechanical

Carburettor data - USA models

	Primary barrel	Secondary barrel
Main venturi	0.866 in (22 mm)	0.866 in (22 mm)
Main jet	0.043 in (1.10 mm)	0.043 in (1.10 mm)
Idle jet	0.018 in (0.45 mm)	0.024 in (0.60 mm)
Main air corrector	0.079 in (2.00 mm)	0.077 in (1.95 mm)
Idle air corrector	0.043 in (1.10 mm)	0.028 in (0.70 mm)
Accelerator pump jet	0.020 in (0.50 mm)	—
Emulsion tube type	F30	F30
Extra fuel device jet	—	0.027 in (0.70 mm)
Extra fuel device jet	—	0.033 in (0.85 mm)
Choke type	Throttle valve	
Primary throttle opening (choke on)	0.035 to 0.394 in (0.90 to 10 mm)	
Needle seat valve	0.059 in (1.50 mm)	
Float level, closed (distance from cover face, in vertical position, with gasket)	0.24 in (6 mm)	

Carburettor data - early European models

	Primary barrel	Secondary barrel
Main jet	0.043 in (1.10 mm)	0.045 in (1.15 mm)
Venturi	0.866 in (22 mm)	0.866 in (22 mm)
Idle jet	0.020 in (0.50 mm)	0.028 in (0.70 mm)
Idle air corrector	0.043 in (1.10 mm)	0.028 in (0.70 mm)
Accelerator pump jet	0.016 in (0.40 mm)	—
Float level, closed (distance from cover face, in vertical position, with gasket)	0.24 in (6 mm)	

Carburettor data - later European models

	Primary barrel	Secondary barrel
Main jet	0.043 in (1.10 mm)	0.045 in (1.15 mm)
Venturi	0.866 in (22 mm)	0.866 in (22 mm)
Idle jet	0.020 in (0.50 mm)	0.020 in (0.50 mm)
Idle air corrector	0.043 in (1.10 mm)	0.028 in (0.70 mm)
Accelerator pump jet	0.016 in (0.40 mm)	—
Float level, closed (distance from cover face, in vertical position, with gasket)	0.24 in (6 mm)	
Float level, open (distance from cover face, in vertical position, with gasket)	0.55 in (14 mm)	

1 General description

1 The carburettor fitted to the X1/9 is of Weber downdraught, twin venturi (choke) type. The cold starting choke is of manually operated type. A carburettor cooling fan, supplying air through the air cleaner, is controlled by a thermostatic switch in the carburettor and a relay mounted on the fan support.

2 The mechanical fuel pump is mounted on the front of the engine and is driven by an eccentric on the auxiliary shaft.

3 A fuel filter is mounted in the line between the carburettor and the fuel pump.

4 A 11 Imp. gallon (49 litres/12 US galls) fuel tank is mounted in a compartment behind the passenger seat.

5 The engine fuel feed system is provided with a fuel recirculation (closed circuit) and evaporative emission control system. Crankcase emission control is provided by recirculation of blow-by gases and oil vapour. The exhaust emission control system reduces air pollution from exhaust-gases and is of the post-combustion type. Not all cars have all the emission control systems, this depends on the country in which they are being marketed.

2 Filters (fuel pump and fuel line) - general

1 A filter is fitted in the fuel pump and some have filters fitted in the fuel line.

2 On mechanical pumps the filter is removed by undoing the central screw and removing the cover. The filter disc should be washed in clean petrol. Always fit a new gasket on reassembly.

3 On electric pumps the filter disc is between the main body and bottom part. Before stripping the pump it is essential that the outside of the pump is cleaned.

4 The line filter (if fitted) is the disposable type and is changed at the 6,000 mile (10,000 km) service. Make sure when refitting it, that the arrow indicating the direction of flow through the filter is pointing in the right direction (towards the carburettor).

3 Mechanical fuel pump - removal and refitting

1 Before removing the pump get a selection of gaskets for the pump to engine joint and either a pump overhaul kit, or a reconditioned pump, if the existing one is faulty. Engine to pump gaskets are supplied in thicknesses of 0.012 - 0.027 - 0.047 in (0.3 - 0.7 - 1.2 mm).

2 Clean the outside of the pump and the area of the cylinder block around the pump.

3 Remove the inlet and outlet fuel pipes from the pump.

4 Remove the two nuts securing the pump to the engine block and take off the pump, spacer and gaskets. Lift out the pump actuating rod.

3.4a Remove the mechanical fuel pump

3.4b ... and then the insulating spacer and gaskets

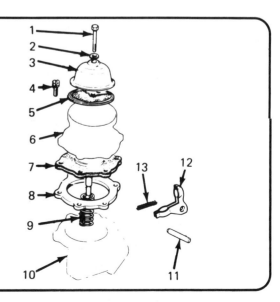

Fig. 3.1. Exploded view of mechanical fuel pump

1	Cover screw	8	Spacer
2	Lockwasher	9	Spring
3	Cover	10	Lower body
4	Screw	11	Pivot pin
5	Filter	12	Control lever
6	Upper body	13	Spring
7	Diaphragm		

5   Clean the gasket joint faces on the block, insulator and fuel pump.
6   When refitting the pump, have a trial fit of the insulating spacer with a gasket each side to check that the actuating rod protrudes between 0.59 and 0.61 in (15 and 15.5 mm). Any adjustment is made by using different thickness gaskets between the insulation spacer and the block. One 0.3 mm gasket is used between the insulation block and the pump. If too much protrudes, the pump may get damaged. If too little protrudes, pump output may be low. Adjust to get the setting correct by selection of the gasket thickness.   Smear the gaskets with grease when refitting the pump.
7   Run the engine and check for leaks after refitting the pump and connecting the fuel lines.

4   Mechanical fuel pump - dismantling and reassembly

1   The pump will need partial dismantling to clean the filter and remove sediment. This was described in Section 2. Here full dismantling is considered, either as a result of failure, or as preventative maintenance after some 60,000 miles (97,000 km).
2   Remove the pump from the engine.
3   Take off the domed filter cover.
4   Undo the ring of screws holding the two halves of the body together. Prise the body apart. It is unwise to undertake this unless new diaphragms are available, as they are likely to get torn.
5   Carefully take out the valves, but only if suspect.
6   Push out the pin for the actuating lever, and take it and its spring out, and unhook the diaphragm.
7   The diaphragms are in two layers, one to do the pumping, and one to prevent fuel leaking into the engine.
8   Use a new gasket under the domed cover, new diaphragms, and if necessary new valves.
9   Assemble the diaphragms so they are spread without undue stretch. Tighten the screws holding the body together evenly.

5   Electric fuel pump - removal and refitting

1   Some cars are fitted with electric fuel pumps. These make fault diagnosis much easier as the pump will work whenever the ignition is switched on, so flow can be checked without having to operate the starter. If an electric pump is fitted to an American version the pump is actuated by the engine's oil pressure system via a relay.
2   To remove the pump, clean off the dirt around the pipe unions. Disconnect the pipe unions and electrical leads. Remove the pump from its bracket by removing the two retaining bolts.
3   The two parts of the pump can be split to give access to the filter.
4   If the electrical operation or the diaphragm and valves fail, it is recommended that a new unit is fitted. The two separate halves of the pump are supplied as spares, but it is usual only to stock the complete unit, as if one part has failed the other is likely to be near the end of its life.

6   Air cleaner - removal and refitting

1   Remove the clamp holding the airline to the non-return valve. Disconnect the line from the valve and move it to the side, out of the way.
2   Loosen the clamp holding the fresh air duct from the carburettor cooling fan.
3   Remove the three nuts holding the cover on the air cleaner. Remove the cover and the paper element.
4   Remove the nut holding the bracket on the air cleaner to the camshaft housing cover.
5   Disconnect the bypass hose from the air cleaner and disconnect the hose from the bottom of the air cleaner.
6   Remove the four nuts holding the air cleaner to the carburettor. Lift off the air cleaner and fresh air duct.
7   Refitting is the reverse of the removal sequence.

7   Carburettor cooling fan - removal and refitting

1   The cooling fan is controlled by a thermostatic switch in the carburettor and a relay mounted on the fan support.
2   Disconnect the black lead from the terminal of the fan relay. Remove the fan relay and voltage regulator.
3   Loosen the clamp and disconnect the flexible, fresh air duct from the fan duct.

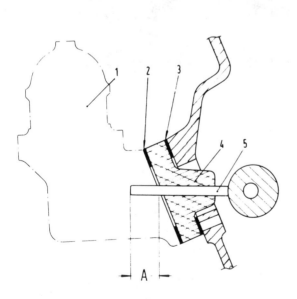

Fig. 3.2. Fuel pump installation adjustment

1 Pump	4 Insulating support
2 Gasket between pump and support	5 Rod
3 Gasket between support and crankcase	
A = 0.59 to 0.61 in (15 to 15.5 mm)	

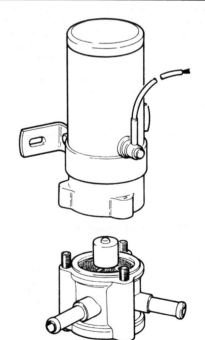

Fig. 3.3. The electric fuel pump

4   Remove the nuts, right front side of support, and the two bolts at the left rear side of the support, holding it to the body.
5   Remove the fan and support.
6   Remove the four screws holding the fresh air duct to the fan and the four screws attaching the fan to the support.
7   Refitting is the reverse of the removal sequence. Make sure the black lead from the fan is under the mounting nut for the fan relay.

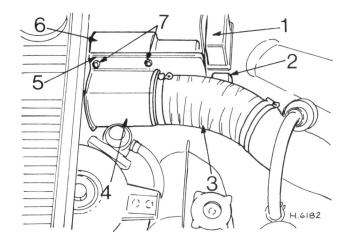

Fig. 3.4. Removing the carburettor cooling fan

1 Regulator	5 Support
2 Fan relay	6 Fan
3 Fresh air duct	7 Screws
4 Fan duct	

6.3a Lift off the air cleaner cover ...

6.3b ... and take out the paper element

6.6a Remove the four nuts holding the air cleaner to the carburettor ...

6.6b ... and lift off the air cleaner base

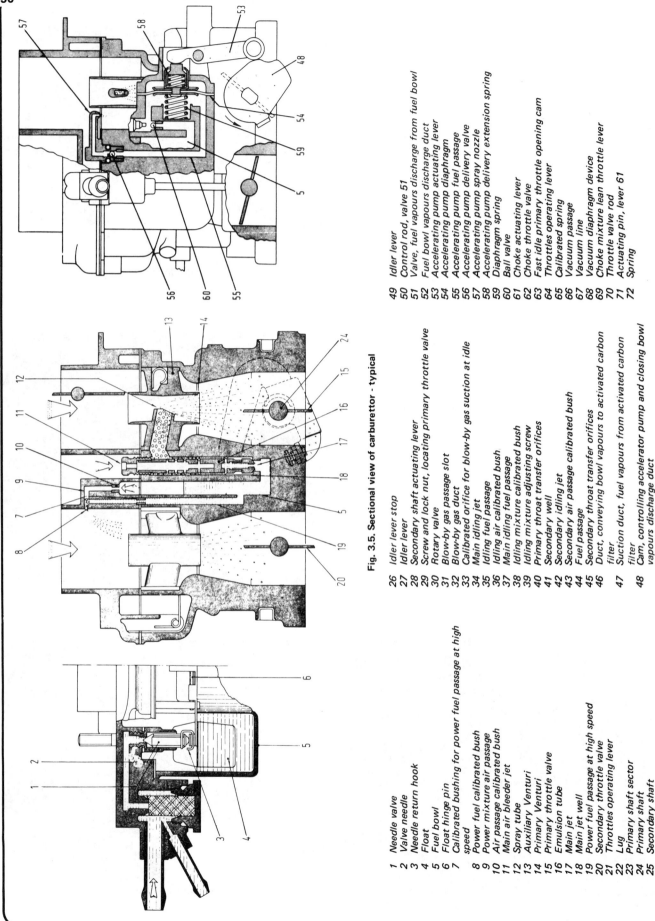

Fig. 3.5. Sectional view of carburettor - typical

1 Needle valve
2 Valve needle
3 Needle return hook
4 Float
5 Fuel bowl
6 Float hinge pin
7 Calibrated bushing for power fuel passage at high speed
8 Power fuel calibrated bush
9 Power mixture air passage
10 Air passage calibrated bush
11 Main air bleeder jet
12 Spray tube
13 Auxiliary Venturi
14 Primary Venturi
15 Primary throttle valve
16 Emulsion tube
17 Main jet
18 Main jet well
19 Power fuel passage at high speed
20 Secondary throttle valve
21 Throttles operating lever
22 Lug
23 Primary shaft sector
24 Primary shaft
25 Secondary shaft

26 Idler lever stop
27 Idler lever
28 Secondary shaft actuating lever
29 Screw and lock nut, locating primary throttle valve
30 Rotary valve
31 Blow-by gas passage slot
32 Blow-by gas duct
33 Calibrated orifice for blow-by gas suction at idle
34 Main idling jet
35 Idling fuel passage
36 Idling air calibrated bush
37 Main idling fuel passage
38 Idling mixture calibrated bush
39 Idling mixture adjusting screw
40 Primary throat transfer orifices
41 Secondary well
42 Secondary idling jet
43 Secondary air passage calibrated bush
44 Fuel passage
45 Secondary throat transfer orifices
46 Duct, conveying bowl vapours to activated carbon filter
47 Suction duct, fuel vapours from activated carbon filter
48 Cam, controlling accelerator pump and closing bowl vapours discharge duct

49 Idler lever
50 Control rod, valve 51
51 Valve, fuel vapours discharge from fuel bowl
52 Fuel bowl vapours discharge duct
53 Accelerating pump actuating lever
54 Accelerating pump diaphragm
55 Accelerating pump fuel passage
56 Accelerating pump delivery valve
57 Accelerating pump spray nozzle
58 Accelerating pump delivery extension spring
59 Diaphragm spring
60 Ball valve
61 Choke actuating lever
62 Choke throttle valve
63 Fast idle primary throttle opening cam
64 Throttles operating lever
65 Calibrated spring
66 Vacuum passage
67 Vacuum line
68 Vacuum diaphragm device
69 Choke mixture lean throttle lever
70 Throttle valve rod
71 Actuating pin, lever 61
72 Spring

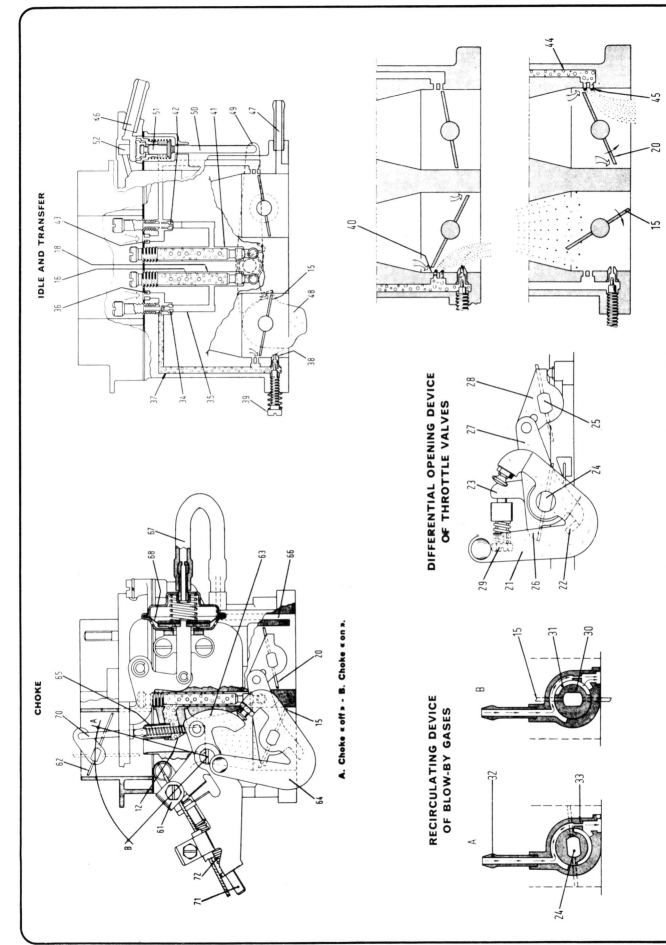

57

IDLE AND TRANSFER

CHOKE

A. Choke « off » - B. Choke « on ».

DIFFERENTIAL OPENING DEVICE OF THROTTLE VALVES

RECIRCULATING DEVICE OF BLOW-BY GASES

Fig. 3.5. (contd.) Sectional view of carburettor - typical

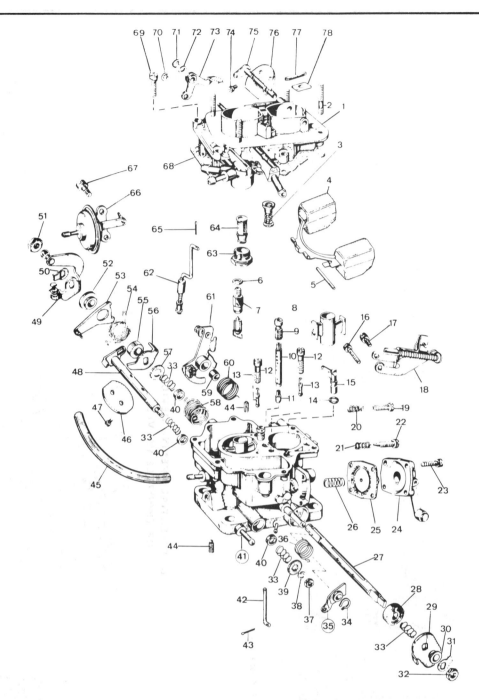

Fig. 3.6. Exploded view of carburettor - typical for USA models

1	Carburettor cover	20	Spring	40	Bush	59	Bushing
2	Stud	21	Spring	41	Carburettor body	60	Spring
3	Bowel vent valve	22	Idle mixture screw	42	Lever	61	Lever
4	Float	23	Screw	43	Cotter pin	62	Rod
5	Pin	24	Accelerator pump cover	44	Secondary throttle stop	63	Filter plug
6	Gasket	25	Diaphragm		screw	64	Filter
7	Needle valve	26	Spring	45	Hose	65	Cotter pin
8	Venturi	27	Throttle shaft, primary	46	Throttle	66	Choke override
9	Air metering jet	28	Bush	47	Screw	67	Screw
10	Emulsion tube	29	Lever	48	Secondary throttle shaft	68	Cover gasket
11	Main jet	30	Bush	49	Lever	69	Screw
12	Idle jet holder	31	Lockwasher	50	Lockwasher	70	Ring
13	Idle jet	32	Nut	51	Nut	71	Ring
14	Gasket	33	Spring	52	Bushing	72	Washer
15	Acceleration pump nozzle	34	Ring	53	Lever	73	Choke override control
16	Screw	35	Rod	54	Spring	74	Screw
17	Screw	36	Spring	55	Spring	75	Choke throttle shaft
18	Support	37	Nut	56	Primary shaft lever	76	Choke throttle
19	Idle screw	38	Lockwasher	57	Washer	77	Plug
		39	Washer	58	Spring	78	Dust cover

8 Carburettor - removal and refitting

1 Remove the air cleaner, as described in Section 6.

2 Disconnect the leads from the carburettor thermostatic switch connection.

3 Loosen the clamps on the fuel lines and vent hose. Disconnect the fuel lines and plug the ends to prevent ingress of dirt.

4 Disconnect the pre-heat hoses and plug them to prevent loss of coolant.

5 Disconnect the choke and throttle control linkage.

6 Remove the carburettor securing nuts and lift it off. Cover the opening in the manifold to prevent any dirt or foreign bodies falling in.

7 Refitting is the reverse of the removal sequence.

9 Carburettor - partial dismantling for cleaning

1 Remove the air cleaner as described in Section 6.

2 Remove the filter plug. Undo the fuel feed to the carburettor and the return pipe. Disconnect the choke to throttle linkage.

3 Remove the screws holding the top onto the carburettor body, and the brackets that span the two parts.

4 Take the top off carefully, so as to lift the float out of the float chamber without bending it. Place it where it cannot get damaged, or the float pivot pin can fall out.

5 Clean out the fuel and dirt from the bottom of the float chamber. Be careful not to get dirt in the ducts to the jets.

6 If the carburettor is found to be very dirty, then the jets must be removed. These should be blown through to clear them.

7 When reassembling the carburettor make sure that everything is clean and that dirt does not enter during assembly.

10 Carburettor - dismantling and reassembly

1 Dirt and water contamination is usually responsible for carburettor malfunction. Careful dismantling and reassembly is essential if damage is to be avoided. Carburettor repair kits are available and they provide all the parts necessary for complete overhaul of the carburettor. Throttle and choke spindles and butterfly valves are not available as individual parts.

2 Clean the outside very thoroughly, but keep the carburettor upright, so any dirt inside will be prevented from washing into fuel passages or the jets.

3 Take off the external fittings. Take out the screws holding the two halves together.

4 Clean out the float chamber, and the filter.

5 Take out all the jets, laying them out in systematic order so they will not get muddled up.

6 Clean all jets, by blowing through them. On no account must they be poked at with wire or a pin, as they are machined to very close tolerances, and even a slight rounding of a corner will vary the amount of petrol that will flow.

7 Clean out all the passages in the body.

8 Examine the float and needle valve. If the latter is badly worn it will need renewal. Shake the float to check it has no leak. Diaphragms, in such things as the accelerator pump, should be replaced unless in very good condition.

9 Reassemble carefully, using new gaskets etc.

10 The idle will need resetting. In order to get the car to start, screw the throttle stop out till the throttle is shut, then in one turn. The mixture screw should be screwed in gently as far as it will go, and then out 1½ turns.

11 Start-up with the air cleaner off, so the movement of the choke can be seen when the throttle is blipped. The function of the accelerator pump can be sensed by judging the engine's response.

11 Float - level setting

1 Remove the top of the carburettor as described in Section 9.

2 Make sure the float moves freely on the pivot pin.

3 Hold the carburettor top vertical and bring the float in contact with the needle valve until the valve is closed. Do not compress the spring-loaded ball into the needle.

4 Measure the distance between the float and the gasket surface of the carburettor top with a gasket fitted. It should be 0.236 in (6 mm). If it is not, bend the tang as required.

5 Extend the float without bending the arm and measure the maximum distance of float from the cover face (refer to Fig. 3.7). It should be 0.590 in (15 mm), if not, bend the stop lug as required to obtain the correct setting. Total distance of float travel should be 0.354 in (9 mm).

12 Carburettor inlet filter - cleaning

1 The inlet filter is cleaned every 6,000 miles (10,000 km).

2 Remove the filter plug, located on the float chamber near the fuel inlet, and take out the filter.

3 Wash the filter in petrol.

4 Refit the filter and the filter plug.

8.6 If the inlet manifold has to be removed it can be taken off with the carburettor attached

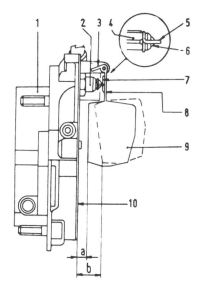

Fig. 3.7. Float level adjustment

1	Carburettor cover	6	Movable ball
2	Needle valve	7	Tang
3	Lug	8	Float arm
4	Valve needle	9	Float
5	Return hook	10	Gasket

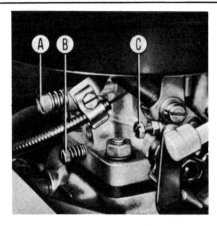

Fig. 3.8. Carburettor adjusting screws

A   Slow running adjusting screw
B   Mixture screw
C   Throttle stop screw (factory sealed)

13 Idling - adjustment

1   From time to time the idling speed of the engine will become erratic and need resetting. After dismantling and reassembly of the carburettor the idling speed will require setting.
2   Warm up the engine until it stabilises at the normal operating temperature.
3   Adjust the slow running screw so that the idle speed is correct according to that specified on the tag located on the underside of the bonnet.
4   Screw the mixture adjusting screw in and out gradually until the point at which the engine runs fastest and smoothest with a steady exhaust note, is reached. This will probably increase the engine speed, in this case re-adjust the slow running screw to obtain the correct speed and then recheck the mixture setting.
5   Depending on model and year, the carburettor may be 'tamper-proof', ie the mixture screw is sealed with a locking cap or sleeve. If it is wished to remove the seal in order to make adjustments, ensure first that local laws do not forbid adjustment by unqualified personnel.

14 Fuel evaporative emission control system (N. American models) - general

1   The evaporation of fuel from the tank is one of the main sources of pollution. To prevent this, the fuel tank is sealed. Air is allowed into the tank by the venting when the engine is running, to let the fuel flow out. When the engine is stopped, and fuel is evaporating, particularly when parked in the sun, the vapour is absorbed by an activated carbon trap. In the pipe from the tank to the carbon trap is a liquid vapour separator to separate the liquid fuel and pass it back to the tank.
2   When the engine is running air is drawn through the carbon trap to purge it of the absorbed fuel vapours and convey them to the inlet manifold, where they are drawn into the engine and burned.

3   The carbon trap is located in the engine compartment. In time the carbon trap loses its efficiency and it should be renewed every 24,000 miles (40,000 km).
4   To remove the carbon trap, note the run of the pipes, then disconnect them. Slacken the mounting bolts and remove the carbon trap.
5   Refit the carbon trap the same way up. Do not get the pipes mixed up. The vapour and fumes go in at the bottom and the purge pipe out at the top.

15 Crankcase emission control system - general

1   Engine gases that blow past the pistons must be ventilated. The crankcase emission control system is a closed system designed to prevent any emission of blow-by gases directly into the atmosphere.
2   At closed throttle (see detail 4b in Fig. 3.10), the blow-by gases are drawn into the inlet manifold through the calibrated orifice of the control valve incorporated in the carburettor.
3   At fully open throttle (detail 4a in Fig. 3.10), part of the blow-by gases are drawn into the inlet manifold through the open duct of the control valve. The remainder flows directly to the 'clean' side of the air cleaner.
4   To clean the control valve, undo the nut on the end of the throttle spindle. The valve must be cleaned in a carbon solvent and washed off rather than scraped.

16 Exhaust emission control system (N. American models) - general

1   This system is designed to control the emission of noxious gases from the exhaust and is based on the post-combustion principle of injecting clean air to the exhaust ports in order to promote the complete combustion of the exhaust gases before they are emitted from the system. The air supply is taken from the 'clean' side of the air cleaner, compressed by the air pump which is belt-driven from a pulley on the camshaft and ejected through a nozzle.
2   To remove the air injection manifold, first remove the air cleaner, as described in Section 6.
3   Remove the bolt holding the clamp on the non-return valve to the bracket on the engine.
4   Remove the two bolts holding the manifold to the engine. Disconnect the four injectors from the engine.
5   Remove the manifold with the non-return valve. Remove the valve from the engine.
6   Refitting is the reverse of the removal sequence.

Catalytic converter

Later models of the X1/9 sold in California, have a catalytic converter incorporated in the exhaust system. This device 'absorbs' many of the harmful elements from the exhaust gas before it is emitted into the atmosphere. This unit has a limited working life, after which it must be renewed.

At 25,000 miles (40,000 km) the catalytic converter service light will start to glow. When this happens, the car should be taken to a FIAT agent to have a new converter installed, the converter over-heating warning light system checked and the service warning light system reset.

Fig. 3.9. Fuel evaporative control system

A Fuel tank	*I Line from carbon trap to carburettor (downstream of throttle)*	*d Safety outlet*
B Liquid vapour separator		*e Air filter*
C Line from separator to 3-way valve	*L To carburettor bowl*	*f To carburettor (downstream of throttle)*
D 3-way control valve	*M Lines between separator and fuel tank*	*g Synthetic filter*
E Activated carbon trap		*h Activated carbon*
F Line from 3-way valve to carbon trap	*a From fuel tank*	*i Air purge paper filter*
G Hot air purge tube	*b To activated carbon trap*	*l Fuel vapour inlet from tank*
H Exhaust manifold	*c Fuel tank air inlet*	*m Hot air purge inlet*
		n Fuel vapour inlet from carburettor

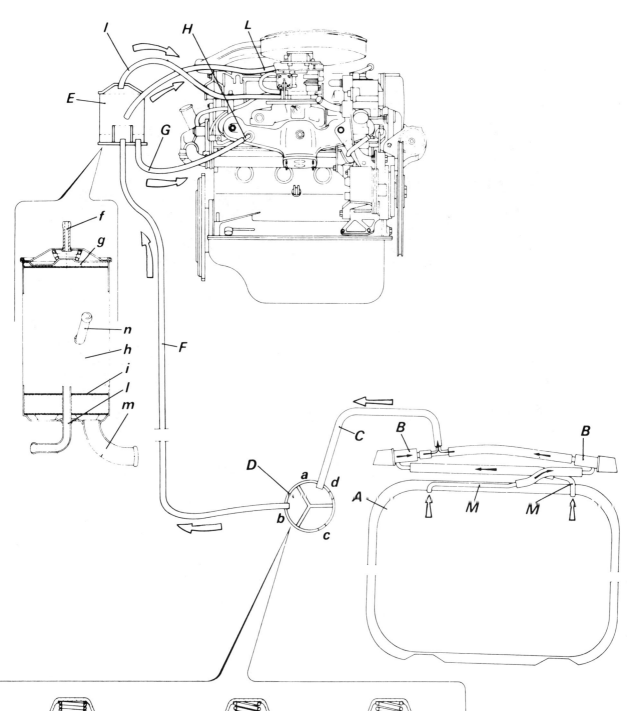

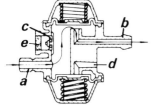

Position 1.
From fuel tank to activated
carbon vapor trap.

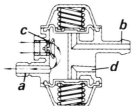

Position 2.
Air from ambient
into tank.

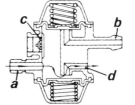

Position 3 (safety).
Vapor from tank to ambient
(excess pressure in the tank).

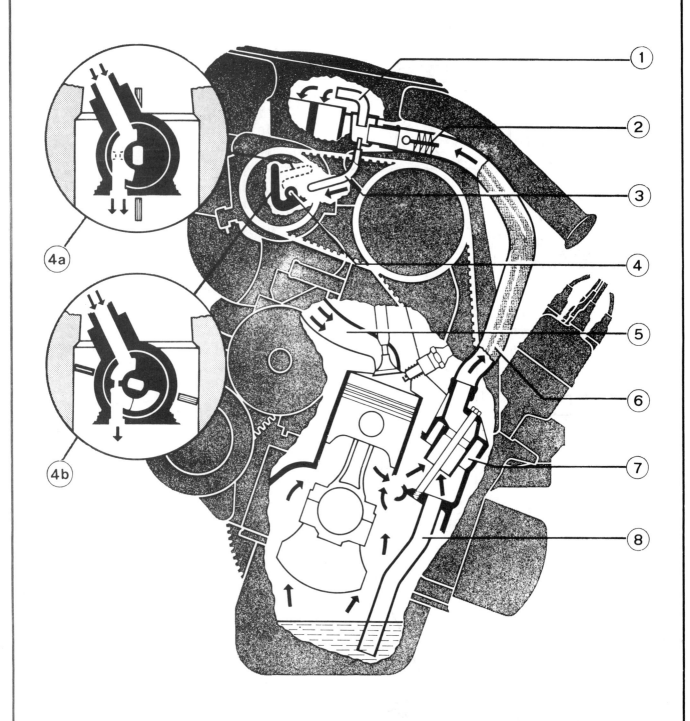

Fig. 3.10. Crankcase emission control system

1 Emission feed back line to air cleaner
2 Flame trap
3 Air cleaner-to-control valve line

4 Control valve
4a Control valve in engine beyond idle condition
4b Control valve in engine idling condition

5 Inlet manifold
6 Sump-to-air cleaner line
7 Cyclone liquid/vapour separator
8 Oil drain line into sump

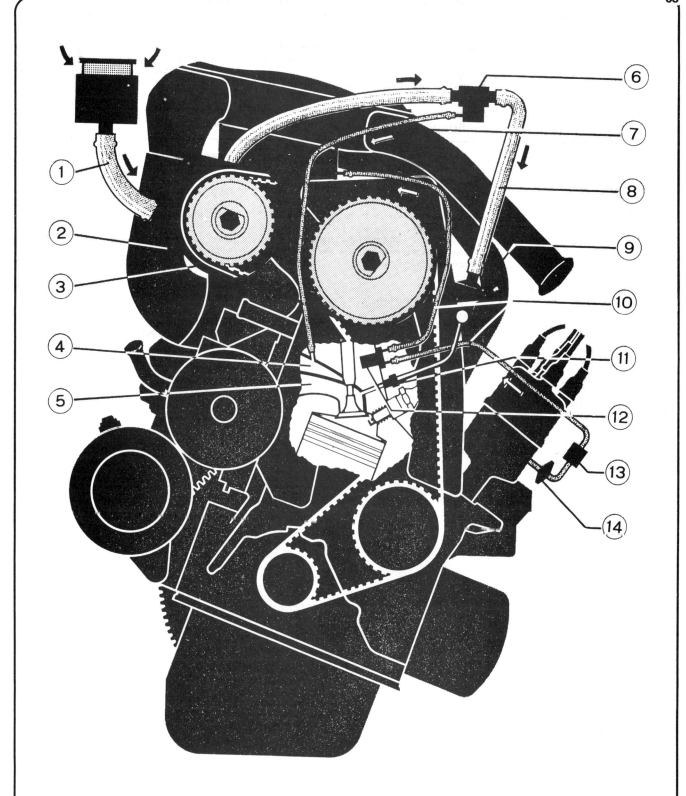

Fig. 3.11. Exhaust emission control system (N. American models)

1 Intake line with filter	4 Intake manifold	8 Air distributor line	12 Vacuum control thermovalve
2 Pump discharge safety valve	5 Exhaust manifold	9 Non-return valve	13 Delay valve
3 Air pump	6 Diverter valve	10 Vacuum line for carburettor diaphragm	14 Distributor advance diaphragm control unit
	7 Vacuum line for diverter valve	11 Air injector	

17 Fault diagnosis - carburation and fuel system

Unsatisfactory engine performance and excessive fuel consumption are not necessarily the fault of the fuel system or carburettor. In fact they more commonly occur as a result of ignition and timing faults. Before acting on the following it is necessary to check the ignition system first. Even though a fault may lie in the fuel system, it will be difficult to trace unless the ignition is correct. The faults below, therefore, assume that this has been attended to first (where appropriate).

Symptom	Reason/s	Remedy
Smell of petrol when engine is stopped	Leaking fuel lines or unions Leaking fuel tank	Repair or renew as necessary. Fill fuel tank to capacity and examine carefully at seams, unions and filler pipe connections. Repair as necessary.
Smell of petrol when engine is idling	Leaking fuel line unions between pump and carburettor Overflow of fuel from float chamber due to wrong level setting or ineffective needle valve or punctured float	Check line and unions and tighten or repair. Check fuel level setting and condition of float and needle valve and renew if necessary.
Excessive fuel consumption for reasons not covered by leaks or float chamber faults	Worn jets Sticking choke flap	Renew jets. Check correct movement of strangler flap.
Difficult starting, uneven running, lack of power, cutting out	One or more jets blocked or restricted Float chamber fuel level too low or needle valve sticking Fuel pump not delivering sufficient fuel Intake manifold gaskets leaking, or manifold fractured	Dismantle and clean out float chamber and jets. Dismantle and check fuel level and needle valve. Check pump delivery and clean or repair as necessary. Check tightness of mounting nuts and inspect manifold.

Chapter 4 Ignition system

For modifications, and information applicable to later models, see Supplement at end of manual

Contents

Specifications

Distributor

Type	Ducellier or Marelli
Firing order	1 - 3 - 4 - 2 (No 1 nearest timing belt)
Static advance	10°
Centrifugal advance	28° ± 2°
Vacuum advance correction	10° ± 1° 30'
Contact breaker points gap (Marelli)	0.015 to 0.017 in (0.37 to 0.43 mm)
Contact breaker points gap (Ducellier)	0.014 to 0.020 in (0.35 to 0.50 mm)
Condenser capacity	0.22 to 0.23 mfd at 50 to 100 Hz
Dwell angle	55° ± 3°
Rotation:	
Crankcase-mounted	Clockwise
Camshaft housing-mounted	Anti-clockwise

Ignition timing

Europe:	
Pre-1976 models	10° BTDC static or idling
1976 on models	5° BTDC static or idling
USA	0° at 850 rpm

Ignition coil

Type	**Marelli BE 200 B**	or	**Martinetti G52S**
Resistance at 68°F (20°C):			
Primary winding	3.1 to 3.4 ohms		3 to 3.3 ohms
Secondary winding	6750 to 8250 ohms		6500 to 8000 ohms

Spark plugs

Make and type	Champion RN7YCC or RN7YC
Electrode gap:	
Champion RN7YCC	0.032 in (0.8 mm)
Champion RN7YC	0.028 in (0.7 mm)

HT leads

HT leads	Champion CLS4 (boxed set)

1 General description

1 For the engine to run correctly it is necessary for an electrical spark to ignite the fuel/air mixture in the combustion chamber at exactly the right moment in relation to engine speed and load. The ignition system is based on feeding low tension voltage from the battery to the coil where it is converted to high tension voltage. The high tension voltage is powerful enough to jump the spark plug gap in the cylinders under high compression pressures, providing that the system is in good condition and that all adjustments are correct.

2 The ignition system is divided into two circuits, the low tension circuit and the high tension circuit.

The low tension (sometimes known as the primary) circuit consists of the battery, lead to the control box, lead to the ignition switch,

lead from the ignition switch to the low tension or primary coil windings, and the lead from the low tension coil windings to the contact breaker points and condenser in the distributor.

The high tension circuit consists of the high tension or secondary coil windings, the heavy ignition lead from the centre of the coil to the centre of the distributor cap, the rotor arm, and the spark plug leads and spark plugs.

The system functions in the following manner: High tension voltage is generated in the coil by the interruption of the low tension circuit. The interruption is effected by the opening of the contact breaker points in this low tension circuit. High tension voltage is fed from the centre of the coil via the carbon brush in the centre of the distributor cap to the rotor arm of the distributor.

The rotor arm revolves at half engine speed inside the distributor cap, and each time it comes in line with one of the four metal segments in the cap, which are connected to the spark plug leads, the opening of the contact breaker points causes the high tension voltage to build up, jump the gap from the rotor arm to the appropriate metal segment, and so via the spark plug lead to the spark plug, where it finally jumps the spark plug gap before going to earth.

3   The ignition is advanced and retarded automatically, to ensure the spark occurs at just the right instant for the particular load at the prevailing engine speed.

The ignition advance is controlled mechanically. Some N. American models also have a vacuum advance system. The mechanical governor mechanism comprises two weights, which move out from the distributor shaft as the engine speed rises, due to centrifugal force. As they move outwards they rotate the cam relative to the distributor shaft, and so advance the spark. The weights are held in position by two springs and it is the tension of the springs which is largely responsible for correct spark advancement.

4   Maintenance of the ignition system is part of the 6,000 mile (10,000 km) task. Lack of maintenance of the ignition system is the prime cause of difficult starting. In particular, cleanliness of the leads and distributor cap is vital.

2   Contact breaker points - cleaning and adjustment

1   Mechanical wear of the contact breaker reduces the gap. Electrical wear builds up a lump of burned metal on one of the contacts. This

prevents the gap being measured for re-adjustment, and also spoils the electric circuit.

2   At 6,000 mile (10,000 km) intervals the points must be removed for cleaning, or renewal. They can be cleaned once, then the next time replacement points should be fitted.

3   Unclip and remove the distributor cap. Pull off the rotor arm. On Ducellier distributors, do not disturb the setting of the star wheel otherwise the advance curve of the unit will be upset.

4   Slacken the insulated terminal on the side of the distributor body enough for the contact breaker lead to slide out. Undo the two screws holding the contact breaker to the distributor plate, and lift out both the moving and the fixed contacts.

5   Clean the points by rubbing the surfaces on a fine abrasive such as an oil stone. The point surface should be shaped to a gentle convex curve. All the lump burned onto one contact must be removed. It is not necessary to go on until all traces of the hole have been removed from the other. There is enough metal on the contacts to allow this to be done once. At alternate services, fit new points. Wash debris off cleaned points, and preservative off new ones, with methylated spirit.

6   Whilst reassembling, lubricate the distributor as detailed in the next Section.

7   Now adjust the contact breaker gap. Turn the engine over by putting the car in top gear, and moving it forward till the contact breaker points are open as wide as they go, with the heel of the moving contact on the top of the cam. Insert a feeler for 0.015 in (0.4 mm)

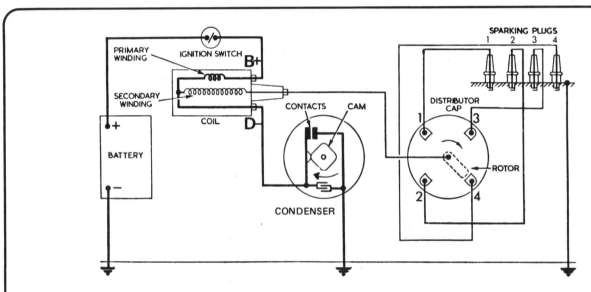

Fig. 4.1. Ignition system layout (typical)

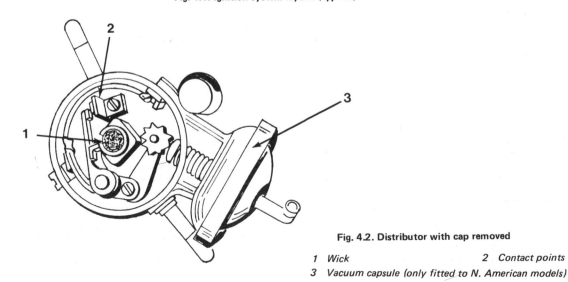

Fig. 4.2. Distributor with cap removed

1   Wick   2   Contact points
3   Vacuum capsule (only fitted to N. American models)

Are your plugs trying to tell you something?

Normal.
Grey-brown deposits, lightly coated core nose. Plugs ideally suited to engine, and engine in good condition.

Heavy Deposits.
A build up of crusty deposits, light-grey sandy colour in appearance.
Fault: Often caused by worn valve guides, excessive use of upper cylinder lubricant, or idling for long periods.

Lead Glazing.
Plug insulator firing tip appears yellow or green/yellow and shiny in appearance.
Fault: Often caused by incorrect carburation, excessive idling followed by sharp acceleration. Also check ignition timing.

Carbon fouling.
Dry, black, sooty deposits.
Fault: over-rich fuel mixture.
Check: carburettor mixture settings, float level, choke operation, air filter.

Oil fouling.
Wet, oily deposits. Fault: worn bores/piston rings or valve guides; sometimes occurs (temporarily) during running-in period.

Overheating.
Electrodes have glazed appearance, core nose very white – few deposits. Fault: plug overheating. Check: plug value, ignition timing, fuel octane rating (too low) and fuel mixture (too weak).

Electrode damage.
Electrodes burned away; core nose has burned, glazed appearance. Fault: pre-ignition. Check: for correct heat range and as for 'overheating'.

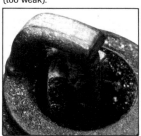

Split core nose.
(May appear initially as a crack). Fault: detonation or wrong gap-setting technique. Check: ignition timing, cooling system, fuel mixture (too weak).

WHY DOUBLE COPPER IS BETTER FOR YOUR ENGINE.

Unique Trapezoidal Copper Cored Earth Electrode — **50% Larger Spark Area** — **Copper Cored Centre Electrode**

Champion Double Copper plugs are the first in the world to have copper core in both centre <u>and</u> earth electrode. This innovative design means that they run cooler by up to 100°C – giving greater efficiency and longer life. These double copper cores transfer heat away from the tip of the plug faster and more efficiently. Therefore, Double Copper runs at cooler temperatures than conventional plugs giving improved acceleration response and high speed performance with no fear of pre-ignition.

Champion Double Copper plugs also feature a unique trapezoidal earth electrode giving a 50% increase in spark area. This, together with the double copper cores, offers greatly reduced electrode wear, so the spark stays stronger for longer.

 FASTER COLD STARTING

 FOR UNLEADED OR LEADED FUEL

 ELECTRODES UP TO 100°C COOLER

 BETTER ACCELERATION RESPONSE

 LOWER EMISSIONS

 50% BIGGER SPARK AREA

 THE LONGER LIFE PLUG

Plug Tips/Hot and Cold.
Spark plugs must operate within well-defined temperature limits to avoid cold fouling at one extreme and overheating at the other.
Champion and the car manufacturers work out the best plugs for an engine to give optimum performance under all conditions, from freezing cold starts to sustained high speed motorway cruising.
Plugs are often referred to as hot or cold. With Champion, the higher the number on its body, the hotter the plug, and the lower the number the cooler the plug. For the correct plug for your car refer to the specifications at the beginning of this chapter.

Plug Cleaning
Modern plug design and materials mean that Champion no longer recommends periodic plug cleaning. Certainly don't clean your plugs with a wire brush as this can cause metal conductive paths across the nose of the insulator so impairing its performance and resulting in loss of acceleration and reduced m.p.g.
However, if plugs are removed, always carefully clean the area where the plug seats in the cylinder head as grit and dirt can sometimes cause gas leakage.
Also wipe any traces of oil or grease from plug leads as this may lead to arcing.

CHAMPION

DOUBLE COPPER

Fig. 4.3. Ignition timing marks on belt cover and crankshaft pulley

1   10° btdc   3   tdc
2   5° btdc

5.1 On some engines the distributor is mounted on the end of the camshaft housing and driven by the camshaft

5.7a When fitting the gasket make sure the cut-out is at the bottom

between the contacts. Slacken the clamping screws so the fixed contact can just be moved. Prise it into position so that the feeler is lightly brushed by the contacts. Carefully tighten the screws so as not to disturb the contact. Recheck the gap, trying feelers slightly larger and smaller to see if it is right. Turn the engine to come up on another cam, to recheck.

8   Setting the points gap as described will only give an approximately correct adjustment. Ideally a dwell meter should be used in accordance with the maker's instructions and the points gap adjusted to achieve the specified dwell angle.

9   Dwell angle is the number of degrees of distributor cam rotation during which the contact breaker points are closed during the ignition cycle of one cylinder. Reducing the points gap increases the dwell angle, and vice versa.

10 After any alteration of the points gap, check, and if necessary, adjust the ignition timing as described in Section 4.

11 Wipe the rotor arm and distributor cap inside clean. Check the metal segments are not badly burned, nor have been in metal to metal contact due to incorrect fitting of the rotor arm. If badly worn, they will need renewal. Clean the outside of the distributor cap, and all the leads.

3   Distributor - lubrication

1   At the 6,000 mile (10,000 km) service, whilst the contact breaker points are being cleaned, the distributor should be lubricated. This lubrication is important for the correct mechanical function of the distributor, but excess lubrication will ruin the electrical circuits, and give difficult starting.

2   Whilst the contact breaker is off, squirt some engine oil into the bottom part of the distributor, onto the centrifugal advance mechanism below the plate.

3   Wet with oil the felt pad on the top of the distributor spindle, normally covered by the rotor arm.

4   Put just a drip of oil on the pivot for the moving contact.

5   Smear a little general purpose grease onto the cam, and the heel of the moving contact breaker.

4   Ignition timing - adjustment

1   The timing must be checked whenever the contact breaker points are cleaned or renewed. If this is not done engine power and efficiency will be lowered, and the idling may be uneven or unreliable. If the timing is retarded the idle will be smooth, but slow. If advanced, it will tend to be fast, but uneven. If the timing has been completely lost, as opposed to needing resetting, refer first to the next Section.

2   For static timing turn the engine over by putting the car in gear and moving it forwards, till the correct mark on the camshaft belt cover is opposite the notch in the crankshaft belt pulley. Do not turn the engine backwards, as then backlash in the distributor drive will upset the timing (see Fig. 4.3).

3   With the engine at this position the points should be at the moment of opening. The ideal way to see when the points open is to wire a 12 volt bulb between the distributor LT terminal (disconnect the coil wire) and the battery.

4   Slacken the nut on the distributor clamping plate.

5   Turn the distributor slightly in the direction of rotation of the cam to make sure the points are shut. Then carefully turn it to advance the ignition, against the direction of rotation, until the points open, as shown by the light going out. If not using a light, then with the ignition on, a spark can sometimes be seen at the points, or if an ammeter is fitted, an assistant can watch this for a flicker, the ignition being on.

6   Reclamp the distributor.

7   Now recheck, by turning the engine over, forwards again, till the timing notch on the pulley is coming up to the mark again. Watch the timing light and the pulley. Turn the engine smoothly and slowly, and see where the notch was when the timing light went out. It should of course be by the same mark. Remake the original connections.

8   The timing can be set with the engine running, using a stroboscope. This method is more accurate, and such accuracy is needed to meet the American emissions regulations.

9   Connect up the timing light to No. 1 cylinder plug lead in accordance with the makers instructions. Start-up the engine. Check the idle speed is correct with a tachometer. Shine the light on the timing marks. Slacken the distributor, and move it as required to get the correct

relationship of the notch on the pulley with the mark on the cover, as 'frozen' by the light. Reclamp the distributor. Speed up the engine, and check the automatic advance is working.

10 Unless an accurate tachometer is in use, setting the timing by stroboscope will be inaccurate, as the automatic advance is varying the timing as the engine speeds up.

5 Distributor - removal and refitting

1 The distributor is mounted, either on the crankcase and driven by the oil pump driveshaft or at the flywheel end of the engine and driven by the camshaft.

2 If the distributor is removed and the engine is turned the timing will be upset. If there will be no need to turn the engine over whilst the distributor is off, turn the engine over until the timing mark on the crankshaft pulley is opposite the timing mark on the belt cover and the mark on the camshaft pulley is opposite the pointer on the engine support. Take off the distributor cap and check that the rotor arm is pointing to the segment for No. 4 cylinder plug lead.

3 For engines with the distributor fitted on the crankcase, remove the nut on the clamp holding the distributor to the engine and take off the clamp. Disconnect the vacuum hose (N. America only) and the : primary lead. Lift the distributor out of its mounting.

4 On engines with the distributor mounted on the end of the camshaft housing, remove the three securing nuts and take off the distributor and its drive spindle.

5 Whenever the distributor is off, check the contact breaker gap as this is easier to do with the distributor on the bench than it is when fitted on the engine.

6 If the engine has not been turned over while the distributor was off, position the rotor arm so that it is at the appropriate position for cylinder No. 4. If the crankshaft has been rotated, reset the timing marks on the crankshaft pulley and the belt cover. With the contact end of the rotor arm positioned opposite the terminal in the distributor cap for cylinder No. 4, insert the distributor into the engine block, then fit the clamp and retaining nut.

7 When refitting distributors fitted on the end of the camshaft housing, always use a new gasket. Do not forget to fit the drive spindle (photos).

8 Connect up a timing light and check the static timing, as described in Section 4.

9 Refit the distributor cap and ensure that all the leads are connected to the correct plugs.

6 Distributor - dismantling and inspection

1 Apart from the contact points the other parts of a distributor which

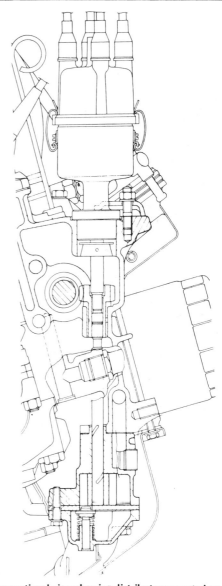

Fig. 4.4. Cross-sectional view showing distributor mounted on the crankcase and drive from auxiliary shaft

5.7b Fit the drive spindle in the end of the camshaft

5.7c Refit the distributor

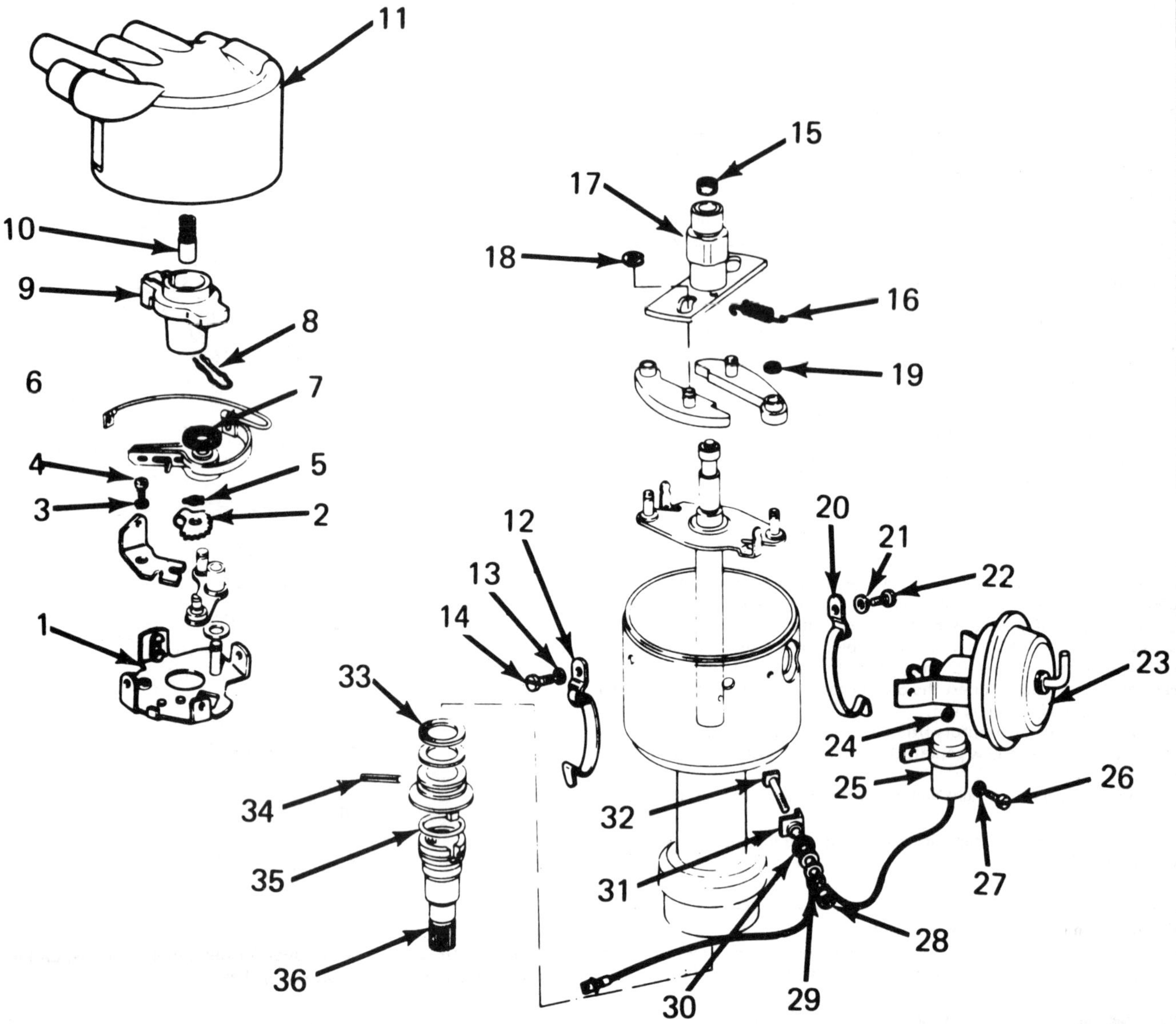

Fig. 4.5. Exploded view of distributor (Ducellier)

1	Contact breaker plate	13	Washer	25	Condenser
2	Star gear	14	Screw	26	Screw
3	Washer	15	Rubber ring	27	Washer
4	Screw	16	Spring	28	Nut
5	Clip	17	Cam	29	Lockwasher
6	Contact breaker points	18	Clip	30	Insulator
7	Washer	19	Washer	31	Terminal
8	Clip	20	Clip	32	Bolt
9	Rotor	21	Washer	33	Washer
10	Spring contact	22	Screw	34	Pin
11	Cap	23	Vacuum diaphragm capsule (N. America only)	35	Seal
12	Clip	24	Washer	36	Splines

deteriorate with age and use, are the cap, the rotor, the shaft bushes, and the bob weight springs.

2   The cap must have no flaws or cracks and the HT terminal contacts should not be severely corroded. The centre spring loaded carbon contact is renewable. If in any doubt about the cap buy a new one.

3   The rotor deteriorates minimally but with age the metal conductor tip may corrode. It should not be cracked or chipped and the metal conductor must not be loose. If in doubt renew it. Always fit a new rotor if fitting a new cap.

4   To gain access to the centrifugal advance mechanism refer to Fig. 4.5. Do not disturb the star wheel on Ducellier distributors.

5   Remove the contact breaker. Take out completely the insulated terminal from the side of the distributor, noting how the insulators are fitted. Remove the screws that hold the plate on which is mounted the contact breaker, and lift out the plate.

6   There is no way to test the bob weight springs other than by checking the performance of the distributor on special test equipment, so if in doubt fit new springs anyway. If the springs are loose where they loop over the posts it is more than possible that the post grooves are worn in which case the various parts which include the shaft will need renewal. Wear to this extent would mean that a new distributor is probably the best solution in the long run. Be sure to make an exact note of both the engine number and any serial number on the distributor when ordering.

7   The cam, with its lugs for the centrifugal advance mechanism, fits as a sleeve over the spindle. To remove it, first prise out the felt oil wick at the top. Hold the bottom of the shaft in a padded vice, and undo the screw at the top (it is a washer on the Ducellier). Take off the centrifugal advance springs, being careful not to stretch them. Note how the bob weights are fitted, then pull the cam up, off the spindle. Before reassembly, put plenty of engine oil on the bearing between the cam and spindle, as not much comes from the wick.

8   If the main shaft is slack in its bushes or the cam on the spindle, allowing sideways play it means that the contact points gap setting can only be a compromise because the cam position relative to the cam follower on the moving point arm is not constant. It is not practical to re-bush the distributor body unless you have a friend who can bore and bush it for you. The shaft can be removed by driving out the roll pin from the retaining collar at the bottom. (The collar also acts as an oil slinger to prevent excess engine oil creeping up the shaft).

7   Condenser - removal, testing and refitting

1   The purpose of the condenser (sometimes known as capacitor) is to ensure that when the contact breaker points open there is no sparking across them which would weaken the spark and cause rapid deterioration of the points.

2   The condenser is fitted in parallel with the contact breaker points. If it develops a short circuit, it will cause ignition failure as the points will be prevented from interrupting the low tension circuit.

3   If the engine becomes very difficult to start or begins to misfire whilst running and the breaker points show signs of excessive burning, then suspect the condenser has failed with open circuit. A further test can be made by separating the points by hand with the ignition switched on. If this is accompanied by a bright spark at the contact points it is indicative that the condenser has failed.

4   Without special test equipment the only sure way to diagnose condenser trouble is to renew a suspected unit with a new one and note if there is any improvement.

5   To remove the condenser from the distributor, take out the screw which secures it to the distributor body and slacken the insulated terminal nut enough to remove the wire connection tag.

6   When fitting the condenser it is vital to ensure that the fixing screw is secure and the condenser tightly held. The lead must be secure on the terminal with no chance of short circuiting.

8   Spark plugs - general

1   The correct functioning of the spark plugs is vital for the correct running and efficiency of the engine. It is essential that the plugs fitted are appropriate for the engine (the correct type is specified at the beginning of this Chapter). If this type is used, and the engine is in good condition, the spark plugs should not need attention between scheduled service renewal intervals. Spark plug cleaning is rarely necessary, and should not be attempted unless specialised equipment

is available, as damage can easily be caused to the firing ends.

2   At intervals of 6,000 miles (10,000 km)/6 months, the plugs should be removed and regapped, or if worn excessively, renewed. The condition of the spark plugs will also tell much about the condition of the engine.

3   If the insulator nose of the spark plug is clean and white, with no deposits, this is indicative of a weak mixture, or too hot a plug. (A hot plug transfers heat away from the electrode slowly - a cold plug transfers it away quickly).

4   If the tip of the insulator nose is covered with sooty black deposits, then this is indicative that the mixture is too rich. Should the plug be black and oily, then it is likely that the engine is fairly worn, as well as the mixture being rich.

5   If the insulator nose is covered with light tan to greyish brown deposits, then the mixture is correct and it is likely that the engine is in good condition and correctly tuned.

6   Clean around the plug seats in the cylinder head before removing the plugs to prevent dirt getting into the cylinder. Plugs should be cleaned by a sand blasting machine, which will free them from carbon more thoroughly than cleaning by hand. The machine will also test the behaviour of the plugs under compression. Any plug that fails to spark at the recommended pressure should be renewed. It is recommended a new set of plugs is fitted, then the others can be taken later for cleaning, when more convenient. The two sets are then used concurrently, plugs can only last about 12,000 miles (20,000 km) before their points are burned too far. So they will not require cleaning often, as renewal will be at alternative services.

7   The spark plug gap is of considerable importance, as, if it is too large or too small the size of the spark and its efficiency will be seriously impaired. The spark plug gap should be set to the gap shown in the Specifications for the best results.

8   To set it, measure the gap with a feeler gauge, and then bend open, or close, the outer plug electrode until the correct gap is achieved. The centre electrode should never be bent as this may crack the insulation and cause plug failure, if nothing worse.

9   When refitting the plug see that the washer is intact and carbon free, also that the plug seat in the cylinder head is quite clean.

10   Note that, as the cylinder head is of aluminium alloy, it is recommended that a little anti-seize compound (such as Copaslip) is applied to the plug threads before they are fitted. Screw in the plugs by hand until the sealing washer just seats, then tighten by no more than a quarter-turn using a spark plug spanner.

11   Refit the leads from the distributor in the correct firing order, which is 1 - 3 - 4 - 2; No. 1 cylinder being the one nearest the camshaft belt.

9   Distributor cap, rotor arm and HT leads - general

1   The distributor cap, leads, and the rotor arm distribute the high tension current to the plugs. They should all last long mileages without renewal. But in a very short mileage their state can be responsible for frustration and annoyance.

2   If the components of the HT circuit are dirty, they will attract damp. This damp will allow the HT current to leak away. This will give difficulty in starting the engine when cold. All this is agravated as when cold and damp the battery only gives a slightly low voltage. The oil will be thick, so making the starter take more voltage and current, even so only cranking the engine slowly. The voltage drop due to the starter's demands means reduced voltage in the primary circuit, so a corresponding fall in that in the secondary, the HT. This at the very time when a strong spark is needed to fire the cold cylinder.

3   It is but a temporary palliative to spray the ignition leads with an aerosol damp repellant. The leads, the spark plug insulators, the outside and inside of the distributor cap, and the rotor arm must be clean and dry. In winter this will need doing at least at 3,000 mile (5,000 km) intervals.

4   Some plug leads are 'resistive'. They are made of cotton impregnated with carbon, to give the necessary radio interference suppression without separate suppressors. After a time flexing makes the leads break down inside. If difficult starting persists, then new leads, with normal metal core, and suppressor end fittings, could effect a cure. End fittings should not be taken off the resistive wire, as it is difficult to fit them so that a good contact is achieved.

10   Ignition coil - general

1   Coils normally run the life of the car. The most usual reason for a

10.1 The coil is mounted on the bulkhead

coil to fail is after being left with the ignition switched on but the engine not running. There is then constant current flowing, instead of the intermittent flow when the contact breaker is opening. The coil then overheats, and the insulation is damaged.

2   The contact breaker points should preferably not be flicked without a lead from the coil centre to some earth, otherwise the opening of the points will give a HT spark which, finding no proper circuit, could break down the insulation in the coil. When connecting a timing light for setting the ignition, this should come from the switch side of the coil, the coil itself being disconnected.

3   If the coil seems suspect after fault finding, the measurement of the resistance of the primary and secondary windings can establish the matter definitely. But if an ohmmeter is not available, then it will be necessary to try a new one.

11   Fault diagnosis - ignition system

There are two general symptoms of ignition faults. Either the engine will not fire, or the engine is difficult to start and misfires. If it is a regular misfire, ie; the engine is only running on two or three cylinders, the fault is almost sure to be in the high tension circuit. If the misfiring is intermittent, the fault could be in either the high or low tension circuits. If the engine stops suddenly, or will not start at all, it is likely that the fault is in the low tension circuit. Loss of power and overheating, apart from faulty carburettor settings, are normally due to faults in the distributor, or incorrect ignition timing.

Engine fails to start

1   If the engine fails to start and it was running normally when it was last used, first check that there is fuel in the petrol tank. If the engine turns over normally on the starter motor and the battery is evidently well charged, then the fault may be in either the high or low tension circuits. First check the HT circuit. **Note:** If the battery is known to be fully charged, the ignition light comes on, and the starter motor fails to turn the engine, **check the tightness of the leads on the battery terminals** and also the secureness of the earth lead to its **connection to the body.** It is quite common for the leads to have worked loose, even if they look and feel relatively secure. If one of the battery terminal posts gets very hot when trying to operate the starter motor this is a sure indication of a faulty connection to that terminal.

2   One of the commonest reasons for bad starting is wet or damp spark plug leads and distributor. Remove the distributor cap. If condensation is visible internally, dry the cap with a rag and also wipe over the leads. Refit the cap. Also wipe the top of the ignition coil. Alternatively, using a moisture dispersant such as Holts Wet Start can be very effective in starting the engine. To prevent the problem recurring, Holts Damp Start can be used to provide a sealing coat, so excluding any further moisture from the ignition system. In extreme difficulty, Holts Cold Start will help to start a car when only a very poor spark occurs.

3   If the engine still fails to start, check that current is reaching the plugs by disconnecting each plug lead in turn at the spark plug end, and holding the end of the cable about 3/16 in (4.8 mm) away from the cylinder block. Spin the engine on the starter motor.

4   Sparking between the end of the cable and the cylinder block should be fairly strong with a regular blue spark. Hold the lead with rubber or plastic gloves to avoid electric shocks. If current is reaching the spark plugs, then remove and examine them. If they appear to be in good condition, regap and refit them, if not, renew them as a set. the engine should now start.

5   If there is no spark at the plug leads take off the HT lead from the centre of the distributor cap and hold it to the cylinder block as before. Spin the engine as before, when a rapid succession of blue sparks between the end of the lead and the block indicate that the ignition coil is in order, and that the distributor cap is cracked, the rotor faulty, or the carbon brush in the top of the distributor cap is not making good contact with the spring on the rotor. Possibly the contact breaker points are burnt, pitted or dirty. If the points are in bad shape, clean and reset them as described in Section 2.

6   If there are no sparks from the end of the lead from the ignition coil, then check the connections of the lead to the coil and distributor cap, and if they are in order, check out the low tension circuit starting with the battery.

7   Switch on the ignition and turn the crankshaft so that the contact breaker points have fully opened. Then with either a 20v voltmeter or a bulb and two lengths of wire check that open current is flowing along the low tension wire to the ignition coil terminal 'B' or '+' by putting the test wire ends on the aforementioned terminal and earth. No reading indicates a break in the supply from the ignition switch. Check the connections at the switch to see if any are loose. Refit them. A reading shows a faulty coil or condenser or broken lead between the coil and distributor.

8   Detach the condenser wire from the points assembly and with the points open, test between the moving point and earth. If there now is a reading, then the fault is in the condenser. Fit a new one as described in Section 7.

9   With no reading from the moving contact breaker point to earth, take a reading between earth and the 'D' or '−' terminal of the coil. A reading here shows a broken wire which will need to be replaced between the coil and distributor. No reading confirms that the coil has failed and must be renewed. Remember to refit the condenser wire to the points assembly. For these tests it is sufficient to separate the points with a piece of dry paper while testing with the points open.

Engine misfires

1   If the engine misfires regularly, run it at a fast idling speed, and short out each of the spark plugs in turn by placing an insulated screwdriver across the plug terminal to the cylinder block.

2   No difference in engine running will be noticed when the plug in the defective cylinder is short circuited. Short circuiting the working plugs will accentuate the misfire.

3   Remove the plug lead from the end of the defective plug and hold it about 3/16 in (5 mm) away from the block. Restart the engine. If sparking is fairly strong and regular the fault must lie in the spark plug.

4   The plug may be loose, the insulation may be cracked or the electrodes may have burnt away giving too wide a gap for the spark to jump across. Worse still, the earth electrode may have broken off. Either renew the plug, or reset the gap and then test it.

5   If there is no spark at the end of the plug lead, or if it is weak and intermittent, check the ignition lead from the distributor to the plug. If the insulation is cracked or damaged, renew the lead. Check the connections at the distributor cap.

6   If there is still no spark, examine the distributor cap carefully for signs of tracking. This can be recognised by a very thin black line running between two or more segments, or between a segment and some other part of the distributor. These lines are paths which now conduct electricity across the cap thus letting it run to earth. The only answer is to fit a new distributor cap.

7   Apart from the ignition timing being incorrect, other causes of misfiring have already been dealt with under the Section dealing with failure of the engine to start.

8   If the ignition timing is too far retarded, it should be noted that the engine will tend to overheat, and there will be quite a noticeable drop in power. If the engine is overheating and power is down, and the ignition is correct, then the carburettor should be checked, as it is likely that this is where the fault lies. See Chapter 3 for details.

Chapter 5 Clutch

For modifications, and information applicable to later models, see Supplement at end of manual

Contents

Specifications

Type	Single dry plate, diaphragm spring
Control	Hydraulic
Clutch disc	
Lining outer diameter	7.126 in (181.5 mm)
Lining inner diameter	5 in (127 mm)
Maximum run-out of disc linings	0.01 in (0.25 mm)
Clutch pedal free-travel	1 in (25 mm)
Master cylinder bore	0.75 in (19.05 mm)
Slave cylinder bore	0.75 in (19.05 mm)

Torque wrench settings

	lb f ft	kg f m
Clutch to flywheel bolt	11	1.5
Clutch release arm bolt	18	2.5

1 General description

1 The clutch is a single dry-disc type with a diaphragm spring. The unit comprises a steel cover which is dowelled and bolted to the face of the flywheel and contains the pressure plate, pressure plate diaphragm spring and fulcrum rings.

2 The clutch disc is free to slide along the splined input shaft of the gearbox and is held in position between the flywheel and the pressure plate by the pressure of the pressure plate spring. Friction lining material is riveted to the clutch disc, and it has a spring cushioned hub to absorb transmission shocks.

3 The release mechanism consists of an operating arm and bearing which is actuated hydraulically by a master and slave cylinder.

2 Clutch - adjustment

1 As the friction linings on the clutch plate wear, the pressure plate moves closer to the flywheel, and the withdrawal mechanism must move back to allow for this movement. There must always be clearance between the withdrawal mechanism and the clutch, otherwise the full clutch spring pressure will not be available, and the clutch will slip, and quickly ruin itself. Also the life of the withdrawal bearing will be shortened.

2 The small clearance of 2 mm at the clutch itself appears as 1 inch (25 mm) at the pedal.

3 This free movement at the pedal can be felt as movement against only the pull-off spring on the clutch withdrawal lever, before the firmer pressure needed to free the clutch itself.

4 Adjust by slackening the locknut on the slave cylinder operating rod and screwing the adjuster nut in, or out, to obtain the correct free-travel.

5 Tighten the locknut and check the operation of the clutch.

3 Clutch life - general

1 Some drivers allow their clutches to outlast the engine and transmission. Others need new ones almost as often and regularly as their 12,000 miles (20,000 km) service. The clutch is one of the prime examples of a component cheap to buy, but expensive (or lengthy for the home mechanic) to fit.

2 The short life is due to abuse.

Fig. 5.1. Clutch cover assembly and clutch disc with linings

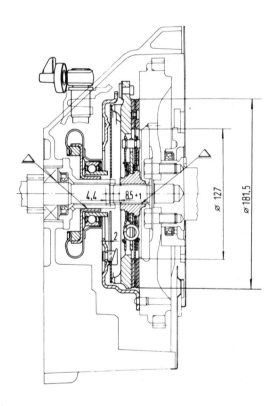

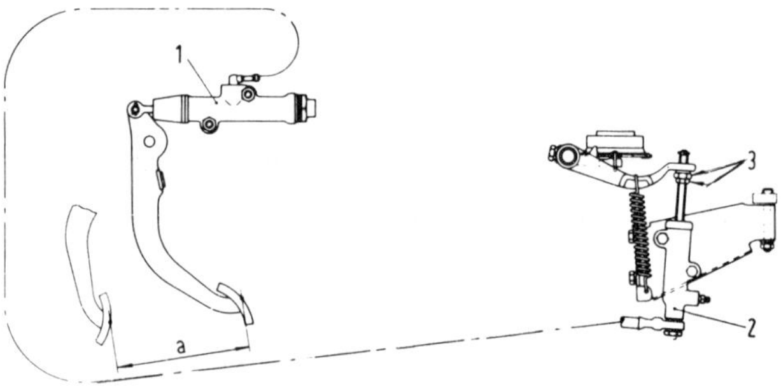

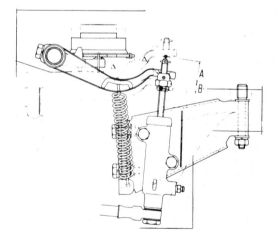

Fig. 5.3. Clutch release hydraulic circuit

1 Master cylinder   3 Adjusting nut
2 Operating cylinder
a Pedal travel = 6.7 in (170 mm)

Fig. 5.2. Cross-section of clutch showing major dimensions

2 mm	=	clutch free-travel
4.4 mm	=	maximum acceptable movement with worn linings
8.5 mm	=	declutching travel
127 mm	=	inner diameter of friction lining
181.5 mm	=	outer diameter of friction lining

Fig. 5.4. Cross-section through operating arm

A 1.25 in (28.5 mm) declutching travel
B 0.5 in (12.5 mm) travel of operating arm as a result of disc lining wear

3 Common abuses can be avoided as follows:
4 Do not sit for long periods, such as traffic lights, with the clutch disengaged. Put the gearbox in neutral until the lights go yellow. This extends the withdrawal bearing life.
5 Always remove the foot completely from the clutch pedal once under way. Riding the clutch lightly ruins the withdrawal bearing. Riding it heavily allows it to slip, so quickly wears out the lining.
6 Whenever the clutch is disengaged, hold it completely so, the pedal down as far as it will go. You find drivers holding the car on a hill by slipping the clutch. This wears it quickly.
7 Always move off in first gear.

4 Clutch hydraulic system - bleeding

Whenever the clutch hydraulic system has been overhauled, a part renewed, or the level in the reservoir is too low, air will have entered the system necessitating its bleeding. During this operation the level of hydraulic fluid in the reservoir should not be allowed to fall below half full, otherwise air will be drawn in again.

1 Obtain a clean and dry jam jar, plastic tubing at least 12 inches (300 mm) long and able to fit tightly over the bleed screw of the slave cylinder, a supply of Brake and Clutch Fluid and the services of an assistant.
2 Check that the master cylinder reservoir is full and if not, fill it. Cover the bottom inch of the jar with hydraulic fluid.
3 Remove the rubber dust cap (if fitted) from the bleed screw on the slave cylinder and, with a suitable spanner, open the bleed screw one turn.
4 Place one end of the tube securely over the end of the bleed screw and insert the other end in the jar so that the tube end is below the level of the fluid.
5 An assistant should now depress the clutch pedal and whilst in the fully down position the bleed screw should be tightened.
6 Allow the clutch pedal to return slowly.
7 Repeat the above sequence, until no more air bubbles appear. Tighten the bleed screw on the next pedal downstroke.
8 Do not forget to check the reservoir frequently to ensure that the hydraulic fluid does not drop too far so letting air into the system.
9 Replace the rubber dust cap over the bleed screw. Note: Never re-use the fluid bled from the hydraulic system.

5 Clutch - removal and inspection

1 Remove the transmission (see Chapter 6).
2 Mark the position of the clutch cover relative to the flywheel.
3 Slacken off the bolts holding the cover to the flywheel in a diagonal sequence, undoing each bolt a little at a time. This keeps the pressure even all round the diaphragm spring and prevents distortion. When all the pressure is released on the bolts, remove them, lift the cover off the dowel pegs and take it off together with the friction plate which is between it and the flywheel.
4 Examine the diaphragm spring for signs of distortion or fracture.
5 Examine the pressure plate for signs of scoring or abnormal wear.
6 If either the spring or the plate is defective it will be necessary to renew the complete assembly with an exchange unit. The assembly can only be taken to pieces with special equipment and, in any case, individual parts of the assembly are not obtainable as regular spares.
7 Examine the friction plate for indications of uneven wear and scoring of the friction surfaces. Contamination by oil will also show as hard and blackened areas which can cause defective operation. If there has been a leak from engine or transmission this must be cured before reassembling the clutch. If the clearance between the heads of the securing rivets and the face of the friction lining material is less than 0.020 in (0.5 mm) it would be worthwhile to fit a new plate. Around the hub of the friction disc are six springs acting as shock absorbers between the hub and the friction area. These should be intact and tightly in position.
8 The face of the flywheel should be examined for signs of scoring or uneven wear and, if necessary, it will have to be renewed or reconditioned. See Chapter 1 for details of flywheel removal.
9 Also check the clutch withdrawal bearing (Section 7) before reassembly.
10 Clutch parts are relatively cheap compared with the great labour of removal, so it is best to renew parts if there is any doubt.

5.3 Removing the clutch assembly and friction disc

6 Clutch - refitting

1 Hold the clutch friction, (driven) plate up against the flywheel. The disc holding the cushion springs must be away from the flywheel.
2 Put the clutch cover assembly over the plate, lining up the dowel holes, and fit the bolts. Tighten the bolts finger-tight, just enough to take the weight of the friction plate between the pressure plate and the flywheel.
3 Now centralise the clutch plate. The splines in the plate must be accurately lined up with the end of the crankshaft, otherwise when the clutch is clamped up tight, and the friction plate cannot be moved, the shaft will not fit through, and reassembly of transmission to engine will be impossible. FIAT use a special mandrel. The alignment can be done satisfactorily using a metal or wooden bar, and checking carefully by eye.
4 Tighten the bolts round the edge of the clutch cover carefully and diagonally, gradually compressing the clutch spring.
5 Tighten the bolts to a torque of 11 lb f ft (1.5 kg f m).
6 Refit the transmission, as described in Chapter 6.

7 Clutch release mechanism - general

1 To release the clutch, so that the drive is disengaged, the pressure plate is withdrawn from the flywheel. The driver's pedal action, actuates the slave cylinder which operates the withdrawal lever on the outside of the transmission case, and the fork inside pushes the withdrawal bearing against the clutch.
2 The pivot for the lever fork should outlast the car.
3 The withdrawal or release bearing should not give trouble either. But should it fail the transmission must be removed from the car to reach it. So when the transmission is out, even though for some other work, the bearing should be looked at very critically, and if there is any doubt it should be renewed.
4 The bearing is clipped to the withdrawal fork. It should not be immersed in cleaning fluid, as it is sealed. Liquid will get in, but can not be dried out, nor can new lubricant be got in. The bearing should be rotated. It should be completely smooth in action, but the smooth resistance of the grease should be felt. It should not make any noise.
5 When fitting a new bearing the clips and the bearing surfaces of the fork should be lubricated with grease.
6 If the bearing is suspect, but the transmission is still in the car, the bearing's failure can only be assessed by noise. If the actual bearings are breaking up, this will be shown by a squawking or groaning noise when the clutch pedal is pressed down. If the bearing is loose, it may rattle at speed, and this rattle can be quietened if the pedal is lightly pressed to hold the bearing. The car should not be driven in this condition, for if the bearing breaks up, repair is likely to be expensive, as other parts will be damaged.

7.3a Removing the clutch release bearing

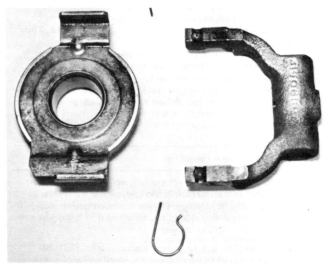

7.3b The clutch release bearing, operating fork and bearing retaining clips

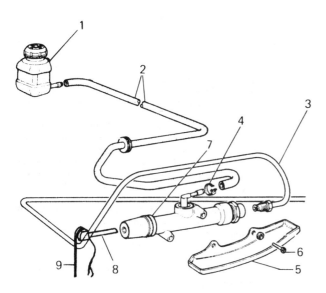

Fig. 5.5. Master cylinder, reservoir and piping

1 Reservoir	6 Bolt
2 Hose	7 Cylinder
3 Tube	8 Rod
4 Clamp	9 Pedal
5 Bracket	

7.4 The clutch release bearing fitted, and held in position by the retaining clips

8 Master cylinder - removal and refitting

1   Depending upon the model, remove the steering column lower shroud or the complete steering column itself. See Chapter 9 for removal instructions.

2   Disconnect the pipe from the master cylinder outlet and blank off the pipe. Use a container and rags to prevent fluid getting on to the carpet.

3   Remove the two bolts and washers securing the master cylinder to the support bracket. Pull the cylinder out and off the operating rod.

4   Remove the clamp securing the hose from the reservoir to the cylinder, pull the hose off and drain the fluid into the container.

5   Refitting is the reverse of the removal sequence. Fill the reservoir with fresh hydraulic fluid, then operate the pedal a few times and check for leaks.

6   Bleed the hydraulic system, as described in Section 4 and refit the steering column, as described in Chapter 9.

9 Master cylinder - dismantling, examination and reassembly

1   Clean off all external dirt.

2   Carefully remove the rubber boot from the operating rod and using a pair of circlip pliers remove the circlip.

3   Remove the plunger, complete with seals, and the spring. Remove the seals from the plunger.

4   Clean and carefully examine all parts, especially the seals, for signs of distortion, swelling, splitting or other damage and check the plunger and cylinder for wear or scoring. Renew any parts that are suspect. It is recommended that whenever a master cylinder is dismantled, new seals are always fitted.

5   To reassemble, fit the seals and gasket on the plunger, wet the assembled parts with fresh fluid and fit in the cylinder together with the spring.

6   Refit the circlip and rubber boot.

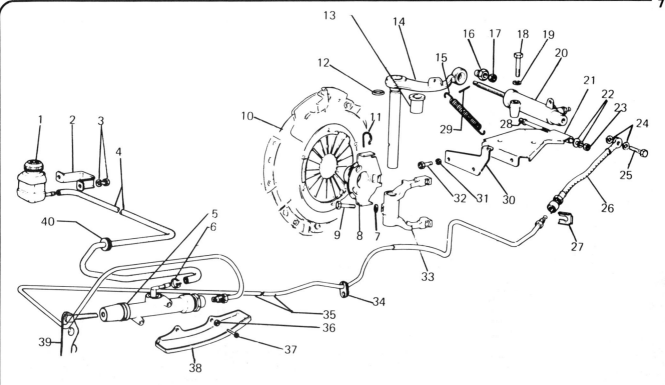

Fig. 5.6. Clutch release components

1	Reservoir	11	Spring	21	Bracket	31	Washer
2	Bracket	12	Seal	22	Washer	32	Bolt
3	Lockwasher and nut	13	Bushing	23	Nut	33	Fork
4	Tube	14	Shaft	24	Gasket	34	Rubber ring
5	Master cylinder	15	Spring	25	Connector	35	Tube
6	Clamp	16	Nut	26	Hose	36	Washer
7	Washer	17	Nut	27	Clip	37	Screw
8	Throw out bearing	18	Bolt	28	Bolt	38	Cover
9	Bolt	19	Washer	29	Cotter pin	39	Pedal
10	Clutch	20	Operating cylinder	30	Bracket		

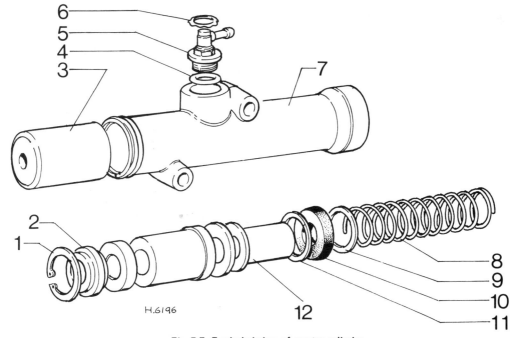

H.6196

Fig. 5.7. Exploded view of master cylinder

1	Lockring	4	Gasket	7	Cylinder	10	Seal
2	Seal	5	Connector	8	Spring	11	Gasket
3	Boot	6	Lockplate	9	Seal	12	Plunger

10 Slave cylinder - removal and refitting

1   Disconnect the hose from the end of the slave cylinder.
2   Remove the split pin from the end of the operating rod, and
remove the clutch return spring from the release arm.
3   Remove the two retaining bolts and washers, and the slave cylinder.
4   Refitting is the reverse of the removal procedure. Use a new split
pin and a new gasket on the hose union.
5   Bleed the hydraulic system, as described in Section 4 and adjust the
clutch pedal free-movement as described in Section 2. Check the
operation of the clutch.

11 Slave cylinder - dismantling, examination and reassembly

1   Clean off all external dirt.

2   Remove the rubber boot and the operating rod.
3   Remove the circlip and collect the washer, spring and bush. Remove
the seals from the piston.
4   Clean and examine all parts. Check the cylinder bore and the piston
for scoring. Always fit new seals at each dismantling.
5   Reassemble the parts and fit in the cylinder. Fit the operating rod
and rubber boot.

12 Clutch pedal travel - adjustment

1   The clutch pedal travel should be approximately 6.7 in (170 mm),
'a' in Fig. 5.4.
2   To adjust, slacken the locknut and screw the adjusting screw in, or
out, as required. Screw out to reduce travel, screw in to increase travel.

10.1 The clutch slave cylinder, operating arm and return spring

10.3 Clutch slave cylinder mounting bracket

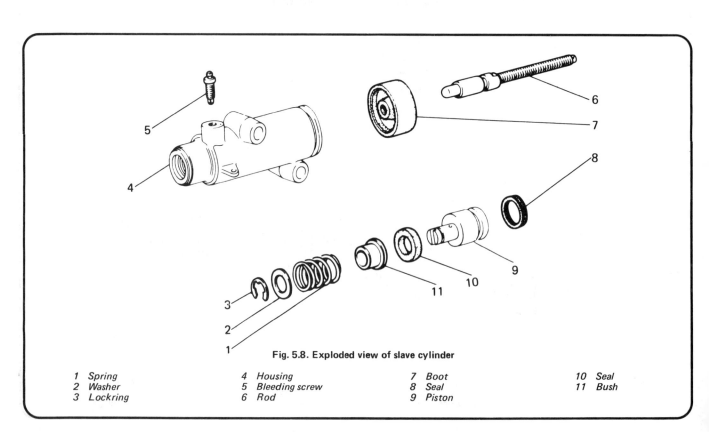

Fig. 5.8. Exploded view of slave cylinder

1	Spring	4	Housing	7	Boot	10	Seal
2	Washer	5	Bleeding screw	8	Seal	11	Bush
3	Lockring	6	Rod	9	Piston		

13 Fault diagnosis - clutch

Symptom	Reason/s	Remedy
Judder when taking up drive	Loose engine/gearbox mountings or over flexible mountings	Check and tighten all mounting bolts and replace any 'soft' or broken mountings.
	Badly worn friction surfaces or friction plate contaminated with oil carbon deposit	Remove transmission and renew clutch parts as required. Rectify the oil leak which caused contamination.
	Worn splines in the friction plate hub or on the gearbox input shaft	Renew friction plate and/or input shaft.
	Badly worn transmission or drive shafts	Renew bearings and shafts.
Clutch drag (or failure to disengage) so that gears cannot be meshed	Clutch actuating and clearance too great	Adjust clearance.
	Clutch friction disc sticking because of rust on splines (usually apparent after standing idle for some length of time)	As temporary remedy engage top gear, apply handbrake, depress clutch and start engine. (If very badly stuck engine will not turn). When running rev-up engine and slip clutch until disengagement is normally possible. Renew friction plate at earliest opportunity.
	Damaged or misaligned pressure plate assembly	Renew pressure plate assembly.
Clutch slip - (increase in engine speed does not result in increase in car speed - especially on hills)	Clutch actuating clearance from fork too small resulting in partially disengaged clutch at all times	Adjust clearance.
	Clutch friction surfaces worn out or clutch surfaces oil soaked	Renew friction plate and remedy source of oil leakage.
	Damaged clutch spring	Fit reconditioned assembly.

Chapter 6 Transmission

For modifications, and information applicable to later models, see Supplement at end of manual

Contents

Specifications

Gears	Four forward and one reverse

Synchromesh

Spring-ring type	1st and 2nd gears
Slip-ring type	3rd and 4th gears
Gear type	
Forward	Constant mesh, helical toothed
Reverse	Straight toothed, with sliding idler gear

Gear ratios

First	3.583 : 1
Second	2.235 : 1
Third	1.454 : 1
Fourth	0.959 : 1
Reverse	3.714 : 1

Final drive gears	Helical toothed
Final drive ratio	4.077 : 1 (13/53)
Differential case bearings	Two
Bearing type	Taper roller
Bearing preload setting	By shims
Side to planet gear backlash adjustment	By thrust washers
Gear backlash	0.004 in (0.1 mm)
Differential preload	0.003 - 0.005 in (0.08 - 0.12 mm)

Torque wrench settings	lb f ft	kg f m
Bolt, final drive ring gear	51	7
Nuts, clutch housing to gearbox casing	18	2.5
Nuts and bolts, transmission to engine	58	8
Bolt, transmission casing halves	18	2.5
Bolt, selector fork and levers to rods	14.5	2
Other nuts/bolts (size M6) (10 mm AF)	7	1

1 General description

1 Two items of the transmission, the clutch and the driveshafts, are dealt with in separate Chapters. In this one the combined gearbox,

final drive and differential are described.

2 Figure 6.1 shows the three shaft layout of the transmission on the left end of the engine. Because the components are arranged so differently from gearboxes in-line with the engine, the normal names, such as mainshaft, and layshaft, are not applicable. The top shaft, in

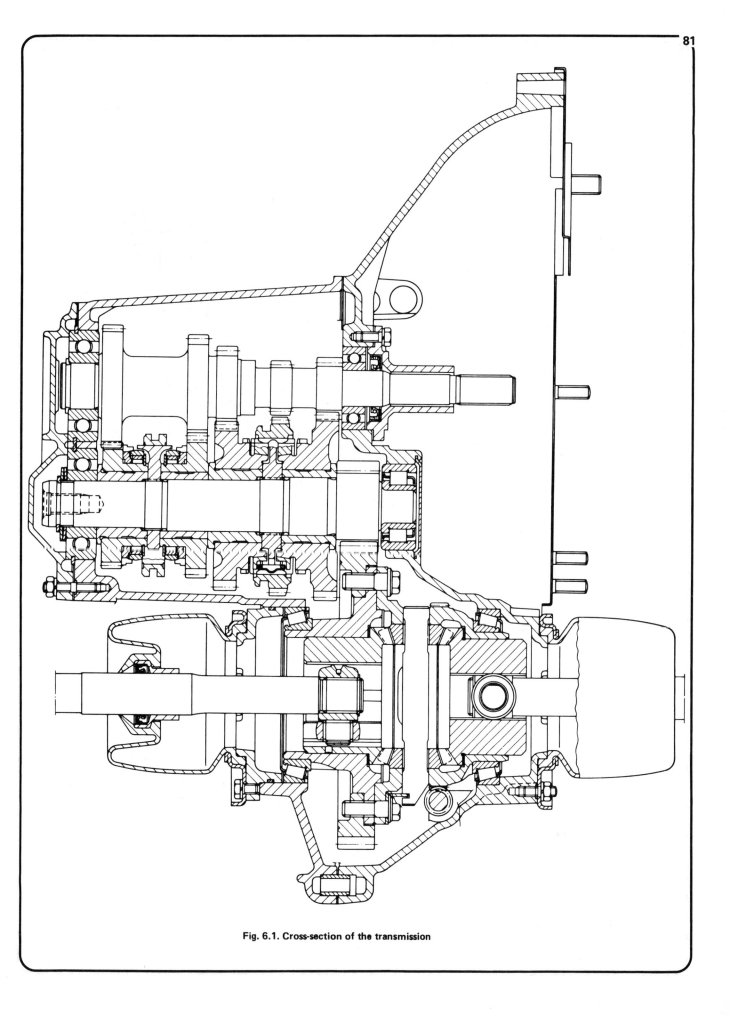

Fig. 6.1. Cross-section of the transmission

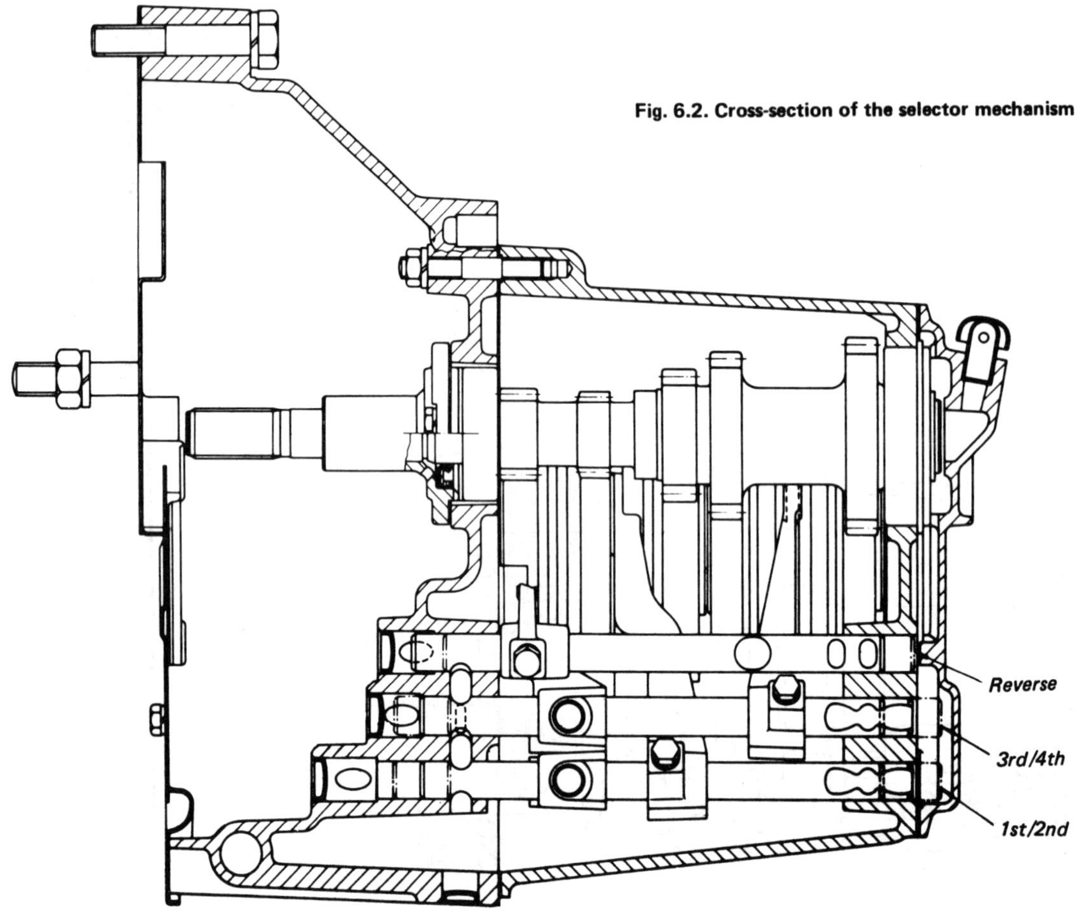

Fig. 6.2. Cross-section of the selector mechanism

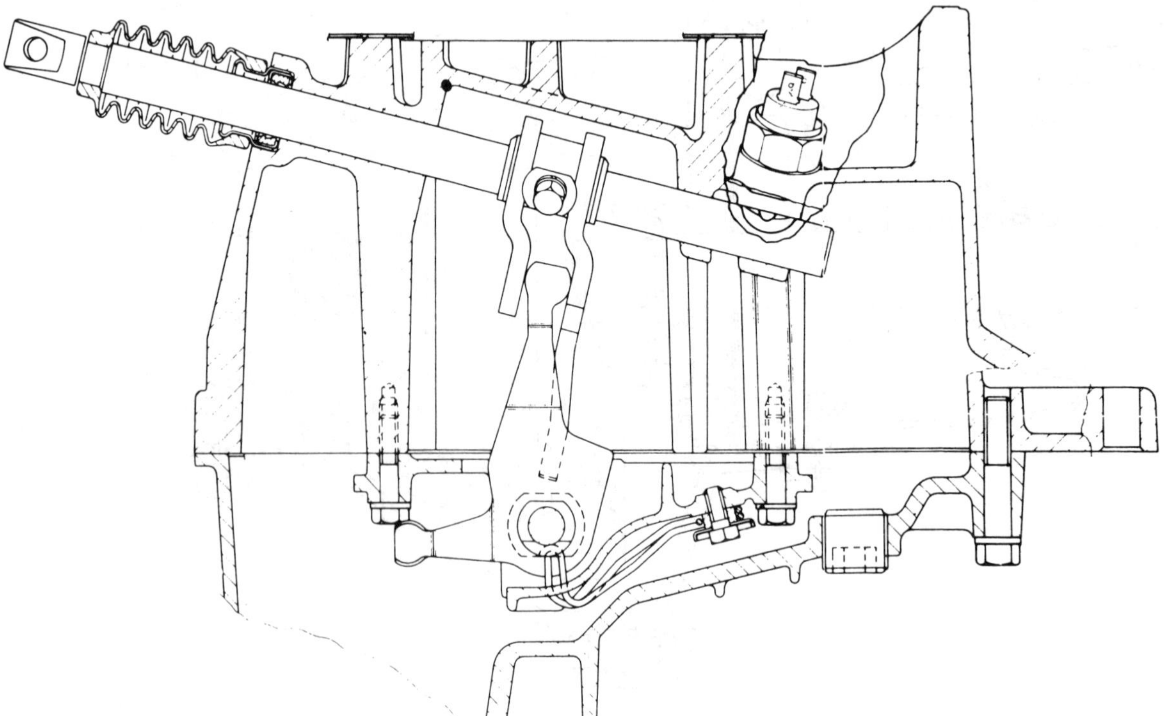

Reverse

3rd/4th

1st/2nd

Fig. 6.3. Section of gear selector rod

line with the engine, is called the input shaft. The next one, with all the sliding dog clutches for engaging the gears, is the 'second shaft'. Below this is the final drive with differential.

3 The synchromesh is of the spring-ring type on 1st/2nd gear and the slip-ring type on 3rd/4th gear.

4 The transmission can be removed from the car leaving the engine in place. Conversely the engine cannot be removed without the transmission, and as this involves disconnecting the driveshafts, it is responsible for much of the labour of engine removal. The transmission must be removed to give access to the clutch. Removal of the transmission, unlike that of the engine, does not involve use of lifting tackle, but two good jacks, and plenty of stout timber blocks will be needed. The most likely reason to remove the transmission is to cure an oil leak, or to overhaul the clutch. If the transmission itself is badly worn, then its overhaul is quite possible without special tools. But to be sure of a successful outcome, with absence of noise, then the overhaul must be exceedingly thorough. The cost and the difficulty in obtaining all the parts makes the case for fitting a FIAT reconditioned unit worth considering.

2 Transmission - removal

1 Drain the transmission oil into a container. Remove the air cleaner and duct for carburettor cooling as described in Chapter 3.
2 Disconnect the battery leads.
3 Slacken the clutch slave cylinder retaining bolts. Slacken the bleed screw on the cylinder to allow the operating rod to retract. Disconnect the return spring from the clutch operating arm. Remove the split pin from the end of the rod, remove the retaining bolts and lift the cylinder to the side out of the way.
4 Remove the upper nuts and bolts, accessible from above, securing the transmission to the engine.
5 Slacken the rear wheel nuts, raise the rear of the car and support it on axle stands or blocks at the jacking points. Remove the rear wheels.
6 Remove the three splash guards on the left-hand side.

7 Scribe a line on the side of the gearchange linkage joint, so that it can be reassembled in the same position, and remove the two bolts. Slacken the bolt connecting the flexible link to the transmission gearchange rod and swing the link out of the way.
8 Disconnect the speedometer cable from the transmission casing.
9 Disconnect the wires to the various switches on the transmission casing. These vary for different markets. For North America, a seatbelt interlock warning switch is fitted. There is also a reversing light switch. Note the colour of the wires going to each switch.
10 Disconnect the solenoid lead and the heavy cable from the starter motor. Remove the starter motor retaining bolts and lift out the starter.
11 Disconnect the earth strap from the transmission.
12 Refer to Chapter 2, and remove the exhaust pipe and silencer assembly.
13 Remove the driveshaft boot retainer bolts from the transmission. On models with 5-speed transmission, simply disconnect the driveshaft flanges from the transmission.
14 Remove the bolts which attach the control arms to the body. Note the number and location of shims so that they can be refitted correctly.
15 Pull the hubs and pillars outwards to free the driveshaft Tripode joints from the differential. Tie the driveshafts to the control arms so that they do not come out of the hubs.
16 Support the engine with blocks under the sump. Remove the flywheel bottom guard and the engine bottom support beam.
17 Support the transmission and remove the remaining bolts holding the transmission to the engine.
18 Withdraw the transmission to the left, taking care not to put any strain on the input shaft, and lower it to the ground.

3 Transmission - dismantling

1 Clean the outside of the casing, and the inside of the clutch housing, checking in the dirt for runs indicating oil leaks, particularly from the

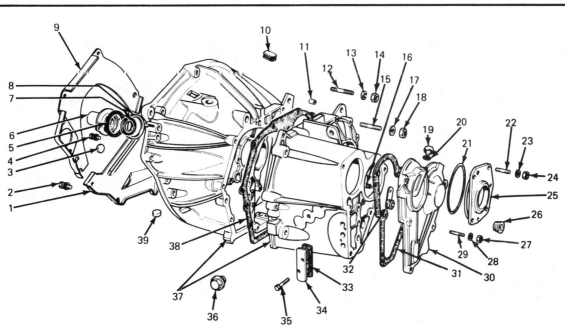

Fig. 6.4. Exploded view of transmission case and covers

1	Cover	11	Dowel	21	Seal	31	Gasket
2	Bolt and washer	12	Stud	22	Stud	32	Magnet
3	Plug	13	Lockwasher	23	Lockwasher	33	Gasket
4	Bolt and washer	14	Nut	24	Nut	34	Cover
5	Gasket	15	Stud	25	Flange	35	Bolt
6	Cover	16	Bolt and washer	26	Plug	36	Plug
7	Seal	17	Lockwasher	27	Nut	37	Case
8	Plug	18	Nut	28	Lockwasher	38	Gasket
9	Cover	19	Vent	29	Stud	39	Plug
10	Plug	20	Gasket	30	Cover		

core plug.

2   Take the clutch pull-off spring off the clutch withdrawal lever. Pivot the lever round so the withdrawal bearing is nearer, and unclip it from the fork.

3   Remove the nuts with spring washers on the studs inside the clutch housing that hold it onto the gearbox casing.

4   Stand the transmission up on end, clutch housing downwards.

5   Remove the nuts on the studs holding the end cover, now at the top of the gearbox. Take off the cover, and the old gasket.

6   Take off the two bolts holding the plate over the detents.

7   Take out the three springs. Note one is green and two are blue. The green one is the shortest, and is for reverse.

8   Remove the three detent balls.

9   Take off the inner circlips, on the end of the input and second shafts. Note that the one on the second shaft has behind it two belleville washers. These put a heavy load on the circlip. If it will not readily come out of its groove, then the load must be taken off it using a clamp. This clamp will definitely be needed for assembly. See Section 7, paragraph 5.

10 The belleville washers can be compressed by screwing into the threaded end of the shaft one of the bolts that holds the transmission to the engine, using a large socket spanner to press down on the belleville washers. Between the socket and the washer must go a semicircle of steel so the socket clears the circlip, and through the gap in it the ends of the circlip can be reached.

11 Having removed the circlips from both shafts, see if the two bearings will come off the shafts and out of the casing readily, prising with screwdrivers. If they do not, leave them on the shafts for now, but take off the large circlips round the outer races.

12 Remove the nuts on the other studs on the outside holding the gearbox casing to the clutch housing.

13 Pull the gearbox casing up off the shafts and selector rods.

14 Remove the nut holding the locking plate for the reverse idler shaft, on the face at present uppermost of the gearbox side of the clutch housing.

15 Take out the reverse shaft.

16 Remove the bolts securing the three selector forks and the selector levers to the three selector rods.

17 Pull the reverse selector rod up, out of the housing, and lift off the reverse fork with the idler gear.

18 Pull up the 3rd/4th, the centre of the three, selector rod, leaving the fork and lever still engaged, until the rod is clear of its seat, then the rod with the fork and lever can be lifted out. Keep the rods with their levers and forks. Though they cannot be muddled up, it saves sorting out later.

19 Repeat for the 1st/2nd selectors.

20 Remove the two interlock plungers from the passages either side of the central, 3rd/4th rod. Remove from the 3rd/4th rod the thin interlock plunger. Put these, and the detent balls in a small box so they cannot get lost.

21 Lift out the input and second shafts. They come most easily as a pair, because of the gears being in mesh.

22 Lift out the final drive/differential.

23 It is recommended the gear selector linkage is removed so that new seals can be fitted. Undo the three bolts holding the selector pivot to the housing.

24 Take out the bolt holding the finger on the inner end of the selector rod. On the outside of the housing take off the flange guiding rod, on which the rubber boot fits. Pull out the rod, retrieving from inside the spring and oil seals and washers.

25 Take out of the housing the engine end bearing (roller) of the second shaft. It might just tip out if the housing is turned over.

26 Turn the housing over, and from inside the clutch housing take off the oil seal for the input shaft, in its carrier.

27 The outer races for the final drive can be left in the housing and casing unless it is decided to renew them. Unless they need renewing, the preload plate on the casing, with behind it a shim, need not be removed.

28 There is no need to take the bearings off the input shaft unless they are being renewed.

3.3 Remove the nuts inside the clutch housing

3.5 Then turn it up on end and remove the endcover

3.6 Remove the bolts and cover plate and collect the three springs and detent balls

3.11 It will probably be easier to remove the big circlip from both bearings ...

3.13 .. leaving the bearings on their shafts when lifting off the half casing

3.14 Take out the locking plate for the reverse idler shaft, and remove the shaft

Fig. 6.5. Gear selector parts

1	Selector shafts	3	Interlock plungers	5	Seals
2	Selector forks	4	Detent balls (only two shown)	6	Selector rod

3.17 Remove the reverse idler with its selector rod

3.18 Next comes the 3rd/4th selector rod, after taking out the bolts holding its fork and lever ...

3.19 ... and then the 1st/2nd selector rod, and the fork and lever

3.20 Remove the two interlock plungers from between the passages. There is also a thin plunger in the end of the 3rd/4th selector rod

3.21 Lift out the input and second shafts complete

3.22 The differential/final drive is now lifted out

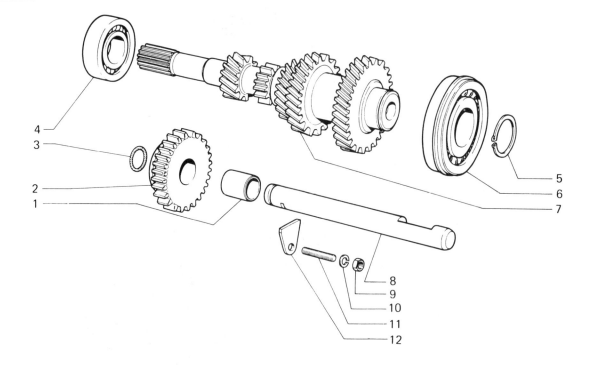

Fig. 6.6. Input and reverse gear shafts

1	Bush	4	Bearing	7	Input shaft	10	Lockwasher
2	Reverse idler gear	5	Circlip	8	Idler shaft	11	Stud
3	Seal	6	Bearing	9	Nut	12	Plate

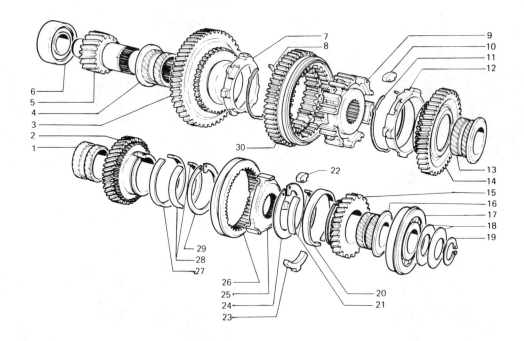

Fig. 6.7. Second shaft gear cluster

1	Bush	9	Hub	17	Bearing	24	Snap-ring
2	Driven gear	10	Pad	18	Spring washer	25	Hub
3	Driven gear	11	Spring	19	Snap ring	26	Sleeve
4	Bush	12	Synchronizer	20	Synchronizer	27	Synchronizer
5	Countershaft	13	Bush	21	Spring	28	Spring
6	Bearing	14	Driven gear	22	Pad	29	Snap-ring
7	Synchronizer	15	Gear	23	Pad	30	Sleeve
8	Spring	16	Bush				

4 Second shaft gear cluster - dismantling and reassembly

1 If the bearing has not yet been removed when taking the shaft out of the gearbox, take it off now, by holding the outer race in the hand, and hitting the end of the shaft with a soft hammer.

2 One by one take the gears with their bushes, and the gear-engaging dog-clutches on their hubs off the shaft, keeping them all in order, and the same way round.

3 If the synchromesh was in good order, do not dismantle it, as reassembly is difficult due to the strength of the circlip.

4 To strip the synchromesh, simply take the circlip off the gear wheel side. See how all the rings, half rings, and stops, fit inside and then lift them out.

5 Keep all parts laid out in order. Though many parts are interchangeable (otherwise how they go is obvious from examining them and from the photos in this book), it saves having to work everything out. It is also better to fit everything back where it came from.

6 Reassembly of the components is the reverse. Check that all is correct by referring to the drawings and photos.

7 To refit the circlip on a synchromesh unit is difficult. Mount the gearwheel in a soft jawed, clean vice, gripping the flanks of the gearwheel. Part the circlip with circlip pliers, or else prise it apart with a screwdriver, to get it part way into position. Then work all the way round with more screwdrivers, to force it into position. An assistant with another screwdriver is almost essential.

5 Differential - dismantling and reassembly

1 The differential cage acts as the final driver carrier.

2 Undo the ring of bolts holding the final drive wheel to the differential, and the two halves of the differential cage together.

3 This will also release the locking plate for the planet pinion shaft.

4.1a Now that the second shaft is out of the casing it is easier to get the circlip off, against the considerable pressure of the Belleville washers

4.1b Driving the shaft out of the bearing

4.2 Slide the gearwheels and synchromesh units off the shafts

5.2 The differential cage is clamped together by this ring of bolts

5.3 Two of the bolts hold the lockplate for the planet pinions shaft

5.4 Undoing the bolts allows the whole assembly to come apart

5.6 The planet pinions come off their shaft

5.7 Both bevel side gears have a washer behind them to take side thrust, and set the backlash with the teeth of the planet pinions

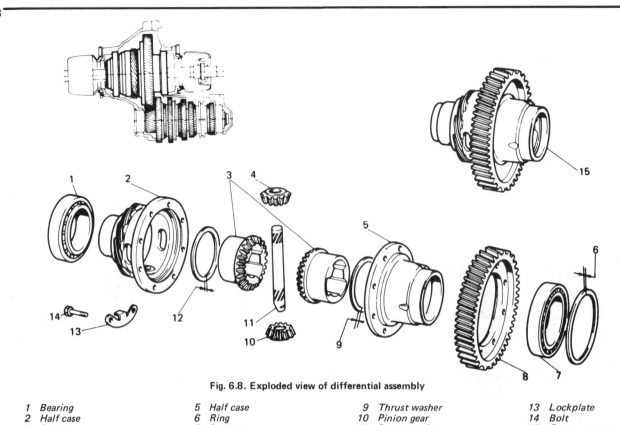

Fig. 6.8. Exploded view of differential assembly

1	Bearing	5	Half case	9	Thrust washer	13	Lockplate
2	Half case	6	Ring	10	Pinion gear	14	Bolt
3	Side gears	7	Bearing	11	Pinion shaft	15	Gears and case
4	Pinion gear	8	Ring gear	12	Thrust ring		

7.2 With all the gears, etc., fitted on the shafts, they should look like this

7.3 Fit the bearing, then the two Belleville washers back-to-back, followed by the circlip

7.5a A transmission-to-engine bolt has a suitable thread to make a press to compress the Belleville washers ...

7.5b ... till the circlip is level with its groove and can be tapped into it

7.6 Fit the roller bearing on the second shaft

7.8 Fitting the final drive

4　Lift off the final drive wheel.

5　Mark the two halves of the differential cage, with punch dots, for reassembly.

6　Prise the two halves apart. Remove the shaft and the two planet pinions.

7　Take out the two bevel side gears, with their thrust washers, from the two halves of the cage. Leave the taper roller bearings in place unless they are being renewed.

8　Reassembly is the reverse of dismantling procedure. The backlash of the side and planet gears must not exceed 0.004 in (0.1 mm). It can be adjusted by fitting different thicknesses of thrust washers behind the side gears. Tighten them both evenly in a diagonal sequence to a torque of 51 lb f ft (7 kg f m). If new bearings are being fitted, drive them into place carefully and evenly, doing so by the rollers. Setting the preload of these bearings as described in Section 7.

6　Inspection and renewal of components

1　Check all the components for signs of damage. All the gear teeth should be smooth and shiny, without any chips. The ball and rollers of the bearings should be unblemished.

2　The races of the final drive taper roller bearings, still in the casing, should be a smooth, even colour without any mark. As the lubricant does not have the extreme pressure (EP) additives necessary with hypoid gears of conventional rear axles, these bearings are likely to last well. But should either the rollers or the races be marked at all, then the complete bearing must be renewed. In this case the outer races must be extracted from the casing, and the rollers with the inner races pulled off the differential cage halves. The latter is strong, so it will be simple to prise them off. But the casing being soft, great care must be taken to pull the outer races out straight. FIAT have a special puller. It would be advisable to get this job done by your agent.

3　Check the clearance of the gearwheels on their hubs against the Specifications.

4　Check the synchromesh rings for signs of wear. Check their fit in their respective gears. If the gears are being renewed, then the synchromesh should also be renewed. One point easy to miss in examining the gears is fracture of the small ends of the teeth that are on the outside of the synchro-ring, and are an extension of the teeth for the dog clutch to engage. If any of these are chipped the gear must be renewed.

5　Check the casings for cracks. If there are leaks at a core plug, it must be renewed. This must be tapped carefully into place, sufficient to expand it but not enough to distort it too much. If a new plug is not available, or its security is in doubt after fitting, it can be secured in place with a layer of eposy resin, two part adhesive, such as Araldite, round its rim. This type of adhesive requires two days to set fully at ambient temperature but can be used in a few hours if heated in an oven.

6　Renew seals and gaskets at each dismantling.

7　Check the movement of the selector rods in their bores in the casing. They should move freely but without appreciable sideplay. Inspect the sliding surfaces of the selector forks for wear or damage.

7　Transmission - reassembly

1　Refit all the differential components and the final drive gear wheel to the differential cage, so it is ready as a sub-assembly. Use appropriate thrust washers behind the bevel side gears to get the correct backlash with the planet gears.

2　Fit all the gearwheels, with their synchromesh units already assembled, on their bushes and hubs respectively onto the second shaft.

3　Fit the bearing on the end of the second shaft, with the groove for the circlip in the outer race outermost. Use some piping over the shaft on the inner race to drive it down.

4　Fit the two Belleville washers, their outer rims next to each other on the end of the shaft.

5　Fit the circlip. Fit this to get into its groove against the considerable pressure of the pair of washers, the latter must be compressed by a clamp. The end of the shaft is internally threaded, and the bolts fixing the transmission to the engine are the same thread. Select a socket just large enough to span the shaft but press on the circlip. The bolts are a bit long, so another socket makes a handy distance piece to use up the extra length of bolt. Screw in the bolt to push the two washers and the circlip down the shaft, watching carefully at the gap in the circlip to see when it is lined up with the groove in the shaft. Tap the circlip, which is trapped by the socket, with a small screwdriver, to push it into the groove. Release the press.

6　Insert the roller bearing for the second shaft in the clutch housing. Fit both bearings to the input shaft, and the circlip to the end, if these have been removed for renewal.

7　Refit the gear selector rod to the housing with the new seals inside and rubber boot outside.

8　Put the differential into the housing.

9　Fit the gear selector linkage bracket onto its studs, engaging the lever with the rod linkage.

10　Fit the input and second shafts with their bearings as a pair, so the gears can be meshed, into the housing, the two shafts standing on their bearings in the housings. The large circlips should be removed from the upper bearings, (those at the left end of the shafts) outside races so that the casing can be fitted over the bearings.

11　Put the reverse idler gear in its selector fork, and the fork on the selector rod, and put them in position in the housing, and then fit the reverse shaft to the idler. Lock the reverse shaft with its plate, and the fork with its bolt.

12　Fit an interlock plunger into the passage between the reverse and 3rd/4th selector rods. To get it in, attach it to a screwdriver with grease, and lower it into place.

13　Fit the 3rd/4th selector rod, with fork and lever. This rod can be recognised by the small hole through the end for the thin interlock plunger. Do not forget to fit this little plunger before fitting the rod. Lodge the lever and fork in place in the selectors and synchro clutch respectively. Then slide the rod down into the housing. Fit the bolts to secure the lever and the fork to the rod.

14　Fit the next interlock plunger into the passage between 3rd/4th and 1st/2nd selector rods.

15　Fit the 1st/2nd selector fork into its clutch groove, and swivel it

7.9 After fitting the gear selector rod with its new seals, fit the lever bracket

7.10 The input and second shafts go in as a pair ...

7.11a ... then the reverse idler in its selector fork, on the selector rod ...

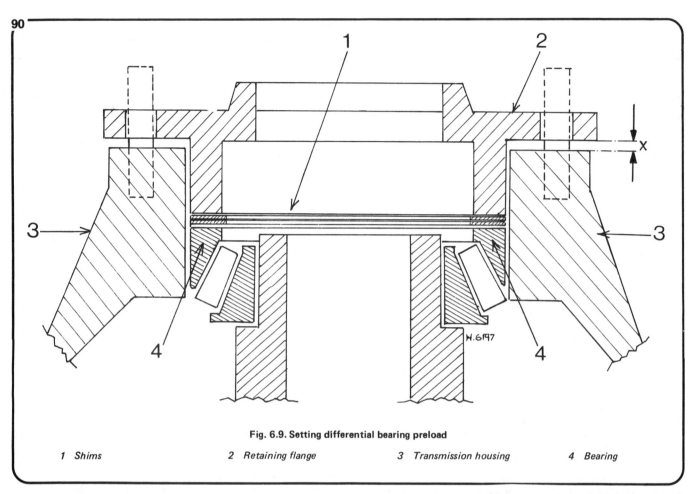

Fig. 6.9. Setting differential bearing preload

| 1 Shims | 2 Retaining flange | 3 Transmission housing | 4 Bearing |

7.11b ... followed by the shaft

7.13 Don't forget this thin interlock plunger in the 3rd/4th selector rod

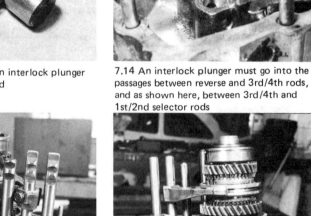

7.14 An interlock plunger must go into the passages between reverse and 3rd/4th rods, and as shown here, between 3rd/4th and 1st/2nd selector rods

7.15 Thread the 1st/2nd fork into position

7.16 Finally all the gears and rods should be in place

7.17 Fit a new gasket ...

into place. Pass its selector rod through it and the lever into its seat. Bolt the fork and lever to their rod.

16 The selector rods should now all be in place with the grooves for the detents all in line at the top.

17 Fit the new gasket to the housing.

18 Fit the gearbox casing, lowering it down over the input and second shafts, the differential, and the selector rods. If the differential bearings have been replaced, the outer races should of course be in place, but the bearing preload plate should not be fitted yet to the casing.

19 Fit the nuts to the studs holding the casing to the housing that are at present uppermost, on the outside.

20 If the differential bearings have been removed, now set the bearing preload. Put two shims above the bearing race then fit the bearing plate, and tighten it gently down to push the bearing into place. This will be helped if a gear is engaged, and the gears rotated by the input shaft, to allow everything to roll into place. As there are two shims fitted the flange of the plate should not go right down. Release the

nuts, so the plate is still in contact through the shims with the bearing, by its own weight only, and not strained. Measure the gap between the flange and its seat on the casing. This can be done by inserting feelers between the two. Remove the plate, and measure the total thickness of the shims in use. Add or remove shims that will leave a gap ('X' in Fig. 6.9), of 0.003 to 0.005 in (0.08 to 0.12 mm) between the bearing preload plate and the casing with no load on the fixing nuts. When the nuts are tightened to a torque of 18 lb f ft (2.5 kg f m), then they will give the correct preload on the bearings.

21 Fit the large circlips to the outer races of the bearings on the ends of the input and second shafts. The bearings may need levering up a little, bringing their shafts with them, to get the grooves clear.

22 Fit the three detent balls and their springs. The one odd spring, the green one, goes in the left hole, for reverse. Put on the new gasket, and fit the cover.

23 Fit the new gasket to the end of the casing, and put on the endplate.

24 Turn the transmission over, clutch end up.

7.18 ... and then the casing can be fitted

7.20a If the differential bearings have been renewed, the casing should be fitted without the bearing plate

7.20b Measure the thickness of shim needed to give specified preload. Then fit it under the plate

7.21 Fit the large circlips on the bearings. The bearings may need prising up a little

7.22a Fit the three detent balls, then the springs, the green one which is shorter than the other two, is for reverse

7.22b Fit the detent balls and springs cover plate

7.23 Place a new gasket on the casing and fit the endplate

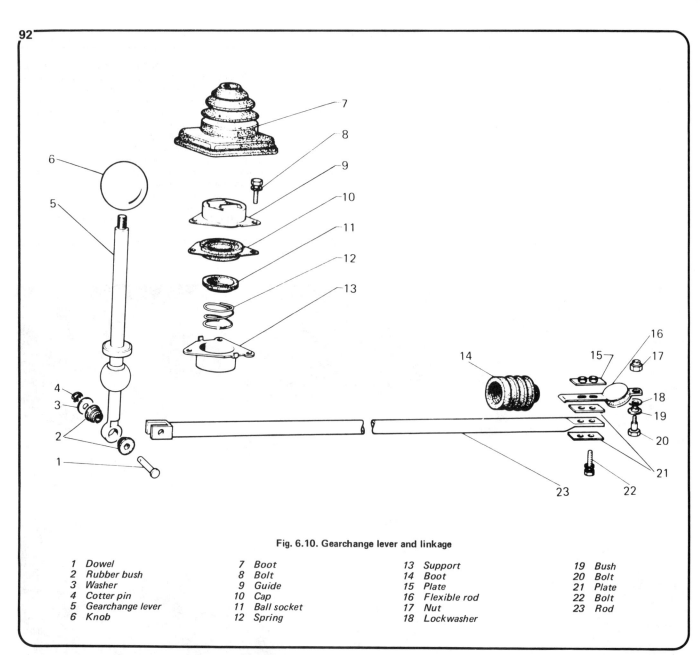

Fig. 6.10. Gearchange lever and linkage

1 Dowel	7 Boot	13 Support	19 Bush
2 Rubber bush	8 Bolt	14 Boot	20 Bolt
3 Washer	9 Guide	15 Plate	21 Plate
4 Cotter pin	10 Cap	16 Flexible rod	22 Bolt
5 Gearchange lever	11 Ball socket	17 Nut	23 Rod
6 Knob	12 Spring	18 Lockwasher	

9.2 Removing the gearchange lever

10.1 Gearchange linkage sandwich joint and flexible link

25 Fit the nuts with their spring washers to the large studs inside the clutch housing.
26 Fit the new oil seal into its carrier, so that its lips will be towards the gearbox. Fit it carefully over the input shaft, and bolt it in place, using a new gasket between it and the housing.
27 Clip the clutch withdrawal race into place on its fork, putting a trace of grease on its seats.

8 Transmission - refitting in car

1 Refitting is the reverse of the removal procedure. Do not forget the earth strap and the electrical connections. When fitting the control arms make sure the shims are replaced exactly as they were removed. Tighten the control arm bolts to 72 lb f ft (10 kg f m).
2 Adjust the clutch as described in Chapter 5.
3 Do not forget to fill the transmission with oil, this is easily done with a plastic bottle and length of tubing. Refit the filler/level plug and check that the drain plug is tightened.
4 Road test the car. Check for leaks.

9 Gearchange controls - removal and refitting

1 Remove the dust boot off the support, from inside the car.

2 Remove the three bolts holding the support and lift the support. Remove the clip and withdraw the pin, connecting the link rod to the gearlever, bushes and washer.
3 From under the car remove the bolt holding the flexible link to the selector rod. Remove the boot and pull the rod out of the car from the rear.
4 Refitting is the reverse of the removal procedure. Adjust the gearlever position, as described in Section 10.

10 Gearchange linkage - adjustment

1 Place the transmission in neutral and slacken the two bolts connecting the flexible link to the link rod. The bolt holes in the flexible link are elongated to allow for adjustment.
2 Have an assistant hold the gearlever centered in the guide, with the lever straight up and down, and then tighten the two bolts in the flexible link sandwich joint.
3 Road test the car to check the engagement of each gear.

11 Fault diagnosis - transmission

Symptom	Reason/s	Remedy
Gearbox		
Difficulty in changing gear	Clutch not disengaging	Check the clutch operation and rectify as necessary.
	Defective synchromesh	Renew.
	Gearchange control linkage maladjusted	Adjust control linkage.
Jumping out of gear	Interlock plunger worn	Renew.
	Detent balls worn or weak spring	Renew faulty parts.
	Gearteeth worn	Renew defective gear.
	Defective synchromesh	Renew.
	Gearchange control linkage out of adjustment	Re-adjust linkage.
Excessive noise	Lack of lubrication	Fill up with correct grade of oil.
	Worn bearings and gears	Renew.
Oil leakage	Defective oil seals and gaskets	Renew as necessary.
	Cracked transmission casing	Renew casing.

Differential

Symptom	Reasons and remedies
Excessive noise	Final drive noises are only heard on the move. Noise when cornering, if not caused by the driveshafts, is most likely due to excessive tightness or play in the bevel side gears or planet gears. A humming noise indicates incorrect backlash adjustment of the differential. If ignored, rapid tooth wear will take place with the noisy increasing to a growling sound. This should be seen to right away so that new gears will not be required.

Chapter 7 Driveshafts

Contents

Specifications

Shaft joints

Outer end (4-speed)	Constant velocity type
Inner end (4-speed)	Sliding 'Tripode' type
Both ends (5-speed)	Constant velocity type

Lubricant

Constant velocity joint	Molybdenum disulphide grease 3.3 oz (95 g)
Tripode joint	Transmission oil

Torque wrench settings

	lb f ft	kg fm
Ball joint nut	72	10
Shock absorber to pillar nut	43	6
Oil boot flange nut	7	1
Driveshaft flange bolts (5-speed)	25	3.5

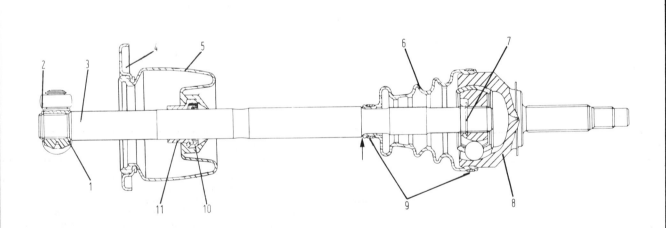

Fig. 7.1. Left-hand driveshaft assembly

1	Tripode joint	3	Driveshaft	5	Rubber boot	8 Constant velocity joint
2	Circlip	4	Flange	6	Rubber boot	9 Boot clamps
				7	Lockring	10 Sealing ring
						11 Bush

Arrow indicates shoulder against which boot (6) should be located.

1 General description

1   From the final drive and differential under the engine the drive is transmitted to the two rear wheels by the driveshafts. As the transmission is to the left of the engine the shafts are of different length, the long shaft on the right and the short one on the left side.

2   At the inner ends of the shafts are universal joints of the Tripode type. These allow for axial movement as well as wheel movement on the suspension.

3   At the outer ends are constant velocity joints. These allow for the movement of the wheels on the suspension and the swivelling of the steering.

4   The main part of the shaft fits into the joints at both ends by splines, held by circlips. Rubber boots keep the lubricant in, and the road dirt out.

5   The Tripode joints are located in the bevel side gears of the differential, and are lubricated by the transmission oil. The constant velocity joints are packed for life with molybdenum disulphide grease.

6   Provided the rubber boots are in good condition and keep out the dirt, the constant velocity joints last well, though on cars used in towns or hills, with a high proportion of driving hard in low gears, they are unlikely to last as long as the rest of the transmission. The Tripode joints should last the life of the transmission.

7   The driveshafts can be removed for overhaul, boot or seal renewal, etc without removing the transmission from the car. They have to be disconnected for removal of the transmission and engine.

2 Driveshafts - removal and refitting

1   Jack-up the rear of the car and support it on axle stands. Remove the rear wheels.

2   Remove the transmission drain plug and drain off approximately two pints (1.2 litres) of oil. Refit the drain plug.

3   Remove the two bolts and nuts holding the shock absorbers to the pillars.

4   Remove the brake calipers from the pillars and tie them up so that they do not hang on the brake pipes.

5   Remove the two bolts and nuts holding the shock absorbers to the pillar (Fig. 7.2). Remove the nut securing the ball joint for the control arm in the pillar. Remove the ball joint from the pillar. Remove the nut holding the ball joint for the strut in the pillar and withdraw the ball joint. For removal of the ball joints use a universal ball joint puller.

6   Remove the three bolts and washers securing the oil seal boot flanges to the differential and pull the driveshaft out of the differential.

7   Remove the clamps holding the rubber boots to the constant velocity joints and pull the boot back to uncover the joints. Clean the grease off the joints. Using pliers compress the lockring (Fig. 7.4) from the constant velocity joint and withdraw the driveshafts from the joints.

8   Refitting of the driveshaft is the reverse of the removal sequence. After fitting the lockrings in the constant velocity joints, move the shaft in, and out, to make sure the lockrings are properly seated in their grooves.

9   Pack the joints with 3 3/8 oz of molybdenum-disulphide grease before refitting the rubber boots.

10 Torque tighten the ball joint nuts to 72 lb f ft (10 kg fm) and the shock absorber to pillar nuts to 43 lb f ft (6 kg fm).

3 Inspection and renewal of parts

1   The need to renew the constant velocity joints can usually be assessed without removing them. If the rubber boot has failed, the joint is almost certain to do so too soon after, unless the hole was spotted, and a new boot fitted, in very good time. By failure, it is not meant that the joints break, but they will become noisy. The clicking noise, later becoming a tearing noise, is a sign of excessive wear inside the joint.

2   The shaft splines and the inner Tripode joint should outlast perhaps two constant velocity joints. Their condition should be examined when taken out for other reasons.

3   The shafts are not serviced as complete assemblies, so individual

Fig. 7.2. Removal of driveshafts

1	Bolts and nuts	4	Control arm
2	Shock absorber	5	Balljoint nut
3	Strut		

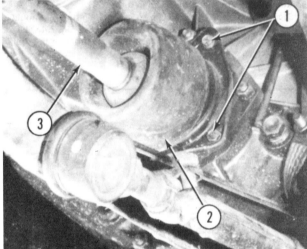

Fig. 7.3. Removing the oil seal boot flange

1	Bolts	3	Driveshaft
2	Boot		

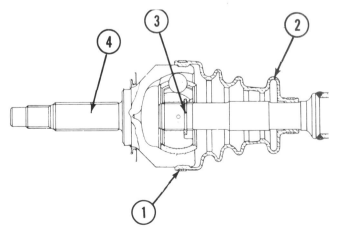

Fig. 7.4. Removing the driveshaft from the constant velocity joint

1	Clamp	3	Lockring
2	Boot	4	Constant velocity joint

parts must be ordered as required. The constant velocity joints do come complete, though without the rubber boot. It is not practicable, nor are the parts available, to renovate the constant velocity joints.

4   The shafts and joints will last well provided the remarks in the next Section on the care of them is heeded.

4   Lubrication and rubber boots - general

1   No specific maintenance tasks have to be done on the driveshafts or their joints. But the visual examination of the condition of the rubber boots is an important item of the check underneath the car in the 3,000 miles (5,000 km) task.

2   The rubber boot on the constant velocity joint at the outer end of the shaft must be examined to ensure there are no tears or slits in it, and that it is properly secured to the joint and the shaft, by clips at each end.

3   The constant velocity joint is lubricated with a molybdenum disulphide grease. Normally this will not need renewing. If the rubber boot is removed, either for renewal or when splitting the driveshaft at the constant velocity joint, then the old grease should be wiped out with clean rag to take out any dirt. Ensure complete cleanliness when doing this, or more dirt will get in, and the joint will not last long. Then pack in new grease, pushing it well in around the joint balls, and leaving a coating on the outside on the splines. Then put on the rubber boot, with a trace of grease inside it and on the shaft. Do not fill the boot with grease. Too much grease will prevent the boot from working as a concertina as the steering turns.

4   Secure the boot to the rim of the joint, making sure the moulded groove of the boot is in the groove of the joint. See Fig. 7.4. The small end of the boot should butt against the shoulder on the shaft.

For preference use the metal tape straps. If these are not available, put round two turns of soft-copper wire, and twist the ends together with pliers to draw the wire firmly round the boot, but not so tightly it cuts into the rubber, or is under such tension it will break after a short time. Bend the twisted ends backwards, the way they will tend to go due to shaft rotation, so they lie out of the way.

5   The Tripode joint at the inner end of the shaft is lubricated by the transmission oil, so no attention need be paid to that. The rubber boot at the inner end must seal in the transmission oil. Two aspects of the boot are therefore important. The baggy portion must be free from cuts. The oil seal in which the shaft rotates must be in good condition.

6   New rubber boots should be fitted to the inner ends of the shafts whenever the transmission is dismantled. Fitting them is also advisable whenever the driveshafts are removed, and there is the slightest suspicion that the boots are near the end of their life, otherwise the work of removing the shafts may soon have to be repeated.

5   Driveshafts (later models) — general

1   Later models are fitted with driveshafts having constant velocity joints at both ends, the inner ends bolting to flanges on the transmission.

2   Removal and refitting of these later type shafts is achieved after removing the socket-headed (Allen key) type bolts securing the CV joints to the flanges. It is recommended that whenever the bolts are removed, new bolts are used on reassembly.

3   The remarks made in the Sections above concerning the inspection and maintenance of the earlier type constant velocity joints apply also to the later type. Oil seals are not fitted to the inboard ends.

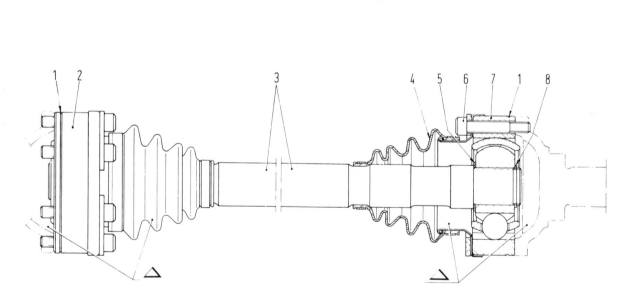

Fig. 7.5 Later type driveshaft with two constant velocity joints

1   Reference grooves (must be nearest flange)
2   CV joint (gearbox side)
3   Driveshaft
4   Rubber boot
5   Spring washer
6   Bolt
7   CV joint (wheel side)
8   Snap-ring
△   Lubrication areas

Chapter 8 Braking system

For modifications, and information applicable to later models, see Supplement at end of manual

Contents

Specifications

Type	Hydraulic, disc brakes on all wheels with independent circuits at front and rear

Front and rear footbrakes
Brake discs:

Diameter	8.937 in (227 mm)
Normal thickness	0.392 - 0.400 in (9.95 - 10.15 mm)
Minimum thickness after refacing	0.368 in (9.35 mm)
Minimum thickness from wear	0.354 in (9 mm)
Maximum run-out	0.006 in (0.15 mm)
Brake calipers	Floating type, single cylinder
Minimum thickness of brake friction material	0.06 in (1.5 mm)

Caliper cylinder bore:

Front	1.772 in (48 mm)
Rear	1.338 in (34 mm)
Master cylinder bore	0.750 in (19.05 mm)

Handbrake	Cable operated, acting on rear calipers
Brake fluid	DOT 3 Motor vehicle brake fluid to FMVSS No. 116

1 General description

1   The dual circuit, hydraulically operated braking system has disc brakes on all wheels. The single cylinder sliding calipers are self-adjusting.
2   The tandem master cylinder operates separate circuits for the front and rear brakes. In the event of failure in one circuit, the other circuit will provide sufficient braking effort, if the car is driven carefully, to allow you to drive to a location where the failed circuit can be repaired.
3   A pressure failure warning switch lights up a warning light on the instrument panel if pressure in either circuit (front or rear) is excessively low due to leakage or line failure. The switch under the handbrake lever allows the driver to check if the bulb is all right and at the same time indicates when the handbrake is applied with the ignition switched on.
4   The handbrake is cable operated and acts on a plunger, on the rear brake calipers, which locks the pads to the brake discs.
5   Always use the specified type of brake fluid, any other can ruin the rubber seals. When cleaning brake parts always wash them with brake fluid or methylated spirit.

2 Front and rear brakes - inspection

1   The brake pads must be checked every 6000 miles (10,000 km). Jack-up the car and remove the wheels. Check the thickness of the pad lining. If the lining is 0.060 in (1.6 mm) or less the pads must be renewed as described in Section 3.
2   Always fit new pads in sets, both pads on both wheels (front or rear) even if only one pad is defective.
3   Check that there is no sign of fluid leakage. Check for chafing or deterioration of the brake hoses.
4   Check the surface of the discs. They should be shiny and smooth.

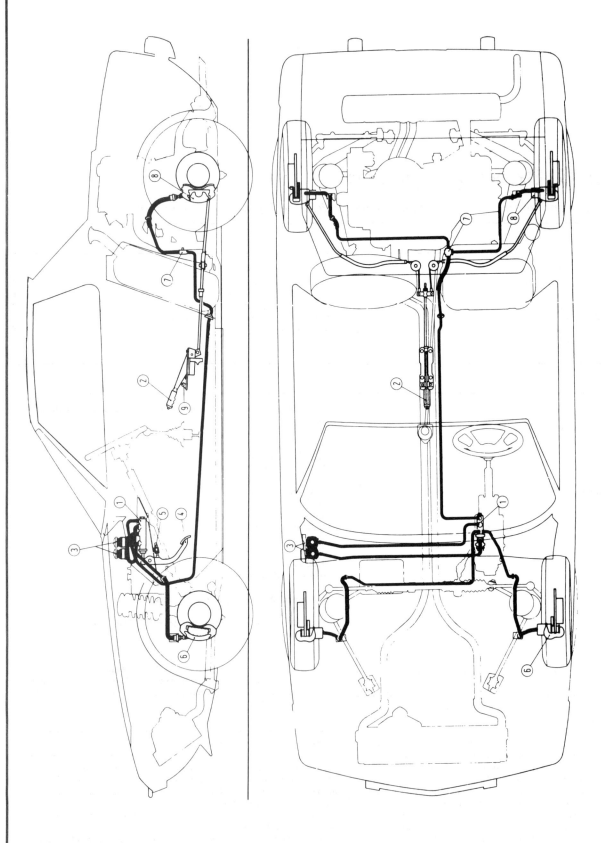

Fig. 8.1 Braking system layout (LHD)

1 Master cylinder
2 Handbrake lever
3 Brake fluid reservoir

4 Brake pedal
5 Stoplight switch
6 Front brake calipers

7 Rear brake 'T' connection
8 Rear brake calipers
9 Handbrake indicator switch

3 Front and rear brakes - pad renewal

1   Jack-up and remove the relevant wheel.

2   Pull out the spring clips that hold the two caliper locking blocks. Disconnect the handbrake cable on the rear brakes.

3   Pull out the locking blocks.

4   Lift off the caliper, and lodge it on the suspension so its weight will not hang on the flexible pipe.

5   Take out the old pads, noting the anti-chatter springs.

6   Wipe the caliper clean, especially the flanks of the piston that are sticking out due to the thinness of the old pads. If very dirty, wash the caliper with ordinary detergent and water, and dry it. Do not use petrol or other solvents.

7   Push the piston into the caliper cylinder (front brakes) or screw it clockwise (rear brakes) until the scribed line is horizontal and above the slot.

8   These operations will cause the level in the fluid reservoir to rise, so anticipate this by syphoning out some of the fluid.

9   If the front brake piston is stubborn, push it in by using a carpenter's clamp. Take care the rim of the piston is not burred. On the rear calipers, make sure that the piston is screwed onto the plunger (see Section 8).

10   Reassemble using the new pads, and checking all the anti-chatter springs are in position.

11   Press the brake pedal to bring the piston and pads up the disc.

12   Check the hydraulic fluid level.

13   Repeat for the other side.

14   Note that the pad lining type used is denoted by colour code daubs of paint. Both pads on both sides must all have the same lining. More than one type is supplied by FIAT. Ensure that the lining used is approved by FIAT.

15   Use the brakes gently for at least a dozen applications so the pads can bed in.

3.2a These spring clips hold the locking blocks in the caliper

3.2b The handbrake cable has to be disconnected from the rear wheel calipers

3.3 The locking plates are pulled out ...

3.4 ... and the caliper is lifted off. Place the caliper on the suspension so that it does not hang on the hydraulic flexible hose

3.5 Remove the brake pads ...

3.6... and the anti-chatter springs

3.7 Scribed line on rear caliper piston (arrowed)

3.10a The caliper is refitted ...

3.10b ... and locked in position with the locking plates. The locking plates may require tapping with a hammer to get them in, take care they don't pick up any burrs

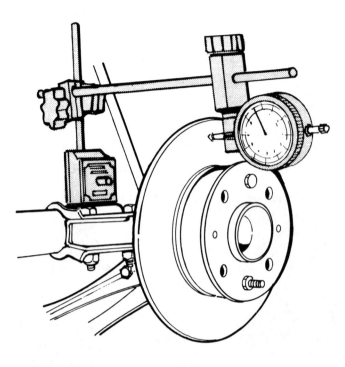

Fig. 8.2. Checking the brake disc run-out

4 Bleeding the hydraulic brake system

1   The system should need bleeding only when some part of it has been dismantled which would allow air into the fluid circuit; or if the level in the fluid reservoirs has been allowed to drop below the minimum level so that air has entered the master cylinder.
2   Have a supply of fresh fluid of the correct specification to hand in order to replenish the reservoirs during the bleeding operations. A clean glass jar and a length of plastic or rubber tubing of 0.125 in (3.2 mm) internal diameter, which will fit tightly over the bleed nipples, are also required.
3   The help of an assistant will be required to pump the brake pedal during the bleeding process.
4   Top-up the reservoirs. Clean all dirt from around the bleed nipples and remove the dust caps.
5   Bleed one system first. Put a small amount of fluid in the jar. Fit the bleed tube on the bleed nipple with the other end submerged in the fluid in the jar. Keep it under the surface throughout the bleeding operations.
6   Slacken the bleed screw on the caliper and get the assistant to depress and release the brake pedal in short sharp strokes when you direct him. Short sharp strokes are better than long slow ones as they will force any air bubbles along the line ahead of the fluid rather than pump the fluid past them. It is not essential to remove all the air the first time. If both systems are being bled, attend to each wheel for three or four strokes and then repeat the process. On the second time round operate the pedal sharply in the same way until no more bubbles are apparent. The bleed nipple should be tightened and closed with the brake pedal depressed, which ensures that no aerated fluid can get back into the system. Do not forget to keep the reservoirs topped-up throughout the bleeding process.
7   When all four wheels have been satisfactorily bled depress the brake pedal, which should offer a firm resistance with no trace of 'sponginess'. The pedal should not go down under sustained pressure. If it does there is a leak in the system or the master cylinder is faulty.
8   After bleeding the system, road test the car to make sure the brakes are working correctly.

5 Brake calipers - removal and refitting

1   Have a container ready to catch the brake fluid.
2   Remove the spring clips and locking blocks as described in Section 3.
3   Plug the outlet port of the reservoir. Disconnect the brake hose and then remove the bolt holding the bracket to the caliper. On rear brakes disconnect the brake hose and the handbrake cable from the caliper.
4   Refitting is the reverse of the removal operations. Top-up the reservoir and bleed the brakes.

6 Brake disc - inspection and renewal

1   After removing the brake caliper, as described in Section 5, and without removing the disc, mount a dial test indicator as shown in Fig. 8.2 and check the run-out of the disc.
2   If the reading on the dial indicator shows a run-out exceeding 0.006 in (0.15 mm) or the disc is scored or damaged, it must be refaced or renewed.
3   Remove the bolts holding the disc to the hub and take off the flange followed by the disc.
4   After renewing the disc check that the run-out is within limit specified. Refit the caliper and bleed the brakes.

7 Front brake caliper - overhaul

1   Remove the brake caliper as described in Section 5. Remove the dust boot and using a thin rod, depress the locking dowel and separate the cylinder from the support.
2   Apply air pressure at the fluid inlet port to push the piston out of the cylinder.
3   Remove the seal from the caliper.
4   Clean all the parts thoroughly. Do not use solvents other than

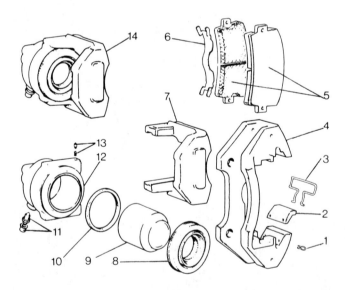

Fig. 8.3. Exploded view of front brake caliper and support bracket

1 Cotter pin	8 Dust boot
2 Caliper locking block	9 Piston
3 Spring	10 Seal
4 Caliper support bracket	11 Bleed nipple and dust cap
5 Disc pad	12 Cylinder
6 Pad retainer spring	13 Spring and dowel
7 Cylinder housing	14 Complete caliper

methylated spirit or brake fluid.

5 Check that the caliper cylinder and the piston are free from scores or other damage. If not, they must be renewed.

6 Examine the flexible pipe. If there is any doubt, fit a new one.

7 As parts are reassembled, lubricate them with brake fluid. Fit the seal in the cylinder, making sure it is completely seated in its groove.

8 Fit the piston in the cylinder, pushing it in as far as it will go. Fit the dust boot and ensure it is seated in the recess in the cylinder. Always fit a new seal and dust boot after each dismantling.

9 Refit the brake caliper as described in Section 5. Top-up the reservoir and bleed the brakes as described in Section 4. Check for leaks and road test the car to check the brakes.

8 Rear brake caliper - overhaul

1 Remove the caliper as described in Section 5.

2 Remove the dust boot. Unscrew the piston from the plunger and remove it from the cylinder. Remove the seal and discard it.

3 Pull back the top of the rubber boot located behind the caliper and remove the circlip from the handbrake shaft. Pull the shaft out of the caliper and remove the pawl, plunger, seal and spring washers.

4 Clean and examine the parts as described for the front caliper in Section 7. In addition, examine the handbrake shaft, the pawl and the plunger. Renew any worn or damaged parts. Renew rubber seals and dust boot. Examine the rubber boot for deterioration, and renew if necessary.

5 Fit a new seal on the plunger and fit the plunger and washers in the caliper.

6 Grease the groove in the plunger, the pawl and the handbrake shaft. Fit the pawl and handbrake shaft. Fit the spacer and circlip on the shaft. Fit the rubber boot.

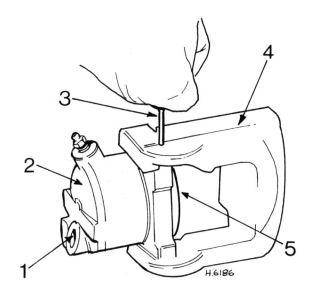

Fig. 8.4. Dismantling the front brake caliper

1 Inlet port	4 Support
2 Cylinder	5 Dust boot
3 Thin rod	

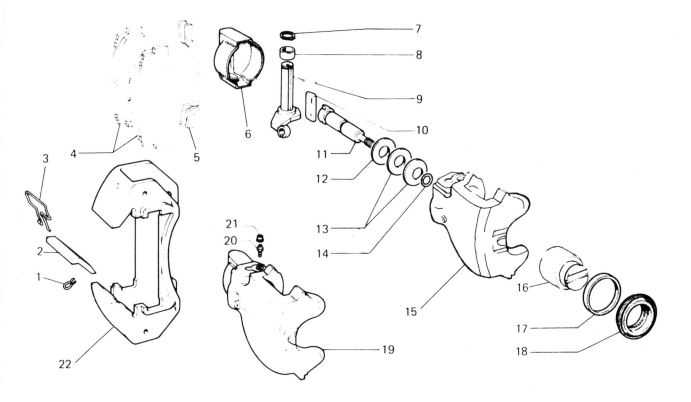

Fig. 8.5. Exploded view of rear brake caliper and support bracket

1 Cotter pin	6 Rubber boot	11 Plunger	17 Seal
2 Caliper locking block	7 Locking ring	12 Spring washers	18 Dust boot
3 Spring	8 Spacer	13 Spring washers	19 Complete caliper
4 Disc pad	9 Handbrake shaft	14 Seal	20 Bleed screw
5 Pad retainer spring	10 Pawl	15 Caliper cylinder	21 Bleeder dust cap
		16 Piston	22 Support bracket

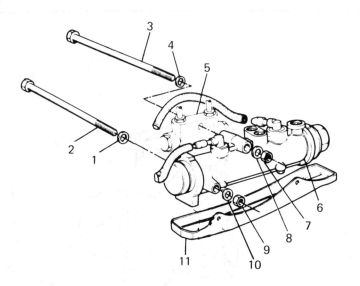

Fig. 8.6. Master cylinder mounting components

1	Washer	7	Nut
2	Bolt	8	Washer
3	Bolt	9	Nut
4	Washer	10	Washer
5	Switch	11	Support
6	Master cylinder		

Fig. 8.7. Cross-section of master cylinder

1 Body
2 Outlet to rear brakes
3 Secondary piston return spring
4 Cup
5 Spacer
6 Inlet from reservoir
7 Secondary piston
8 Outlet to front brakes
9 Cup pressure spring
10 Cup
11 Inlet from reservoir
12 Spacer
13 Primary piston
14 Dust boot
15 Seal
16 Stop screw
17 Fluid ports
18 Primary piston spring
19 Washer
20 Secondary cup
21 Stop screw
22 Secondary cup pressure spring
23 Fluid port
24 End plug

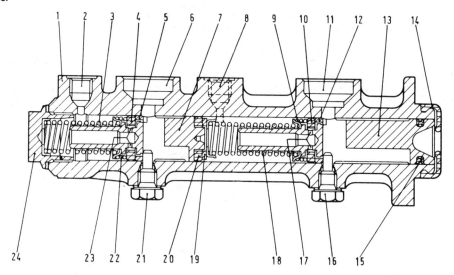

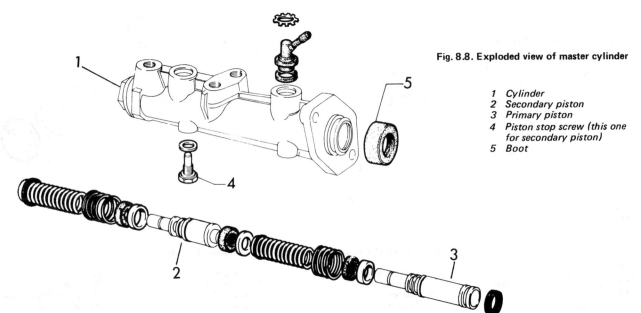

Fig. 8.8. Exploded view of master cylinder

1 Cylinder
2 Secondary piston
3 Primary piston
4 Piston stop screw (this one for secondary piston)
5 Boot

7   Fit a new seal in the caliper cylinder and make sure it is seated in its groove. Lubricate the cylinder and piston with brake fluid.
8   Insert the piston in the cylinder and screw it on to the plunger. Make sure that the mark on the piston is horizontal and towards the side of the caliper on which the bleed screw is located.
9   Fit the dust boot and ensure it is seated in the groove in the cylinder.
10   Refit the caliper, as described in Section 5. Top-up the fluid reservoir. Bleed the brakes and check for leaks. Road test the car to check the brakes.

9   Master cylinder - removal and refitting

1   The master cylinder is mounted under the dashboard above the steering column and to remove it the steering column has to be removed as described in Chapter 9, Section 6. On some models it may only be necessary to remove the steering column lower shroud.
2   With the steering column or shroud out of the way, have a container ready and disconnect the hoses from the reservoir. Drain the fluid into the container, some thick rags on the floor of the car to prevent fluid getting on the carpet is a sound precaution.
3   Remove the nuts holding the cylinder to the support and pull the cylinder off the operating rod.
4   Disconnect the delivery pipes to the front and rear brakes and drain the fluid in the cylinder into the container.
5   Refitting is the reverse of the removal sequence. Make sure the hoses are connected properly. Fill the reservoir and bleed the brakes, as described in Section 4.
6   Check for leaks. Road test the car for brake check.

10   Master cylinder - overhaul

1   Clean the outside of the master cylinder, but only use brake fluid or methylated spirit. If other solvents such as petrol are used, traces will remain afterwards, and could destroy the rubber cups.
2   Refer to Fig. 8.7.
3   Remove the rubber boot from the cylinder end.
4   Remove the two piston stop screws (16 and 21) from the underneath of the cylinder.
5   Take out of the open end of the cylinder such pistons, cups etc as are willing to come out easily at this instance, laying them out in the order in which they were fitted.
6   Take out the plug (24) from the other end of the cylinder.
7   With a pencil push the remaining components out.
8   Discard all the rubber parts.
9   Examine the cylinder bore and the pistons for scratches or pitting. They must have a smooth surface, otherwise there will be seepage of fluid past the cups, and the latters' lips will wear rapidly. If the surface is not good, then a new cylinder is needed.
10   On reassembly wet all parts liberally with brake fluid.
11   Fit all the cups into place using the fingers only to push them gently into place. Cups with lips must have the lips towards the high pressure side, away from the actuating rod. Push the secondary piston down with a pencil, then fit its stop screw. The stop screw must engage with the groove in the piston. Check it moves freely. Then fit all the primary piston parts.
12   After fitting the cylinder in the car, check that there is a little free-play between the pedal's pushrod and the rear end of the piston. Otherwise the pushrod cannot return to the end of its stroke to recoup fluid through the ports.

11   Hydraulic pipes and hoses - general

1   Periodically all brake pipes, pipe connections and unions should be completely and carefully examined.
2   First examine for signs of leakage where the pipe unions occur. Then examine the flexible hoses for signs of chafing and fraying and, of course, leakage. This is only a preliminary part of the flexible hose inspection, as exterior condition does not necessarily indicate the interior condition, which will be considered later.
3   The steel pipes must be examined equally carefully. They must be cleaned off and examined for any signs of dents, or other percussive

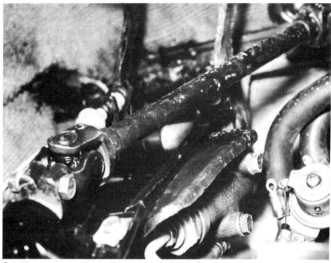

9.1 The master cylinder is mounted above the steering column

9.2 The brake and clutch fluid reservoirs

damage and rust and corrosion. Rust and corrosion should be scraped off and, if the depth of pitting in the pipes is significant, they will need renewal. This is particularly likely in those areas underneath the car body and along the rear axle where the pipes are exposed to full force of road and weather conditions.
4   If any section of pipe is to be taken off, first of all drain the fluid, or remove the fluid reservoir cap and line it with a piece of polythene film to make it air tight, and replace it. This will minimise the amount of fluid dripping out of the system, when pipes are removed. It is normally best to drain all the fluid, as a change is probably due anyway.
5   Rigid pipe removal is usually quite straightforward. The unions at each end are undone, the pipe and union pulled out, and the centre sections of the pipe removed from the body clips where necessary. Underneath the car, exposed unions can sometimes be very tight. As one can use only an open ended spanner and the unions are not large burring of the flats is not uncommon when attempting to undo them. For this reason a special brake union spanner or self-locking grip wrench (Mole) is often the only way to remove a stubborn union.
6   Flexible hoses are always mounted at both ends in a rigid bracket attached to the body or a sub-assembly. To remove them it is necessary first of all to unscrew the pipe unions of the rigid pipes which go into them. The hose ends can then be unclipped from the brackets. The mounting brackets, particularly on the body frame, are not very heavy gauge and care must be taken not to wrench them off.

7 With the flexible hose removed, examine the internal bore. If it is blown through first, it should be possible to see through it. Any specks of rubber which come out, or signs of restriction in the bore, mean that the inner lining is breaking up and the hose must be renewed.

8 Replacements for faulty rigid pipes can usually be purchased at any garage where they have the pipe, unions and special tools to make them up. All they need to know is the total length of the pipe, the type of flare used at each end with the union, and the length and thread of the union. FIAT is metric remember.

9 Fitting of pipes is a straightforward reversal of the removal procedure. If the rigid pipes have been made up it is best to get all the sets (bends) in them before trying to install them. Also if there are any acute bends, ask your supplier to put these in for you on a tube bender. Otherwise you may kink the pipe and thereby restrict the bore area and fluid flow.

10 When refitting the flexible pipes check they cannot be under tension, or rub, when the wheels are at the full range of suspension or steering movement.

12 Handbrake - adjustment

1 Jack-up both rear wheels.
2 Operate the brake pedal a few times.
3 Pull the handbrake lever up three clicks of the ratchet from the fully released position.
4 Under the car remove the cover plate for the handbrake adjusting nut.
5 Slacken the locknut and tighten the adjusting nut until the rear wheels are just locked. Try to turn the wheels manually. Tighten the locknut.
6 Release the handbrake and check that the wheels are free to turn.
7 Refit the cover plate and lower the car to the ground.
8 The handbrake should be fully applied after it has been pulled over four or five clicks of its ratchet.

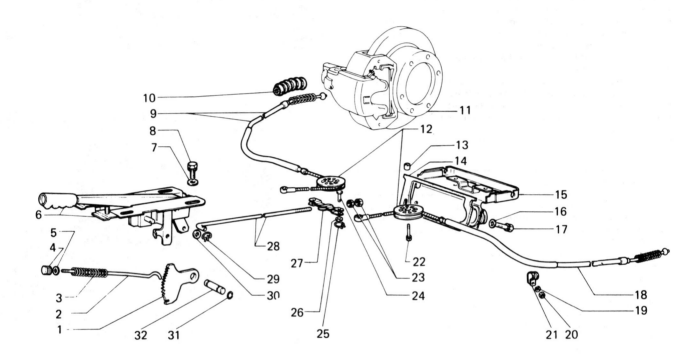

Fig. 8.9. Handbrake linkage

1	Ratchet	9	Cable	17	Bolt	25	Clip
2	Rod	10	Boot	18	Cable	26	Washer
3	Spring	11	Caliper	19	Lockwasher	27	Swinging arm
4	Button	12	Pulley	20	Nut	28	Tie-rod
5	Rubber ring	13	Spacer	21	Clamp	29	Clip
6	Lever	14	Gasket	22	Bolt	30	Washer
7	Washer	15	Support	23	Nuts	31	Lockring
8	Bolt	16	Washer	24	Pin	32	Pin

13 Fault diagnosis - braking system

Before diagnosing faults in the braking system, check that any irregularities are not caused by the following:

1 Uneven and incorrect tyre pressures
2 Incorrect mix of radial and crossply tyres
3 Wear in steering mechanism
4 Defects in the suspension
5 Misalignment of the bodyframe

Symptom	Reason/s	Remedy
Pedal travels a long way before the brakes operate	Failure of half the hydraulic system	Check for leaks.
Stopping ability poor, even though pedal pressure is firm	Pads and/or discs worn or scored Failure of half the system Brake pads contaminated with oil	Dismantle and renew as necessary. Check for leaks. Renew pads and rectify source of oil contamination.
Car pulls to one side when the brakes are applied	Brake pads on one side contaminated with oil Brake caliper seized on one side	Renew pads and rectify oil leak. Dismantle and rectify as necessary.
Pedal feels spongy	Air present in the hydraulic system	Bleed the brake system and check for leaks.
Pedal goes down gradually under sustained pressure	Small leak Master cylinder cups being bypassed	Check for leak. If none, dismantle and check master cylinder.
Brakes binding, overheating	Master cylinder cups defective Master cylinder no free play Handbrake maladjusted	Overhaul master cylinder. Check pedal clearance. Re-adjust.

Chapter 9 Steering

Contents

Specifications

Steering gear type	Rack and pinion
Ratio	
Steering wheel turns (lock-to-lock)	3
Corresponding rack travel	4.606 in (117 mm)
Pinion bearing	Ball
Adjustment	By shims
Turning circle (approx)	33 ft (10 m)
Steering column	Three sections, with two universal joints
Front wheel toe-in (car unladen)	0.079 to 0.236 in (2 to 6 mm)
Steering box oil	SAE 90 EP

Torque wrench settings

	lb f ft	kg f m
Nut, steering wheel to column	36.2	5
Nut, trackrod ball bearing	36	5
Nut, steering arm ball bearing	25.3	3.5
Nut, steering box to body bolt	18	2.5
Nut, universal joint	18	2.5
Nut, upper steering column support	10.8	1.5

1 General description

1 The layout of the steering is shown in Fig. 9.1 and 9.2. It is of the rack and pinion type with self-centring action.
2 The steering column is in three parts with two universal joints and a collapsible joint which prevents the steering column from being forced into the car in the event of an accident.
3 The condition of the rear suspension can affect the steering. The adjustment for the toe-in and camber of this are described in Chapter 11.
4 No routine lubrication is needed on the steering. An important item of routine maintenance is the checking and inspection of the steering.

2 Ball joints - checking

1 There are ball joints at the outer ends of the trackrods and at the swivels at the bottom of the steering knuckle that carries the hub.
2 When carrying out the visual checks of the steering during routine maintenance, ensure that the rubber boots, fitted to prevent the ingress of dirt and water, are not damaged and are fitted correctly. If dirt or water gets into the joints they will have a very short life. The joint should be removed, and a new boot fitted without delay.
3 When checking the steering for wear get an assistant to rock the steering wheel to-and-fro just enough to make the front wheels move. Watch the ball joints, there should be no visible free-movement. Now hold the front wheel with the hands at three and nine o'clock

on the wheel. Try to twist the wheel while the assistant holds the steering wheel firmly. The rocking should be felt at the steering wheel, but no lost motion should be felt.

4   There are also ball joints at the inner end of the trackrods, where these join to the rack. But these are well protected and lubricated, and providing the rubber boots are maintained in good condition, no wear should develop there for considerable mileages.

5   The steering knuckle ball joint is more difficult to check. Again grip the wheel, but this time with both hands at the top. Rock the wheel to-and-fro vigorously, with an assistant watching the joint. If

any free-movement is seen or felt, the joint must be renewed.

3   Trackrod ball joints - removal and refitting

1   The ball joints on the outer end of the trackrod fit into the steering arm with a tapered pin which is retained by a nut at the bottom. They have to be removed to disconnect the steering when the suspension is being worked on. They have to be taken off the steering arm when a new rubber boot is being fitted.

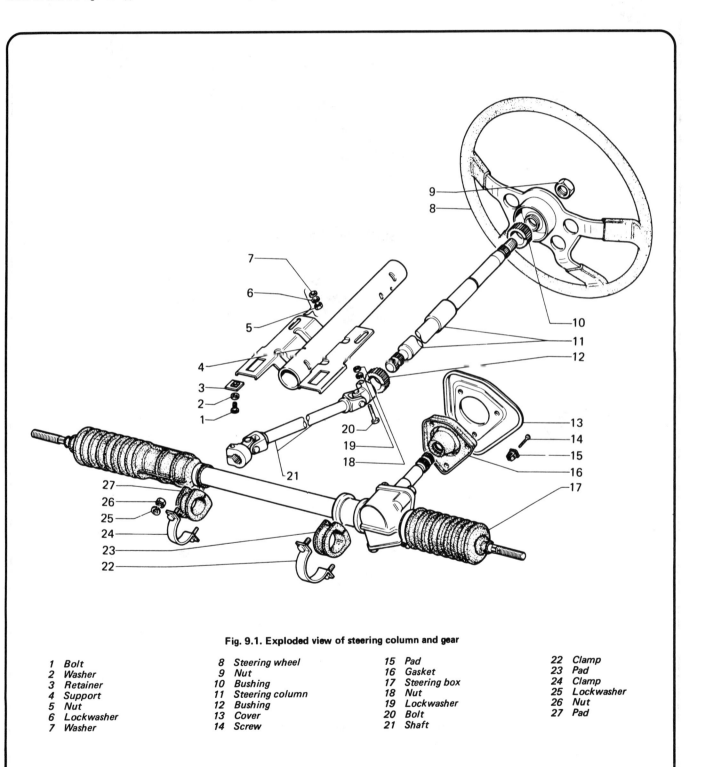

Fig. 9.1. Exploded view of steering column and gear

1	Bolt	8	Steering wheel	15	Pad	22	Clamp
2	Washer	9	Nut	16	Gasket	23	Pad
3	Retainer	10	Bushing	17	Steering box	24	Clamp
4	Support	11	Steering column	18	Nut	25	Lockwasher
5	Nut	12	Bushing	19	Lockwasher	26	Nut
6	Lockwasher	13	Cover	20	Bolt	27	Pad
7	Washer	14	Screw	21	Shaft		

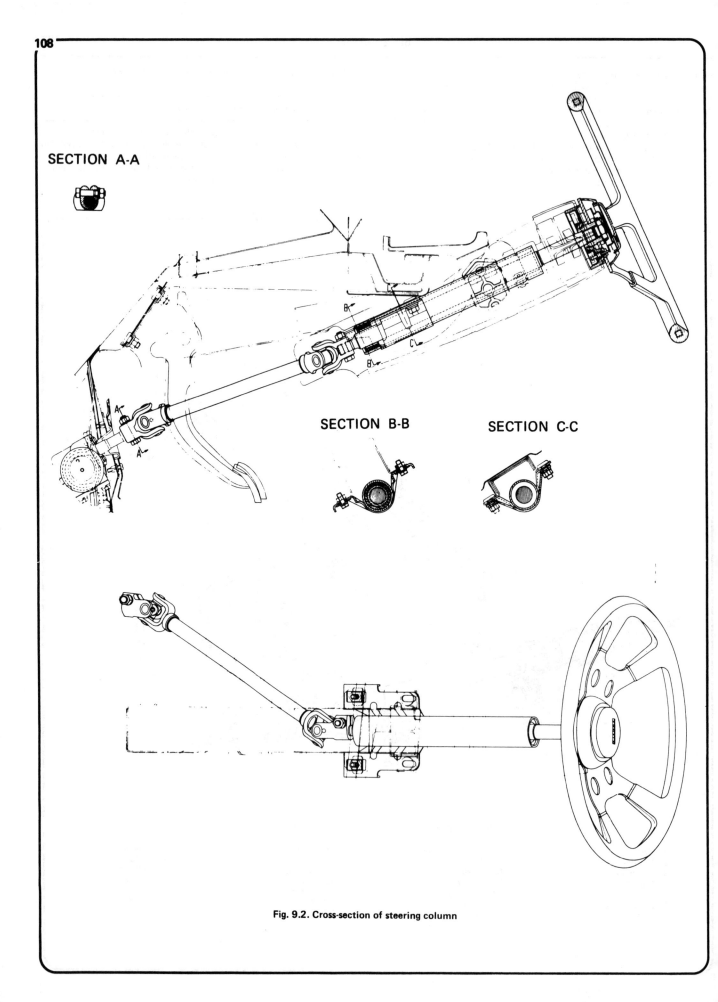

SECTION A-A

SECTION B-B

SECTION C-C

Fig. 9.2. Cross-section of steering column

2   Jack-up and support the car. Remove the relevant front wheel.
3   Remove the self-locking nut on the bottom of the tapered pin
under the steering arm.
4   Now remove the ball joint taper from the steering arm. If you have
a universal steering ball joint separator this is not too difficult. The
purchase of one could be a good investment. They can be used
on most makes of cars as ball joints are pretty well standardised.
Without a separator, the taper may be freed by impact. Hold a
heavy hammer against the steering arm at the ball joint, now hit the
steering arm a hard blow with another hammer on the opposite side.
It must be struck firmly with a heavy hammer. Do not try to drive the
ball joint by direct hammer blows, as the threads at the end will be
damaged. If the ball joint proves very hard to move, using either a
separator or the two hammer method, allow some penetrating oil
to soak in and then try again.
5   When fitting the ball joint never grease the taper pin of the ball joint.
6   If fitting a new rubber boot to the existing ball joint, clean off all
dirt and old grease. Smear some molybdenum-disulphide grease over
the joint, fill the boot with the grease and then fit the boot, squeezing
it down tight to force out excess grease and get the boot close into the
joint.
7   To renew the balljoint, proceed as follows. Hold the inboard balljoint by means of the spanner flats and release the locknut. Unscrew
the rack balljoint from the tubular trackrod. Grease the rack balljoint
threads before screwing the trackrod onto the balljoint threads. Check
that the rack boot is correctly fitted. Connect the trackrod (outboard)
balljoint to the eye of the steering arm and tighten the taper pin nut to
specified torque. If the taper pin rotates when tightening the nut, apply
pressure downwards on the balljoint using a long lever inserted under
the body side member as a fulcrum point.
8   Fit the road wheel, lower the car and check the front wheel
alignment, as described in Section 13.

4   Steering knuckle ball joint - general

1   The steering ball joint at the swivel for the steering knuckle on the
suspension control arm is an integral part of the arm. If it needs
renewal, the whole suspension control arm is renewed. The ball joint
need not be removed from the steering knuckle unless it is being
renewed. At other times it is easier to remove the suspension arm
from the car at its inner end than the knuckle from the ball joint,
should it be necessary to remove the steering knuckle for
some other reason.
2   Removal and refitting is described in Chapter 11.

5   Steering wheel - removal and refitting

1   Remove the horn button. This is done by gripping it on opposite
sides, squeezing in the sides and lifting it out.
2   Remove the nut securing the steering wheel to the steering column.
3   Remove the steering wheel. The wheel should lift off but you may
find it needs a knock with the heel of your hand, from behind the
spokes, to free it.
4   When refitting the steering wheel tighten the retaining nut to 36
lb f ft (5 kg f m).

6   Steering column - removal and refitting

1   Disconnect the lead from the battery earth terminal.
2   Remove the steering wheel, as described in Section 5.
3   Remove the five screws holding the steering column cover and lift
off the two halves of the cover.
4   Disconnect the three connectors and one lead.
5   Remove the pinch bolt from the bottom universal joint.
6   Remove the two nuts and washers holding the steering column to
the dashboard at the top and the two bolts, washers and retainers
securing it at the bottom of the dashboard.
7   Slide the lower shaft of the steering gear pinion shaft and remove
the complete column from the car.
8   Remove the turn indicator switch unit retaining bolt and slide the
unit off the shaft.
9   To separate the lower shaft from the upper shaft, remove the pinch
bolt from the universal joint.

Fig. 9.3. Disconnecting the trackrod from the steering arm

1   Nut   3   Steering arm
2   Trackrod

5.1 Steering wheel with horn button removed

6.3 Steering column with covers removed

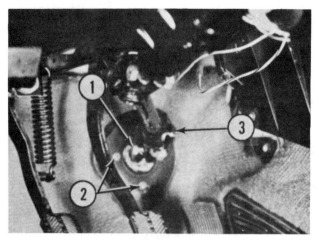

Fig. 9.4. Removing the gasket cover

1	Pinch bolt	3	Universal joint
2	Screws		

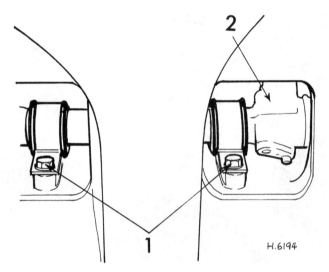

H.6194

Fig. 9.5. Removing the steering box mounting bolts

1   Mounting bolts and clamps   2   Steering box

Fig. 9.6. Dismantling the steering gear

1	Rubber boots	4	Cover plate
2	Clamps	5	Earth lead
3	Cover plate		

10 Refitting is the reverse of the removal sequence. Tighten the universal joint pinch bolts to 18 lb f ft (2.5 kg f m) and the steering column mounting bolts to 11 lb f ft (1.5 kg f m).
11 Refit the steering wheel, as described in Section 5.

7 Steering column bushes - renewal

1 To remove the bottom bush from the steering column, push the shaft down to remove the bush, and then remove the top bush.
2 When fitting the new bushes, fit the bottom bush first, the shaft and then the top bush.

8 Steering column lock - general

1 The ignition switch is combined with a steering lock.
2 If the lock sticks, rock the steering wheel slightly while trying to turn the key. This takes the load off the locking pawl.
3 If the lock has be be changed, difficulty will be experienced getting the securing screws out. To remove them, a hole must be drilled in each screw and a stud extractor used to remove them. When the switch is fitted, the screws are tightened until the heads shear off.

9 Steering gear - removal and refitting

1 Remove the pinch bolt securing the bottom universal joint to the steering gear pinion shaft.
2 Remove the two screws securing the gasket cover (Fig. 9.4) to the steering box.
3 Jack-up the car and support it securely. Make sure there is enough room on the right-hand side to allow for the removal of the steering gear, which is withdrawn on that side. Remove the front wheel.
4 Working from underneath the car, disconnect the trackrod from the steering arms, as described in Section 3.
5 Remove the four bolts securing the steering box to the body and pull the box down to withdraw the pinion shaft from the bottom universal joint. Remove the steering gear from the car through the right-hand side.
6 Before refitting the steering gear, fill it with oil and check the adjustment of the damping yoke, as described in Section 11.
7 Inside the car set the steering wheel in the 'straight-ahead' position. Position the steering rack in the midway position by setting it to the end of its travel in one direction, then counting the number of turns, wind the pinion fully to the other end of its travel. Divide the number of turns of the pinion in half and then set the rack in the mid-position The pinion can be turned by protecting the splines and gripping it with a self-grip (mole) type of wrench.
8 Refit the steering gear from the right-hand side, and mount it in the clamps, making sure the rubber pads are in good condition. Note that the clamps are handed left and right. Tighten the mounting bolts to 18 lb f ft (2.5 kg f m). Tighten the pinch bolt in the lower universal joint to 18 lb f ft (2.5 kg f m).
9 Before connecting the trackrods to the steering arms, turn the steering wheel from lock-to-lock to check that the steering column is correctly aligned.

10 Steering gear - overhaul

1 The rack and pinion should last for high mileages, particularly if the rubber boots are maintained in good condition. The most likely need is to reset the damping yoke after a high mileage. This is described in Section 11. If the rack and pinion and the ball joints at the inner end are worn, then it is worth considering renewing the complete assembly. This is certainly the case if there is accident damage.
2 First remove the trackrods from the inner ball joints of the rack. There are flats on the ball joints so that they can be held by an open-ended spanner.
3 Remove the mounting clamps, that hold the steering gear to the car, and their rubber packing.
4 Take off the cover plate and remove the rack damping yoke, with spring, shims and oil sealing ring.
6 Remove the two bolts holding the pinion bearing plate to the

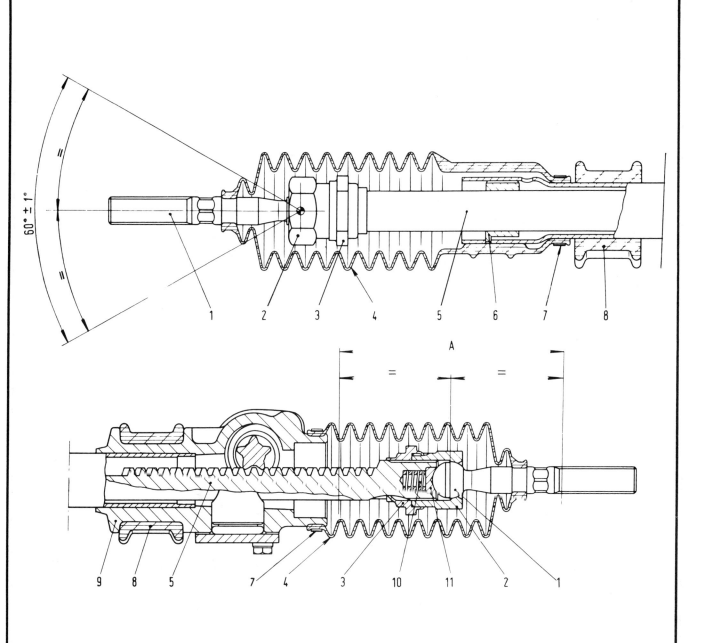

Fig. 9.7. Cross-section of early type rack and steering gear

1 Ball joints	4 Rubber bellows	7 Clamps	10 Spring
2 Adjustable ball joints	5 Rod and rack	8 Rubber pads	11 Ball pin cup
3 Locknuts for adjustable ball joints	6 Bush	9 Steering housing	

A = Travel *4.606 ± 0.059* in (117 ± 1.5 mm)
    60° ± 1° ball joint stroking angle

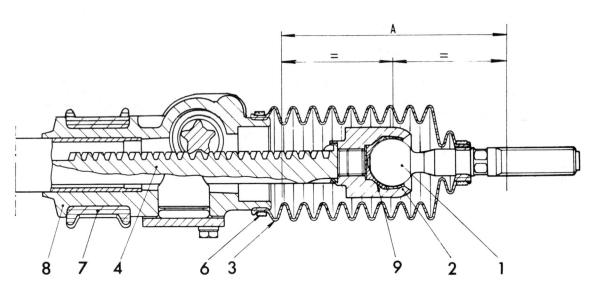

H.6195

Fig. 9.8. Cross-section of later type rack and steering gear

1 Ball joints	3 Rubber bellows	5 Bush	7 Resilient pads
2 Ball joint heads	4 Rod and rack	6 Clamps	8 Steering gear housing
			9 Ball joint socket

A = Travel 4.606 $\pm$ 0.059 in (117 $\pm$ 1.5 mm)
a = Ball joint stroking angle 62° $\pm$ 4°

housing. Remove the pinion, oil seal, gasket, shim and top ball bearing.
Note: On later type steering boxes the ball joints have a threaded
collar. If the joint is removed it must be renewed, therefore, remove
only one joint when removing the rack.

7 Mount the steering box in a vice, taking care not to damage the
casing.

8 On the later type box unstake the lock on the collar and ball joint.
Unscrew the ball joint. On early type box unstake the lock for the
locknuts and unscrew the nuts. Slide off the ball joints with sockets
and springs.

9 Slide the rack out of the steering box and remove the lower bearing
for the drive pinion.

10 Clean and check all parts for excessive wear or damage or
corrosion. Always fit new gaskets, rubber boots and pinion shaft oil
seal at reassembly.

11 As all parts are refitted, lubricate them thoroughly with an SAE
90 EP oil. Take care the rack teeth do not damage the housing bearings
when being refitted.

12 Fit the pinion bearing plate with extra shims and screw in its
retaining bolts gently to settle the bearing. Release the bolts until they
are finger-tight. Measure the gap between the housing and the plate.
Measure the thickness of the gasket with a micrometer and calculate
the thickness of shims needed. The shims should be thicker than the
gap between the housing and plate allowing for the gasket, by
0.001 - 0.005 in (0.025 - 0.13 mm). Shims are available in four
thicknesses: 0.0047, 0.0079, 0.0098, 0.0984 in (0.12, 0.2, 0.25, 2.5 mm).

13 Fit the shims. Coat the gasket and bolts for the cover plate with
a non-setting gasket compound. Fit the gasket, cover plate, washers and
bolts. Fit the pinion shaft oil seal.

14 Check that the pinion turns freely without sticking, even without
the damping yoke fitted. The force required to turn the pinion shaft
should not exceed 0.3 lb f ft (0.04 kg f m).

15 Adjust the damping yoke, as described in Section 11.

16 Reassemble the ball joints to the ends of the rack.

 a) On later type steering gear, screw the collar of the joint onto the
    rack to the end of the threaded section. Tighten the collar to
    54 lb f ft (7.5 kg f m). Stake the inside collar over the edge of
    the trackrod.
 b) On early type steering gear, tighten the adjustable heads till a
    torque of 1.5 to 3.25 lb f ft (0.2 to 0.5 kg f m) is needed to
    turn the ball joints in their seats.

17 Check that the ball joints can swivel and rotate through 60° ± 1
(see Fig. 9.7).

18 Lock the heads in position with the locknuts and stake them where
indicated by arrows in Fig. 9.10.

19 Fit the boots over the ball joints and slip the ends of the boots over
the steering box.

20 Position the clamping screws as shown in Fig. 9.11 and 9.12

21 Fit the trackrods and fill the steering box with oil, as described in
Section 12.

Fig. 9.9. Fitting the pinion bearing plate

1 Bearing plate   3 Rack
2 Seal

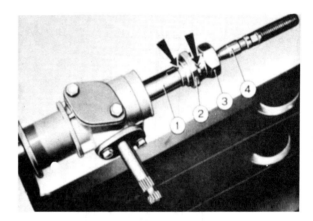

Fig. 9.10. Locking the adjustable heads

1 Rack   3 Adjustable head
2 Locknut   4 Ball pin

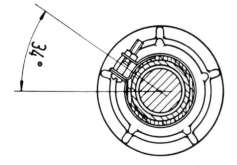

Fig. 9.11. Position of boot clamp screws - early type steering

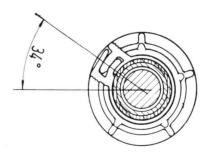

Fig. 9.12. Position of boot clamp screw - later type steering

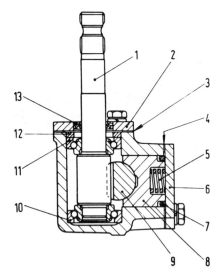

Fig. 9.13. Section through steering rack and pinion

1	Drive pinion shaft	8	Rack yoke
2	Cover plate	9	Rack
3	Gasket	10	Drive pinion lower bearing
4	Rack yoke shims	11	Drive pinion upper bearing
5	Spring	12	Drive pinion shims
6	Yoke cover plate	13	Seal
7	Seal ring		

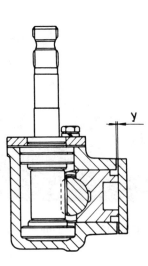

Fig. 9.14. Rack damping yoke adjustment

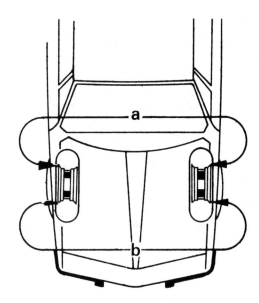

Fig. 9.15. Checking the front wheel toe-in
a greater than b for toe-in

Fig. 9.16. Adjusting the front wheel toe-in

1   Locknut   2   Inboard balljoint

11 Steering rack damping yoke - adjustment

1 The damping yoke presses the rack into mesh with the pinion. This prevents backlash between the gears and due to the pressure applied, dampens excessive reaction from the road to the steering wheel.
2 The pressure is controlled by the yoke cover plate and spring and is adjustable to compensate for wear.
3 The need for adjustment of the yoke after the car has run a high mileage is not easy to detect. On rough roads the shock induced through the steering will give a feeling of play. In extreme cases free play in the steering may be felt. If the steering is compared with that of new steering gear on another car, the lack of friction damping is quite apparent in the ease of movement of the steering wheel of the worn one.
4 Access to the yoke with the steering box fitted in the car is difficult and there is also the risk of getting dirt into the casing, so it is much easier done on the bench after removing the steering gear, as described in Section 9.
5 Turn the steering to the 'straight-ahead' position.
6 Take the cover plate off the damping yoke, remove the spring and shims and then refit the cover plate. Tighten the cover plate bolts just enough to hold the yoke firmly against the rack.
7 Turn the pinion through 180° in both directions to settle it between it and the rack.
8 Measure the gap between the cover plate and the rack housing ('Y' in Fig. 9.14).
9 Select shims to a thickness of 0.002 to 0.005 in (0.5 to 0.13 mm) more than the measured gap. Shims are available in 0.0039 and 0.0059 in (0.1 and 0.15 mm) thickness.
10 Remove the cover plate and fit the spring.
11 Coat surfaces of shims with non-setting gasket compound. Fit the shims, cover plate and bolts.

12 Steering gear - lubrication

1 The steering rack and pinion is lubricated for 'life'. If it is dismantled, it must be reassembled with a new supply.
2 The lubricant is gear oil of SAE 90 EP. The amount is 0.14 litre (0.24 Imp pt, 0.3 US pt).

3 The oil is inserted into the rack at the pinion end, that is the driver's end. If this is being done on the bench before refitting the rack to the car, fit the rubber boot to the other end, pour in the oil at the pinion end, then fit that boot. Turn the rack to-and-fro to spread the oil and check the boots are not being blown out by excess oil.
4 If there has been a leak, and it is required to refill the rack on the car, undo the rubber boots, and allow any old oil left to drain out, so there will not be much in it after refilling.
5 Refit the boot on the passenger's side. Jack up the car very high on the driver's side.
6 Pour the oil into the end of the rack and the boot, and quickly refit the boot to prevent any dribbling out.
7 Turn the rack from lock-to-lock to distribute the oil and check the rubber boots are relaxed, and showing no signs of the rack being over full.
8 Refit the clamping clips to the large ends of the rubber boots.

13 Front wheel toe-in - checking and adjustment

1 Position the car on level ground with the wheels in the 'straight-ahead' position. Make sure the steering wheel spokes are positioned properly, if not, refer to Section 9, and alter as necessary.
2 Using a wheel alignment gauge measure the distance between the rear of the wheel rims as shown in Fig. 9.15. Mark the wheel (dimension 'A').
3 Push the car forward to turn the wheels through 180° until the mark is in front. Measure the distance between the rims at this point (dimension 'B').
4 For correct toe-in dimension 'A' must be greater than dimension 'B' by the amount given in the Specifications.
5 To adjust the toe-in, release the locknuts at the inboard ends of the trackrods. Turn the rack balljoints, by means of their spanner flats, in the same direction and by the same amount until the toe-in is correct when rechecked.
6 The position of the steering wheel spokes should not have altered if both rack balljoints have been turned equally. Tighten the locknuts on completion.

14 Fault diagnosis - steering

Before assuming that the steering mechanism is at fault when mishandling is experienced make sure that the trouble is not caused by:—

1 *Binding brakes*
2 *Incorrect mix of radial and crossply tyres*
3 *Incorrect tyre pressure*
4 *Misalignment of the body or faulty suspension*

Symptom	Reason/s	Remedy
Steering wheel can be moved before any sign of movement of the wheels is apparent	Wear in the steering linkage, gear and column coupling	Check movement in all joints and steering gear and overhaul and renew as required.
Vehicle difficult to steer in a consistent straight line; wandering: unstable on corners	As above	As above.
	Wheel alignment incorrect (indicated by excessive or uneven tyre wear)	Check toe-in.
	Rear suspension toe-in camber wrong	See Chapter 11.
	Front wheel hub bearings loose or worn	Adjust or renew as necessary.
	Worn ball joints, trackrods or suspension arms	Renew as necessary.
Steering stiff and heavy	Incorrect wheel alignment (indicated by excessive or uneven tyre wear)	Check wheel alignment.
	Excessive wear or seizure in one or more of the joints in the steering linkage or suspension arm ball joints	Renew as necessary.
	Excessive wear in the steering gear unit	Dismantle, check, relubricate the rack and pinion.
Wheel wobble and vibration	Road wheels out of balance	Balance wheels. (See Chapter 11).
	Road wheels buckled	Check for damage.
Excessive pitching and rolling on corners and during braking	Defective shock absorbers	Check and renew as necessary. (See Chapter 11).

Chapter 10 Electrical system

For modifications, and information applicable to later models, see Supplement at end of manual

Contents

Specifications

Voltage ... ... 12 volts

Polarity ... ... Negative earth

Battery
Nominal capacity (at 20 hour discharge rate) ... ... 60 AH

Alternator

Type	Marelli FIMM A124 - 14V - 44A VAR 3
Nominal voltage	12
Cut-in speed at 12V at 77°F (25°C)	1000 ± 50 rpm
Current output at 14V to battery at 7000 rpm	Not below 44A
Maximum current output	53A approx.
Maximum speed	13000 rpm
Rotation, drive end	Clockwise
Ratio - engine to alternator	1 : 2

Voltage regulator

Type	Bosch AD1/14V or Marelli RC2/12D (later models)
Resistance between positive terminal and earth at 77° ± 18°F (25° ± 10°C)	85 ± 4.5 ohms

Starter motor

Type	Pre-engaged by solenoid
Model	FIAT E84 - 0.8/12 VAR 1
Nominal output	0.8 kw
Number of poles	4
Field winding	Series
No load test (11.9 volts)	30 amps or less at 6000 - 8000 rpm
Solenoid winding resistance	0.39 ± 0.02 ohms

Lubrication:
Armature brushes	Engine oil
Armature spiral grooves	SAE 10(W) oil
Free wheel splines	General purpose grease

Heater fan motor 20W

Radiator fan motor 55W

Windscreen wiper motor 25W

Wiper blades ... ...   Champion X-3803

Bulbs

	SAE standard	FIAT part no. or rating
	Sealed beam unit No. 7031	(UK has standard bulbs)
Headlights		
Turn indicators	1073 (32C)	Norm. 1/41460/90
Brake light	1073 (32C)	Norm. 1/41460/90
Reversing light	1073 (32C)	Norm. 1/41460/90
Number plate light	1073 (32C)	Norm. 1/41460/90
Parking lights	67 (4C)	Norm. 1/41459/90
Interior light	—	12V - 5W
Instrument lights	—	12V - 3W

Fuses

Number and rating	2 three-amp fuses; 8 eight-amp fuses; 2 sixteen-amp fuses; 1 eight-amp fuse in separate holder

Protected circuits:

A (8 amp)	Brake lights
	Reversing lights
	Brake system effectiveness and handbrake 'ON' indicator
	Ignition - seatbelt interlock system (US only)
	Turn signal and indicator
	Tachometer
	Oil pressure gauge and indicator
	Windscreen washer motor
	Fuel gauge and fuel reserve indicator
	Engine water temperature gauge
	Heater fan motor
	Windscreen wiper
	Fasten seatbelts indicator ⎱(US only)
	Fasten seatbelts buzzer relay ⎰
B (8 amp)	Retractable headlamp motors
	Interlock system control unit ⎱(US only)
	Fasten belts and remove key buzzer ⎰
C (8 amp)	Left headlamp high beam
D (8 amp)	Right headlamp high beam
E (8 amp)	Left headlamp low beam
F (8 amp)	Right headlamp low beam
G (8 amp)	Front left parking light
	Parking and tail lights indicator
	Rear right side marker light (US only)
	Rear right tail light
	Front left side marker light (US only)
	Number plate light (one bulb only)
	Light source, ideograms optical fibre illumination
	Cigar lighter spotlight
	Light source, heater from ideogram illumination
H (8 amp)	Front right parking light
	Front right side marker light (US only)
	Rear left tail light
	Rear left marker light (US only)
	Number plate light (one bulb only)
I (16 amp)	Cigar lighter
	Vehicle hazard warning signal and indicator
L (16 amp)	Radiator fan motor
	Horns and relay
M (3 amp)	Retractable headlamps control relay (closing)
N (3 amp)	Retractable headlamps control relay (opening)
28/3 (8 amp)	Carburettor fan motor and relay
	Interior light
Unprotected circuits:	Alternator
	Radiator fan motor relay field winding
	Ignition
	Instrument cluster lights
	Starting
	Starter motor relay field winding
	Battery charge indicator

1 General description

1   The electrical system is of the 12 volt type and the major
components comprise a 12 volt battery, of which the negative terminal
is earthed, a voltage regulator, an alternator which is mounted on the
right-hand end of the engine and belt driven from the pulley on the
front of the crankshaft, and a starter motor fitted at the left-hand end
of the engine.
2   The battery supplies a steady amount of current for starting,
ignition, lighting and other electrical circuits and provides a reserve of
electricity when the current consumed by the electrical equipment
exceeds that being produced by the alternator.
3   When fitting electrical accessories to cars with a negative earth
system it is important, if they contain silicone diodes or transistors,
that they are connected correctly, otherwise serious damage may
result to the components concerned. Items such as radios, tape
recorders, and electrical tachometers should all be checked for correct
polarity.
4   It is important that the battery is always disconnected if it is to
be boost charged from an external source, or when electric welding
equipment is to be used for work on the car, otherwise the alternator
may be damaged.

2 Battery - removal and refitting

1   The battery is located on a shelf in the left-hand side of the front
luggage compartment. Remove the battery cover.
2   Slacken the clamp retaining nuts and disconnect the battery leads
from the terminal posts, negative first.
3   Remove the retaining bolt from the battery clamp bar, remove the
bar and lift out the battery.
4   Refitting is the reverse of the removal sequence. Coat the terminals
with petroleum jelly (do not use a mineral grease). Connect the positive
lead first.

3 Battery - maintenance and inspection

1   Normal weekly battery maintenance consists of checking the
electrolyte level of each cell to ensure that the separators are covered
by ¼ in (6.3 mm) of electrolyte. If the level has fallen, top-up the
battery using distilled water only. Do not overfill. If the battery is
overfilled or any electrolyte spilled, immediately wipe away excess as
electrolyte attacks and corrodes any metal it comes into contact with
very rapidly.
2   If the battery is of a special type, full instructions as to how these
should be checked will be given on the battery.
3   As well as keeping the terminals clean and covered with petroleum
jelly, the top of the battery, and especially the top of the cells, should

be kept clean and dry. This helps to prevent corrosion and ensures that
the battery does not become partially discharged by leakage through
dampness and dirt.
4   Once every three months remove the battery and inspect the
battery securing nuts, battery clamp plate, tray and battery leads for
corrosion (white fluffy deposits on the metal which are brittle to
touch). If any corrosion is found, clean off the deposit with ammonia
and paint over the clean metal with an anti-rust, anti-acid paint.
5   At the same time inspect the battery case for cracks. If found,
clean and plug it with a proprietary compound. If leakage through the
crack has been excessive then it will be necessary to refill the appropriate cell with fresh electrolyte as described later. Cracks are frequently
caused at the top of the battery case by pouring in distilled water in
the middle of winter *after* instead of *before* a run. This gives the water
no chance to mix with the electrolyte and so the former freezes and
splits the battery case.
6   If the topping-up becomes excessive and the case has been inspected
for cracks that could cause leakage, but none are found, the battery is
being overcharged and the voltage regulator will have to be checked
and reset.
7   With the battery on the bench at the three monthly interval check,
measure the specific gravity with a hydrometer to determine the state
of charge and condition of the electrolyte. There should be very little
variation between the different cells and, if a variation in excess of
0.025 is present, it will be due to:

a) *Loss of electrolyte from the battery at some time caused by
   spillage or a leak, resulting in a drop in the specific gravity
   of the electrolyte when the deficiency was replaced with
   distilled water instead of fresh electrolyte.*
b) *An internal short circuit caused by buckling of the plates
   or similar malady pointing to the likelihood of total
   battery failure in the near future.*

8   The specific gravity of the electrolyte for fully charged conditions
at the electrolyte temperatures indicated, is listed in Table A. The
specific gravity of a fully discharged battery at different temperatures
of the electrolyte is given in Table B.

Table A
Specific gravity - battery fully charged

1.268 at 100^{0}F or 38^{0}C electrolyte temperature
1.272 at 90^{0}F or 32^{0}C electrolyte temperature
1.276 at 80^{0}F or 27^{0}C electrolyte temperature
1.280 at 70^{0}F or 21^{0}C electrolyte temperature
1.284 at 60^{0}F or 16^{0}C electrolyte temperature
1.288 at 50^{0}F or 10^{0}C electrolyte temperature
1.292 at 40^{0}F or 4^{0}C electrolyte temperature
1.296 at 30^{0}F or -1.5^{0}C electrolyte temperature

2.1 The battery cover is removed ...

2.2 ... and the battery leads are disconnected from the battery.
The negative terminal is disconnected first

Table B

Specific gravity - battery fully discharged

1.098 at 100°F or 38°C electrolyte temperature
1.102 at 90°F or 32°C electrolyte temperature
1.106 at 80°F or 27°C electrolyte temperature
1.110 at 70°F or 21°C electrolyte temperature
1.114 at 60°F or 16°C electrolyte temperature
1.118 at 50°F or 10°C electrolyte temperature
1.122 at 40°F or 4°C electrolyte temperature
1.126 at 30°F or -1.5°C electrolyte temperature

4 Battery - electrolyte replenishment

1   If the battery is in a fully charged state and one of the cells maintains a specific gravity reading which is 0.025 or lower than the others and a check of each cell has been made with a voltage meter to check for short circuits (a four to seven second test should give a steady reading of between 1.2 and 1.8 volts), then it is likely that electrolyte has been lost from the cell with the low reading at some time.
2   Top-up the cell with a solution of 1 part sulphuric acid to 2.5 parts of water. If the cell is already fully topped-up draw some electrolyte out of it with a pipette.
3   When mixing the sulphuric acid and water **never add water to sulphuric acid** always pour the acid slowly onto the water in a glass container. **If water is added to sulphuric acid it will explode.**
4   Continue to top-up the cell with the freshly made electrolyte and then recharge the battery and check the hydrometer readings.

5 Battery - charging

1   It is a good idea to occasionally have the battery fully charged from an external source at a rate of 3.5 or 4 amps, particularly after heavy loading.
2   Continue to charge the battery at this rate until no further rise in specific gravity is noted over a four hour period.
3   Alternatively, a trickle charge, charging at the rate of 1.5 amps can be safely used overnight.
4   Special rapid 'boost' charges which are claimed to restore the power of the battery in 1 to 2 hours are most dangerous unless they are thermostatically controlled as they can cause serious damage to the battery plates through overheating.
5   While charging the battery note that the temperature of the electrolyte should never exceed 100°F (37.8°C).

6 Alternator - description and testing

1   The alternator develops its current in the stationary windings, the rotor carrying this field. The brushes therefore carry only a small current, so they last a long time, and only simple slip rings are needed instead of a commutator.
2   The AC voltage is rectified by a bank of diodes. These also prevent battery discharge through the alternator.
3   Very little servicing is needed. Every 24,000 miles (40,000 km) the alternator should be stripped and the brushes cleaned and checked.
4   Fault-finding is more a matter of confirming the fault is in the alternator, and it is probable then that a new unit will have to be fitted. However, if parts are available, component repair is possible. To fit new rectifiers or stator windings requires experience with a soldering iron, and should not be done by someone completely inexperienced.
5   To prevent damage to the rectifying diodes, the alternator leads should be disconnected whenever electric welding repairs are being carried out on the car, or when the battery is being charged from an external power supply.
6   Before suspecting a fault in the alternator, make sure that its electrical connections are secure and that the drivebelt is correctly tensioned. Also make sure that the battery is in good condition.
7   Start the engine and allow it to idle. Connect a voltmeter (range 0 to 20 volts dc) across the battery terminals. The voltmeter should read between 12 and 13 volts.
8   Increase the engine speed to approximately 2500 rpm: the voltmeter reading should increase to between 13 and 14 volts. No increase, or an increase to 15 volts or more, suggests that the alternator or voltage regulator is faulty.
9   Further testing should be left to an electrical expert. The home mechanic with an interest in electrical systems will find further test procedures in the *Automobile Electrical Manual,* available from the publishers of this book.

7 Alternator - removal and refitting

1   Disconnect the battery earth lead.
2   Disconnect the plug from the rear of the alternator. Remove the undershield.
3   Slacken the pivot and lock bolts, and remove the drivebelt from the pulley.
4   Hold the alternator and remove the lock bolt and pivot bolt and withdraw the alternator either upwards or downwards.
5   Refitting is the reverse of the removal procedure. Tension the drivebelt by pulling on the alternator and then tightening the pivot and lockbolt. The correct tension is a deflection of 0.5 in (12 mm) midway between the water pump and the drive pulley when a pressure of 20 lb (10 kg) is applied.
Note: If the belt is too slack it will slip and cause the engine to overheat and the alternator output will be low. If it is too tight it will overload the water pump and alternator bearings resulting in rapid bearing failure.

8 Alternator - servicing

1   It is assumed at this stage that the alternator is only being stripped either to clean and check the brushes, or to trace a fault. So only partial dismantling is necessary. Fault-finding and repair should be left to the official agent if you have no experience of electricity and electronics.
2   Undo the long bolts clamping the two parts of the body together. Prise them apart, keeping the two straight. Pull the front part away, with the rotor still inside.
3   Clean all the parts, but do not dip them in any liquid. Check the condition of the slip rings, which should be smooth and shiny. The brushes' minimum length is 2/3 of their original.
4   If the alternator has failed, it is now stripped enough to check the field windings on the rotor, and the stator windings. As a repair will need knowledge of radio techniques, such as soldering without overheating the diodes; some knowledge is assumed here. Check the windings are neither open circuit, or shorted to their rotor/stator. The resistance of the field windings on the rotor should be about 4 ohms. Check the diodes only allow current in one direction.
5   If the diodes or stator coils need renewal, they must be unsoldered and removed from the brush-end of the body. Note all leads so that they can be reconnected correctly.
6   If the rotor or the bearings need renewal the drive-end must be dismantled. Undo the nut on the end of the shaft holding on the pulley. Pad the rotor, and put it in a vice with soft jaws, and then undo the nut. Press the drive-end bracket with the bearing off the shaft. The brush-end bearing can be pulled off the other end of the shaft.
7   The bearings are lubricated and then sealed on assembly. If they feel dry or rough, they should be renewed.
8   When reassembling, the brushes have to be fitted into their holders, and put into position after fitting the rotor.

9 Voltage regulator - checking

1   Before checking the regulator, refer to Section 6 and ensure that the alternator is operating correctly.
2   Start the engine and allow it to idle. Disconnect the battery earth lead.
3   Connect the positive lead of a voltmeter to the battery positive terminal and the negative lead to the battery earth lead.
4   Gradually increase the engine speed to between 4000 and 5000 rpm and check that the voltmeter reading is between 13.8 and 14.6 volts.
5   If the regulator requires adjusting this is best left to your FIAT

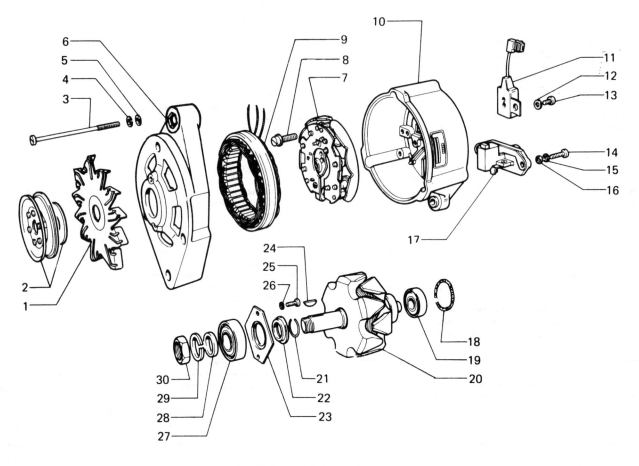

Fig. 10.1. Exploded view of alternator

1	Fan	9	Stator	17	Brush holder	25	Screw
2	Pulley	10	Body	18	Backing washer	26	Washer
3	Bolt	11	Condenser	19	Bearing	27	Bearing
4	Lockwasher	12	Washer	20	Rotor	28	Thrust ring
5	Washer	13	Washer	21	Clip	29	Lockwasher
6	Drive-end bracket	14	Screw	22	Thrust ring	30	Nut
7	Diode plate	15	Lockwasher	23	Plate		
8	Plate screw	16	Washer	24	Key		

agent or an auto-electrician.

6   If the alternator and voltage regulator are in order and the ignition warning light (charge indicator) remains on then the charge indicator relay, which is located in the voltage regulator, is suspect. The testing of this relay is a job for your FIAT agent or auto-electrician.

10 Starter motor - description and checks

1   The starter is of the pre-engaged type. When the ignition switch is turned through to the starter position, the solenoid on the top of the starter is switched on, by the thin red wire. The solenoid slides along, pulling on the starter's gear lever. This slides the starter's gear into mesh with the starter ring on the flywheel. Having done this, the solenoid comes to the end of its travel, when a button on it switches the heavy cable direct from the battery to the starter motor itself. The starter now cranks the engine. Should the teeth of the starter and the flywheel have been out of alignment, the starter gear is spring loaded, so will actually mesh as soon as they come in line. This is helped by the spiral splines. Once the engine fires, it would run up to speed very quickly taking the starter with it, and the latter would turn so fast its windings would be damaged. In the drive is a freewheel to prevent this over speeding.

2   If the starter fails some fault-finding can be done with it still on the car. Check the ignition warning light comes on, and does not go

out when the starter is switched on. If it goes out then the fault is probably in the battery. If it stays bright, get an assistant to work the switch, whilst listening to the starter. Listen to find out if the solenoid clicks into position. If it does not, pull out the red solenoid wire, and check it with a test bulb. If the wire is live when the key is turned, but the solenoid does not move, then take off the starter to work more comfortably on the bench.

11 Starter motor - removal and refitting

1   Disconnect the earth lead from the negative terminal of the battery.
2   Disconnect the lead from the starter solenoid and the heavy cable from the battery.
3   Remove the mounting bolts and lift out the starter.
4   Refitting is the reverse of the removal sequence. Make sure the electrical connections are secure.

12 Starter motor - overhaul

1   Having removed the starter from the engine, first clean the outside.
2   If the starter has been removed because it will not work, before stripping it, test to see where the defect is, and decide whether to try repairing it, or if it is better to obtain a replacement. Connect a lead

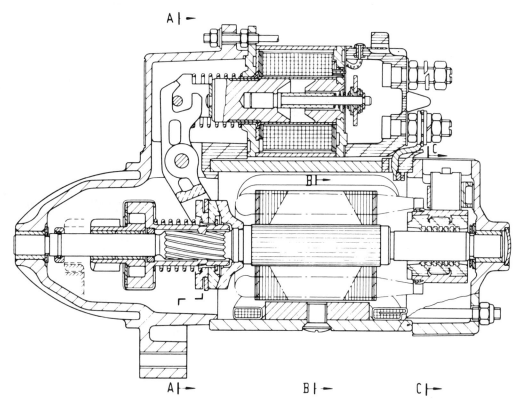

A |←

A |←   B |←   C |←

Longitudinal section of starter assembly.

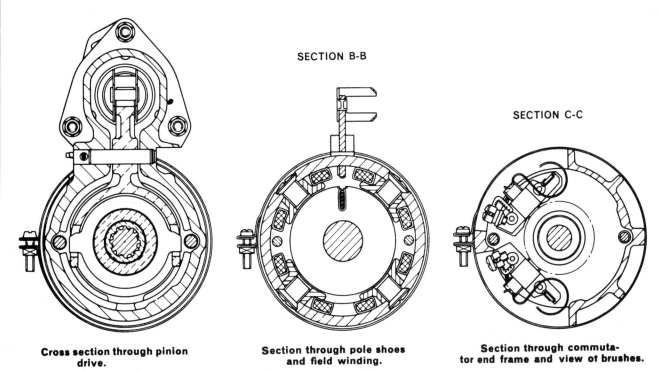

SECTION A-A

SECTION B-B

SECTION C-C

Cross section through pinion drive.

Section through pole shoes and field winding.

Section through commutator end frame and view of brushes.

Fig. 10.2. Sectional views of starter motor

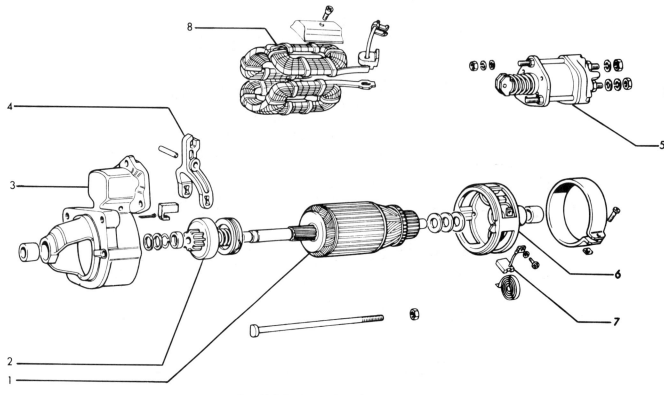

Fig. 10.3. Exploded view of starter motor

1	Armature	3	Pinion end bracket	5	Solenoid	7	Brush
2	Pinion with free wheel	4	Gear lever	6	Brush end plate	8	Field windings

from the battery negative terminal to the starter body, using one of the bolts that held it to the engine. Connect the positive battery terminal to the little solenoid terminal. The solenoid should slide the starter's gear along the shaft, but the starter will not turn because at present no wire is on the starter's motor terminal. Now add another wire to that terminal. With the solenoid live, the starter should turn after the gear has slid into engagement. If it does not, try the wire direct to the motor's lead on the solenoid terminal nearer the motor main body, on which is the lead into the motor. If the motor now turns it shows that the switch part of the solenoid is faulty.

3   The starter should be dismantled for cleaning and renewing of the brushes every 24,000 miles (40,000 km).

4   Take off the nut on the solenoid, and disconnect the cable from the solenoid into the motor, the field connection.

5   Remove the nuts and washers on the long studs holding the solenoid to the end frame. Lift off the solenoid, unhooking it from the gear lever.

6   Slacken and slide off the dust cover on the end of the yoke, to uncover the brushes.

7   Disconnect the wire from the field winding to its brush.

8   Hook up the brush springs on the sides of the brush holders, so the load is taken off them.

9   Undo the nuts on the long through bolts holding the whole motor together.

10 Take off the brush-end endplate, and retrieve the one fibre and two steel washers from the end of the armature shaft.

11 Tip the motor pinion end down, and lift the yoke off the armature and pinion end frame.

12 Take out its split pin, and remove the pivot pin for the gear lever from the 'waist' of the pinion housing.

13 Take the pinion housing off the assembly of armature, pinion and gear lever.

14 Clean all the parts by wiping. Do not immerse in cleaning liquid, especially the free wheel and the armature bushes in the end frames, as the liquid will get into the freewheel race and the pores of the bushes.

15 Check the condition of the commutator. If it is dirty and blackened, clean it with a rag, dampened with petrol. If the commutator is in good condition the surface will be smooth and free from pitting or burnt areas, and the insulated segments clearly defined.

16 Scrape the dirt out of the undercut gaps of insulator between the metal segments with a narrow screwdriver.

17 If, after the commutator has been cleaned, pitted and burnt spots are still present, wrap a strip of fine glass paper round the commutator. Rub the patches off while turning the armature so that the rubbing is spread evenly all over. Finally polish the commutator with metal polish, then clean out the gaps.

18 In extreme cases of wear the commutator can be mounted in a lathe. With the lathe turning fast, take a very fine cut. Then polish with fine glass paper, followed by metal polish.

19 If the commutator is badly worn or has been skimmed the segments may be worn down level with the insulator in between the segments. In this case the insulator must be undercut. This is done to a depth of 0.040 in (1.0 mm). The best tool for this job is a hacksaw blade, if necessary ground down to make it thinner. The undercutting must extend the full width of the insulator, right out to the metal segments on each side.

20 Clean every part thoroughly when finished and ensure that no rough edges are left as any roughness will cause excessive brush wear.

21 Before reassembly lubricate the splines of the freewheel with general purpose grease. Use a thin oil on the spiral splines. Use engine oil for the armature brushes, allowing it time to soak in before assembly.

22 Fit the brushes in their guides, but clip them back so that they will clear the commutator by putting the springs on their side. The springs can be hooked into place after the brush endplate has been fitted.

---

13 Windscreen wiper motor - fault diagnosis, removal and refitting

1   Fault diagnosis is complicated by the complex wiring due to the intermittent wiper mode, and the self-parking arrangements. Fault

diagnosis will need reference to the wiring diagram for the colours of the wires from switch to the timing device, and on to the motor. If the wiper does not work either intermittently or continuously then there is a strong chance that the defect is in the motor. The wiper shares the fuse of the heater fan, so this is easily checked, and eliminated before tackling the wiring.

2   Unplug the wires near the motor, and using a test bulb or volt meter with probes to reach into the terminals, test the circuit with the switch on the steering column in its three positions. Note that because of the self-parking facility, the circuit is always partially live.

3   Once a defect in the motor is suspected, it must be removed with the blade mechanism, all on the mounting plate.

4   Disconnect the plug for the leads.

5   Pull off the wiper arms.

6   Take off the fixtures on the ends of the arms spindles so that these can be withdrawn through the brushes in the body below the windscreen.

7   Undo the two bolts holding the motor mounting frame to the bracket on the bulkhead.

8   Remove the whole assembly.

9   When refitting, grease the arm spindles in their brushes, and all the other links for the connecting levers.

10 Operate the motor before fitting the blade arms. Once the motor has put the spindles in the parked position, the arms can be fitted in their correct orientation. Make sure the assembly is refitted without distortion which could make the linkage stiff.

11 If the operation of the wiper becomes very sluggish due to the need for lubrication of the interconnecting mechanism, or in heavy snow, there is risk of burning out the motor. Always switch off the wiper if it stalls, and if it cannot get back to the parked position, unplug the motor.

14 Lighting - general

1   As bulbs blow without warning and at inconvenient times always carry spare ones in the car. When going to get a new bulb, or light unit, take the old one with you to be sure of getting the right type;

2   The headlamps are renewable sealed-beam units. Both the high-beam and low-beam circuits and filaments are included in one unit. If one circuit fails, the sealed-beam unit must be renewed. Note that Holts Amber Lamp is useful for temporarily changing the headlight colour to conform with the normal usage on Continental Europe.

3   If an indicator flashing light bulb fails, it will give a different flashing speed to the indicators.

4   Except for the headlamps, which have individual fuses, the failure of one lamp only is usually the bulb. Only very occasionally is it a wiring failure, as these failures are usually short circuit rather than an open one. But failure of the earth contact at the lamp is likely in older cars.

5   Remember when checking the brake lights that the ignition must be switched on. These lights can be checked by reversing close to a wall, this also checks the reversing lights.

15 Headlamps - removal and refitting

1   Remove the three screws holding the headlamp outer frame. Slacken the screws securing the headlamp retaining rim and rotate the rim counterclockwise until the lugs are clear, then remove the rim.

2   Take out the lamp unit, disconnect the plug and remove the lamp unit.

3   Connect the plug to a new lamp and fit it in position, by lining up the lugs of the lamp with the recesses in the headlamp inner mounting ring. Fit the retaining ring over the retaining screws and turn it clockwise. Tighten the screws.

4   Fit the outer frame and retaining screws.

16 Front indicators and sidelights - bulb renewal

1   Remove the two retaining screws and lift off the lens.

2   Remove the relevant bulb by pushing in and twisting anticlockwise to release the bulb.

3   Fit a new bulb by pushing it in and turning it clockwise. Fit the

13.3 To get at the windscreen motor remove the grille

13.5 Pull off the wiper arms

13.8 The windscreen wiper mechanism is housed in a compartment in front of the bulkhead

15.1a The headlamp outer frame is removed first ...

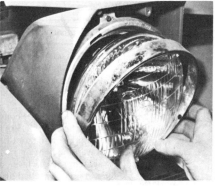
15.1b ... then after removing the securing screw turn the rim counterclockwise to release it

15.2 Disconnect the plug and remove the headlamp

16.3 When refitting the lens to the front flasher and sidelights, make sure the seal is in good condition

17.1 The lens for the rear cluster is in three parts

17.5 When refitting the lens in the rear cluster, ensure the seal is in good condition. Don't overtighten the securing screws

lens and retaining screws. Take care not to overtighten the screws as this may crack the lens.

17 Rear light cluster - bulb renewal

1 Remove the two screws securing the lens and remove the lens for access to the indicator bulb.
2 Remove the four screws and lens for access to the brake light bulb and tail light bulb.
3 For access to the reversing light bulb remove two screws and the relevant lens.
4 All these bulbs are of the bayonet coupling type.
5 When refitting the lenses for the indicator and reversing lights, position their lugs in the recesses in the brake and tail light lens before tightening the securing screws.

18 Number plate light - bulb renewal

1 Undo the retaining screw and remove the lens-body unit. Remove the bulb.
2 When refitting the lens-body unit locate the lug in the recess in the lens before tightening the screw.

19 Side marker lights - bulb renewal (US models only)

1 The bulb cannot be renewed separately. In the event of failure, change the complete unit.
2 To remove, free the spring retainers from inside each headlamp motor housing and pull the unit from the outside.

20 Headlamp motors - checking

1 If the headlamp motors do not raise the headlamps, check the fuses 'B' and 'N' in the fusebox. If the motors fail to lower the headlamps check the fuses 'B' and 'M'.
2 If the fuses are in order check the circuit with a voltmeter or a test lamp to isolate the fault (ie; wiring, relays or motors).
3 The motors and relays are in housings behind the headlamps in the front luggage compartment.
4 If the motors fail to operate, the headlamps can be raised to the open position manually. Remove the cover plate from the motor housing and turn the knob on the headlamp motor shaft until the unit is fully raised.

21 Headlamp motor - removal and refitting

1 Remove the bolt securing the headlamp arm to the motor shaft.
2 Remove the three motor retaining bolts. Disconnect the electrical connector and remove the motor.
3 Refitting is the reverse of the removal procedure. Do not forget to connect the earth wire to the retaining bolt. Avoid turning the headlamp adjuster rod when refitting a motor, but in any event it is advisable to have the beam alignment check carried out.

22 Seatbelt interlock system - general

1 Cars going to the USA and neighbouring countries have a number of special electrical items.
2 A buzzer warns if the door is opened, but the ignition key is still in the switch steering lock. The same buzzer is used for the seatbelt warning system.
3 Instead of the convenient European combined lap and shoulder belt, the seatbelts are in separate parts. The warning system to remind the driver and front passenger to do them up operates the buzzer and a warning light on the dash. The system is triggered by the ignition switch, the gearlever, and for the passenger a pad in the seat. The system is switched off by a contact in the lap strap belt reel each side.
4 The engine can be started for maintenance or turning operations by reaching in through a window so that no weight is placed on either of the front seats.

18.2 When refitting the lens-body unit make sure the lug is located in its recess

19.2 When changing the side marker light the complete unit is pulled out and renewed

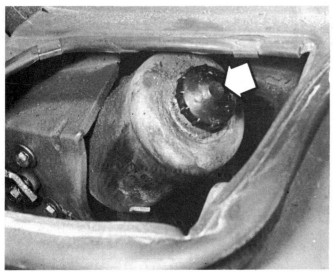

20.3a The headlamp motors (manual knob arrowed) ...

20.3b ... and relays are in housings behind the headlamps

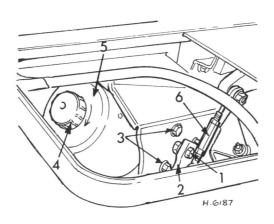

H.6187

Fig. 10.4. Removing the headlamp motor

1 Bolt	3 Bolts	5 Motor	6 Adjusting rod
2 Arm	4 Manual knob		

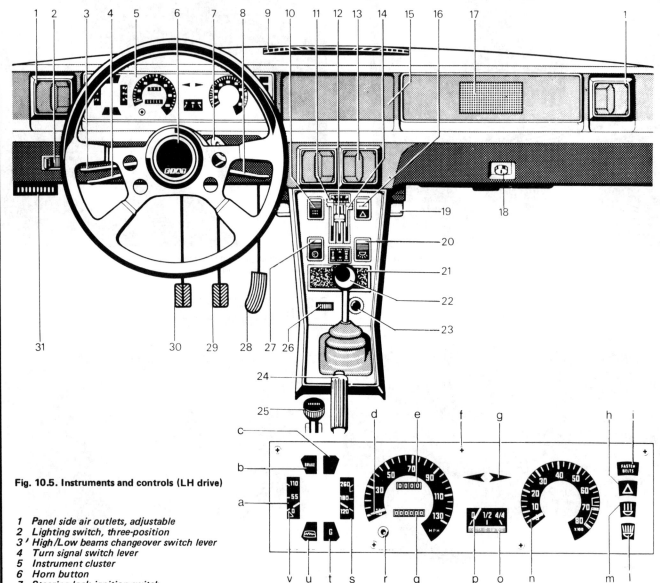

Fig. 10.5. Instruments and controls (LH drive)

1 Panel side air outlets, adjustable
2 Lighting switch, three-position
3 High/Low beams changeover switch lever
4 Turn signal switch lever
5 Instrument cluster
6 Horn button
7 Steering lock ignition switch
8 Windscreen wiper/washer switch lever, three-position
9 Air diffuser, windscreen
10 Two-speed heater fan switch, three-position
11 Air volume control lever
12 Heater outlet flap lever
13 Panel center air outlets, adjustable
14 Air temperature control lever
15 Radio housing blanking lid
16 Vehicular hazard warning signal switch
17 Loudspeaker grill, optional radio
18 Drop tray button (with lock). Front trunk latch release handle is housed in tray recess
19 Heater outlet flap
20 Courtesy light switch
21 Front ashtray
22 Gearchange lever
23 Cigar lighter
24 Handbrake lever. To release, thumb in the button on top of handgrip
25 Choke knob
26 Ideogram illumination intensity rheostat
27 Instrument cluster light switch
28 Accelerator pedal
29 Service brake pedal
30 Clutch pedal
31 Fusebox

a Oil pressure gauge
b Brake system effectiveness indicator (red)
c Spare indicator
d Speedometer
e Trip recorder
f Cluster panel mounting screws
g Turn signal arrow indicator
h Vehicular hazard warning indicator
i Fasten seatbelts indicator (red) and buzzer
l High beams indicator (blue)
m Parking and tail lights indicator (green)
n Tachometer
o Fuel reserve indicator (red)
p Fuel gauge
q Odometer
r Trip recorder zeroing knob
s Engine water temperature gauge
t Battery charge indicator (red)
u Back window demister indicator (amber)
v Low oil pressure indicator (red)

23 Horns - fault diagnosis

1   The use of twin horns makes fault diagnosis simple. If only one
sounds, then the fault is particular to the one that is silent. If both are
silent, then it is a wiring or horn button defect.
2   If a horn fails, it can be adjusted by a screw on the back. Try
screwing the screw in first: only a turn or so. Once the horn works
again, adjust the screw in or out for the best note. Afterwards put
some paint on the screw to seal out water, and to lock it.
3   The fuse is easily checked as it is shared with the interior light.
4   The horn button is the earth return, the black wire. Join a short
length of wire from that terminal on one of the horns to a bright metal
part and see if that makes the horn work. Check the live side, the
violet wires, with a test bulb.
5   Carefully prise off the horn button from the steering wheel and
try earthing the wire to the steering column if the contacts are suspect.

24 Turn indicator and flasher relays - general

1   The turn indicator and flasher relays are mounted beneath the
dashboard. The connectors are plug-in type.
2   Failure of a bulb will be shown by a change in the speed of flashing,
and the sound of the clicking. If the bulb and wiring is in order,
unplug the unit and fit a new one.

25 Instruments - checking

1   Access to the instruments is gained by removing the panel as
described in Chapter 12.
2   The fuel oil pressure temperature gauges and lights have their
senders whose electric resistance varies according to the circumstances
they are recording. The temperature, and oil pressure senders are both
on the front of the engine. The fuel gauge sender is mounted in the
top of the tank, with access only by removing the tank. To check the
function of the actual instrument, remove the wire from the sender.
Turn on the ignition. Note the reading with the lead off. Then put the
lead direct to a good earth. These two tests should give full scale
deflections in the two directions. Warning lights should come on
when the lead is earthed. If this is successful, then the fault is in the
sender. If unsuccessful, the same test should be done at the instrument, first establishing which is the live wire from the ignition switch
with a test lamp. This will then show whether the fault is in the
wiring to the sender or the instrument itself.

26 Fuses - general

1   The fusebox is below the dashboard, on the left-hand side, covered
by a plastic lid. The fuse functions are given in the Specifications at
the beginning of this Chapter.
2   Fuses normally seldom blow. Sometimes when a lamp bulb fails
it may blow the fuse as it goes, which can cause confusion in the fault
diagnosis. Tracing the fault is easiest on those fuses that serve more
than one component.
3   If a fuse consistently blows, it is indicating a short in that
circuit, usually intermittent. Do not be tempted to replace the
fuse by one of higher capacity than standard. The result will be that as
the short gets worse, the wiring of the car will overheat, causing
widespread harm, and even the risk of burning the whole car.
4   Whilst searching for the cause of blowing fuses it is economical
to use household fusewire laid in the clips and held by the burned
out fuse cartridge. The cause of the trouble is likely to be frayed
wire, chafing where it passes through a hole in the sheet metal.

27 Fault diagnosis - preliminaries

1   Tracing an electrical fault follows the usual principle of the
methodical check along the system.
2   First check for foolish errors, such as the wrong switch
turned on, or for such things as an over-riding control like the
accessory position of the ignition/steering lock. Also, if other
components have failed simultaneously, then a fuse appears to be
the fault.
3   If the fault is a light failure, try changing the bulb before proceding
with other checks.
4   On old cars a common fault is a poor earth return. If this is suspected then strip the component and de-rust it to ensure a good contact.
5   The proper systematic tracing of a more elusive fault requires a
voltmeter or a test lamp. The latter is a small 12 volt bulb with two
wires fitted to it; either using a bulb holder, or soldered direct. To test
a circuit one wire is put to earth, and the other used to test the live
side of a component. Work back from the component till the point is
found where the bulb lights, indicating that the circuit is live until then.
To test the earth side, the test bulb is wired to a live source, such as the
starter solenoid. Then if the other wire is put to a component properly
earthed it will light the bulb.
6   Trace methodically back until a correct result is obtained.
Inaccessible circuits can be bridged with a temporary wire to see if it
effects a cure.
7   With the wiring in a loom, defective wiring must be replaced with
a separate wire. This must be securely fixed so it cannot chafe.

26.1 The fusebox is mounted under the dashboard

28 Fault diagnosis - electrical system

See Section 27

Symptom	Reason/s	Remedy
Starter motor fails to turn engine		
No electricity at starter motor	Battery discharged	Charge battery.
	Battery defective internally	Fit new battery.
	Battery terminal leads loose or earth lead not securely attached to body	Check and tighten leads.
	Loose or broken connections in starter motor circuit	Check all connections and tighten any that are loose .
	Starter motor switch or solenoid faulty	Test and renew faulty components with new.
Electricity at starter motor: faulty motor	Starter brushes badly worn, sticking, or brush wires loose	Examine brushes, renew as necessary, tighten brush wires.
	Commutator dirty, worn, or burnt	Clean commutator, recut if badly burnt.
	Starter motor armature faulty	Overhaul starter motor, fit new armature.
	Field coils earthed	Overhaul starter motor.
Starter motor turns engine very slowly		
Electrical defects	Battery in discharged condition	Charge battery.
	Starter brushes badly worn, sticking, or brush wires loose	Examine brushes, renew as necessary, tighten brush wires.
	Loose wires in starter motor circuit	Check wiring and tighten as necessary.
Starter motor operates without turning engine		
Free wheel in drive faulty	Seized or stuck	Remove, examine, renew as necessary.
Mechanical damage	Pinion or ring gear teeth broken or worn	Fit new gear ring, and new pinion to starter motor drive.
Starter motor noisy or excessively rough engagement		
Lack of attention or mechanical damage	Pinion or ring gear teeth broken or worn	Fit new ring gear, or new pinion to starter motor drive.
	Starter motor retaining bolts loose	Tighten starter motor securing bolts. Fit new spring washer if necessary.
Battery will not hold charge for more than a few days		
Wear or damage	Battery defective internally	Remove and fit new battery.
	Electrolyte level too low or electrolyte too weak due to leakage.	Top-up electrolyte level to just above plates.
	Drive belt slipping	Check belt for wear, renew if necessary, and tighten.
	Short in lighting circuit causing continual battery drain	Trace and rectify.
	Regulator unit not working correctly	Check setting, clean, and renew if defective.
Alternator shows no charge: Battery runs flat in a few days		
Alternator not charging	Drivebelt loose and slipping, or broken	Check, renew and tighten as necessary.
	Brushes worn, sticking, broken or dirty	Examine, clean, or renew brushes as necessary.
	Brush springs weak or broken	Examine and test. Renew as necessary.
	Slip rings worn	Fit new item or reconditioned alternator.
	Rotor windings faulty	Fit new or reconditioned item or alternator.
	Regulator faulty	Check, renew.
Wipers		
Wiper motor fails to work	Blown fuse	Check and renew fuse if necessary.
	Wire connections loose, disconnected, or broken	Check wiper wiring. Tighten loose connections.
	Brushes badly worn	Remove and fit new brushes.
	Armature worn or faulty	Remove and overhaul and fit replacement armature.
	Field coils faulty	Purchase reconditioned wiper motor.
Wiper motor works very slowly and takes excessive current	Commutator dirty, greasy or burnt	Clean commutator thoroughly.
	Drive linkage bent or unlubricated	Examine drive and straighten out curvature. Lubricate.
	Wiper arm spindle binding or damaged	Remove, overhaul, or fit replacement.
	Armature bearings dry or unaligned	Replace with new bearings correctly aligned.
	Armature badly worn or faulty	Remove, overhaul, or fit replacement armature.

Wiper motor works slowly and takes little current	Brushes badly worn	Remove and fit new brushes.
	Commutator dirty, greasy, or burnt	Clean commutator thoroughly.
	Armature badly worn or faulty	Remove and overhaul armature or fit replacement.
Wiper motor works but wiper blades remain static	Driving linkage disengaged or faulty	Examine and if faulty renew.
	Wiper motor gearbox parts badly worn	Overhaul or fit new wiper motor.

Lights

Lights do not come on	If engine not running, battery discharged	Charge battery.
	Light bulb filament burnt out or bulb broken	Test bulbs in live bulb holder.
	Wire connections loose, disconnected or broken	Check all connections for tightness and wire cable for breaks.
	Light switch faulty	Bypass light switch to ascertain if a fault is in switch and fit new switch as appropriate.
Lights come on but fade out	If engine not running, battery discharging	Push start car, and charge battery.
Lights give very poor illumination	Lamp glasses dry	Clean glasses.
	Reflector tarnished or dirty	Fit new light unit.
	Lamps badly out of adjustment	Adjust lamps correctly.
	Incorrect bulb with too low wattage fitted	Remove bulb and renew with correct grade.
	Existing bulb old and badly discoloured	Renew bulbs.
	Electrical wiring too thin not allowing full current to pass	Rewire lighting system

Wiring diagrams - overleaf

(See Chapter 13 for later models)

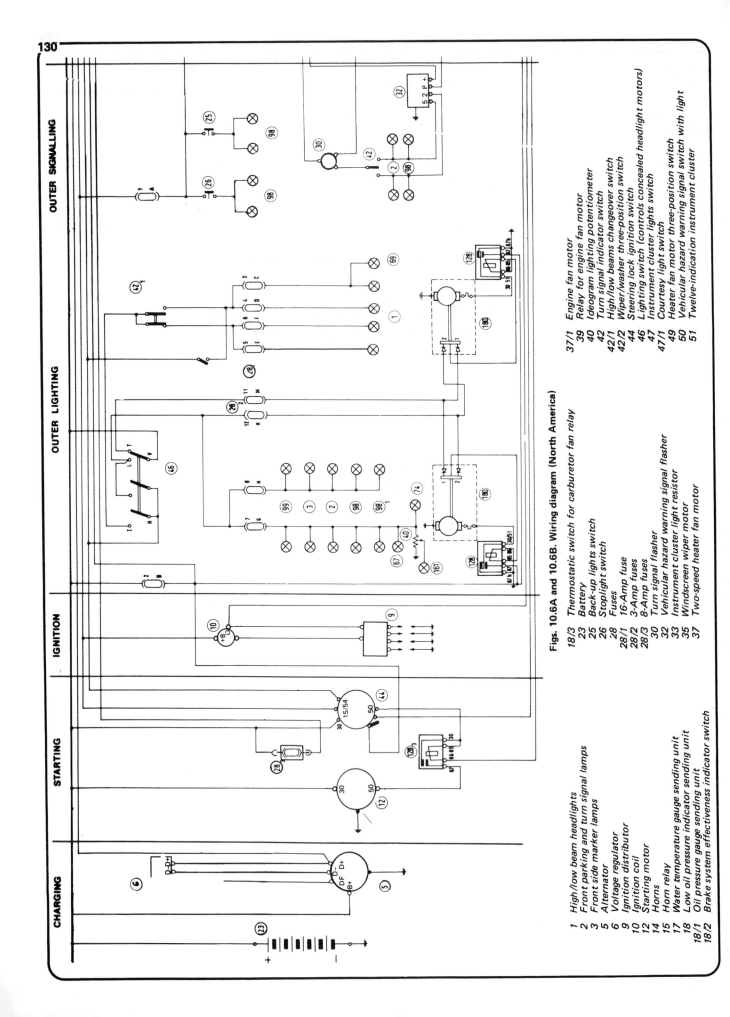

Figs. 10.6A and 10.6B. Wiring diagram (North America)

1   High/low beam headlights
2   Front parking and turn signal lamps
3   Front side marker lamps
5   Alternator
6   Voltage regulator
9   Ignition distributor
10 Ignition coil
12 Starting motor
14 Horns
15 Horn relay
17 Water temperature gauge sending unit
18 Low oil pressure indicator sending unit
18/1 Oil pressure gauge sending unit
18/2 Brake system effectiveness indicator switch

18/3 Thermostatic switch for carburetor fan relay
23 Battery
25 Back-up lights switch
26 Stoplight switch
28 Fuses
28/1 16-Amp fuse
28/2 3-Amp fuses
28/3 8-Amp fuses
30 Turn signal flasher
32 Vehicular hazard warning signal flasher
33 Instrument cluster light resistor
35 Windscreen wiper motor
37 Two-speed heater fan motor

37/1 Engine fan motor
39 Relay for engine fan motor
40 Ideogram lighting potentiometer
42 Turn signal indicator switch
42/1 High/low beams changeover switch
42/2 Wiper/washer three-position switch
44 Steering lock ignition switch
46 Lighting switch (controls concealed headlight motors)
47 Instrument cluster lights switch
47/1 Courtesy light switch
49 Heater fan motor three-position switch
50 Vehicular hazard warning signal switch with light
51 Twelve-indication instrument cluster

OUTER SIGNALLING

OUTER LIGHTING

IGNITION

STARTING

CHARGING

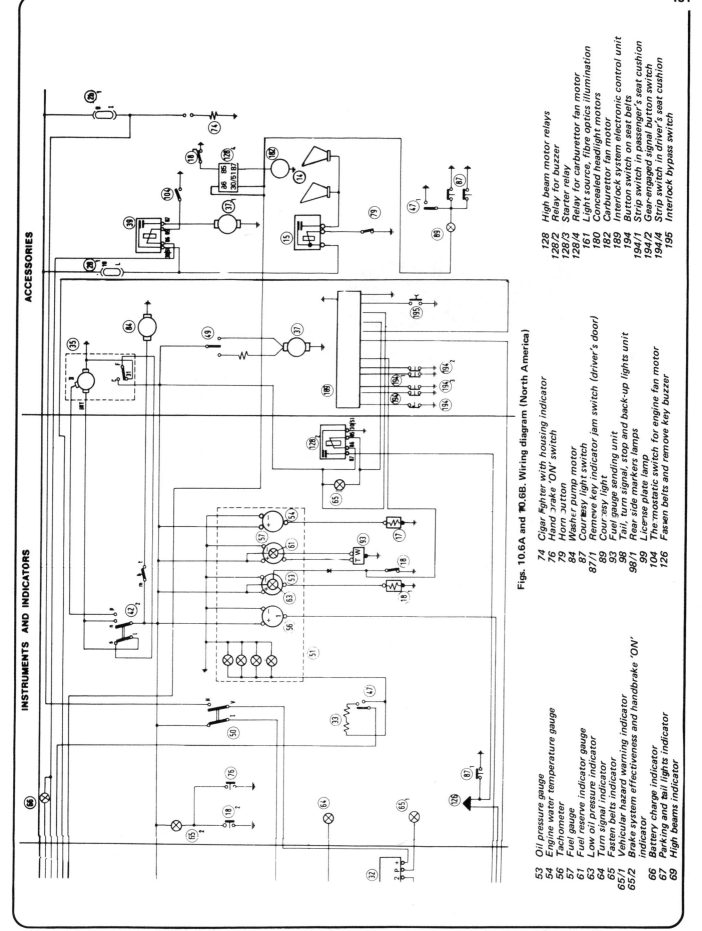

Figs. 10.6A and 10.6B. Wiring diagram (North America)

53 Oil pressure gauge
54 Engine water temperature gauge
56 Tachometer
57 Fuel gauge
61 Fuel reserve indicator gauge
63 Low oil pressure indicator
64 Turn signal indicator
65 Fasten belts indicator
65/1 Vehicular hazard warning indicator
65/2 Brake system effectiveness and handbrake 'ON' indicator
66 Battery charge indicator
67 Parking and tail lights indicator
69 High beams indicator

74 Cigar lighter with housing indicator
76 Hand brake 'ON' switch
79 Horn button
84 Washer pump motor
87 Courtesy light switch
87/1 Remove key indicator jam switch (driver's door)
89 Courtesy light
93 Fuel gauge sending unit
98 Tail, turn signal, stop and back-up lights unit
98/1 Rear side markers lamps
99 License plate lamp
104 Thermostatic switch for engine fan motor
126 Fasten belts and remove key buzzer

128 High beam motor relays
128/2 Relay for buzzer
128/3 Starter relay
128/4 Relay for carburettor fan motor
161 Light source, fibre optics illumination
180 Concealed headlight motors
182 Carburettor fan motor
189 Interlock system electronic control unit
194 Button switch on seat belts
194/1 Strip switch in passenger's seat cushion
194/2 Gear-engaged signal button switch
194/4 Strip switch in driver's seat cushion
195 Interlock bypass switch

ACCESSORIES

INSTRUMENTS AND INDICATORS

Continued on page 133

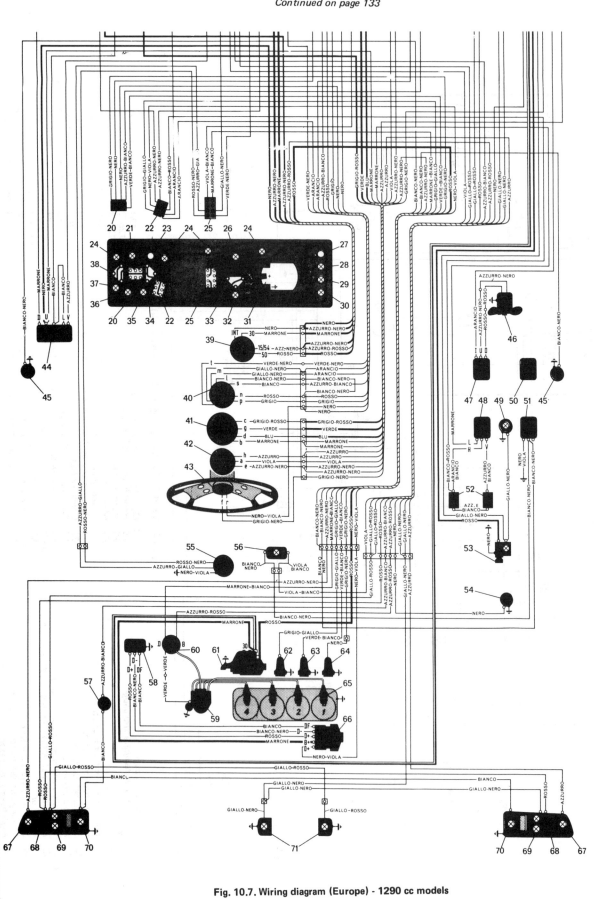

Fig. 10.7. Wiring diagram (Europe) - 1290 cc models

w/l = Warning light
w/b = Wedge base

1 Front direction indicators (21 W, spherical)
2 Side lights (5W, spherical)
3 Concealed headlamps (45/40W, spherical, double filament)
4 Headlamp motor relay
5 Radiator fan relay
6 Horns
7 Radiator fan motor
8 Radiator fan thermostatic switch
9 Horn relay
10 Headlamp drive motors
11 Repeater lights (4W, tubular)
12 Headlamp change-over relay
13 Fuse unit
14 Screen washer pump
15 Wiper motor
16 Direction indicator flasher
17 Stop light switch
18 Handbrake warning flasher
19 Battery
20 Connector
21 Handbrake w/l (1.2W, w/b)
22 Connector
23 Spare w/l socket
24 Panel lights (3W, w/b)
25 Connector
26 Direction indicator w/l (1.2W, w/b)
27 Spare w/l socket
28 Hazard w/l (where mandatory)
29 Side light w/l (1.2W, w/b)
30 Main beam w/l (1.2W, w/b)
31 Electronic tachometer
32 Fuel w/l (1.2W, w/b)
33 Fuel gauge
34 Water temperature gauge

35 Ignition w/l (1.2W, w/b)
36 Heated backlight w/l (optional) (1.2W, w/b)
37 Oil pressure w/l (12W, w/b)
38 Oil pressure gauge
39 Ignition switch
40 Wiper/washer switch
41 Headlamp switch
42 Direction indicator switch
43 Horn switch
44 Lighting/headlamp raise switch
45 Door switches
46 Heater fan motor
47 Heater fan switch
48 Panel light switch
49 Heater control light bulb (3W, tubular)
50 Spare switch
51 Courtesy light switch
52 Panel light ballast resistors
53 Cigar lighter/lamp (4W, tubular)
54 Handbrake warning transmitter
55 Fuel transmitter
56 Courtesy light (5W, festoon)
57 Reversing light switch
58 Voltage regulator
59 Distributor
60 Ignition coil
61 Starter
62 Oil pressure warning transmitter
63 Water temperature transmitter
64 Oil pressure transmitter
65 Spark plugs
66 Alternator
67 Rear direction indicators (21W, spherical)
68 Rear lights (5W, spherical)
69 Stop lights (21W, spherical)
70 Reversing lights (21W, spherical)
71 Number plate lights (5W, spherical)

Cable Colour Code

Arancio	=	Amber	Giallo	=	Yellow	Rosa	=	Pink
Azzurro	=	Light blue	Grigio	=	Grey	Rosso	=	Red
Bianco	=	White	Marrone	=	Brown	Verde	=	Green
Blu	=	Dark blue	Nero	=	Black	Viola	=	Mauve

Note: Always make sure that the new bulbs are identical with those they replace. Remember that bulbs of insufficient rating give poor lighting whereas overrated bulbs will draw excessive current.

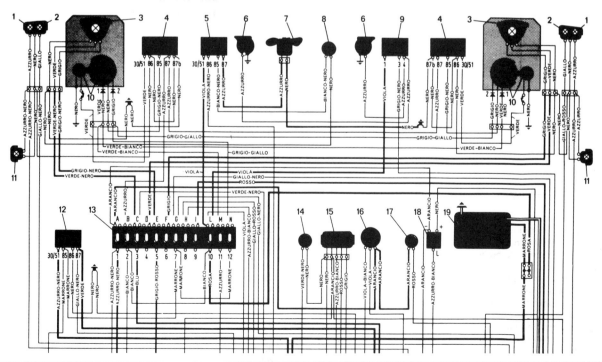

Chapter 11 Suspension and wheels

For modifications, and information applicable to later models, see Supplement at end of manual

Contents

Specifications

Front suspension

Type	MacPherson strut
Length of coil springs:	
Class 'A' (yellow) under load of 474 lbs (215 kg)	More than 6.693 in (170 mm)
Class 'B' (green) under load of 474 lbs (215 kg)	6.693 in (170 mm) or less
Minimum load to achieve above length	441 lb (200 kg)
Camber angle (front wheels) *	$-0^o\,30' \pm 30'$
Toe-in (front wheels) *	0.079 to 0.236 in (2 to 6 mm)

Rear suspension

Type	MacPherson strut
Length of coil springs:	
Class 'A' (yellow) under load of 562 lb (255 kg)	More than 7.874 in (200 mm)
Class 'B' (green) under load of 562 lb (255 kg)	7.874 in (200 mm) or less
Minimum load to achieve above length	518 lb (235 kg)
Camber angle (rear wheels) *:	
Four-speed models	$-1^o\,40' \pm 30'$
Five-speed models	$-1^o\,15' \pm 30'$
Toe-in (rear wheels) *:	
Four-speed models	+0.158 to 0.315 in (4 to 8 mm)
Five-speed models	+0.197 to 0.354 in (5 to 9 mm)
Toe-in adjustment (rear wheels)	By threaded sleeves on tie-rods

* Unladen

Wheels

Type	Pressed disc
Size	4½J x 13 in or 5J x 13 in

Tyres

	Four-speed	Five-speed
Type and size	Radial ply, 145HR - 13	Radial ply, 165/70 SR 13
Tyre pressures:		
Front	26 psi (1.8 kg/Sq. cm)	27 psi (1.9 kg/sq cm)
Rear	28 psi (2 kg/Sq. cm)	30 psi (2.1 kg/sq cm)

Torque wrench settings

	lb f ft	kg f m
Hub nuts	101	14
Steering knuckle balljoint nut	58	8
Nut, strut to top mounting bracket	50.6	7
Nut, strut to control arm	50.6	7
Strut top mounting nuts to body	7.2	1
Wheel stud	50.6	7
Nut, front control arm to body	29	4
Strut mounting to knuckle	43.4	6
Nut, tie-rod to control arm bolt	50.6	7
Nut, tie-rod sleeve clamp bolt	14.4	2
Rear control arm pivot pin nut	72.3	10
Rear control arm balljoint to filler	72.3	10
Hub bearing ring nut	43.4	6
Roadwheel bolt	63	9

1 General description

1   The suspension is independent all round, having MacPherson type struts (integrated coil spring and hydraulic shock absorber) and lower control arms on all wheels.
2   There are forward facing radius arms on the front suspension to give more exact control of the steering geometry. The rear suspension has adjustable tie-rods which adds to the stability of the suspension and provides a means of adjusting the toe-in of the rear wheels.
3   The front hubs are carried in a bearing in the front steering knuckles. The rear suspension pillars carry the rear hubs which are driven through the constant velocity joint of the driveshafts.

2 Front and rear suspension - checking

1   Checking the suspension is part of the 6,000 mile (10,000 km) task.
2   Inspect the outside of the struts for leaks, and check their operation by bouncing.
3   With the car parked on level ground, check that it sits level from left to right, and does not appear to be drooping at one end, particularly down at the back.
4   Examine all the rubber bushes of the suspension arms and rear spring mountings. The rubber should be firm, not softened by oil or cracked by weathering. The pin pivoted in the bush should be held

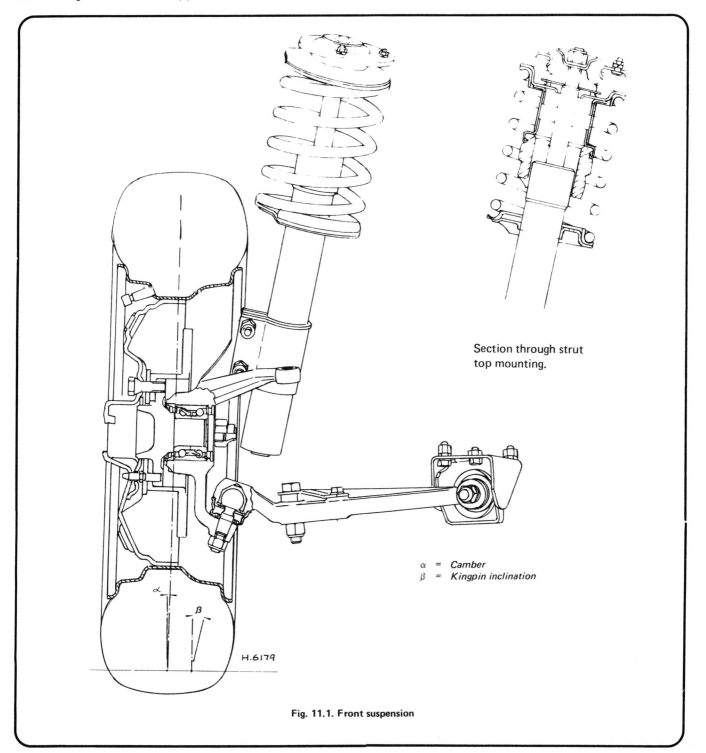

Section through strut top mounting.

α = Camber
β = Kingpin inclination

H.6179

Fig. 11.1. Front suspension

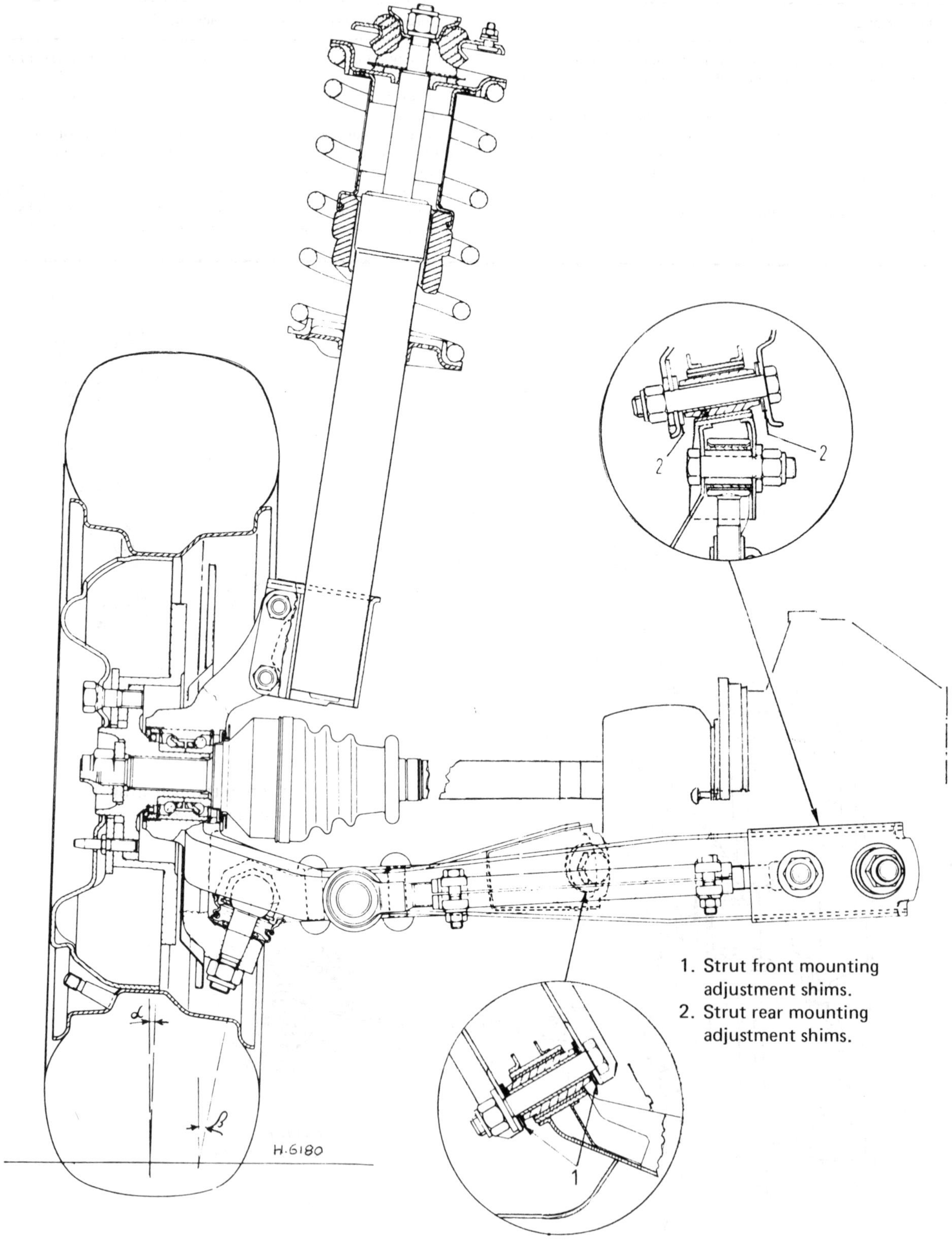
2
2
1
H.6180
1. Strut front mounting adjustment shims.
2. Strut rear mounting adjustment shims.

Fig. 11.2. Rear suspension

α = Camber
β = Kingpin inclination

central, and not able to make metal to metal contact.

5   Check the outside of the springs. If rusting, they should be sprayed with oil.

6   Check the tightness of all nuts, particularly those holding the front suspension strut to the steering knuckle, and the rear strut to the pillar.

7   Grip the top of each wheel, in turn, and rock vigorously. Any looseness in the bearings, or the suspension can be felt, or failed rubber bushes giving metal to metal contact can be heard.

8   Free wheel slowly with the engine switched off, and listen for unusual noises.

3   Front suspension strut - removal and refitting

1   Jack-up the front of the car and support it securely on axle stands or wooden blocks. Remove the front wheels.

2   If the front strut is to be removed without dismantling anything else, unscrew the two bolts which attach the strut to the steering knuckle and then remove the three upper mounting nuts accessible in the front luggage compartment, and lift out the strut. Do not release the piston rod (centre) nut.

3   Refitting is the reverse of the removal sequence. Tighten the top mounting nuts to 7.5 lb f ft (1 kg f m) and the bottom attaching bolts to 43 lb f ft (6 kg f m).

4   Front spring or shock absorber - renewal

1   The front suspension strut consists of a coil spring and shock absorber. When removed from the car, the shock absorber is held fully extended by the spring.

2   To release the spring the load must be taken off the shock absorber, then, the nut can be removed from the shock absorber's central stem, and the spring allowed to expand. This must be done using a special spring compressor. Without the use of one of these tools, the nut must not be taken off the shock absorber. Many makes of cars have MacPherson strut suspension, so if you are not near a FIAT agent where this can be done, some other local garage should be able to release the spring.

3   The most likely reason for needing to separate the two will be to renew the shock absorber, as this has a shorter life than the spring. Even so, the spring should be carefully examined when free, as should all the component parts of the top bush and the spring seat at the bottom.

4   Springs come in two grades of length. It will usually be found that the front one on the driver's side will have settled more than the other. This one alone could be renewed by a short one, (class B), which will then match the old one on the passenger side. The springs are marked with paint on the outside of the coils at their centre, yellow for 'class A' and green for 'class B'. On the rear suspension springs having the same colour code should be used.

5   Front suspension - removal and refitting

1   Jack-up the front of the car and support it on axle stands or wooden blocks. Remove the roadwheels.

2   Remove the brake caliper mounting bolts and lift the brake caliper off the disc and the caliper up with cord, so that it does not hang from the brake hose.

3   Disconnect the trackrod from the steering arm, as described in Chapter 9, Section 3.

4   Remove the bolts and plate attaching the radius arm to the control arm and the bolt securing the control arm to the mounting bracket on the body.

5   Disconnect the strut at its top mounting by removing the three nuts, accessible from inside the luggage compartment, and lower the suspension out of the car.

6   If the hub bearing has to be renewed, see Section 9.

7   Refitting is the reverse of the removal sequence. When fitting the suspension do not fully tighten the control arm and radius arm attachment, as these bolts and nuts must be tightened with the car loaded. Tighten the strut top mounting nuts to 7.5 lb f ft (1 kg f m).

8   Lower the car to the ground and with the car laden tighten nuts '1',

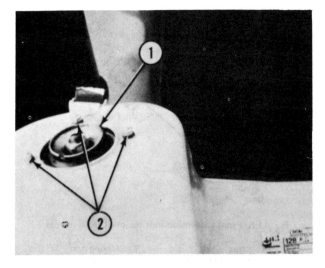

Fig. 11.3. Strut top attachment in the front luggage compartment

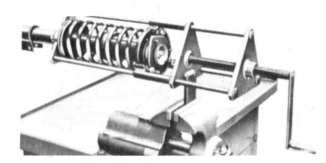

Fig. 11.4. Using FIAT tool A74241 to remove the spring from the strut

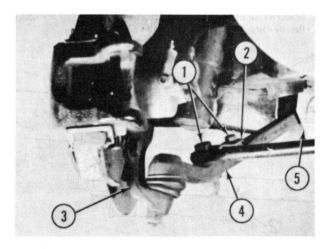

Fig. 11.5. Removing the front suspension

1   Bolts
2   Plate
3   Steering knuckle

4   Track control arm
5   Bracket

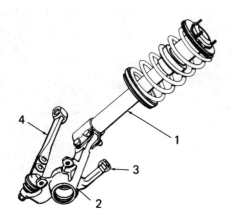

Fig. 11.6. Front suspension unit removed from the car

1 Strut   3 Steering arm
2 Steering knuckle   4 Control arm

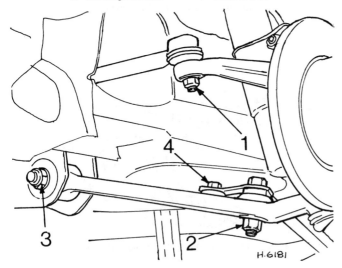

**Fig. 11.7. Tighten the suspension nuts and bolt with the car loaded
(2 persons + 44 lbs [20 kg])**

1 Trackrod balljoint nut   3 Track control arm inner pivot nut
2 Radius rod bolt   4 Radius rod nut

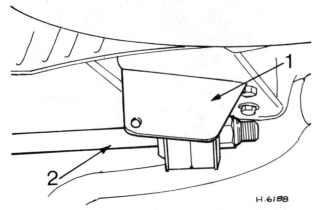

**Fig. 11.8. When removing radius arms always note the number of
shims fitted**

1 Support   2 Radius arm

'2' and '3' and bolt '4' (refer to Fig. 11.7.), to a torque of:

(1)   *58 lb f ft (8 kg f m)*
(2)   *51 lb f ft (7 kg f m)*
(3)   *29 lb f ft (4 kg f m)*
(4)   *29 lb f ft (4 kg f m)*

6 Camber and caster of front wheels - general

1   It is not practical for the owner to check front wheel camber.
Camber (negative) is the amount the wheel slopes inwards from
bottom to top. It is not adjustable, and does not cause abnormal tyre
wear. It will normally only be upset by accident damage. Re-alignment
of the body and suspension mounting points must then be done by a
garage with the jigs, measuring equipment, and experience for such
work.
2   Again it is not practical for the owner to do anything about
caster. Caster is the arrangement whereby the ground contact point of
the wheel is behind its centre of pivot for steering, so the wheel is
self-centering. Caster is adjusted by removing or adding shims between
the radius arms and their supports. Remove shims to increase caster.
The adjustment is easily made, but the difficulty is the measurement
of the angle which requires special equipment. Small variations of
caster do not noticeably affect the handling of the car and the owner
can limit these by always ensuring that the same shims are refitted
after each removal of the radius arms. If the car has been in an
accident or the front suspension subjected to excessive shock, the
caster should be checked by a FIAT agent with the appropriate
equipment.

7 Front control arm bush - renewal

1   The rubber bushes at the inner end of the suspension control arm
should be renewed if they perish or soften, which will show in the way
they curl round at the ends, and the way the arm is not held centrally
on the bolt.
2   The metal spacer and end washers are staked in position (See
Fig. 11.10).
3   This staking is done in a power press under a load of 2200 to
2600 lb (1000 to 1200 kg). Unless this is done correctly the bush as a
whole will be too long, and it will prove difficult, if not impossible, to
fit it into its mounting. It is recommended that the job of fitting new
bushes should be given to your FIAT agent.
4   If the rubber bushing needs renewing, the balljoint at the outer end
of the arm must be suspect, and it may well be worth renewing the
complete arm. The complete assembly of arm with balljoint and
bushes is supplied as a spare. The balljoint cannot be renewed
separately. Remove the balljoint from the steering knuckle using the
method described in Chapter 9, Section 3.

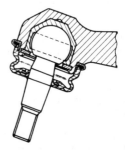
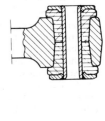

**Fig. 11.9. Cross-sectional view of front control arm balljoint and
rubber bush**

8 Front radius arm - removal, inspection and refitting

1 Remove the bolt attaching the radius arm to the control arm.
2 Remove the nut holding the arm in the support bracket and with-draw the arm. Note the number of shims, if fitted, and retain them for refitting.
3 Inspect the arm for distortions. If the distortion is minor, straighten the arm. If badly distorted renew the arm. Inspect the rubber pad and ring for wear and deterioration (see Fig. 11.12).
4 When refitting the arm fit the same shims as were removed.

9 Front hub bearings - renewal

1 The hub bearings are sealed for life. They are a press fit in the hubs. The force needed to remove them is such that this should only be done when they are to be renewed.
2 Dismantle the suspension, as described in Section 5 to remove the steering knuckle from the car.
3 Remove the brake disc by undoing the attaching bolts.
4 Remove the nut holding the hub to the steering knuckle and drive out the hub as shown in Fig. 11.13. The hub is a tight fit and may have rusted in. A good soak in penetrating oil will help. It may be necessary to use a press to remove the hub, if so, the steering knuckle must be well supported while the hub is pressed from the inside. The mandrel must only rest on the hub, not the bearing inner race. The help of a FIAT agent is recommended as they have the special tools for this.
5 Once the hub is out, the bearing ring nut can be removed. This is screwed in and locked in position by staking. Relieve the staking and remove the ring nut. Access to a press will be necessary to remove the bearing.
6 Clean off the knuckle bearing housing and the hub.
7 Press in the new bearing. Fit a new bearing ring nut and tighten it to 43 lb f ft (6 kg f m). Lock the ring nut by staking.
8 Using a press, fit the hub in the steering knuckle and tighten the retaining nut to 101 lb f ft (14 kg f m). Stake the nut to lock it as shown in Fig. 11.14.

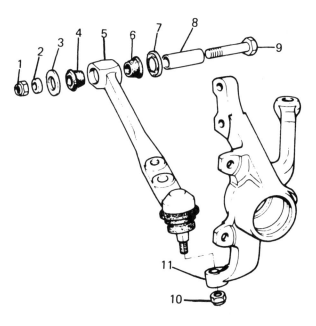

Fig. 11.10. Exploded view of front track control arm

1	Nut	7	Washer
2	Washer	8	Spacer
3	Washer	9	Bolt
4	Rubber bushing	10	Nut
5	Control arm	11	Steering knuckle
6	Rubber bushing		

Fig. 11.11. Front suspension radius arm attachment points

1	Bolt	3	Support	5	Steering knuckle
2	Plate	4	Control arm	6	Radius arm

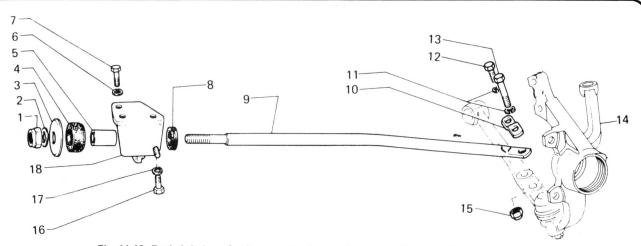

Fig. 11.12. Exploded view of radius arm attachments to body and front track control arm

1	Nut	6	Lockwasher	11	Lockwasher	16	Bolt
2	Washer	7	Bolt	12	Bolt	17	Washer
3	Cup	8	Rubber ring	13	Bolt	18	Support
4	Rubber pad	9	Radius arm	14	Knuckle		
5	Spacer	10	Lockplate	15	Nut		

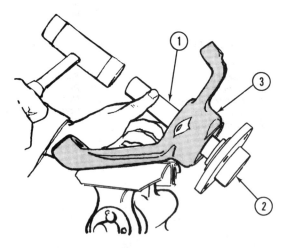

Fig. 11.13. Driving the hub out of the steering knuckle

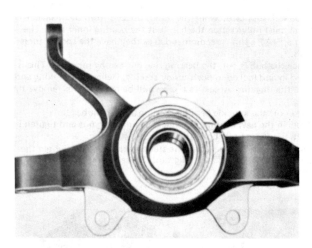

Fig. 11.14. Lock the front hub bearing ring nut by staking

1	Mandrel	2	Hub	3	Steering knuckle

Fig. 11.15. Rear suspension control arm attachment points

1	Bolt	3	Control arm	5	Bracket	6	Hub assembly
2	Bracket	4	Balljoint				

10 Rear suspension strut - removal and refitting

The rear strut removal and refitting procedure is the same as described for the front strut, see Section 3. Renewal of the spring or shock absorber is the same procedure as for the front suspension, see Section 4.

11 Rear suspension - removal and refitting

1   Jack-up the rear of the car and support it on axle stands or wooden blocks . Remove the rear wheels.
2   Remove the brake caliper, as described in Chapter 8, and tie it up with cord so that it does not hang on the brake hose.
3   Remove the exhaust system, as described in Chapter 2.
4   Remove the bolt which attaches the control arm to the bracket at the front of the suspension. Note the number of shims, and position, between the control arm and the bracket. Retain the shims so that they can be refitted in the same position.
5   Remove the bolt attaching the control arm to the bracket at the rear of the suspension. Again note the number of shims and retain them for refitting in the same position.
6   Remove the hub nut. Remove the three nuts securing the strut at its top mounting on the wing valance, accessible in the engine compartment.
7   Slide the suspension assembly off the driveshaft constant velocity joint. Take care that the driveshaft is not pulled out of the differential. Secure the driveshaft to retain it in the differential.
8   Refitting is the reverse of the removal sequence. Ensure that the shims on the control arms are refitted in the same position they were in before removal. Always use a new hub nut and tighten it to 101 lb f ft (14 kg f m). Stake the nut to lock it.
9   Refit the exhaust system, as described in Chapter 2, fit roadwheels and lower the car. Torque tighten the shock absorber mounting nuts to 43 lb f ft (6 kg f m) and the control arm attaching bolts to 72 lb f ft (10 kg f m), with the car loaded.

12 Rear wheel alignment - general

1   Special equipment is required to check the camber. This should be left to your FIAT agent.
2   Check the toe-in of the rear wheels in the same way as for the front wheels: refer to Chapter 9, Section 13. To adjust, slacken the trackrods. The toe-in is given in the specifications. Turn the sleeves on both sides in the same direction and by the same amount.
3   Tighten the adjusting sleeve clamp bolts.

13 Rear suspension control arm - inspection and servicing

1   Inspect the bushes for wear, damage or deterioration and renew them as necessary.
2   Examine the main control arm balljoint boot for damage. If it shows signs of cracking or deterioration it must be renewed.
3   Check the condition of the balljoint. If it is worn or damaged the complete control arm must be renewed.
4   Check the trackrod balljoint for wear.

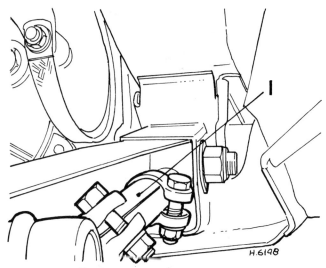

Fig. 11.16. Rear suspension trackrod

1   Adjusting sleeve

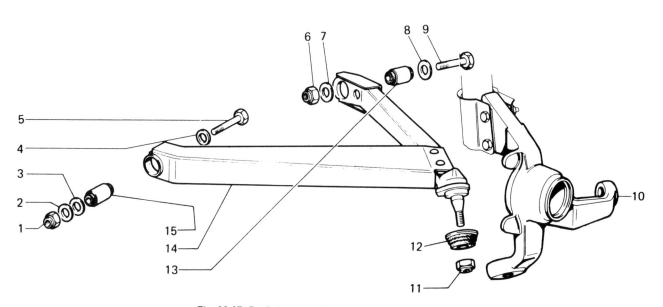

Fig. 11.17. Exploded view of rear suspension control arm

1 Nut	5 Bolt	9 Bolt	13 Bush
2 Washer	6 Nut	10 Hub assembly	14 Control arm
3 Washer	7 Washer	11 Nut	15 Bush
4 Washer	8 Washer	12 Boot	

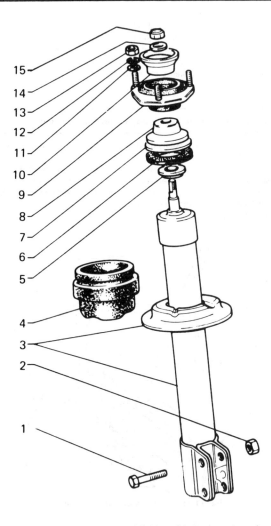

Fig. 11.18. Front strut attachments (spring not shown)

1	Bolt	9	Pad
2	Nut	10	Cup
3	Shock absorber	11	Washer
4	Rubber pad	12	Lockwasher
5	Thrust plate	13	Nut
6	Rubber ring	14	Washer
7	Washer	15	Nut
8	Spacer		

5   If the control arm or trackrod balljoints must be disconnected due to evidence of wear, use the method described in Chapter 9, Section 3. When refitting, tighten all nuts and bolts to the specified torque.

14 Rear hub bearing - removal and refitting

Removal and refitting of the hub bearing is the same procedure as described for the front hub bearing, see Section 9.

15 Shock absorbers - checking

1   Failure comes on gradually, so sometimes loss of damping is not noticed in normal driving.
2   Leaks of fluid from the shock absorber are a sure sign of failure.
3   Loss of performance can be checked by bouncing the car.
4   Bounce vigorously on one end of the car, timing the bouncing to be in phase with the car's spring bounce. When a good movement has been set going, release the car: stop bouncing. It should go on once more only past the normal position; the next time stopping at the static height.
5   Do not renew single shock absorbers unless the failure is an unusual one after a short mileage. Renew them as pairs, front or rear.
6   The removal of the suspension struts is described in Section 3, and the separation of the spring and shock absorber is described in Section 4.
7   It is probable that the FIAT agent will stock the shock absorber in its outer casing. But the inside working parts are serviced as a sub-assembly. To extract them from the casing, the shock absorber should be extended. Then the gland fitting where the rod enters the casing should be unscrewed. Cleanliness is most important.

16 Wheels and tyres - general

1   Wheels can get damaged if a kerb is struck. During routine checks of the suspension, spin the wheels round and check that they are not out of true. If a wheel is suspect have it checked for balance and true running at the earliest opportunity.
2   Tyres are very important for safety. Never allow the tread to get so worn that it is on the legal limit, as they can be dangerous in the wet or at high speeds. Always maintain the tyres at the correct pressure to ensure that you get the maximum wear out of them, and to maintain good steering and braking characteristics.
3   The car is designed for radial tyres, therefore crossply tyre should not be used.
4   Examine the tyres regularly for cracks, bulges and excessive and uneven tyre wear. Tyres with cracks or bulges on the walls should be renewed. If the tyre wear is uneven, and the pressures have been correctly maintained, the wheel alignment should be checked immediately, a wheel out of alignment can ruin a tyre in a very short mileage.

17 Fault diagnosis - suspension

Symptom	Reason/s	Remedy
Uneven tyre wear	Faulty front or rear wheel geometry	Check and adjust as necessary.
	Faulty shock absorbers, worn balljoints	Check and renew as necessary.
	Wrong tyre pressures	Check and adjust as necessary.
Car sags at one end or corner	Weak springs	Check and renew as necessary.
Car pitches and bounces when cornering or on rough road surfaces: handling generally poor	Worn shock absorbers	Check and renew as necessary.
Car rolls and lurches during cornering	Worn shock absorbers and/or weak springs	Check and renew as necessary.

Chapter 12 Bodywork and fittings

For modifications, and information applicable to later models, see Supplement at end of manual

Contents

1 General description

1 The bodyframe is fabricated from steel pressings welded together and has reinforced longitudinal stress members to give added strength. The two doors are specially strengthened to lessen the effect of side impact and roll-over safety is provided by the roll-over bar built into the structure behind the seats.

2 The doors have two safety glass panes, a fixed quarter window and a drop window with winding mechanism. The doors have outside key handles and inside locking devices.

3 There are two luggage compartments, a large one at the front and a smaller one at the rear, behind the engine. The spare wheel is stowed in a compartment behind the driving seat.

4 The detachable fibreglass roof is stowed in the front luggage compartment when it is not in use.

2 Maintenance - bodywork and underframe

The general condition of a vehicle's bodywork is the one thing that significantly affects its value. Maintenance is easy but needs to be regular. Neglect, particularly after minor damage, can lead quickly to further deterioration and costly repair bills. It is important also to keep watch on those parts of the vehicle not immediately visible, for instance the underside, inside all the wheel arches and the lower part of the engine compartment.

The basic maintenance routine for the bodywork is washing – preferably with a lot of water, from a hose. This will remove all the loose solids which may have stuck to the vehicle. It is important to flush these off in such a way as to prevent grit from scratching the finish. The wheel arches and underframe need washing in the same way to remove any accumulated mud which will retain moisture and tend to encourage rust. Paradoxically enough, the best time to clean the underframe and wheel arches is in wet weather when the mud is thoroughly wet and soft. In very wet weather the underframe is usually cleaned of large accumulations automatically and this is a good time for inspection.

Periodically, except on vehicles with a wax-based underbody protective coating, it is a good idea to have the whole of the underframe of the vehicle steam cleaned, engine compartment included, so that a thorough inspection can be carried out to see what minor repairs and renovations are necessary. Steam cleaning is available at many garages and is necessary for removal of the accumulation of oily grime which sometimes is allowed to become thick in certain areas. If steam cleaning

facilities are not available, there are one or two excellent grease solvents available, such as Holts Engine Cleaner or Holts Foambrite, which can be brush applied. The dirt can then be simply hosed off. Note that these methods should not be used on vehicles with wax-based underbody protective coating or the coating will be removed. Such vehicles should be inspected annually, preferably just prior to winter, when the underbody should be washed down and any damage to the wax coating repaired using Holts Undershield. Ideally, a completely fresh coat should be applied. It would also be worth considering the use of such wax-based protection for injection into door panels, sills, box sections, etc, as an additional safeguard against rust damage where such protection is not provided by the vehicle manufacturer.

After washing paintwork, wipe off with a chamois leather to give an unspotted clear finish. A coat of clear protective wax polish, like the many excellent Turtle Wax polishes, will give added protection against chemical pollutants in the air. If the paintwork sheen has dulled or oxidised, use a cleaner/polisher combination such as Turtle Extra to restore the brilliance of the shine. This requires a little effort, but such dulling is usually caused because regular washing has been neglected. Care needs to be taken with metallic paintwork, as special non-abrasive cleaner/polisher is required to avoid damage to the finish. Always check that the door and ventilator opening drain holes and pipes are completely clear so that water can be drained out. Bright work should be treated in the same way as paint work. Windscreens and windows can be kept clear of the smeary film which often appears by the use of a proprietary glass cleaner like Holts Mixra. Never use any form of wax or other body or chromium polish on glass.

3 Maintenance - upholstery and carpets

Mats and carpets should be brushed or vacuum cleaned regularly to keep them free of grit. If they are badly stained remove them from the vehicle for scrubbing or sponging and make quite sure they are dry before refitting. Seats and interior trim panels can be kept clean by wiping with a damp cloth and Turtle Wax Carisma. If they do become stained (which can be more apparent on light coloured upholstery) use a little liquid detergent and a soft nail brush to scour the grime out of the grain of the material. Do not forget to keep the headlining clean

mm.	490	750	965	1174	1335	1343	1570	2202	3900
in.	19.3	29.5	38.0	46.1	52.5	52.9	61.8	86.7	153.5

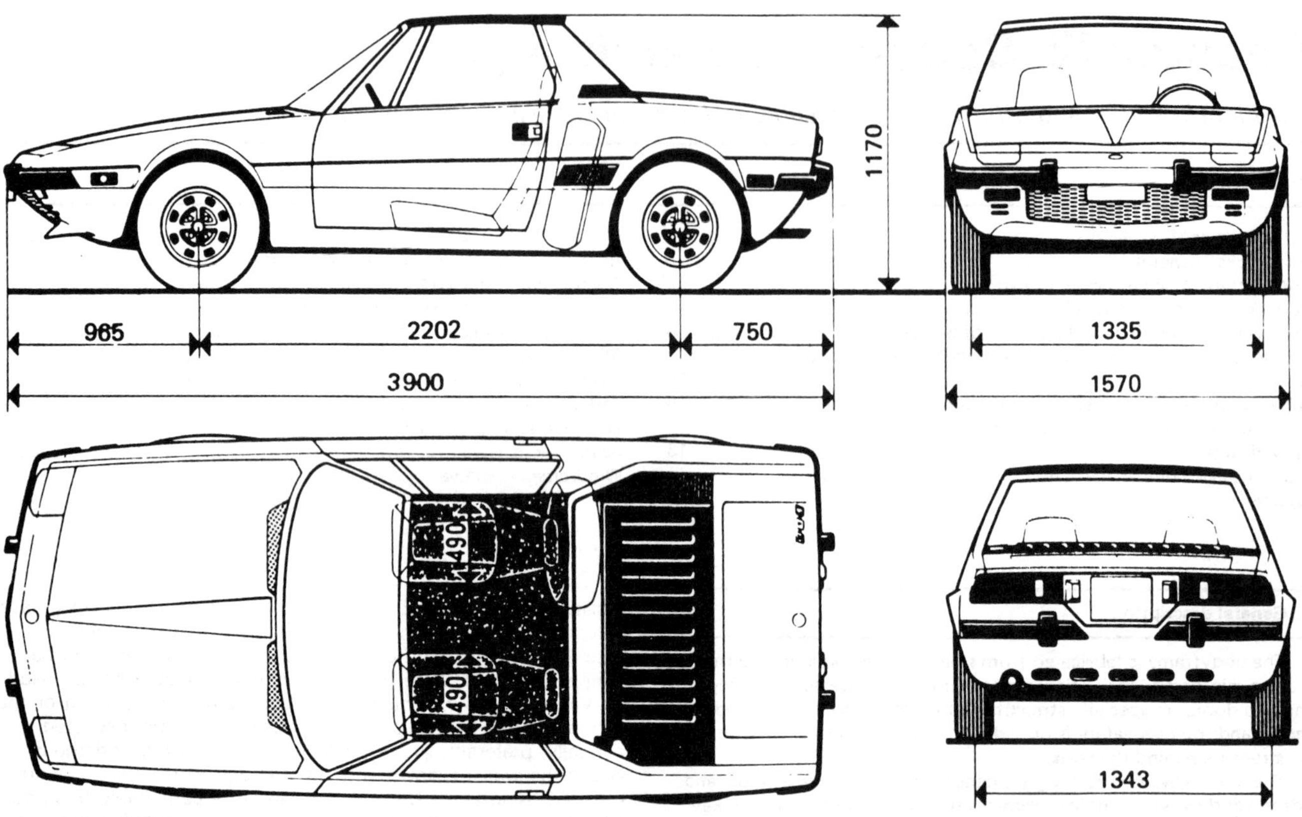

Fig. 12.1. Dimensions (metric) pre 1979 models - see conversion table above

in the same way as the upholstery. When using liquid cleaners inside the vehicle do not over-wet the surfaces being cleaned. Excessive damp could get into the seams and padded interior causing stains, offensive odours or even rot. If the inside of the vehicle gets wet accidentally it is worthwhile taking some trouble to dry it out properly, particularly where carpets are involved. *Do not leave oil or electric heaters inside the vehicle for this purpose.*

4 Minor body damage – repair

The photographic sequences on pages 150 and 151 illustrate the operations detailed in the following sub-sections.
Note: *For more detailed information about bodywork repair, the Haynes Publishing Group publish a book by Lindsay Porter called The Car Bodywork Repair Manual. This incorporates information on such aspects as rust treatment, painting and glass fibre repairs, as well as details on more ambitious repairs involving welding and panel beating.*

Repair of minor scratches in bodywork
If the scratch is very superficial, and does not penetrate to the metal of the bodywork, repair is very simple. Lightly rub the area of the scratch with a paintwork renovator like Turtle Wax New Color Back, or a very fine cutting paste like Holts Body + Plus Rubbing Compound to remove loose paint from the scratch and to clear the surrounding bodywork of wax polish. Rinse the area with clean water.

Apply touch-up paint, such as Holts Dupli-Color Color Touch or a paint film like Holts Autofilm, to the scratch using a fine paint brush; continue to apply fine layers of paint until the surface of the paint in the scratch is level with the surrounding paintwork. Allow the new paint at least two weeks to harden:

then blend it into the surrounding paintwork by rubbing the scratch area with a paintwork renovator or a very fine cutting paste, such as Holts Body + Plus Rubbing Compound or Turtle Wax New Color Back. Finally, apply wax polish from one of the Turtle Wax range of wax polishes.

Where the scratch has penetrated right through to the metal of the bodywork, causing the metal to rust, a different repair technique is required. Remove any loose rust from the bottom of the scratch with a penknife, then apply rust inhibiting paint, such as Turtle Wax Rust Master, to prevent the formation of rust in the future. Using a rubber or nylon applicator fill the scratch with bodystopper paste like Holts Body + Plus Knifing Putty. If required, this paste can be mixed with cellulose thinners, such as Holts Body + Plus Cellulose Thinners, to provide a very thin paste which is ideal for filling narrow scratches. Before the stopper-paste in the scratch hardens, wrap a piece of smooth cotton rag around the top of a finger. Dip the finger in cellulose thinners, such as Holts Body + Plus Cellulose Thinners, and then quickly sweep it across the surface of the stopper-paste in the scratch; this will ensure that the surface of the stopper-paste is slightly hollowed. The scratch can now be painted over as described earlier in this Section.

Repair of dents in bodywork
When deep denting of the vehicle's bodywork has taken place, the first task is to pull the dent out, until the affected bodywork almost attains its original shape. There is little point in trying to restore the original shape completely, as the metal in the damaged area will have stretched on impact and cannot be reshaped fully to its original contour. It is better to bring the level of the dent up to a point which is about $\frac{1}{8}$ in (3 mm) below the level of the surrounding bodywork. In cases where the dent is very shallow anyway, it is not worth trying to pull it out at all. If the underside of the dent is accessible, it can be hammered out gently from behind, using a mallet with a wooden or plastic

head. Whilst doing this, hold a suitable block of wood firmly against the outside of the panel to absorb the impact from the hammer blows and thus prevent a large area of the bodywork from being 'belled-out'.

Should the dent be in a section of the bodywork which has a double skin or some other factor making it inaccessible from behind, a different technique is called for. Drill several small holes through the metal inside the area – particulary in the deeper section. Then screw long self-tapping screws into the holes just sufficiently for them to gain a good purchase in the metal. Now the dent can be pulled out by pulling on the protruding heads of the screws with a pair of pliers.

The next stage of the repair is the removal of the paint from the damaged area, and from an inch or so of the surrounding 'sound' bodywork. This is accomplished most easily by using a wire brush or abrasive pad on a power drill, although it can be done just as effectively by hand using sheets of abrasive paper. To complete the preparation for filling, score the surface of the bare metal with a screwdriver or the tang of a file, or alternatively, drill small holes in the affected area. This will provide a really good 'key' for the filler paste.

To complete the repair see the Section on filling and re-spraying.

Repair of rust holes or gashes in bodywork

Remove all paint from the affected area and from an inch or so of the surrounding 'sound' bodywork, using an abrasive pad or a wire brush on a power drill. If these are not available a few sheets of abrasive paper will do the job just as effectively. With the paint removed you will be able to gauge the severity of the corrosion and therefore decide whether to renew the whole panel (if this is possible) or to repair the affected area. New body panels are not as expensive as most people think and it is often quicker and more satisfactory to fit a new panel than to attempt to repair large areas of corrosion.

Remove all fittings from the affected area except those which will act as a guide to the original shape of the damaged bodywork (eg headlamp shells etc). Then, using tin snips or a hacksaw blade, remove all loose metal and any other metal badly affected by corrosion. Hammer the edges of the hole inwards in order to create a slight depression for the filler paste.

Wire brush the affected area to remove the powdery rust from the surface of the remaining metal. Paint the affected area with rust inhibiting paint like Turtle Wax Rust Master; if the back of the rusted area is accessible treat this also.

Before filling can take place it will be necessary to block the hole in some way. This can be achieved by the use of aluminium or plastic mesh, or aluminium tape.

Aluminium or plastic mesh or glass fibre matting, such as the Holts Body + Plus Glass Fibre Matting, is probably the best material to use for a large hole. Cut a piece to the approximate size and shape of the hole to be filled, then position it in the hole so that its edges are below the level of the surrounding bodywork. It can be retained in position by several blobs of filler paste around its periphery.

Aluminium tape should be used for small or very narrow holes. Pull a piece off the roll and trim it to the approximate size and shape required, then pull off the backing paper (if used) and stick the tape over the hole; it can be overlapped if the thickness of one piece is insufficient. Burnish down the edges of the tape with the handle of a screwdriver or similar, to ensure that the tape is securely attached to the metal underneath.

Bodywork repairs – filling and re-spraying

Before using this Section, see the Sections on dent, deep scratch, rust holes and gash repairs.

Many types of bodyfiller are available, but generally speaking those proprietary kits which contain a tin of filler paste and a tube of resin hardener are best for this type of repair, like Holts Body + Plus or Holts No Mix which can be used directly from the tube. A wide, flexible plastic or nylon applicator will be found invaluable for imparting a smooth and well contoured finish to the surface of the filler.

Mix up a little filler on a clean piece of card or board – measure the hardener carefully (follow the maker's instructions on the pack) otherwise the filler will set too rapidly or too slowly.

Alternatively, Holts No Mix can be used straight from the tube without mixing, but daylight is required to cure it. Using the applicator apply the filler paste to the prepared area; draw the applicator across the surface of the filler to achieve the correct contour and to level the filler surface. As soon as a contour that approximates to the correct one is achieved, stop working the paste – if you carry on too long the paste will become sticky and begin to 'pick up' on the applicator. Continue to add thin layers of filler paste at twenty-minute intervals until the level of the filler is just proud of the surrounding bodywork.

Once the filler has hardened, excess can be removed using a metal plane or file. From then on, progressively finer grades of abrasive paper should be used, starting with a 40 grade production paper and finishing with 400 grade wet-and-dry paper. Always wrap the abrasive paper around a flat rubber, cork, or wooden block – otherwise the surface of the filler will not be completely flat. During the smoothing of the filler surface the wet-and-dry paper should be periodically rinsed in water. This will ensure that a very smooth finish is imparted to the filler at the final stage.

At this stage the 'dent' should be surrounded by a ring of bare metal, which in turn should be encircled by the finely 'feathered' edge of the good paintwork. Rinse the repair area with clean water, until all of the dust produced by the rubbing-down operation has gone.

Spray the whole repair area with a light coat of primer, either Holts Body + Plus Grey or Red Oxide Primer – this will show up any imperfections in the surface of the filler. Repair these imperfections with fresh filler paste or bodystopper, and once more smooth the surface with abrasive paper. If bodystopper is used, it can be mixed with cellulose thinners to form a really thin paste which is ideal for filling small holes. Repeat this spray and repair procedure until you are satisfied that the surface of the filler, and the feathered edge of the paintwork are perfect. Clean the repair area with clean water and allow to dry fully.

The repair area is now ready for final spraying. Paint spraying must be carried out in a warm, dry, windless and dust free atmosphere. This condition can be created artificially if you have access to a large indoor working area, but if you are forced to work in the open, you will have to pick your day very carefully. If you are working indoors, dousing the floor in the work area with water will help to settle the dust which would otherwise be in the atmosphere. If the repair area is confined to one body panel, mask off the surrounding panels; this will help to minimise the effects of a slight mis-match in paint colours. Bodywork fittings (eg chrome strips, door handles etc) will also need to be masked off. Use genuine masking tape and several thicknesses of newspaper for the masking operations.

Before commencing to spray, agitate the aerosol can thoroughly, then spray a test area (an old tin, or similar) until the technique is mastered. Cover the repair area with a thick coat of primer; the thickness should be built up using several thin layers of paint rather than one thick one. Using 400 grade wet-and-dry paper, rub down the surface of the primer until it is really smooth. While doing this, the work area should be thoroughly doused with water, and the wet-and-dry paper periodically rinsed in water. Allow to dry before spraying on more paint.

Spray on the top coat using Holts Dupli-Color Autospray, again building up the thickness by using several thin layers of paint. Start spraying in the centre of the repair area and then, with a single side-to-side motion, work outwards until the whole repair area and about 2 inches of the surrounding original paintwork is covered. Remove all masking material 10 to 15 minutes after spraying on the final coat of paint.

Allow the new paint at least two weeks to harden, then, using a paintwork renovator or a very fine cutting paste such as Turtle Wax New Color Back or Holts Body + Plus Rubbing Compound, blend the edges of the paint into the existing paintwork. Finally, apply wax polish.

Plastic components

With the use of more and more plastic body components by the vehicle manufacturers (eg bumpers, spoilers, and in some cases major body panels), rectification of more serious damage to such items has become a matter of either entrusting repair work to a specialist in this field, or renewing complete components.

Fig. 12.2. Door trim panel and fittings

1 Plug
2 Armrest
3 Lock knob
4 Door handle

5 Cover
6 Window winding handle
7 Top cover strip

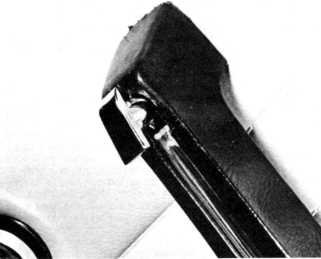

7.1a Remove the plug covering the screw at the top of the armrest ...

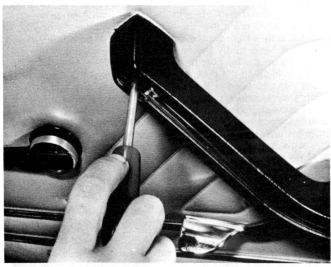

7.1b ... and then remove the screw

Repair of such damage by the DIY owner is not really feasible owing to the cost of the equipment and materials required for effecting such repairs. The basic technique involves making a groove along the line of the crack in the plastic using a rotary burr in a power drill. The damaged part is then welded back together by using a hot air gun to heat up and fuse a plastic filler rod into the groove. Any excess plastic is then removed and the area rubbed down to a smooth finish. It is important that a filler rod of the correct plastic is used, as body components can be made of a variety of different types (eg polycarbonate, ABS, polypropylene).

Damage of a less serious nature (abrasions, minor cracks etc) can be repaired by the DIY owner using a two-part epoxy filler repair material like Holts Body + Plus or Holts No Mix which can be used directly from the tube. Once mixed in equal proportions (or applied direct from the tube in the case of Holts No Mix), this is used in similar fashion to the bodywork filler used on metal panels. The filler is usually cured in twenty to thirty minutes, ready for sanding and painting.

If the owner is renewing a complete component himself, or if he has repaired it with epoxy filler, he will be left with the problem of finding a suitable paint for finishing which is compatible with the type of plastic used. At one time the use of a universal paint was not possible owing to the complex range of plastics encountered in body component applications. Standard paints, generally speaking, will not bond to plastic or rubber satisfactorily, but Holts Professional Spraymatch paints to match any plastic or rubber finish can be obtained from dealers. However, it is now possible to obtain a plastic body parts finishing kit which consists of a pre-primer treatment, a primer and coloured top coat. Full instructions are normally supplied with a kit, but basically the method of use is to first apply the pre-primer to the component concerned and allow it to dry for up to 30 minutes. Then the primer is applied and left to dry for about an hour before finally applying the special coloured top coat. The result is a correctly coloured component where the paint will flex with the plastic or rubber, a property that standard paint does not normally possess.

5 Major body damage - repair

1 Because the body is built on the monocoque principle, major damage must be repaired by a competent body repairer with the necessary jigs and equipment.
2 In the event of a crash that resulted in buckling of body panels, or damage to the roadwheels the car must be taken to a FIAT dealer or body repairer where the bodyshell and suspension alignment may be checked.
3 Bodyshell and/or suspension mis-alignment will cause excessive wear of the tyres, steering system and possibly transmission. The handling of the car will also be affected adversely.

6 Door rattles - tracing and rectification

1 Door rattles are due either to loose hinges, worn or maladjusted catches, or loose components inside the door.
2 Loose hinges can be detected by opening the door and trying to lift it. Any play will be felt. Worn or badly adjusted catches can be found by pushing and pulling on the outside handle when the door is closed. Any movement of the door indicates loose catches.
3 To check the window mechanism, open the door and shake it with the window open and then closed.
4 Loose parts should be tightened and worn parts renewed.

7 Door trim - removal and refitting

1 Remove the plug from the top of the armrest and remove the three

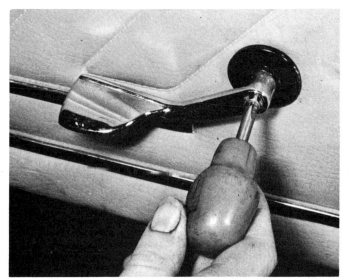

Fig. 12.3. Door window winder adjustment

1 Screws   2 Window   3 Rubber pad

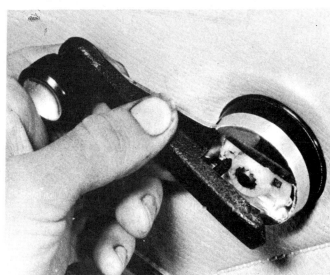

Fig. 12.4. Tensioning the window winder cable

1 Cable   2 Nut   3 Slot

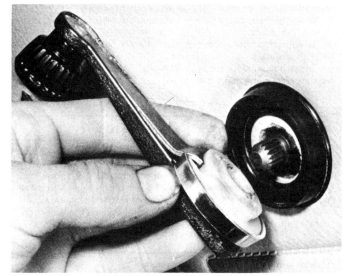

7.2 Removing the door handle retaining screw

7.3a Pull off the window winding handle cover ...

7.3b ... and then remove the handle

7.5 Door with trim removed

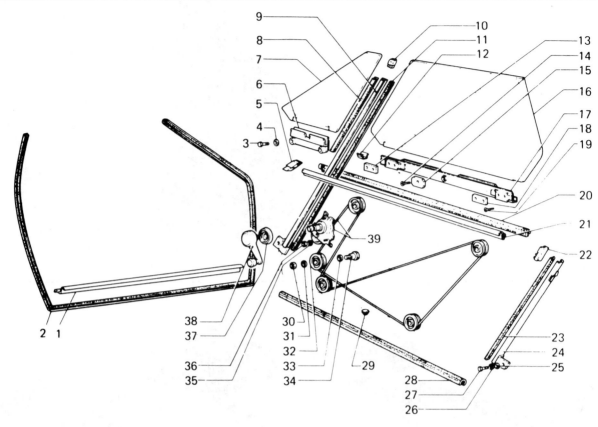

Fig. 12.5. Exploded view of door window and winding mechanism

1	Doorsill moulding	11	Weatherstrip	21	Cover	31	Washer
2	Weatherstrip	12	Clip	22	Boot	32	Pulley
3	Bolt	13	Plate	23	Weatherstrip	33	Washer
4	Washer	14	Screw	24	Channel	34	Bolt
5	Boot	15	Pad	25	Washer	35	Lockwasher
6	Channel	16	Glass	26	Lockwasher	36	Nut
7	Glass	17	Guide	27	Screw	37	Ornament
8	Weatherstrip	18	Plate	28	Weatherstrip	38	Handle
9	Pillar	19	Screw	29	Pad	39	Winding mechanism
10	Pad	20	Weatherstrip	30	Nut		

screws holding the armrest in the door.
2   Remove the screw attaching the door handle and pull off the handle.
3   Prise the cover off the window winding handle and push the handle towards the winding mechanism and pull it off.
4   Unscrew the door lock knob and remove top cover strip.
5   Carefully prise out the trim pad from the door to release the snap-fasteners and lift the panel off.
6   Reverse the removal sequence to refit the trim.

8   Door window winding mechanism - adjustment

1   Remove the door trim as described in Section 7.
2   Loosen the screws in the two window locating plates.
3   Wind the window fully down and tighten the locating plate screws.
4   After adjustment, the glass must be able to run the full length of its travel and the control cable must wind and unwind properly on the winding mechanism pulley.
5   To remove any slack from the control cable, loosen the nut on the adjustable pulley of the winding mechanism and move the pulley, in its slot, to tension the cable then tighten the pulley nut.

9   Door locks - general

1   To gain access to the door locks, remove the door trim, as described

in Section 7.
2   Wind the window to the fully closed position. The lock can then be reached through the access hole in the door inner panel.
3   To adjust the exterior door handle, turn the adjustable head of the tie-rod (Fig. 12.7).
4   To adjust the inside door handle, loosen the holding screws and move the handle spindle as required.
5   The striker plate for the door lock is adjusted by loosening the two securing screws and moving the plate.

10 Windscreen - renewal

1   The windscreen glass is fitted using special sealing adhesive. It cannot be done quickly or easily by the do-it-yourselfer and should be left to a FIAT agent with the proper equipment for applying the sealant.
2   The curing of the adhesive takes 24 hours and the glass and frame needs lengthy preparation. As the glass is of laminated type, any crack will not mean that renewal is a matter of urgency and can wait for a convenient time.

11 Rear window - removal and refitting

1   Remove the engine cover, as described in Section 16.
2   Remove the air scoops on each side, by removing the four securing

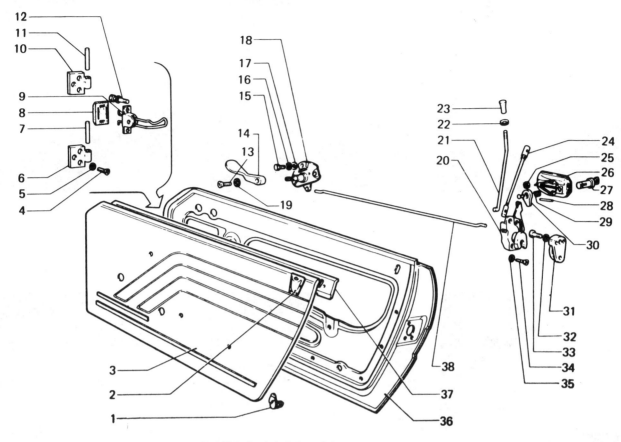

Fig. 12.6. Exploded view of door components

1	Clip	11	Pin	21	Rod	31	Striker plate
2	Lock cover	12	Bolt	22	Rubber ring	32	Lockwasher
3	Door panel	13	Screw	23	Knob	33	Screw
4	Screw	14	Handle	24	Rod	34	Screw
5	Lockwasher	15	Bolt	25	Nut	35	Lockwasher
6	Hinge half	16	Lockwasher	26	Handle	36	Door
7	Pin	17	Washer	27	Lock cylinder	37	Channel
8	Lining	18	Lever	28	Pin	38	Rod
9	Door check	19	Lockwasher	29	Spring		
10	Hinge half	20	Lock	30	Pawl		

9.2 The lock is accessible through a hole in the door inner panel

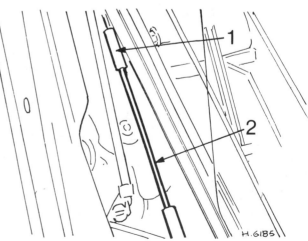

Fig. 12.7. Adjusting the outside door handles

1   Adjustable head   2   Tie-rod

This photographic sequence shows the steps taken to repair the dent and paintwork damage shown above. In general, the procedure for repairing a hole will be similar; where there are substantial differences, the procedure is clearly described and shown in a separate photograph.

First remove any trim around the dent, then hammer out the dent where access is possible. This will minimise filling. Here, after the large dent has been hammered out, the damaged area is being made slightly concave.

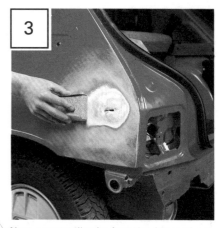

Next, remove all paint from the damaged area by rubbing with coarse abrasive paper or using a power drill fitted with a wire brush or abrasive pad. 'Feather' the edge of the boundary with good paintwork using a finer grade of abrasive paper.

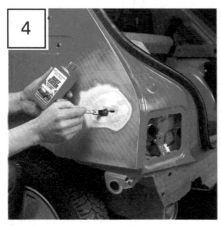

Where there are holes or other damage, the sheet metal should be cut away before proceeding further. The damaged area and any signs of rust should be treated with Turtle Wax Hi-Tech Rust Eater, which will also inhibit further rust formation.

For a large dent or hole mix Holts Body Plus Resin and Hardener according to the manufacturer's instructions and apply around the edge of the repair. Press Glass Fibre Matting over the repair area and leave for 20-30 minutes to harden. Then ...

... brush more Holts Body Plus Resin and Hardener onto the matting and leave to harden. Repeat the sequence with two or three layers of matting, checking that the final layer is lower than the surrounding area. Apply Holts Body Plus Filler Paste as shown in Step 5B.

For a medium dent, mix Holts Body Plus Filler Paste and Hardener according to the manufacturer's instructions and apply it with a flexible applicator. Apply thin layers of filler at 20-minute intervals, until the filler surface is slightly proud of the surrounding bodywork.

For small dents and scratches use Holts No Mix Filler Paste straight from the tube. Apply it according to the instructions in thin layers, using the spatula provided. It will harden in minutes if applied outdoors and may then be used as its own knifing putty.

Use a plane or file for initial shaping. Then, using progressively finer grades of wet-and-dry paper, wrapped round a sanding block, and copious amounts of clean water, rub down the filler until glass smooth. 'Feather' the edges of adjoining paintwork.

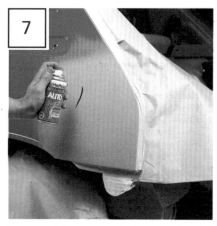

Protect adjoining areas before spraying the whole repair area and at least one inch of the surrounding sound paintwork with Holts Dupli-Color primer.

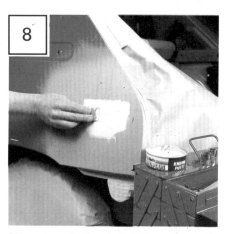

Fill any imperfections in the filler surface with a small amount of Holts Body Plus Knifing Putty. Using plenty of clean water, rub down the surface with a fine grade wet-and-dry paper – 400 grade is recommended – until it is really smooth.

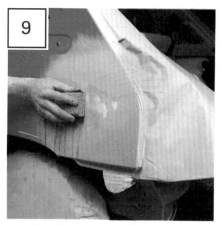

Carefully fill any remaining imperfections with knifing putty before applying the last coat of primer. Then rub down the surface with Holts Body Plus Rubbing Compound to ensure a really smooth surface.

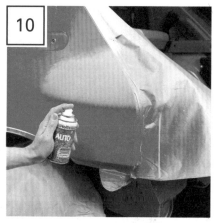

Protect surrounding areas from overspray before applying the topcoat in several thin layers. Agitate Holts Dupli-Color aerosol thoroughly. Start at the repair centre, spraying outwards with a side-to-side motion.

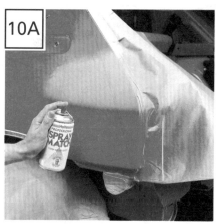

If the exact colour is not available off the shelf, local Holts Professional Spraymatch Centres will custom fill an aerosol to match perfectly.

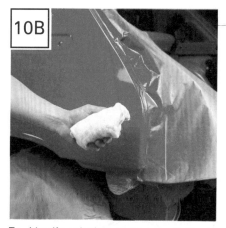

To identify whether a lacquer finish is required, rub a painted unrepaired part of the body with wax and a clean cloth.

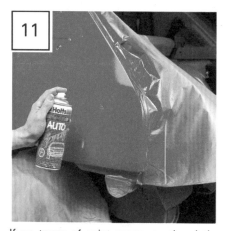

If *no* traces of paint appear on the cloth, spray Holts Dupli-Color clear lacquer over the repaired area to achieve the correct gloss level.

The paint will take about two weeks to harden fully. After this time it can be 'cut' with a mild cutting compound such as Turtle Wax Minute Cut prior to polishing with a final coating of Turtle Wax Extra.

When carrying out bodywork repairs, remember that the quality of the finished job is proportional to the time and effort expended.

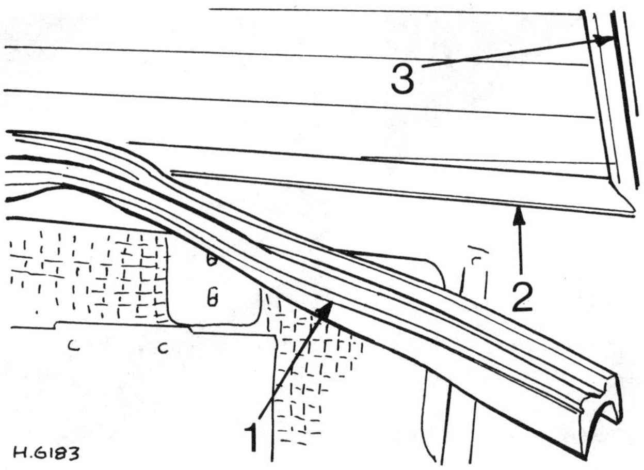

Fig. 12.8. Removing the rear window

1 Rubber seal
2 Window
3 Frame

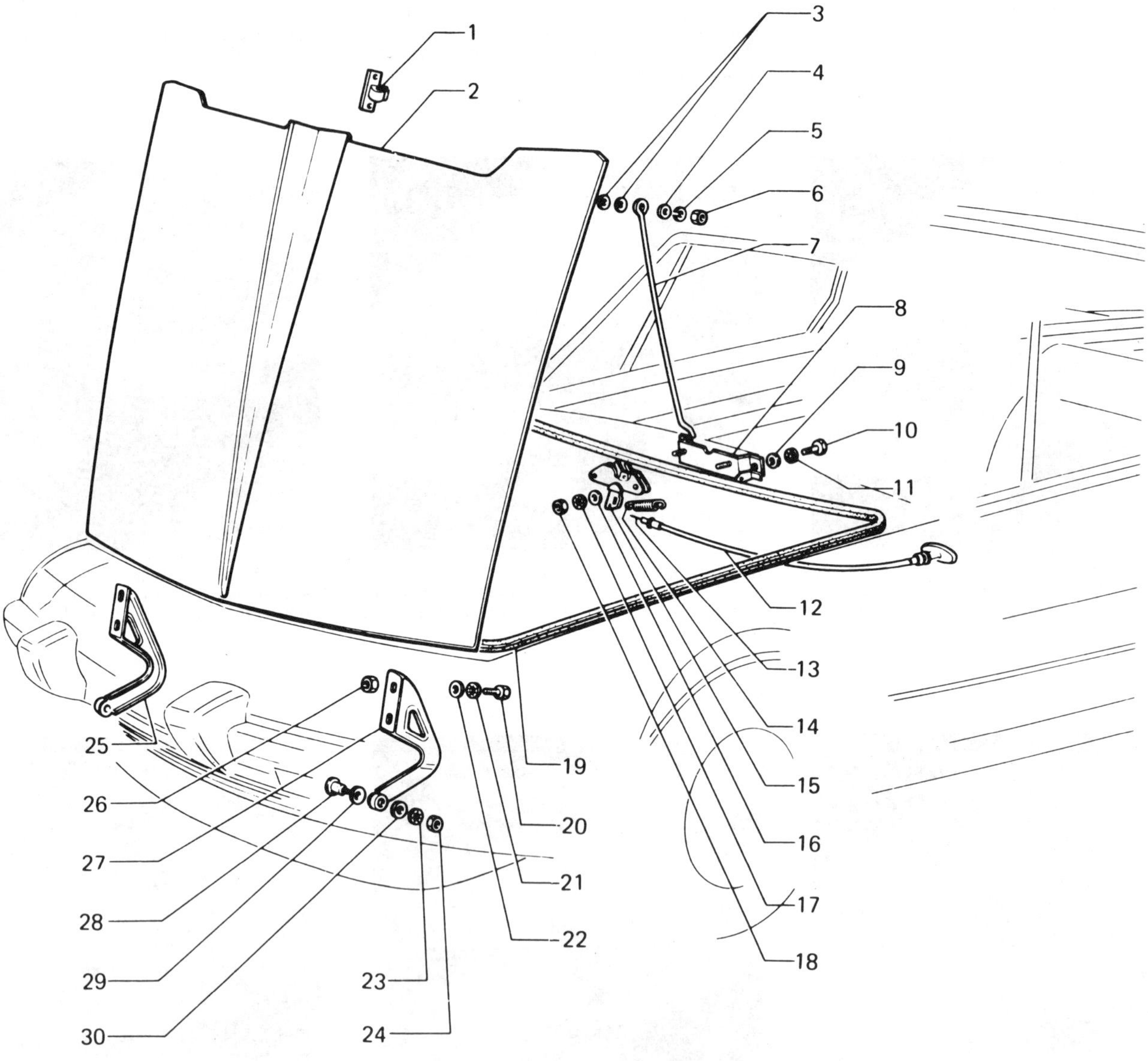

H.6183

Fig. 12.9. Exploded view of front luggage compartment lid components

1	Striker plate	9	Washers	17	Lockwasher	25	Hinge
2	Lid	10	Bolt	18	Nut	26	Nut
3	Spring washer	11	Washer	19	Compartment rubber seal	27	Hinge
4	Washers	12	Latch cable	20	Bolt	28	Bolt
5	Lockwasher	13	Cable	21	Lockwasher	29	Washer
6	Nut	14	Spring	22	Washer	30	Washer
7	Rod	15	Lock	23	Lockwasher		
8	Lock bracket	16	Washer	24	Nut		

screws. One screw is under the rear luggage compartment lid. Remove the petrol tank cap.

3   Remove the six bolts holding the weatherstrip to the body. On cars with a heated rear window disconnect the wire from each side of the window.

4   Pull the rubber seal around the window towards the centre of the window and slide the seal out from under the edge of the window.

5   Pull down the window, remove the top seal and lift out the window.

6   Refitting is the reverse of the removal sequence. Make sure the window is in the centre of the seal and that the seal overlaps the frame.

7   Refit the engine cover, as described in Section 16.

12 Front luggage compartment lid - removal, refitting and adjustment

1   Remove the bolts attaching the lid to the hinges and with the help of an assistant, disconnect the lid support stay and lift the lid off.

2   When refitting the lid, do not tighten the hinge bolts fully, leave them just slack enough to allow the lid to be moved. Close the lid and check for proper alignment. Move the lid as necessary to position it correctly, then fully tighten the hinge bolts. Fit the support stay.

13 Front luggage compartment lid lock - removal, refitting and adjustment

1   Remove the four screws and bolt holding the grille on the right-hand side.

2   Remove the two bolts securing the lock bracket and withdraw the lock out through the grille opening.

3   Disconnect the cable from the lock and remove the two nuts holding the lock to the bracket.

4   When refitting the lock tighten the bolts enough to allow the lock to be moved. Check the operation of the lock, move the lock, if necessary, and fully tighten the bolts.

14 Rear luggage compartment lid and lock - removal, refitting and adjustment

1   Removal, refitting and adjustment of the lid and lock is basically the same as for the front luggage compartment, see Section 13. The release lever for the cable is located in the left-hand door pillar.

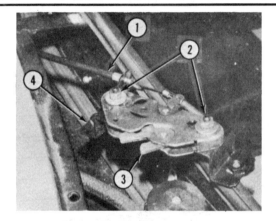

Fig. 12.10. Removing the front luggage compartment lid lock

1   Cable
2   Nuts
3   Lock
4   Bracket

14.1 Rear luggage compartment lid being removed

Fig. 12.11. Exploded view of rear luggage compartment components

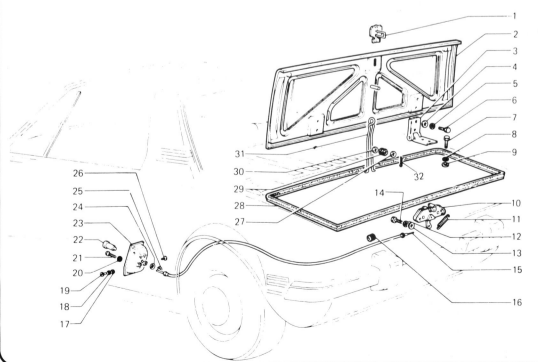

1   Striker plate
2   Lid
3   Hinge
4   Washer
5   Lockwasher
6   Bolt
7   Bolt
8   Lockwasher
9   Washer
10 Lock
11 Spring
12 Lockwasher
13 Washer
14 Bolt
15 Cable
16 Rubber ring
17 Washer
18 Lockwasher
19 Screw
20 Lockwasher
21 Screw
22 Lock cylinder
23 Handle
24 Washer
25 Fork
26 Screw
27 Washer
28 Weatherstrip
29 Bushing
30 Washer
31 Stay
32 Pin

Fig. 12.12. Removing the key lock and release levers for the engine and rear luggage compartment lids

16.1 The engine cover is hinged to the front bulkhead

1	Lever	3	Assembly screw
2	Cable screw	4	Escutcheon

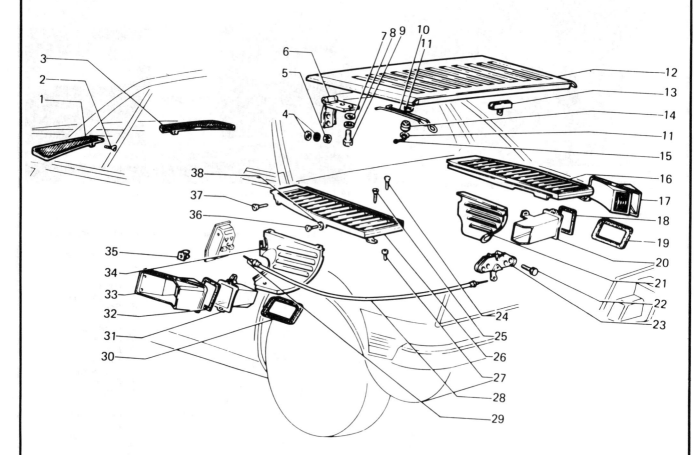

Fig. 12.13. Exploded view of engine compartment lid components and air inlets

1	Grill	11	Washer	21	Conveyor	31	Conveyor
2	Screw	12	Lid	22	Bolt	32	Gasket
3	Grill	13	Striker plate	23	Lock	33	Air intake
4	Washers	14	Bushing	24	Screw	34	Wall
5	Nut	15	Cotter pin	25	Screw	35	Clip
6	Hinge	16	Grill	26	Grill	36	Screw
7	Washer	17	Conveyor	27	Screw	37	Screw
8	Lockwasher	18	Gasket	28	Cable	38	Washer
9	Bolt	19	Gasket	29	Cable		
10	Centre prop	20	Wall	30	Gasket		

154

15 Engine and luggage compartment key lock - removal and refitting

1   The key lock and release levers for the engine and rear luggage compartments are located in the left-hand door pillar.
2   To remove the assembly remove the screws securing the cables in the levers and then the screw holding the assembly in the door pillar. Remove the lock and lever assembly.
3   To refit the assembly, fit the cables into the levers and pull the cables and levers until the lids release. Hold the cables and feed them fully into the levers, then fit the securing screws.
4   Fit the lock and lever assembly retaining screw and check the operation of the release cables.

16 Engine cover and lock - removal, refitting and adjustment

1   With the help of an assistant remove the four hinge bolts and disconnect the support stay at its bottom attachment. Lift off the cover.
2   Take the stay off the bonnet by removing the split pin, washer and bush attaching it to the bonnet.
3   To remove the lock undo the two retaining bolts and disconnect the cable from the lock.
4   When refitting the bonnet and lock, tighten the attaching bolts enough to allow movement, for adjustment of the bonnet and lock. When the bonnet and lock are correctly positioned, fully tighten the attaching bolts.
5   Check the operation of the bonnet release cable.

17 Instrument panel - removal and refitting

1   Disconnect the earth lead from the battery.
2   Remove the five screws holding the panel and slide the panel out part way.
3   Unscrew the speedometer cable and disconnect the three electrical connectors.
4   Remove the instrument panel.
5   Refitting is the reverse of the removal sequence.

18 Detachable roof - general

1   To remove the detachable roof, lower the sun-visors, release the two

16.3 The engine cover lock is bolted to the rear bulkhead

17.2 The instrument panel is secured by five screws

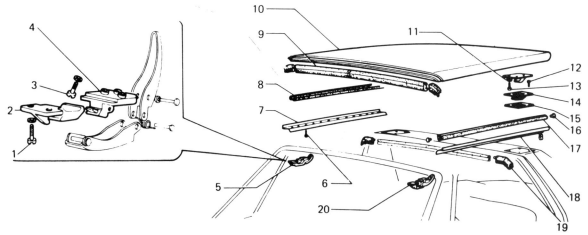

Fig. 12.14. Exploded view of detachable roof components

1 Screw	6 Screw	11 Lug	16 Plug
2 Striker plate	7 Moulding	12 Screw	17 Weatherstrip
3 Screw	8 Weatherstrip	13 Screw	18 Moulding
4 Support	9 Weatherstrip	14 Striker plate	19 Joint
5 Lock	10 Hard top	15 Covering	20 Lock

overcentre catches ('A' in Fig. 12.15), by pulling downwards simultaneously, hold the catches in their seats and push the lever forward to loosen the top.

2 Raise the roof upwards from inside the car until the two retaining lugs are clear of the recesses in the striker plates, and lift off the roof.

3 To adjust the alignment of the roof, slacken the four screws securing the striker plate, move the plate as required and then tighten the securing screws.

19 Seats - removal and refitting

1 Disconnect the seatbelt interlock relay (if fitted) and disconnect the spring from the bracket on the floor.

2 Raise the seat adjusting lever and slide the seat off the floor tracks.

3 Refitting is the reverse of the removal sequence.

Fig. 12.15. Releasing the overcentre catches

Fig. 12.16. Lifting off the roof

B   Retaining lugs   C   Striker plates

Chapter 13 Supplement:
Revisions and information on later models

Contents

1 Introduction

This Supplement describes modifications and changes which have been carried out to the X1/9 during the later years of production. Most alterations have been of a minor nature, with the exception of the introduction of the 1498 cc engine and five-speed transmission in late 1978.

In order to use this Supplement to the best advantage, it is suggested that it is referred to before the main Chapters of the Manual. This will ensure that any relevant information can be collated and absorbed into the procedures described in Chapters 1 to 12 before starting work.

2 Specifications

The following Specifications are supplementary to, or revisions of, those at the beginning of the preceding Chapters.

Engine (1500 cc)
General

Identification code	138 A2 000
Bore	86.4 mm (3.40 in)
Stroke	63.9 mm (2.52 in)
Displacement	1498 cc (91.41 cu in)
Maximum power (DIN)	62.5 kW (85 bhp) at 6000 rpm
Maximum torque (DIN)	118 Nm (87 lbf ft) at 3200 rpm

Cylinder block

Cylinder bore diameter (standard)	86.40 to 86.45 mm (3.402 to 3.404 in)

Crankshaft and main bearings

Main bearing journal diameter	50.775 to 50.795 mm (1.9990 to 1.9998 in)
Main bearing shell thickness	1.834 to 1.840 mm (0.0722 to 0.0724 in)
Main bearing undersizes	0.508, 0.762 and 1.016 mm (0.0200, 0.0300 and 0.0400 in)
Main bearing running clearance	0.032 to 0.077 mm (0.0013 to 0.0030 in)

Pistons and piston rings

Standard piston diameters:
Grade A	86.360 to 86.370 mm (3.4000 to 3.4004 in)
Grade C	86.380 to 86.390 mm (3.4008 to 3.4012 in)
Grade E	86.400 to 86.410 mm (3.4016 to 3.4020 in)
Oversizes	0.008, 0.016 and 0.024 mm (0.0003, 0.0006 and 0.0009 in)
Piston-to-cylinder bore clearance	0.030 to 0.050 mm (0.0012 to 0.0020 in)

Piston ring groove width:
Top	1.535 to 1.555 mm (0.0604 to 0.0612 in)
Second	2.030 to 2.050 mm (0.0799 to 0.0807 in)
Bottom	3.967 to 3.987 mm (0.1562 to 0.1570 in)

Piston ring clearance in groove:
Top	0.045 to 0.077 mm (0.0018 to 0.0030 in)
Second	0.040 to 0.072 mm (0.0016 to 0.0028 in)
Bottom	0.030 to 0.062 mm (0.0012 to 0.0024 in)

Camshatt

Cam lift:
Inlet	9.20 mm (0.362 in)
Exhaust	9.25 mm (0.364 in)

Valve timing:
Inlet	Opens 24° btdc, closes 68° abdc
Exhaust	Opens 64° bbdc, closes 28° atdc

Cylinder head

Valve guide bore in cylinder head (standard)	13.950 to 13.977 mm (0.5492 to 0.5503 in)
Valve guide outside diameter	14.040 to 14.058 mm (0.5528 to 0.5535 in)

Lubrication system

Oil pump:
Gear endfloat	0.05 to 0.20 mm (0.002 to 0.008 in)
Gear-to-body clearance	0.08 to 0.11 mm (0.003 to 0.004 in)
Backlash between gears	0.15 mm (0.006 in)
Oil pressure at 100°C (212°F)	3.5 to 4.8 bar (51 to 70 lbf/in²)

Torque wrench setting

	Nm	lbf ft
Additional cylinder head bolts (where applicable, see text)	30	22

Fuel system (1500 cc engine)

Air cleaner element

Champion W136

Carburettor data

Type	Weber 34 DATR 7/250	
Calibration:	**Primary barrel**	**Secondary barrel**
Venturi	23.0 mm (0.91 in)	26.0 mm (1.02 in)
Main jet	1.07	1.30
Air correction jet	1.60	1.50
Slow running jet	0.47	0.70
Slow running air bleed	1.10	0.70
Emulsion tube	F30	F30
Accelerator pump	0.40	–
Accelerator pump excess fuel discharge orifice	0.40	–
Power fuel jet diameter	–	0.80
Power mixture outlet	–	2.0
Needle valve	1.75	
Float setting	6.75 to 7.25 mm (0.266 to 0.285 in)	
Throttle valve opening with choke on	0.95 to 1.05 mm (0.037 to 0.041 in)	
Choke vacuum pulldown	3.75 to 4.75 mm (0.148 to 0.187 in)	
Idle speed	800 to 850 rpm	
CO level at idle	1.0 to 2.0%	

Ignition system
Ignition timing (1500 cc engine)

Static or dynamic (at idle speed)	5° BTDC

Spark plugs (all models)

Type	Champion RN7YC	Bosch WR6D
	Marelli CW 78 LPR	Fiat 1L45UR

Electrode gap:
Champion	0.7 mm (0.028 in)
All other makes	0.7 to 0.8 mm (0.028 to 0.031 in)

Manual transmission (5-speed)
Gear ratios

1st	3.583 : 1
2nd	2.235 : 1
3rd	1.454 : 1
4th	1.042 : 1
5th	0.863 : 1

Reverse	3.714 : 1
Final drive	4.077 : 1

Synchroniser type
1st/2nd	Baulk ring and cone
3rd/4th/5th	Porsche type

Torque wrench settings

	Nm	lbf ft
Detent spring cover plate bolts	25	18
Bellhousing-to-transmission casing bolts	25	18
Bellhousing-to-engine bolts	78	58
End cover bolts	10	7
Casing front cover (bearing guide) bolts	10	7
Input and output shaft nuts	118	87
Crownwheel bolts	68	50
Driveshaft joint-to-output flange bolts	34	25
Selector fork lockbolts	18	13
Reverse idle shaft lockplate nut	10	7

Electrical system (1500 cc models)
Battery	12V 45Ah

Alternator
Type	45A with integral voltage regulator
Minimum brush length (wear limit)	5.0 mm (0.197 in)

Fuses

Ref	Rating (A)	Circuits protected
A	20	Horns
B	10	Carburettor fan and relay, power-operated aerial
C	20	Heated rear window
D	25	Spare
F	25	Spare
G	10	Spare
H	7.5	Headlamp lift control switch
I	7.5	Headlamp lift motor (LH)
K	7.5	Headlamp lift motor (RH)
L	20	Cigar lighter, clock, hazard warning courtesy lamps and delay
M	25	Radiator cooling fan
N	25	Power-operated windows
O	7.5	Headlamp lowering control switch
P	10	Headlamp main beam (LH)
Q	10	Headlamp main beam (RH)
R	7.5	Direction indicators, clock, windscreen wiper/washer, low fluid level warning lamps, handbrake 'on', tachometer, radio
S	10	Heater blower, stop-lamps, reversing lamps, heated rear window relay
T	7.5	Spare
U	10	Headlamp dipped beam (RH)
V	10	Headlamp dipped beam (LH)
X	7.5	Front parking lamp (RH), tail lamp (LH), rear number plate lamp (RH)
Y	7.5	Front parking lamp (LH), tail lamp (RH), rear number plate lamp (LH), clock, switch and accessory illumination
W	7.5	Spare
Z		Spare fuse (six) storage

Relays

1	Courtesy lamp delay unit
2	Direction indicator/hazard warning flasher
3	Wiper (intermittent) timer
4	Handbrake 'on'
E1	Radiator fan
E2	Parking lamps and headlamp raising control
E3	Headlamp motor (RH)
E4	Headlamp main beam
E5	Headlamp motor (LH)
E6	Power-operated windows
E7	Heated rear window
E8	Horns

Bulbs

	Wattage
Headlamp (Halogen)	60/55
Front direction indicator lamp	21
Side repeater lamps	Renewable as complete lamp
Rear direction indicator lamp	21
Tail lamp	5
Reversing lamp	21

Bulbs (continued)

	Wattage
Stop-lamp	21
Rear foglamp	21
Courtesy lamp	5
Rear number plate lamp	5
Warning lamp (wedge type)	1.2
Instrument panel illumination (wedge type)	3

General dimensions, weights and capacities (1500 cc models)

Dimensions

Overall length	3969 mm (156.3 in)
Height (unladen)	1180 mm (46.5 in)
Track (front)	1355 mm (53.4 in)
Track (rear)	1350 mm (53.2 in)

Weights

Kerb weight	920 kg (2028 lb)
Towing weight	990 kg (2183 lb)

Capacities

Cooling system	11.6 litres (20.4 pints)
Engine oil, including filter change	4.5 litres (7.9 pints)

---

3   Routine Maintenance

In common with most other manufacturers, FIAT have extended their servicing intervals.

Where servicing costs are not of prime importance, however, it is recommended that the intervals remain as given on pages 6 to 8.

The operations affected by the revised schedule are as follows.

Every 7500 miles (12 000 km) or 6 months, whichever comes first

Renew engine oil and filter
Inspect brake disc pads for wear

Every 15 000 miles (24 000 km) or 12 months, whichever comes first

Renew air cleaner element
Renew spark plugs
Adjust alternator drivebelt tension or renew
Check clutch fluid level
Check all suspension and steering components
Lubricate controls, hinges and locks
Check driveshaft joints and boots

Every 30 000 miles (48 000 km) or two years, whichever comes first

Renew transmission lubricant
Renew engine coolant

---

4   Engine (1500 cc)

Description

1   This larger capacity engine was introduced in late 1978 and is very similar to the 1290 cc version described in Chapter 1.
2   The increase in displacement is obtained by lengthening the stroke, and by a slight bore increase.
3   Refer to Specifications at the beginning of this Supplement.

Removal and refitting

4   The operations are essentially as described in Chapter 1, but note the following differences:

     (a)   *Disconnect the coolant hoses from the carburettor automatic choke instead of the choke control cable*
     (b)   *Disconnect the driveshaft flanges (socket-headed Allen screws) from the transmission*
     (c)   *Note the different removal procedure for the gearchange lever (see Section 9, this Chapter)*

5   Note the modified engine mountings (photos).

Cylinder head bolts

6   On later models, either 4 or 5 additional cylinder head bolts are used. These bolts are positioned along the edge of the cylinder head nearest the passenger compartment bulkhead. The additional bolts should be tightened to the specified torque, starting from the centre and working outwards, after the main cylinder head bolts have been tightened.

Toothed drivebelt/camshaft – refitting

7   The procedures are as given in Chapter 1, Sections 5 and 28, but the camshaft pulley timing mark must be aligned with the pointer on the belt guard, **not** the finger on the engine mounting support.

4.5A Left-hand engine mounting

4.5B Lower centre engine mounting

4.5C Engine stabiliser

Engine compartment with air cleaner removed

1 Petrol filler cap
2 Carburettor cooling fan
3 Lid support spring
4 Coil suppressor
5 Engine oil dipstick
6 Engine oil filler cap
7 Ignition coil
8 Rear suspension strut upper mounting
9 Coolant expansion tank
10 Engine stabiliser
11 Carburettor
12 Coolant heated automatic choke
13 Timing belt cover
14 Coolant pump
15 Lid buffer

162

View under front end

1　Track rod outboard balljoint
2　Track control arm
3　Brake caliper
4　Radius rod
5　Steering rack (box) housing
6　Radiator hose
7　Radiator fan motor
8　Radiator lower mounting rail
9　Radiator hose
10　Metal coolant distribution pipes
11　Accelerator cable
12　Steering arm
13　Workshop jack lifting point

View under rear end

1 Fuel tank
2 Handbrake cable
3 Suspension arm
4 Driveshaft
5 Track control arm balljoint
6 Metal coolant distribution
  pipes
7 Engine sump pan
8 Sill jacking point
9 Exhaust silencer
10 Engine/transmission centre
   mounting
11 Workshop jack lifting
   bracket
12 Rear number plate lamp
13 Transmission
14 Gearchange linkage
15 Cover panels
16 Driveshaft

FIAT Bertone X1/9 and X1/9VS

5 Cooling system

Radiator-to-engine distribution pipes

1   The flexible coolant hoses from the engine, heater and radiator are connected to metal pipes which run under the length of the car and are enclosed in a protective cover welded to the floor (photos).
2   Drain screws are fitted to the two larger diameter pipes (photo).
3   Although it is unlikely that a leak would occur in these pipes, where renewal is required, perhaps because of grounding, then the assembly will have to be removed by cutting through the spot welds of the cover.
4   The new assembly can be fitted by spot welding (remove interior floor covering) or by pop riveting.

6 Fuel system

Fuel pump (later models)

1   The fuel pump on later models is a sealed unit which cannot even be cleaned. Any fault will necessitate renewal (photo).

Fuel tank sender unit – removal and refitting

2   Disconnect the battery and then, working at the left-hand side of the engine compartment forward bulkhead, cut through the fuel hose clips and remove them. Extract the screws and remove the cover panel (photos).
3   Disconnect the electrical leads from the sender unit (photo).
4   Unscrew the circle of securing nuts and withdraw the sender unit – taking care not to damage the float.

5.1A Flexible hose connections to rigid distribution pipes (rear end)

5.1B Flexible hose connection to rigid distribution pipe (front end)

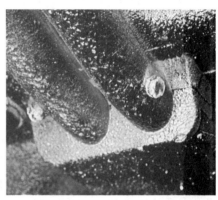

5.2 Coolant distribution pipe drain plugs

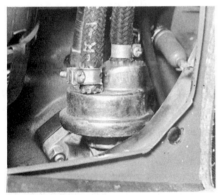

6.1 Sealed type fuel pump

6.2A Fuel hoses at tank sender unit

6.2B Fuel tank sender unit corner panel

6.3 Fuel tank sender unit

6.7 Fuel tank filler hose clips

6.9 Fuel tank mounting bolt and strap

5   Refitting is a reversal of removal, but always use a new flange seal and hose clips.

Fuel tank – removal and refitting

6   The fuel tank is located on the left-hand side, forward of the engine compartment front bulkhead. Before removing the tank it is recommended that it is almost empty of fuel either achieved by normal usage or by syphoning into suitable containers.
7   Working within the engine compartment, disconnect the fuel filler hose clip (photo).
8   Disconnect the sender unit hoses and leads as described in paragraphs 2 to 5 of the preceding sub-section.
9   Working under the car, release the fuel tank support straps and carefully lower the tank and remove it (photo).
10   **Never** *attempt to weld or solder a fuel tank unless it has been thoroughly purged by steaming or boiling out.*
11   To remove sediment or water from the tank, first remove the sender unit and then pour in some paraffin. Shake vigorously repeating as necessary until the tank is clean. Give a final rinse out with petrol.

12   Refitting is a reversal of removal.

Accelerator control cable – renewal

13   Working at the carburettor end with the air cleaner removed, slide the spring sleeve off the ball socket to release the cable from the lever on the camshaft cover (photo).
14   Working inside the car at the driver's footwell, reach around in front of the centre console and peel back the carpet which covers the aperture in the top surface of the tunnel.
15   The cable will now be seen to be attached to the accelerator pedal rod crankarm using a split pin, washer and coil spring (photo).
16   Extract the split pin and disconnect the cable.
17   Working under the car, disconnect the cable from the retaining clips and withdraw the cable through the floorpan grommets (photo).
18   Refit the new cable by reversing the removal operations. Adjust the cable tension by means of the threaded end fitting and locknut at the carburettor end to provide a small amount of slackness in the cable (photo).

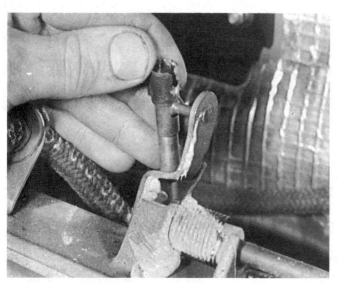

6.13 Removing throttle cable spring clips

6.15 Cable arrangement at accelerator pedal crank rod

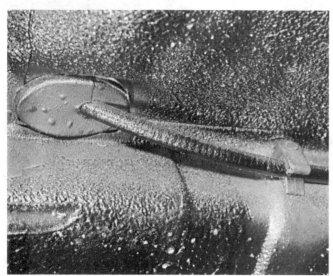

6.17 Accelerator cable under car

6.18 Throttle cable adjuster nut

Accelerator pedal – removal and refitting

19 Working within the driver's side footwell, extract the screws and nuts, and remove the accelerator pedal protective plate and the clutch pedal footrest, and peel back the carpet (photo).
20 The pedal is of cranked cross-rod type, the rod being protected by a cover which should be removed after extracting the fixing screws (photos).
21 Disconnect the accelerator cable from the pedal rod crankarm as previously described.
22 Reaching down into the centre tunnel forward aperture, release the fixing at the left-hand end of the pedal cross-rod (photo).
23 Move the cross-rod as necessary to release it from its support bushes and withdraw the complete pedal/rod assembly.
24 Refitting is a reversal of removal.

Carburettor (Weber 34 DATR) – description
25 This carburettor is fitted to 1498 cc engined models.

26 The unit is of dual barrel, downdraught type with a coolant-heated automatic choke (photos).
27 The carburettor is flow-tested and set during production and adjustment should not normally be required unless it has been dismantled and reassembled, or engine characteristics have radically changed due to wear or carbon build-up.

Carburettor (Weber 34 DATR) – idle speed and mixture adjustment
28 Remove the tamperproof cap, if fitted, from the throttle speed screw.
29 Have the engine at normal operating temperature with valve clearances, spark plugs and ignition timing correctly set.
30 Switch off all electrical components and, with the engine idling, wait until the radiator fan cuts in, then adjust the throttle speed screw until the idle speed is within the specified range (photo).

6.19 Accelerator pedal protection plate. Clutch pedal footrest locating stud (arrowed)

6.20A Accelerator pedal cross-rod cover

6.20B Accelerator pedal and cross-rod

6.22 Pedal cross-rod end fixing

6.26A Weber 34 DATR carburettor, view of automatic choke side

6.26B Weber 34 DATR carburettor, view of accelerator pump side

6.26C Weber 34 DATR carburettor viewed from fuel inlet side

6.26D Weber 34 DATR carburettor viewed from the top

6.30 Adjusting idle speed

31 An exhaust gas analyser will be required to check the fuel mixture precisely. If the exhaust CO level is outside the specified limits, remove the blanking plug from the carburettor flange and turn the adjustment screw inwards to weaken the mixture or unscrew it to enrich the mixture (photo).

32 If the adjustment period exceeds two minutes, increase the engine speed for one minute to clear the intake, return to idle and resume adjustment.

33 Check and adjust the idle speed again if necessary.

Carburettor (Weber 34 DATR) – removal and refitting

34 Remove the air cleaner as described in Chapter 3.

35 Disconnect the throttle link rod from the carburettor (photo).

36 Disconnect the fuel flow and return hoses from the carburettor and plug them.

37 Remove the cap from the coolant expansion tank to release the system pressure. Cover the cap with a rag if the system is hot to prevent scalding.

38 Disconnect the two coolant hoses from the automatic choke housing and quickly tie them up as high as possible to avoid coolant loss (photo).

39 Disconnect the leads from the anti-run-on valve (photo).

40 Unscrew the four fixing nuts and remove the carburettor. Discard the flange gasket (photo).

41 Refitting is a reversal of removal, always use a new flange gasket fitted to perfectly clean mating surfaces.

42 Top up the coolant in the expansion tank on completion.

Carburettor (Weber 34 DATR) – overhaul

43 Overhaul of a modern carburettor should not be regarded as routine and the operations should be restricted to those described for the purpose of cleaning the carburettor interior and the jets.

44 If wear is detected, a new or factory reconditioned unit is recommended as, in any event, small components are becoming increasingly difficult to obtain.

45 Always obtain a repair kit in advance of commencing the work. This will contain all the necessary gaskets and other renewable items.

46 With the carburettor removed from the engine, clean away all external dirt, using a brush and a suitable solvent.

47 Detach the externally mounted diaphragm units (accelerator pump and choke pull down).

48 Extract the securing screws which hold the upper body to the main body, then lift the upper body slowly to avoid damaging the floats (photo).

49 Mop or syphon out the fuel from the float bowl and remove any sediment. Unscrew the plug, remove the filter and clean it (photo).

50 The individual jet may be removed and cleared using air pressure from a tyre pump – never probe with wire as this will ruin their calibration. Remove only one jet at a time to avoid any possibility of refitting it in the wrong position. Always use a screwdriver or spanner of a close fitting type to avoid damage to the jets or bleed orifices (photo).

51 When refitting a jet, tighten it securely, with a new sealing washer (if fitted). Do not overtighten it; its thread may strip out those in the alloy body of the carburettor.

52 A jet of air from a tyre pump may be applied to any or all of the jets and passages which are visible, as a means of clearing the carburettor internal passages.

53 It is not usually necessary to disturb the adjustment screws or the fuel cut-off valve.

54 The accelerator pump diaphragm can be renewed once the pump cover is removed.

55 Flooding or heavy fuel consumption may be due to an incorrect fuel level in the float bowl, or a loose or worn fuel inlet needle valve. First remove the float pivot and detach the float. Using a socket, box or ring spanner, check the security of the needle valve seat. This must be really tight, otherwise fuel will bypass the needle valve and cause the fuel level to rise, even when the float is in the fully raised position.

6.31 Tamperproof plug on mixture screw

6.35 Carburettor throttle link rod

6.38 Automatic choke coolant hoses

6.39 Anti-run-on (anti-diesel) valve leads

6.40 Unscrewing a carburettor mounting nut

6.48 Upper body (with floats) removed

56 If the needle valve has been in service for a long time, it is best to renew it, also the float pivot pin, if it is grooved.

57 Once the fuel inlet valve and the float assembly have been refitted, check the float adjustment.

58 Reassembly is a reversal of the dismantling process; use new gaskets and other parts from the repair kit and, as work progresses, check the other adjustments as described in the following paragraphs.

59 Before fitting the top cover, half fill the fuel bowl with clean fuel as an aid to rapid start-up, but keep the unit in an upright position once this is done.

60 After overhaul and the carburettor is refitted to the engine, adjust the idle as described earlier and check that the choke housing and cover marks are in alignment (photo).

Float level adjustment

61 Remove the cover assembly and hold it vertically so the float hangs downward to lightly seat the fuel inlet needle valve.

62 Measure the distance between the surface of the cover gasket and each float face. This should be between 6.75 and 7.25 mm (0.27 and 0.29 in). Make sure that the gasket-to-float distances are equal. Where adjustment is required, gently bend the float arm or tang.

Fast idle throttle valve opening adjustment

63 With the automatic choke cover removed, close the choke valve completely and position the fast idle screw on the highest cam step.

64 Measure the opening of the primary throttle valve, using a twist drill or gauge rod. If it is outside the specified limits, adjust by turning the fast idle screw.

6.49 Filter screen and plug

6.50 Location of jets

6.60 Choke housing and cover alignment marks

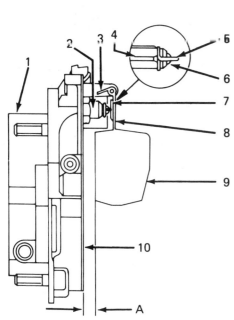

Fig. 13.1 Float adjustment diagram (Sec 6)

1   Top cover   6   Damper ball
2   Fuel inlet valve   7   Float tang
3   Float stroke stop   8   Float arm
4   Needle valve detail   9   Float
5   Valve hook   10   Gasket

A (Float setting dimension) = 6.75 to 7.25 mm (0.266 to 0.285 in)

Fig. 13.2 Fast idle throttle valve opening diagram (Sec 6)

1   Choke valve plate   3   Cam
2   Fast idle screw   4   Primary throttle valve plate

X = 0.95 to 1.05 mm (0.037 to 0.041 in)

Choke unloader (vacuum pulldown) opening adjustment

65 Position the screw on the second step of the cam (2). See Fig. 13.3.

66 A special tool (No 4460, shown in Fig. 13.4) should be obtained and fitted to the rod (7). In the absence of the special tool, the rod can be gripped with pliers, provided its jaws are insulated to prevent scoring the rod.

67 Push the rod until it makes contact with the stop screw (6), and hold it in this position.

68 Now measure the gap (D), which should be between 3.75 and 4.75 mm (0.15 and 0.19 in). Where necessary, adjust the gap by rotating the screw (6) which is accessible once the outer threaded plug (8) is extracted. See Fig. 13.3.

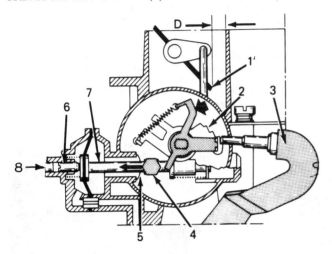

Fig. 13.3 Choke vacuum pulldown (unloader) checking diagram (Sec 6)

1	Choke valve plate
2	Fast idle cam
3	Fast idle linkage
4	Tool No. 4460
5	Bush
6	Stop screw
7	Rod
8	Threaded plug

D = 3.75 to 4.75 mm (0.148 to 0.187 in)

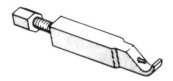

Fig. 13.4 Pullrod gripping tool (Sec 6)

---

7 Ignition system

Distributor (Marelli) — routine servicing

1 At the specified intervals, take off the distributor cap and rotor and prise the contact points apart with the thumb nail. If the faces of the contact points are burned or severely eroded, renew them in the following way.

2 It is worth remembering that better access to the distributor (and fuel pump) is obtained after removal of the spare wheel and then unbolting and withdrawing the inspection plate (photos).

3 Extract the two screws which secure the contact breaker assembly and remove the assembly from the baseplate.

4 Fit the new contact breaker assembly with the securing screws only finger tight.

5 Turn the crankshaft until the plastic heel of the movable contact arm is on a high point of the cam (photo).

7.2A Inspection plate fixing nut

7.2B Removing inspection plate upwards. Distributor cap must be removed first

7.5 Marelli contact breaker

7.6 Checking contact points gap

7.15A Distributor showing clamp plate and nut

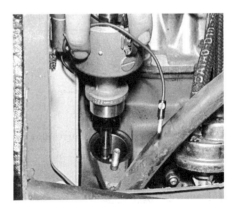

7.15B Removing distributor. Note LT lead

6 Using a feeler blade, check and adjust the points gap to specification. Notches are provided in the contact breaker arms to insert a screwdriver for the purpose of adjustment by twisting the blade (photo).

7 Tighten the contact breaker screws.

8 Apply a smear of grease to the high points of the cam and two drops of engine oil to the felt pad in the recess in the top of the distributor shaft.

9 Refit the rotor and cap.

10 Check the dwell angle with a suitable meter. There is no external adjustment so any alteration required to the points gap will require removal of the distributor cap again.

11 Once the dwell angle is correct, check the ignition timing as described in Chapter 4.

Distributor (Marelli) – removal and refitting

12 Remove the distributor cap, turn the crankshaft pulley nut until

Distributor (Marelli) – HT lead connections

21 The HT lead sockets in the Marelli distributor cap are of side-located type. The positions are shown in Fig. 13.5.

---

8 Clutch

Clutch hydraulic system (1500 cc engine models)

1 The clutch slave cylinder and release lever on these models have been redesigned.

2 Although the clutch release bearing is in constant light contact with the diaphragm spring fingers, and therefore no free movement should be evident at the clutch pedal, the settings shown in Fig. 13.6 should be maintained.

3 Adjustment is carried out by means of the nut and locknut on the pushrod.

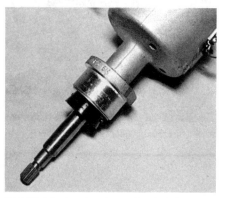

7.16 Distributor showing splined shaft

7.19A Extracting baseplate screw

7.19B Distributor with baseplate removed

the notch in the crankshaft pulley is opposite the TDC mark on the timing belt cover.

13 Mark the rim of the distributor body in alignment with the contact end of the rotor.

14 Remove the cover plate (see paragraph 2) for better access and mark the plinth of the distributor in relation to the crankcase.

15 Unscrew the clamp plate nut, disconnect the LT lead and withdraw the distributor (photos).

16 As the distributor shaft is splined to engage in the recess of the oil pump driveshaft, refitting is simply a matter of aligning the rotor and plinth marks and pushing the distributor into its location, but check that the timing marks are still at TDC before installation (photo).

17 Check the timing after refitting (Chapter 4).

Distributor (Marelli) – overhaul

18 Overhaul operations are very limited on this distributor.

19 The condenser can be renewed and the baseplate removed for access to the advance mechanism. No vacuum advance capsule is fitted (photos).

20 Wear in the shaft bush should be rectified by renewal of the complete distributor.

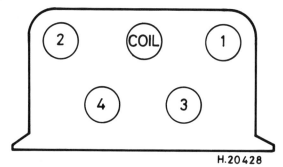

H.20428

Fig. 13.5 HT lead connections to Marelli distributor cap (Sec 7)

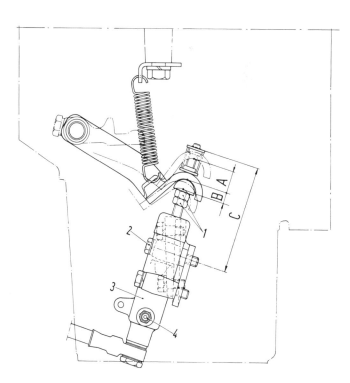

Fig. 13.6 Clutch slave cylinder and release lever on later models (Sec 8)

1	Nut and locknut	A = 19.66 mm (0.774 in)
2	Cylinder mounting bolt	B = 9.10 mm (0.358 in)
3	Slave cylinder	C = 95.00 mm (3.740 in)
4	Bleed screw	

Clutch pedal – removal and refitting

4   Remove the underdash trim panel from the driver's side.
5   Disconnect the pushrod from the pedal arm by extracting the split pin and clevis pin.
6   Unscrew the nut from the end of the pedal cross-shaft, slide out the shaft and take off the pedal (photo).
7   Refitting is a reversal of removal.
8   The foregoing operations will prove to be extremely fiddly. It may be found easier to disconnect the fluid pipes and hoses from the master cylinder and then unbolt and remove them to provide greater working clearance. If this is done, the hydraulic system must be bled in completion of refitting.

9   Manual transmission

Gearchange lever – removal and refitting

1   Using an Allen key, extract the grub screw then unscrew and remove the gear lever knob (photos).
2   Extract the centre tunnel fixing screws (photo).
3   Slide the tunnel upwards off the gear lever, at the same time disconnecting any switch leads and the LED plug from its socket.
4   Unscrew and remove the three screws which secure the gear lever upper plate (photo).
5   Twist the plate until it releases from the fastening clips.

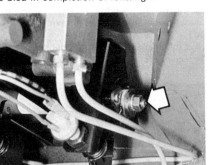

8.6 Pedal cross-shaft nut (arrowed)

9.1A Extracting grub screw from gear lever knob

9.1B Unscrewing gear lever knob

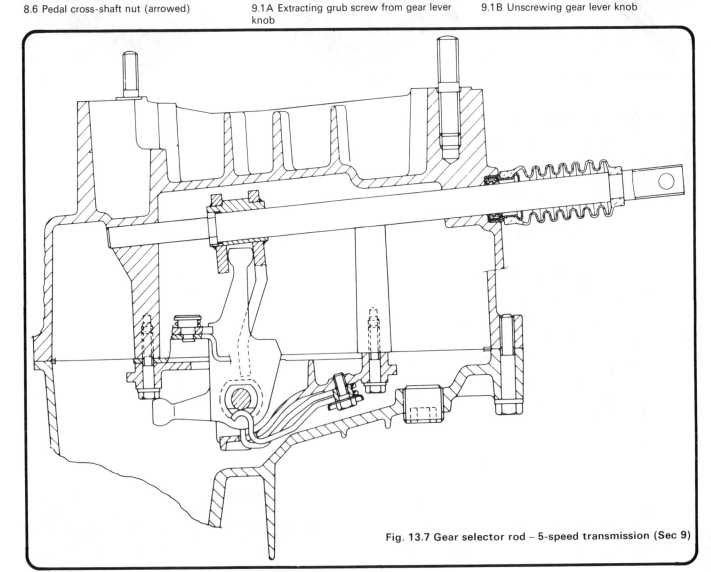

Fig. 13.7 Gear selector rod – 5-speed transmission (Sec 9)

6   Remove the lower plate.
7   Withdraw the gear lever until the connecting bolt and nut can be removed, and the gear lever withdrawn. The insulated link rod can be disconnected after removal of the bolt (photo). When reassembling the linkage or gear lever, adjust if necessary at the elongated holes in the sandwich plate to give smooth side-to-side movement of the lever in neutral (photo).

Transmission (5-speed) – removal and refitting
8   The operations are as described in Chapter 6, but note that the driveshafts must be disconnected from the transmission by extracting the socket-headed bolts with an Allen key (photo).
9   Disconnection of the gearchange linkage is as described in the preceding sub-section.

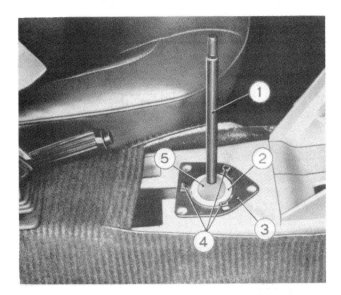

Fig. 13.8 Gearchange lever lower plate (Sec 9)

1 Lever	4 Upper plate fasteners
2 Ball seat	5 Lever ball
3 Lower plate	

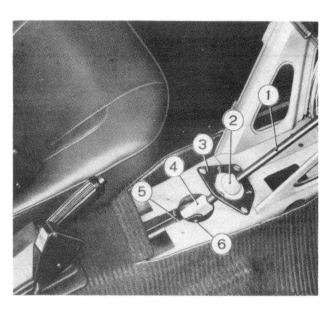

Fig. 13.9 Withdrawing gearchange lever (Sec 9)

1 Gearchange lever	4 Trunnion
2 Ball	5 Linkage
3 Lower plate	6 Connecting bolt and nut

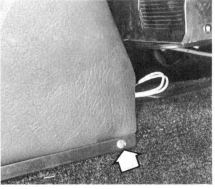

9.2 Centre tunnel fixing screw (arrowed)

9.4 Gear lever upper plate screws

9.7A Gear linkage disconnection bolt (arrowed)

9.7B Gear link rod sandwich plate showing elongated holes

9.8 Driveshaft socket-headed bolts

Transmission (5-speed) – dismantling

10 The operations are essentially as described in Chapter 6, Section 3 for the 4-speed type, but the following additional work will be required after having taken off the transmission casing end cover.

11 Release the 5th gear selector fork lockbolt and slide the fork up its selector shaft, together with the 5th gear synchro sleeve; remove the sleeve from the output shaft.

12 Grip the balljointed end of the gearchange selector rod and push or pull to select any gear.

13 Refit the 5th gear synchro sleeve to the output shaft and depress it fully to lock up 5th gear.

14 With two gears now simultaneously engaged, the input and output shaft nuts can be unscrewed, having first relieved the staking.

15 Remove the 5th gear synchro sleeve for the second time, then withdraw the 5th gear synchro hub, followed by the 5th gear from the input shaft.

16 Take off the 5th gear from the output shaft.

17 Extract the two securing screws and remove the intermediate plate and its paper gasket.

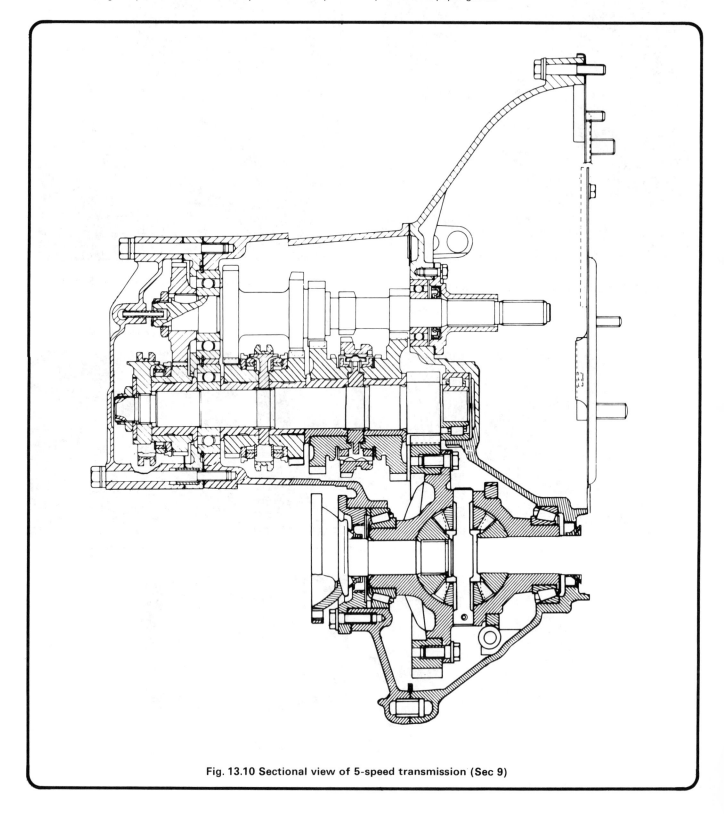

Fig. 13.10 Sectional view of 5-speed transmission (Sec 9)

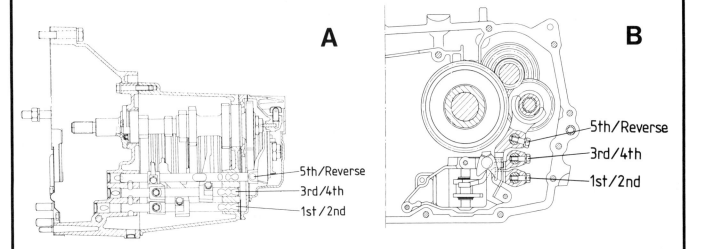

Fig. 13.11 Selector shaft (A) and fork (B) arrangements – 5-speed transmission (Sec 9)

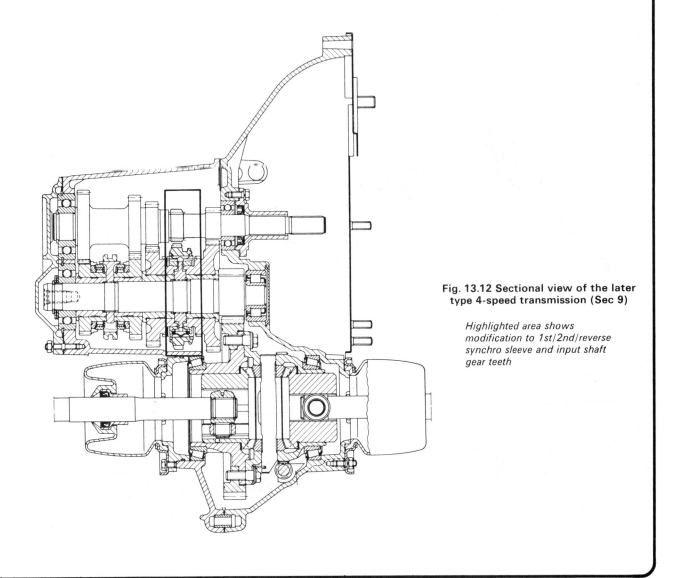

Fig. 13.12 Sectional view of the later type 4-speed transmission (Sec 9)

Highlighted area shows modification to 1st/2nd/reverse synchro sleeve and input shaft gear teeth

Input shaft

18 Only the bearing can be renewed on the input shaft. Use a puller or press to remove and refit it (photo).

Output shaft

19 All components can be removed from the output shaft using hand pressure only, with the exception of the bearing, for which a puller will be required (photos).

20 When reassembling the output shaft, remember to fit the washer and 5th gear bush to the end of the shaft (photo).

Transmission (5-speed) – reassembly

21 The operations are similar to those for the 4-speed type described in Chapter 6, Section 7, but carry out the following additional work (photos).

22 Locate the intermediate plate, using a new gasket.

23 Fit the Woodruff key into its shaft groove and slide the 5th gear over it, onto the input shaft (photos).

24 With the 5th gear bush fitted to the output shaft (oiled liberally) slide on the 5th gear and synchro-hub (photos).

25 Fit the 5th gear synchro sleeve with its chamfered edge away from the gear teeth.

26 Tap the synchro sleeve downward so that the shift fork (not yet lockbolted) slides on its rod at the same time. Fit the shaft thrust washers (photos).

27 Insert a thin screwdriver into the lockbolt hole in the selector rod and prise it upward, so engaging 5th gear.

28 Select another gear by pushing or pulling the main gearchange operating remote control rod (photo).

29 With both shafts now prevented from rotating, screw on their nuts, tighten them to the specified torque and stake them (photos).

30 Release the 5th gear and the other gear which were selected to lock up the input and output shafts; insert and tighten the 5th gear shift fork lockbolt on its selector rod (photo).

31 Fit the end cover with a new gasket (photo).

Transmission (4-speed) – modifications

32 At the beginning of 1978 (from chassis No. 3056610) a major design change occurred, and many of the 4-speed transmission components were extensively modified.

33 The most significant visible change concerns the orientation of the 1st/2nd/reverse synchro sleeve on the second shaft gear cluster. On the modified transmission, the sleeve position is the other way round to that of the earlier transmission, so that the selector fork groove is now towards 1st gear. Consequently, the reverse gear teeth on the input shaft are now positioned closer to the 2nd gear teeth, and the selector forks have been altered accordingly. Reference to Fig. 13.12 in this Supplement, and Fig. 6.1 in Chapter 6 will clearly show the differences between the two types.

34 Apart from these changes, none of the other modifications affect the procedures contained in Chapter 6, which are still valid for later transmissions.

35 Ensure that any replacement parts are correct for the type of transmission being worked on, since the modified parts are not interchangeable with those for the earlier transmission.

10 Braking system

Brake (and clutch) hydraulic systems – alternative bleeding methods

1 In addition to the method described in Chapter 8, Section 4, either of the following methods may be used.

Bleeding – using one way valve kit

2 There is a number of one-man, one-way brake bleeding kits available from motor accessory shops. It is recommended that one of these kits is used wherever possible as it will greatly simplify the bleeding operation and also reduce the risk of air or fluid being drawn back into the system quite apart from being able to do the work without the help of an assistant.

9.18 Input shaft

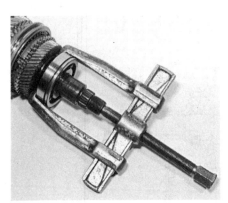
9.19A Removing the output shaft bearing

9.19B Output shaft, stripped

9.20 Fitting the washer and 5th gear bush

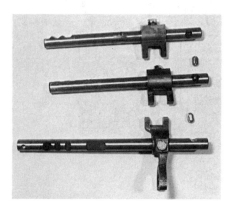
9.21A Gear selector rods
Top 1st/2nd   Middle 3rd/4th
Bottom 5th/reverse

9.21B Selector rods correctly located
Left to right: 5th/reverse
3rd/4th   1st/2nd

9.23A Woodruff key on the input shaft

9.23B Fitting 5th gear to the input shaft

9.24A Fitting 5th gear to the output shaft

9.24B Fitting 5th gear syncrho-hub to the output shaft

9.26A Fitting 5th gear synchro sleeve and selector fork

9.26B Fitting a shaft thrust washer

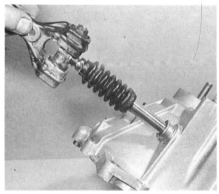

9.28 Gearchange selector remote control rod

9.29A Tightening a shaft nut

9.29B Staking a shaft nut

9.30 Tightening the 5th gear selector lockbolt

9.31 Refitting the end cover to the transmission casing

3   To use the kit, connect the tube to the bleed screw and open the screw one half a turn.
4   Depress the brake pedal fully and slowly release it. The one-way valve in the kit will prevent expelled air from returning at the end of each pedal downstroke. Repeat this operation several times to be sure of ejecting all air from the system. Some kits include a translucent container which can be positioned so that the air bubbles can actually be seen being ejected from the system.
5   Tighten the bleed screw, remove the tube and repeat the operations on the remaining brakes.
6   On completion, depress the brake pedal. If it still feels spongy repeat the bleeding operations as air must still be trapped in the system.

Bleeding – using a pressure bleeding kit

7   These kits too are available from motor accessory shops and are usually operated by air pressure from the spare tyre.
8   By connecting a pressurised container to the master cylinder fluid reservoir, bleeding is then carried out by simply opening each bleed screw in turn and allowing the fluid to run out, rather like turning on a tap, until no air is visible in the expelled fluid.
9   By using this method, the large reserve of hydraulic fluid provides a safeguard against air being drawn into the master cylinder during bleeding which often occurs if the fluid level in the reservoir is not maintained.
10 Pressure bleeding is particularly effective when bleeding 'difficult' systems or when bleeding the complete system at time of routine fluid renewal.

All methods

11 When bleeding is completed, check and top up the fluid level in the master cylinder reservoir.
12 Check the feel of the brake pedal. If it feels at all spongy, air must still be present in the system and further bleeding is indicated. Failure to bleed satisfactorily after a reasonable period of the bleeding operation may be due to worn master cylinder seals.
13 Discard brake fluid which has been expelled. It is almost certain to be contaminated with moisture, air and dirt making it unsuitable for further use. Clean fluid should always be stored in an airtight container as it absorbs moisture readily (hygroscopic) which lowers its boiling point and could affect braking performance under severe conditions.

Brake pedal – removal and refitting

14 The brake and clutch pedals operate on a common cross-shaft, refer to Section 8 for clutch pedal removal and refitting.

11.6 Alternator terminals

11 Electrical system

Battery – low maintenance type

1   The low maintenance type battery fitted to later models should not require regular topping-up, but still check the electrolyte level regularly. The battery is located under a protective cover within the front luggage boot. Knurled thumb nuts secure the cover .
2   The need for anything more than the adding of a small amount of distilled or purified water very infrequently will indicate that the battery is being overcharged (faulty alternator regulator) or that the casing is leaking (photo).
3   Never be tempted to mix or add battery acid. Any such requirement should be left to a battery retailer.
4   Keep the terminals clean and smeared with petroleum jelly.
5   Disconnect the battery leads before using a mains charger.

Alternator (Bosch type) – brush renewal

6   With the alternator removed as described in Chapter 10, clean away external dirt (photo).
7   Unscrew the nuts and take off the plastic rear cover (photo).
8   Extract the two screws and withdraw the brush holder. If the brushes have worn down to their minimum specified length, renew the holder and brushes as an assembly (photos).

11.2 Battery with cell covers removed

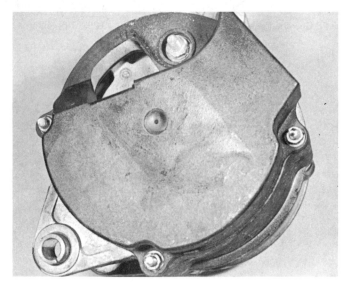

11.7 Alternator rear cover

9   Check the condition of the slip rings. Clean them with a petrol-moistened cloth or fine glasspaper if heavy discolouration must be removed (photo).
10 Refit the brush holder and rear cover.

Fuses and relays
11 Later models have a revised fuse block (see Specifications) which incorporates most of the plug-in type relays (photo).
12 A separate relay for the carburettor cooling fan is located to the left of the spare wheel compartment (photo).

Headlamp bulb – renewal
13 Extract the screws and take off the headlamp filler plate (photo).
14 Release but do not remove the screws which hold the headlamp rim. Turn the rim in an anti-clockwise direction and remove it (photos).

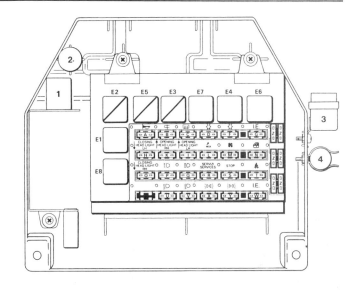

Fig. 13.13 Fuse and relay block on later models (Sec 9)

For key see Specifications

11.8A Brush holder fixing screws

11.8B Removing brush holder

11.9 Alternator slip rings

11.11 Fuse and relay block

15 Withdraw the lamp unit and disconnect the wiring plug (photo).
16 Release the spring clip, remove the bulb holder.
17 Reassembly is a reversal of dismantling, do not touch the bulb glass with the fingers (photo).

Headlamp beams – alignment
18 It is recommended that the headlamp beams are checked and adjusted by your dealer or a service station having optical beam setting equipment.
19 However, the following procedure will give a reasonably accurate setting.
20 Have the car standing on a level surface square to and a distance of 5.0 m (16.0 ft) from a wall or screen.
21 Mark the wall at two points to represent the exact height and distance apart of the two headlamp lens centres.

22 Switch on dipped beam and the bright spots of the lights should be 35.0 mm (1.4 in) below the marks on the wall.
23 Adjust if necessary by turning the screws shown (photos). The screw which is accessible from the side controls horizontal movement while the one at the base controls vertical movement.

Lamp bulbs – renewal
Rear number plate lamp
24 Access to the bulbs is obtained by depressing the catches and withdrawing the lamp body (photo).
Rear foglamp
25 Extract the two screws and remove the lens (photo).
Side repeater lamp
26 Twist the lamp through 90° and withdraw it. Renew the lamp complete with bulb (photo).

11.12 Carburettor fan relay

11.13 Headlamp filler plate screw

11.14A Releasing a rim screw

11.14B Turning the headlamp rim

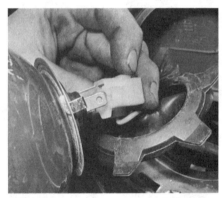

11.15 Disconnecting a headlamp wiring plug

11.17 Headlamp unit locating notch

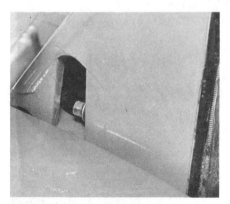

11.23A Headlamp horizontal adjuster

11.23B Headlamp vertical adjuster

11.24 Rear number plate lamp

Courtesy lamp bulb
27 Prise the lamp lens from the door panel using a screwdriver. Remove the bulb (photos).

Warning and illumination lamp bulbs
28 These lamp bulbs can only be renewed after withdrawal of the instrument panel. Note that switches on the centre console are illuminated by fibre optics from a light source located under the centre of the centre console (photos).

Courtesy lamp switch – removal and refitting
29 Open the door wide and extract the screw which holds the switch to the body pillar, then withdraw the switch. If the leads are to be disconnected, tape them to the pillar to prevent them from slipping into the body cavity (photo).
30 Smear the switch terminals and contacts with petroleum jelly before refitting as a means of preventing corrosion.

Push-button and rocker switches – removal and refitting
31 The control switches or switch plate mounted in the centre console are removed by gently prising them out with a small screwdriver (photos).
32 Withdraw the switch until the multi-pin plug can be disconnected.
33 Refitting is a reversal of removal.

Horn switch – removal and refitting
34 Disconnect the battery negative lead.
35 Peel the plastic cover from the centre of the steering wheel (photo).
36 Disconnect the lead from the spade terminal and remove the sealed horn switch capsule (photo).
37 Refitting is a reversal of removal.

11.25 Rear foglamp

11.26 Side repeater lamp

11.27A Removing a courtesy lamp

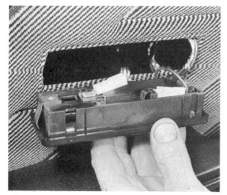
11.27B Courtesy lamp connections and bulb

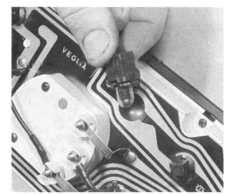
11.28A Instrument panel bulb

11.28B Fibre optic light source

11.29 Courtesy lamp switch

11.31A Withdrawing window lift switches

11.31B Withdrawing push-button switch

Instrument panel – removal and refitting

38 Disconnect the battery negative terminal.

39 Using an Allen key, extract the instrument panel fixing screws – three long ones at the upper edge, two shorter ones at the lower edge (photo).

40 Disconnect the speedometer drive cable. To do this, remove the right-hand scuttle grille and slide back the speedometer cable coupling sleeve. Note the short intermediate section of the speedometer drive cable, and the routing of the main cable through the front luggage boot and underneath the car to the transmission (photos).

41 Pull the instrument panel from the binnacle until the colour-coded multi-pin plugs can be disconnected from the rear of the panel.

42 Slide the panel out sideways behind the steering wheel (photos).

11.31C Switch panel removed

11.35 Steering wheel cover removed

11.36 Horn switch

11.39 Instrument panel screw (arrowed)

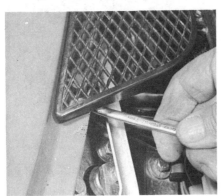

11.40A Unscrewing a grille nut

11.40B Removing a scuttle grille

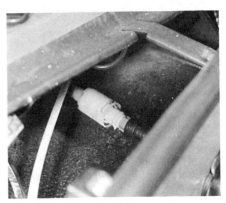

11.40C Speedometer cable connecting sleeve

11.40D Speedometer intermediate cable

11.40E Speedometer cable entry at bulkhead adjacent to master cylinder fluid supply hoses

11.40F Speedometer cable at under car grommet

Windscreen wiper blade – removal and refitting
43 Pull the wiper arm away from the glass until it locks.
44 Using the thumb nail or a small screwdriver, prise the tab to release the peg from its hole and slide the blade from the arm (photo).
45 Refitting is a reversal of removal.

Windscreen wiper arm – removal and refitting
46 Stick a piece of masking tape along the edge of the wiper blade on the glass as a guide to refitting.
47 Pull the wiper arm away from the glass until it locks.
48 Pull the arm from the splined shaft of the wheelbox. If it is tight, insert a screwdriver under opposing edges of the cap and prise the arm upwards against the clip (photo).
49 Before refitting, apply a smear of grease to the shaft splines and only partially push the arm onto the shaft before checking its alignment on the screen. If its position on the glass was not marked

before removal, set the arm so that the blade is parallel to and between 65.0 and 85.0 mm (2.5 and 3.3 in) from the lower edge of the windscreen glass.

Windscreen washer
50 The fluid reservoir for the system is located within the front luggage compartment and incorporates an electric pump (photo).
51 The pump can be removed after disconnecting the leads and prising it out. Use a new seal when refitting the pump (photo).
52 The jet nozzles can be adjusted by means of a screwdriver to give a satisfactory wash pattern on the screen.

Power-operated windows
53 The control switches are located in the centre console (photo).
54 Access to the window winder motor is obtained after removal of the door interior trim panel as described in Chapter 12 (photo).

11.42A Withdrawing the instrument panel

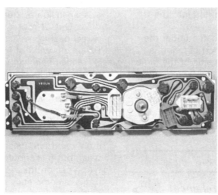
11.42B Rear view of the instrument panel

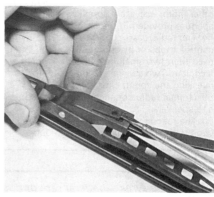
11.44 Using a screwdriver to disconnect a wiper blade

11.48 Wiper arm removed. Retaining clip arrowed

11.50 Washer fluid reservoir retaining bracket

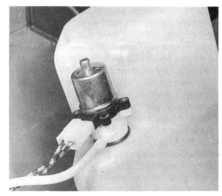
11.51 Washer reservoir pump

11.53 Power window switches in centre console. Note console rear fixing screw

11.54 Window winder motor

55 In the event of a failure, the windows can be raised or lowered manually using the handle which is stored in the glove compartment. This facility does not apply to 1988 models.
56 Fitting the handle is somewhat complicated on the first occasion it is used.
57 Prise out the plastic plug from the door trim panel.
58 Punch a hole in the plastic waterproof sheeting.
59 Depress the handle spring and push the gear end of the handle into the hole in the panel to engage the pin.
60 Release the handle spring and gently pull on the handle to check that it has locked.
61 Turn the handle in the required direction to raise or lower the glass. Never depress the window control switches while the handle is locked in position.
62 To remove the handle, depress the spring and pull.

Radio (FIAT accessory) – removal and refitting

63 The in-car entertainment equipment supplied by FIAT dealers or other motor accessory suppliers will normally be fitted into the aperture provided in the facia panel.
64 The radio/cassette may be secured by nuts located under the control knobs or by spring clips. If the latter method of fixing is used then two small holes will be evident at each side of the radio faceplate. Two special (U-shaped) removal tools will be required for releasing the spring clips.
65 Normal radio connections will be required: power, earth, aerial and speakers.
66 The recommended location for the aerial is on the left-hand rear wing with entry into the luggage boot.

12 Suspension

Wheels and tyres – general care and maintenance

1 Wheels and tyres should give no real problems in use provided that a close eye is kept on them with regard to excessive wear or damage. To this end, the following points should be noted.
2 Ensure that tyre pressures are checked regularly and maintained correctly. Checking should be carried out with the tyres cold and not immediately after the vehicle has been in use. If the pressures are checked with the tyres hot, an apparently high reading will be obtained owing to heat expansion. Under no circumstances should an attempt be made to reduce the pressures to the quoted cold reading in this instance, or effective underinflation will result.
3 Underinflation will cause overheating of the tyre owing to excessive flexing of the casing, and the tread will not sit correctly on the road surface. This will cause a consequent loss of adhesion and excessive wear, not to mention the danger of sudden tyre failure due to heat build-up.
4 Overinflation will cause rapid wear of the centre part of the tyre tread coupled with reduced adhesion, harsher ride, and the danger of shock damage occurring in the tyre casing.
5 Regularly check the tyres for damage in the form of cuts or bulges, especially in the sidewalls. Remove any nails or stones embedded in the tread before they penetrate the tyre to cause deflation. If removal of a nail *does* reveal that the tyre has been punctured, refit the nail so that its point of penetration is marked.

Then immediately change the wheel and have the tyre repaired by a tyre dealer. Do *not* drive on a tyre in such a condition. In many cases a puncture can be simply repaired by the use of an inner tube of the correct size and type. If in any doubt as to the possible consequences of any damage found, consult your local tyre dealer for advice.
6 Periodically remove the wheels and clean any dirt or mud from the inside and outside surfaces. Examine the wheel rims for signs of rusting, corrosion or other damage. Light alloy wheels are easily damaged by 'kerbing' whilst parking, and similarly steel wheels may become dented or buckled. Renewal of the wheel is very often the only course of remedial action possible.
7 The balance of each wheel and tyre assembly should be maintained to avoid excessive wear, not only to the tyres but also to the steering and suspension components. Wheel imbalance is normally signified by vibration through the vehicle's bodyshell, although in many cases it is particularly noticeable through the steering wheel. Conversely, it should be noted that wear or damage in suspension or steering components may cause excessive tyre wear. Out-of-round or out-of-true tyres, damaged wheels and wheel bearing wear/maladjustment also fall into this category. Balancing will not usually cure vibration caused by such wear.
8 Wheel balancing may be carried out with the wheel either on or off the vehicle. If balanced on the vehicle, ensure that the wheel-to-hub relationship is marked in some way prior to subsequent wheel removal so that it may be refitted in its original position.
9 General tyre wear is influenced to a large degree by driving style – harsh braking and acceleration or fast cornering will all produce more rapid tyre wear. Interchanging of tyres may result in more even wear, but this should only be carried out where there is no mix of tyre types on the vehicle. However, it is worth bearing in mind that if this is completely effective, the added expense of replacing a complete set of tyres simultaneously is incurred, which may prove financially restrictive for many owners.
10 Front tyres may wear unevenly as a result of wheel misalignment. The front wheels should always be correctly aligned according to the settings specified by the vehicle manufacturer.
11 Legal restrictions apply to the mixing of tyre types on a vehicle. Basically this means that a vehicle must not have tyres of differing construction on the same axle. Although it is not recommended to mix tyre types between front axle and rear axle, the only legally permissible combination is crossply at the front and radial at the rear. When mixing radial ply tyres, textile braced radials must always go on the front axle, with steel braced radials at the rear. An obvious disadvantage of such mixing is the necessity to carry two spare tyres to avoid contravening the law in the event of a puncture.
12 In the UK, the Motor Vehicles Construction and Use Regulations apply to many aspects of tyre fitting and usage. It is suggested that a copy of these regulations is obtained from your local police if in doubt as to the current legal requirements with regard to tyre condition, minimum tread depth, etc.

Suspension mountings – general

13 Later models have slightly modified suspension mountings (photos).

12.13A Front suspension arm inboard mounting

12.13B Rear suspension arm front mounting

12.13C Radius rod front mounting

13 Bodywork

Radiator grille – removal and refitting

1 The radiator grille is held in place by self-tapping screws and can be removed independently of the front spoiler (photo).
2 Refitting is a reversal of removal.

Front spoiler and end caps – removal and refitting

3 Remove the radiator grille as previously described.
4 Extract the self-tapping screws from the centre section of the spoiler then unscrew the two bolts at each side plastic bracket (photo).
5 Slide the centre spoiler section towards you and remove it.
6 The end caps are secured by nuts and bolts, which are accessible after removal of the cover plate at each front corner of the front luggage boot, and self-tapping screws under the front corners of the floorpan (photos).
7 Refitting is a reversal of removal.

Front bumper – removal and refitting

8 Remove the radiator grille, unbolt the front parking/direction indicator lamps and allow them to hang on their leads (photos).
9 Unscrew the nuts which hold the bumper bar to the tubular brackets and withdraw the bumper (photos).
10 If the bumper upper trim strip must be removed, unscrew the retaining nuts which are accessible under the front lip of the front luggage boot (photo).
11 Refitting is a reversal of removal.

12.13D Rear suspension arm rear mounting

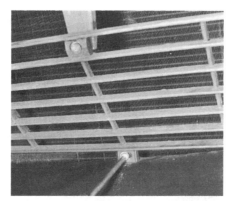
13.1 Extracting a radiator grille screw

13.4 Front spoiler bracket

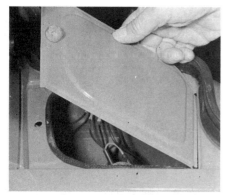
13.6A Removing a front boot cover plate

13.6B End cap fixing screw

13.8A Front parking/indicator lamp bracket

13.8B Releasing front parking/indicator lamp

13.9A Unscrewing a front bumper bracket nut

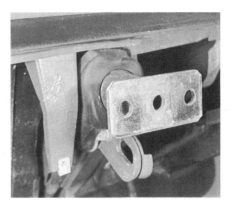
13.9B Front bumper mounting bracket

Rear bumper – removal and refitting

12 Disconnect the rear number plate lamps and the rear foglamp.
13 Unscrew the nuts which hold the bumper bar to the tubular mounting brackets.
14 Withdraw the bumper.
15 The upper trim strip and the end caps are held in position by bolts which are accessible from within the rear luggage boot (photos).
16 Refitting is a reversal of removal.

Door interior trim panel – removal and refitting

17 The procedure is similar to that described in Chapter 12, Section 7, but note that a different type of interior lock handle is used. Push the handle escutcheon plate towards the rear of the car then remove it (photo).
18 The handle itself stays in place while the door trim panel is removed.

Door – removal and refitting

19 Open the door to its full extent and disconnect the door check which is secured by bolts.
20 Remove the door interior trim panel only if power-operated windows are fitted, and disconnect the wiring harness and feed it out of the forward door edge (photo).
21 Support the lower edge of the door on jacks or blocks covered with soft material to prevent damage to the paintwork.
22 Using a large cross-head screwdriver, extract the screws which hold the hinges to the body pillar. Lift the door from the car (photo).
23 Refitting is a reversal of removal.

Wing protective shields

24 Protective shields are fitted underneath the front wings only and they are secured by small self-tapping screws (photo).

13.10 Front bumper upper trim strip fixing nut (arrowed)

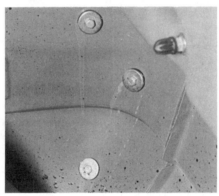

13.15A End cap fixing bolts

13.15B Rear bumper upper trim strip fixing nut

13.17 Removing door interior handle escutcheon

13.20 Door interior trim panel clips

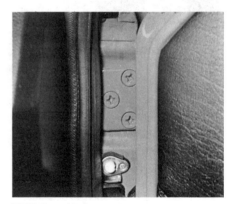

13.22 Door hinge screws

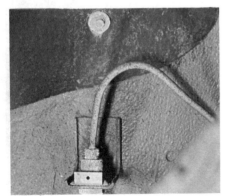

13.24 Wing protective shield fixing screw

13.25 Front boot lid latch control handle

13.26 Front boot lid latch

Lid latch remote control cables

Front luggage boot lid latch

25 The control handle is located under the left-hand side of the facia panel (photo).

26 Disconnect the cable from the latch and from the control handle (photo).

27 Tape the end of the new cable to the end of the old one and draw the new cable into position.

28 After connecting the new cable, adjust the tension using the end fitting nut to give smooth release without excessive movement of the control handle being necessary.

Engine compartment and rear boot lid latches

29 The remote control handles are recessed into the left-hand door closure pillar.

30 Extract the control handle assembly fixing screws (photo).

31 Extract the screws and remove the left-hand engine side air intake grille to expose the cables (photos).

32 Disconnect the cable from the latch (photo).

33 Note that the rear boot lid latch has an emergency cable attached to it with a ring pull located within the engine compartment below the coolant expansion tank (photo).

34 If a new cable is being fitted, tape it to the end of the old one and draw it into position.

13.30 Door pillar control handle fixing screw

13.31A Extracting engine side air intake grille screw

13.31B Removing an engine side air intake grille

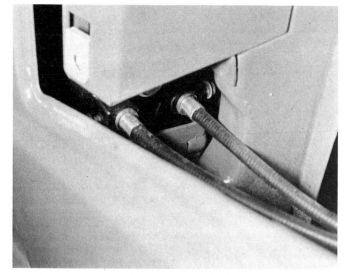

13.31C Cables exposed after withdrawal of grille

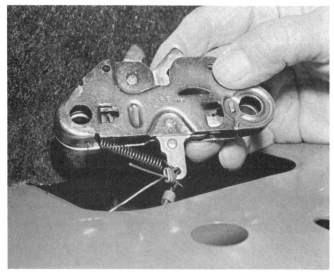

13.32 Rear boot lid latch

Instrument binnacle – removal and refitting

35 Remove the instrument panel as described in Section 11.
36 Disconnect the control cables from the levers on the heater.
37 Remove the radio (Section 11).
38 Extract the screws which are located within the instrument panel aperture and remove the binnacle (photo).
39 Refitting is a reversal of removal.

Seat belts

40 Regularly inspect the seat belts for fraying. If evident, renew the belt complete.
41 Clean seat belts with warm water and detergent only, and do not allow them to retract into their reel housings until they are dry.
42 If a seat belt is to be removed, note the sequence of the anchor plate components (spacer, wave washer etc) for exact replacement.
43 The seat belt inertia reel can be removed after unscrewing its single retaining bolt (photo).

Exterior mirror (1986 on) – removal and refitting

44 This is fixed to the front quarter light glass so exercise reasonable care.
45 Prise off the interior rubber cover (photo).
46 Unscrew the bezel nut now exposed and remove the nut and the buffer (photos).
47 Withdraw the mirror from outside the car (photo).

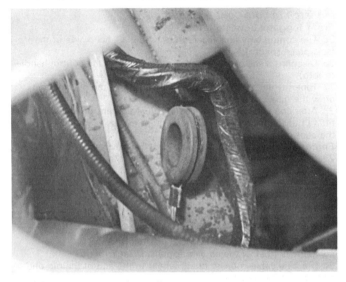

13.33 Emergency cable ring pull

13.38 Instrument binnacle fixing screws (arrowed)

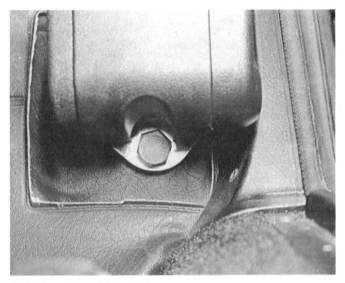

13.43 Seat belt reel fixing bolt

13.45 Removing exterior mirror control handle rubber cover

13.46A Exterior mirror fixing nut

48 If new glass is to be fitted, extract the two countersunk screws and withdraw the glass with mounting plate (photo). Protect the fingers and prise off the mirror or fragments of glass. Clean the surface of the mounting plate.

49 The new glass is supplied with a self-adhesive backing. Remove the paper and stick it correctly to the mounting plate.

50 Reassembly and refitting are reversals of removal and dismantling.

Interior mirror – removal and refitting

51 The mirror stem is secured to the base by a single screw while the base is held to the body by two screws (photo).

Rear grille – removal and refitting

52 This is removed by extracting the self-tapping screws (photo).

53 Once the grille is removed, the exhaust silencer spring-damped mounting bolts are accessible (photo).

54 Refitting is a reversal of removal.

13.46B Exterior mirror mounting buffer

13.47 Withdrawing exterior mirror

13.48 Exterior mirror glass and mechanism withdrawn

13.51 Interior mirror stem screw

13.52 Extracting a rear grille screw

13.53 Exhaust silencer mounting bolts

Wiring diagrams commence overleaf

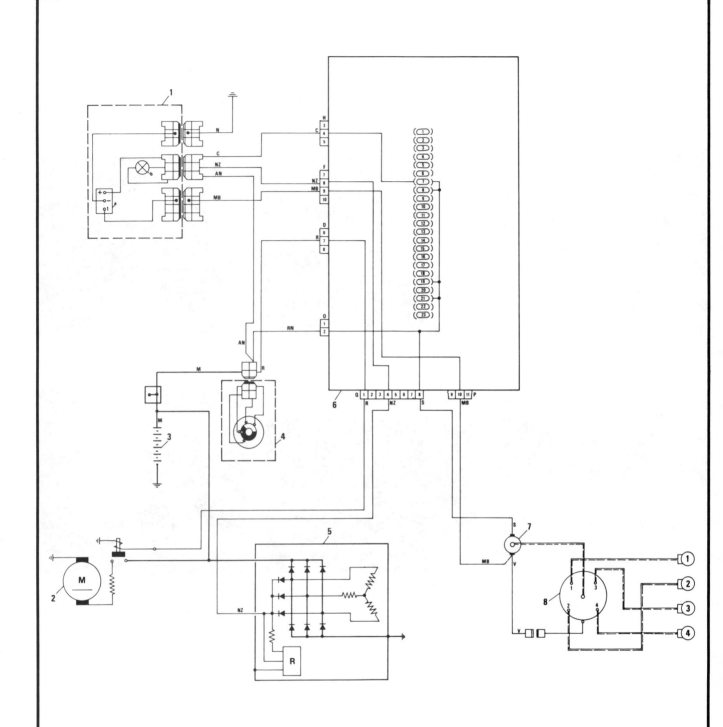

Fig. 13.14 Wiring diagram for 1500 cc models – starting, ignition and charging

1	Instrument cluster	2	Starter	5	Alternator	7	Ignition coil
a	Tachometer	3	Battery	6	Fuse block	8	Ignition distributor
b	Ignition light	4	Ignition switch				

Cable colour coding

A	Light Blue	G	Yellow	M	Brown	S	Pink
B	White	H	Grey	N	Black	V	Green
C	Orange	L	Blue	R	Red	Z	Violet

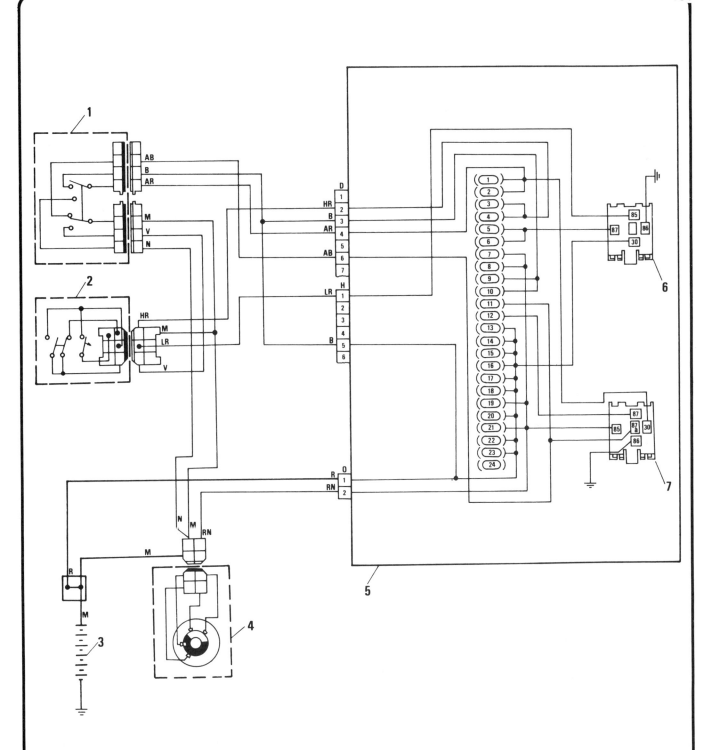

Fig. 13.15 Wiring diagram for 1500 cc models – headlamps

1 Lighting switch
2 Steering column dipper switch
3 Battery
4 Ignition coil
5 Fuse block
6 Headlamp relay
7 Headlamp motor relay

For colour code see key to Fig. 13.14

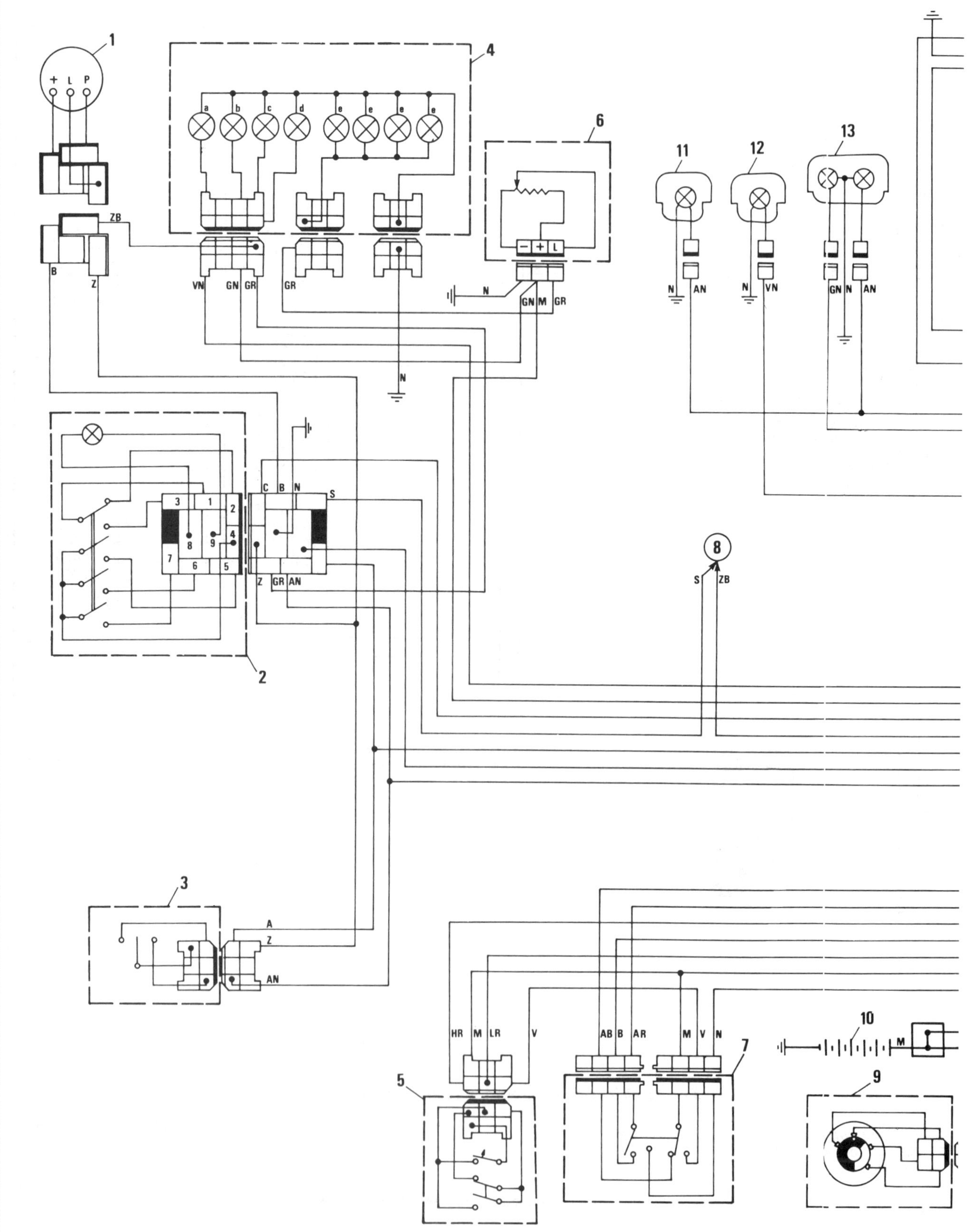

Fig. 13.16 Wiring diagram for 1500 cc models – front lights

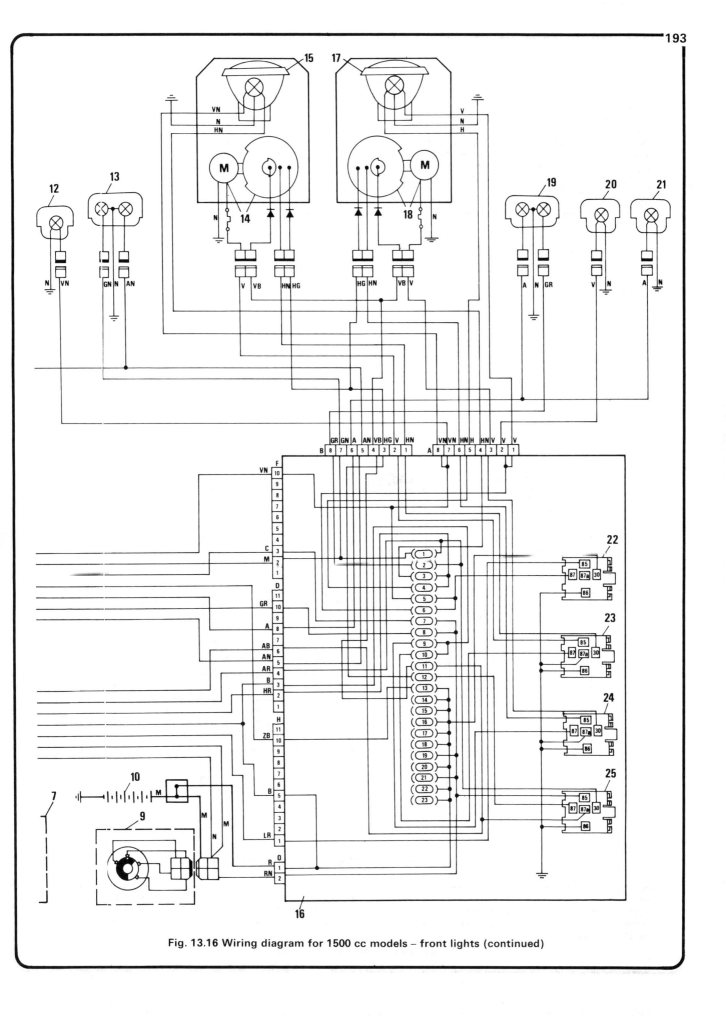

Fig. 13.16 Wiring diagram for 1500 cc models – front lights (continued)

Key to Fig. 13.16

1 Direction indicator/hazard warning relay
2 Hazard warning switch
3 Direction indicator switch
4 Instruments
  a Headlamp main beam warning lamp
  b Parking lamps warning lamp
  c Hazard warning lamp

  d Direction indicator warning lamp
  e Instrument illumination
5 Headlamp dip switch
6 Instrument illumination rheostat
7 Lighting switch
8 Courtesy lamp timer
9 Ignition switch
10 Battery

11 LH side repeater lamp
12 LH auxiliary driving lamp
13 LH front direction indicator/parking lamp
14 LH headlamp lift motor
15 LH headlamp main/dipped bulb
16 Fuse block
17 RH headlamp main/dipped bulb

18 RH headlamp lift motor
19 RH front direction indicator/parking lamp
20 RH auxiliary driving lamp
21 RH side repeater lamp
22 Headlamp beam relay
23 LH headlamp lift motor relay
24 RH headlamp lift motor relay
25 Headlamp raised switch relay

For colour code see key to Fig. 13.14

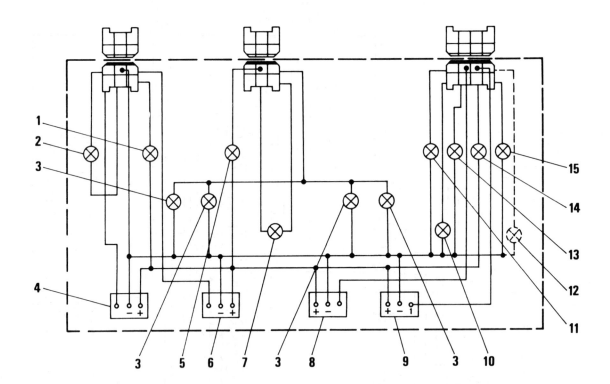

Fig. 13.17 Wiring diagram for 1500 cc models – instrument panel

1 Handbrake 'on' and brake fluid warning lamp
2 Heated rear window warning lamp
3 Panel illumination

4 Oil pressure gauge
5 Oil pressure warning lamp
6 Coolant temperature gauge
7 Ignition warning lamp

8 Fuel level gauge
9 Tachometer
10 Hazard warning lamps
11 Direction indicator warning

12 Rear foglamp warning lamp
13 Parking lamp warning lamps
14 Fuel reserve warning lamp
15 Headlamp main beam warning lamp

For colour code see key to Fig. 13.14

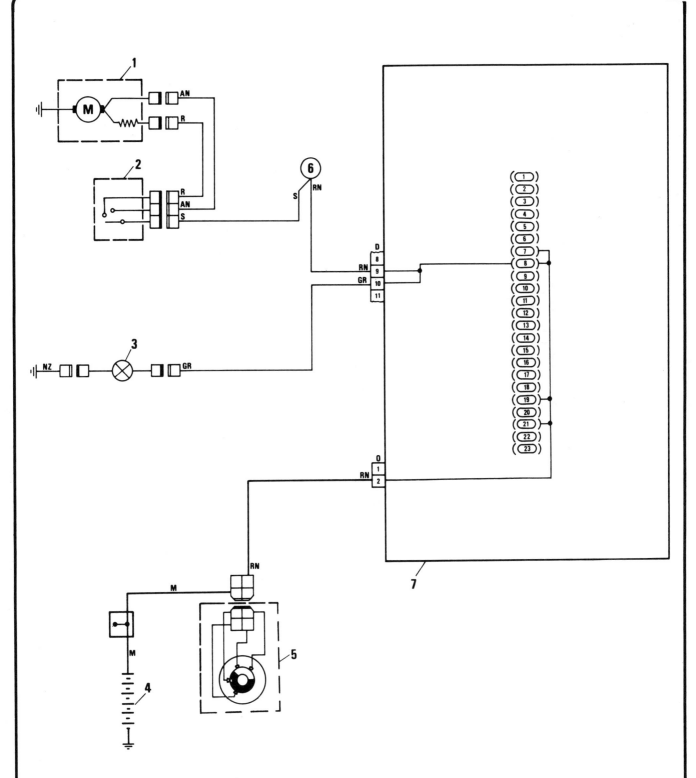

Fig. 13.18 Wiring diagram for 1500 cc models – heater

1	Blower	3	Heater control illumination	5	Ignition coil	7 Fuse block
2	Blower switch	4	Battery	6	Stop-lamp switch	

For colour code see key to Fig. 13.14

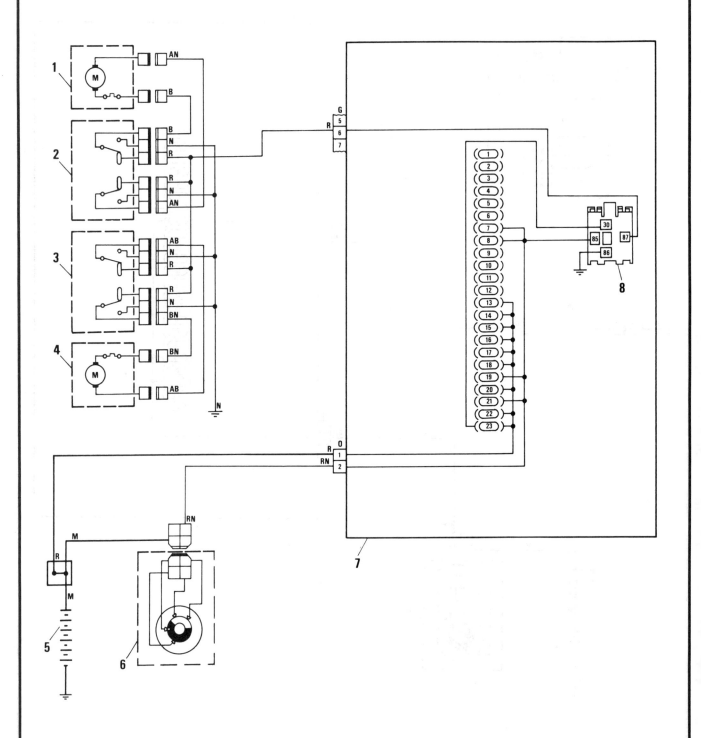

Fig. 13.19 Wiring diagram for 1500 cc models – power-operated windows

1	LH window motor	3	RH control switch	5	Battery	7	Fuse block
2	LH control switch	4	RH window motor	6	Ignition switch	8	Relay

For colour code see key to Fig. 13.14

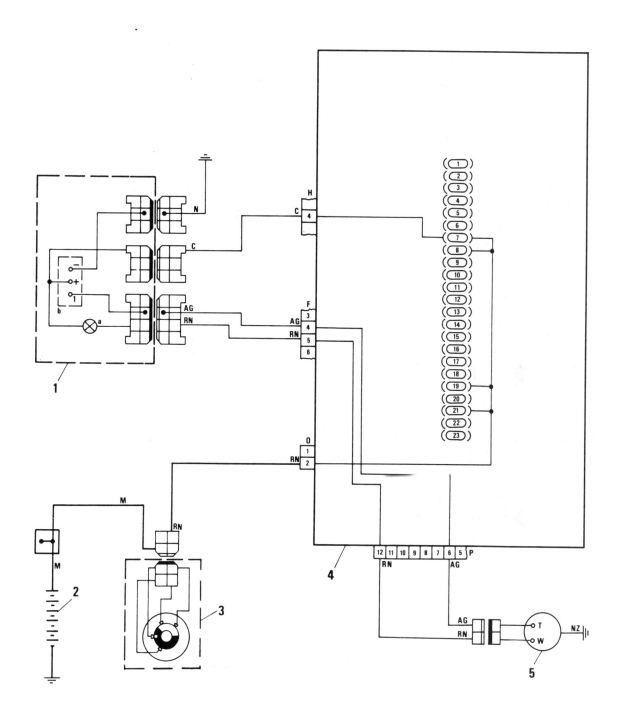

Fig. 13.20 Wiring diagram for 1500 cc models – fuel tank sender unit

1 Instruments
   a   Fuel reserve warning
       lamp
   b   Fuel contents gauge

2 Battery

3 Ignition switch

4 Fuse block
5 Fuel tank sender unit

For colour code see key to Fig. 13.14

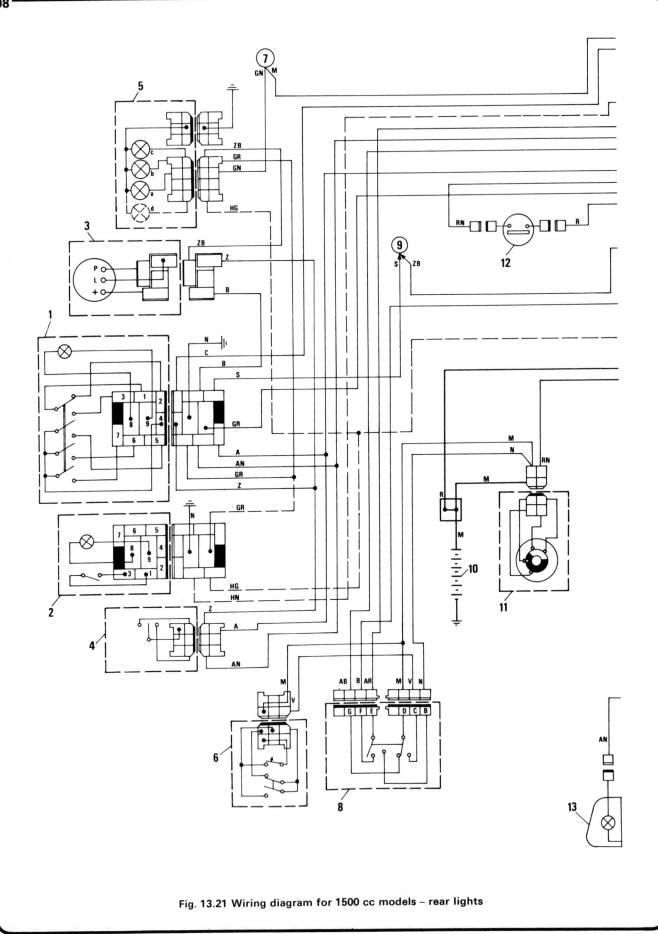

Fig. 13.21 Wiring diagram for 1500 cc models – rear lights

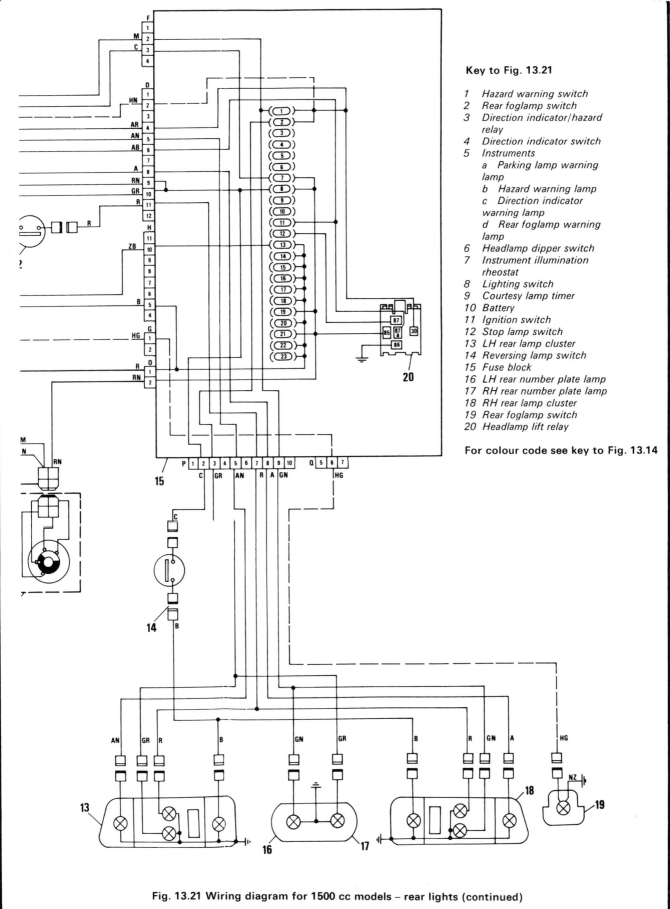

Key to Fig. 13.21

1 Hazard warning switch
2 Rear foglamp switch
3 Direction indicator/hazard relay
4 Direction indicator switch
5 Instruments
  a Parking lamp warning lamp
  b Hazard warning lamp
  c Direction indicator warning lamp
  d Rear foglamp warning lamp
6 Headlamp dipper switch
7 Instrument illumination rheostat
8 Lighting switch
9 Courtesy lamp timer
10 Battery
11 Ignition switch
12 Stop lamp switch
13 LH rear lamp cluster
14 Reversing lamp switch
15 Fuse block
16 LH rear number plate lamp
17 RH rear number plate lamp
18 RH rear lamp cluster
19 Rear foglamp switch
20 Headlamp lift relay

For colour code see key to Fig. 13.14

Fig. 13.21 Wiring diagram for 1500 cc models – rear lights (continued)

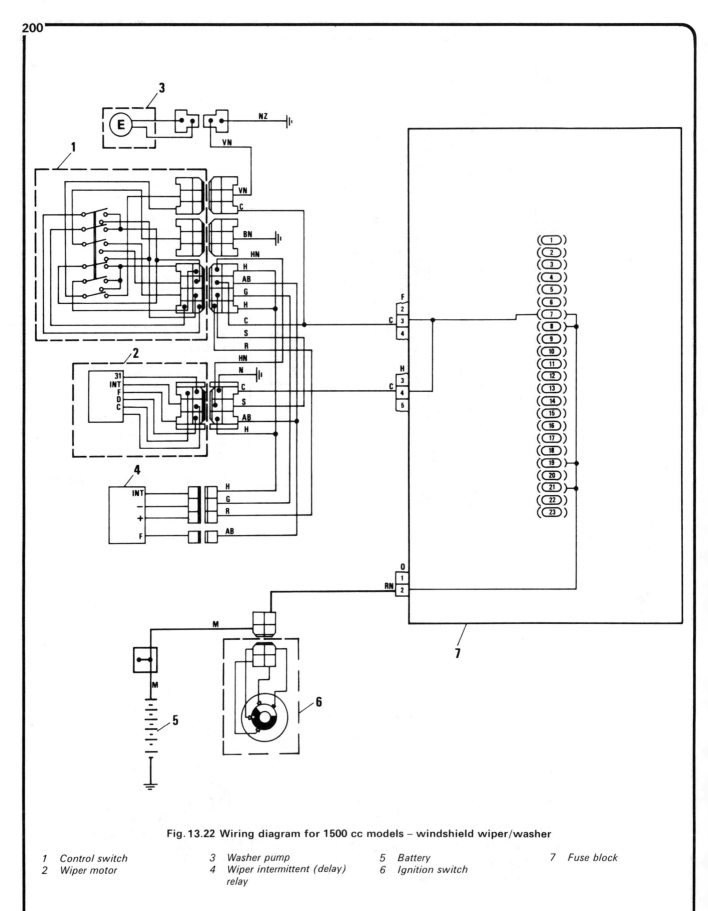

Fig. 13.22 Wiring diagram for 1500 cc models – windshield wiper/washer

1	Control switch	3	Washer pump	5	Battery	7	Fuse block
2	Wiper motor	4	Wiper intermittent (delay) relay	6	Ignition switch		

For colour code see key to Fig. 13.14

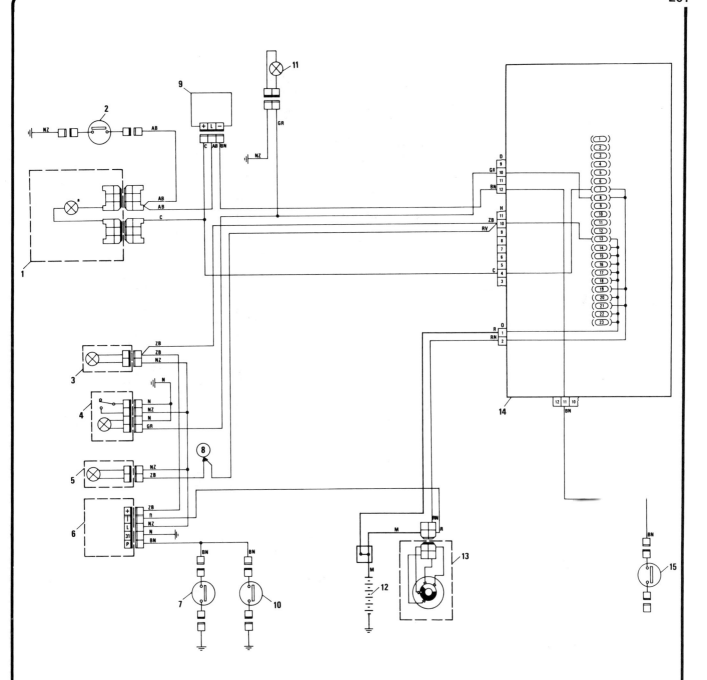

Fig. 13.23 Wiring diagram for 1500 cc models – interior lights and brake warning

1 Instruments	4 Courtesy lamps control	8 Cigar lighter	12 Battery
a Handbrake 'on' and low	switch	9 Handbrake 'on' warning	13 Ignition switch
brake fluid warning lamp	5 RH courtesy lamp	lamp relay	14 Fuse block
2 Low brake fluid level switch	6 Courtesy lamp timer	10 RH courtesy lamp switch	15 Handbrake 'on' warning
3 LH courtesy lamp	7 LH courtesy lamp switch	11 Optical fibre lamp (source)	lamp switch

For colour code see key to Fig. 13.14

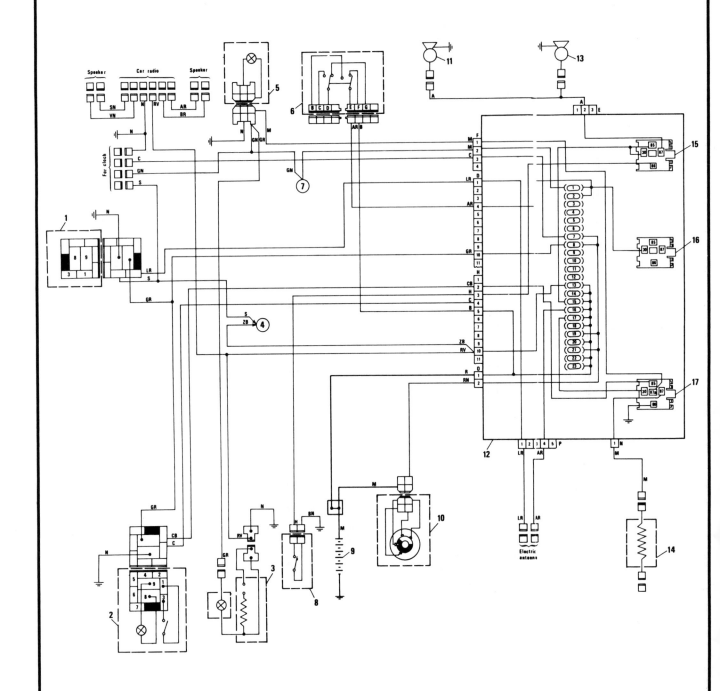

Fig. 13.24 Wiring diagram for 1500 cc models – horns, electric aerial and heated rear window

1 Aerial switch	a Heated rear window	8 Horn switch	13 RH horn
2 Heated rear window switch	warning lamp	9 Battery	14 Heated rear window
3 Cigar lighter	6 Lighting switch	10 Ignition switch	15 Horn relay
4 Courtesy lamp timer	7 Instrument illumination	11 LH horn	16 Headlamp lift relay
5 Instruments	rheostat	12 Fuse unit	17 Heated rear window relay

For colour code see key to Fig. 13.14

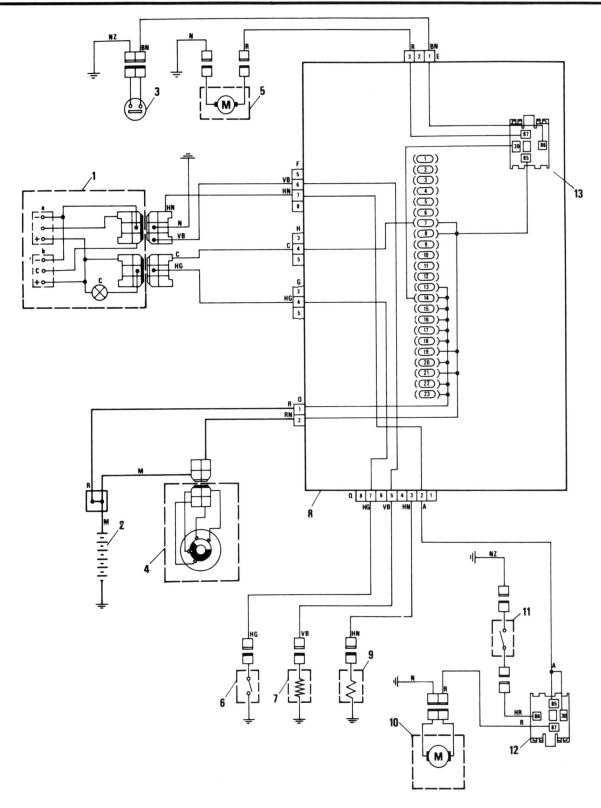

Fig. 13.25 Wiring diagram for 1500 cc models – cooling system

1 Instruments
   a Oil pressure gauge
   b Coolant temperature gauge
   c Oil pressure warning lamp

2 Battery
3 Radiator fan thermostatic switch
4 Ignition coil
5 Radiator fan motor
6 Oil pressure switch

7 Coolant temperature sender unit
8 Fuse block
9 Oil pressure switch
10 Carburettor cooling fan motor

11 Carburettor cooling fan thermostatic switch
12 Carburettor cooling fan relay
13 Radiator cooling fan relay

For colour code see key to Fig. 13.14

Fault diagnosis

Introduction

The vehicle owner who does his or her own maintenance according to the recommended schedules should not have to use this section of the manual very often. Modern component reliability is such that, provided those items subject to wear or deterioration are inspected or renewed at the specified intervals, sudden failure is comparatively rare. Faults do not usually just happen as a result of sudden failure, but develop over a period of time. Major mechanical failures in particular are usually preceded by characteristic symptoms over hundreds or even thousands of miles. Those components which do occasionally fail without warning are often small and easily carried in the vehicle.

With any fault finding, the first step is to decide where to begin investigations. Sometimes this is obvious, but on other occasions a little detective work will be necessary. The owner who makes half a dozen haphazard adjustments or replacements may be successful in curing a fault (or its symptoms), but he will be none the wiser if the fault recurs and he may well have spent more time and money than was necessary. A calm and logical approach will be found to be more satisfactory in the long run. Always take into account any warning signs or abnormalities that may have been noticed in the period preceding the fault – power loss, high or low gauge readings, unusual noises or smells, etc – and remember that failure of components such as fuses or spark plugs may only be pointers to some underlying fault.

The pages which follow here are intended to help in cases of failure to start or breakdown on the road. There is also a Fault Diagnosis Section at the end of each Chapter which should be consulted if the preliminary checks prove unfruitful. Whatever the fault, certain basic principles apply. These are as follows:

Verify the fault. This is simply a matter of being sure that you know what the symptoms are before starting work. This is particularly important if you are investigating a fault for someone else who may not have described it very accurately.

Don't overlook the obvious. For example, if the vehicle won't start, is there petrol in the tank? (Don't take anyone else's word on this particular point, and don't trust the fuel gauge either!) If an electrical fault is indicated, look for loose or broken wires before digging out the test gear.

Cure the disease, not the symptom. Substituting a flat battery with a fully charged one will get you off the hard shoulder, but if the underlying cause is not attended to, the new battery will go the same way. Similarly, changing oil-fouled spark plugs for a new set will get you moving again, but remember that the reason for the fouling (if it wasn't simply an incorrect grade of plug) will have to be established and corrected.

Don't take anything for granted. Particularly, don't forget that a 'new' component may itself be defective (especially if it's been rattling round in the boot for months), and don't leave components out of a fault diagnosis sequence just because they are new or recently fitted. When you do finally diagnose a difficult fault, you'll probably realise that all the evidence was there from the start.

Electrical faults

Electrical faults can be more puzzling than straightforward mechanical failures, but they are no less susceptible to logical analysis if the basic principles of operation are understood. Vehicle electrical wiring exists in extremely unfavourable conditions – heat, vibration and chemical attack – and the first things to look for are loose or corroded connections and broken or chafed wires, especially where the wires pass through holes in the bodywork or are subject to vibration.

All metal-bodied vehicles in current production have one pole of the battery 'earthed', ie connected to the vehicle bodywork, and in nearly all modern vehicles it is the negative (–) terminal. The various electrical components – motors, bulb holders etc – are also connected to earth, either by means of a lead or directly by their mountings. Electric current flows through the component and then back to the battery via the bodywork. If the component mounting is loose or corroded, or if a good path back to the battery is not available, the circuit will be incomplete and malfunction will result. The engine and/or gearbox are also earthed by means of flexible metal straps to the body or subframe; if these straps are loose or missing, starter motor, generator and ignition trouble may result.

Assuming the earth return to be satisfactory, electrical faults will be due either to component malfunction or to defects in the current supply. Individual components are dealt with in Chapter 10. If supply wires are broken or cracked internally this results in an open-circuit, and the easiest way to check for this is to bypass the suspect wire temporarily with a length of wire having a crocodile clip or suitable connector at each end. Alternatively, a 12V test lamp can be used to verify the presence of supply voltage at various points along the wire and the break can be thus isolated.

If a bare portion of a live wire touches the bodywork or other earthed metal part, the electricity will take the low-resistance path thus formed back to the battery: this is known as a short-circuit. Hopefully a short-circuit will blow a fuse, but otherwise it may cause burning of the insulation (and possibly further short-circuits) or even a fire. This is why it is inadvisable to bypass persistently blowing fuses with silver foil or wire.

Spares and tool kit

Most vehicles are supplied only with sufficient tools for wheel changing; the *Maintenance and minor repair* tool kit detailed in *Tools and working facilities,* with the addition of a hammer, is probably sufficient for those repairs that most motorists would consider attempting at the roadside. In addition a few items which can be fitted without too much trouble in the event of a breakdown should be carried. Experience and available space will modify the list below, but the following may save having to call on professional assistance:

Spark plugs, clean and correctly gapped
HT lead and plug cap – long enough to reach the plug furthest from the distributor
Distributor rotor, condenser and contact breaker points
Drivebelt(s) – emergency type may suffice
Spare fuses
Set of principal light bulbs
Tin of radiator sealer and hose bandage
Exhaust bandage
Roll of insulating tape
Length of soft iron wire
Length of electrical flex
Torch or inspection lamp (can double as test lamp)
Battery jump leads

Tow-rope
Ignition water dispersant aerosol
Litre of engine oil
Sealed can of hydraulic fluid
Worm drive clips

If spare fuel is carried, a can designed for the purpose should be used to minimise risks of leakage and collision damage. A first aid kit and a warning triangle, whilst not at present compulsory in the UK, are obviously sensible items to carry in addition to the above.

When touring abroad it may be advisable to carry additional spares which, even if you cannot fit them yourself, could save having to wait while parts are obtained. The items below may be worth considering:

Throttle cables
Cylinder head gasket
Alternator brushes
Tyre valve core

One of the motoring organisations will be able to advise on availability of fuel etc in foreign countries.

Carrying a few spares may save a long walk!

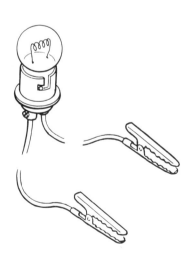

A simple test lamp is useful for tracing electrical faults

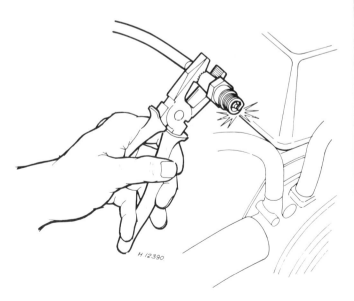

Crank engine and check for spark. Note use of insulated tool to hold plug lead

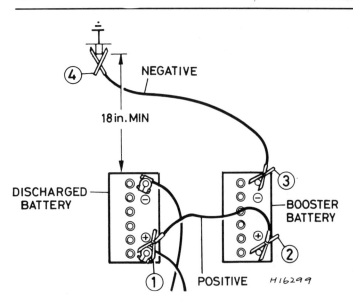

NEGATIVE

18 in. MIN

DISCHARGED BATTERY

BOOSTER BATTERY

POSITIVE H16299

Jump start lead connections for negative earth vehicles - connect leads in order shown

Engine will not start

Engine fails to turn when starter operated
Flat battery (recharge, use jump leads, or push start)
Battery terminals loose or corroded
Battery earth to body defective
Engine earth strap loose or broken
Starter motor (or solenoid) wiring loose or broken
Ignition/starter switch faulty
Major mechanical failure (seizure)
Starter or solenoid internal fault (see Chapter 10)

Starter motor turns engine slowly
Partially discharged battery (recharge, use jump leads, or push start)
Battery terminals loose or corroded
Battery earth to body defective
Engine earth strap loose
Starter motor (or solenoid) wiring loose
Starter motor internal fault (see Chapter 10)

Starter motor spins without turning engine
Flat battery
Starter motor pinion sticking on sleeve
Flywheel gear teeth damaged or worn
Starter motor mounting bolts loose

Engine turns normally but fails to start
Damp or dirty HT leads and distributor cap – crank engine and check for spark, or try a moisture dispersant such as Holts Wet Start
Dirty or incorrectly gapped distributor points (if applicable)
No fuel in tank (check for delivery at carburettor)
Excessive choke (hot engine) or insufficient choke (cold engine)
Fouled or incorrectly gapped spark plugs – remove and regap, or renew as a set
Other ignition system fault (see Chapter 4)
Other fuel system fault (see Chapter 3)
Poor compression
Major mechanical failure (eg camshaft drive)

Engine fires but will not run
Insufficient choke (cold engine)
Air leaks at carburettor or inlet manifold
Fuel starvation (see Chapter 3)
Ballast resistor defective, or other ignition fault (see Chapter 4)

Engine cuts out and will not restart

Engine cuts out suddenly – ignition fault
Loose or disconnected LT wires
Wet HT leads or distributor cap (after traversing water splash)
Coil or condenser failure (check for spark)
Other ignition fault (see Chapter 4)

Engine misfires before cutting out – fuel fault
Fuel tank empty
Fuel pump defective or filter blocked (check for delivery)
Fuel tank filler vent blocked (suction will be evident on releasing cap)
Carburettor needle valve sticking
Carburettor jets blocked (fuel contaminated)
Other fuel system fault (see Chapter 3)

Engine cuts out – other causes
Serious overheating
Major mechanical failure (eg camshaft drive)

Engine overheats

Ignition (no-charge) warning light illuminated
Slack or broken drivebelt – retension or renew (Chapter 10)

Ignition warning light not illuminated
Coolant loss due to internal or external leakage (see Chapter 2)
Thermostat defective
Low oil level
Brakes binding
Radiator clogged externally or internally
Electric cooling fan not operating correctly
Engine waterways clogged
Ignition timing incorrect or automatic advance malfunctioning
Mixture too weak

Note: *Do not add cold water to an overheated engine or damage may result*

Low engine oil pressure

Gauge reads low or warning light illuminated with engine running
Oil level low or incorrect grade
Defective gauge or sender unit
Wire to sender unit earthed
Engine overheating
Oil filter clogged or bypass valve defective
Oil pressure relief valve defective
Oil pick-up strainer clogged
Oil pump worn or mountings loose
Worn main or big-end bearings
Note: *Low oil pressure in a high-mileage engine at tickover is not necessarily a cause for concern. Sudden pressure loss at speed is far more significant. In any event, check the gauge or warning light sender before condemning the engine.*

Engine noises

Pre-ignition (pinking) on acceleration
Incorrect grade of fuel
Ignition timing incorrect
Distributor faulty or worn

Worn or maladjusted carburettor
Excessive carbon build-up in engine

Whistling or wheezing noises
Leaking carburettor or manifold gasket
Blowing head gasket

Tapping or rattling
Incorrect valve clearances
Worn valve gear
Worn timing belt
Broken piston ring (ticking noise)

Knocking or thumping
Unintentional mechanical contact (eg fan blades)
Worn drivebelt
Peripheral component fault (generator, water pump etc)
Worn big-end bearings (regular heavy knocking, perhaps less under load)
Worn main bearings (rumbling and knocking, perhaps worsening under load)
Piston slap (most noticeable when cold)

General repair procedures

Whenever servicing, repair or overhaul work is carried out on the car or its components, it is necessary to observe the following procedures and instructions. This will assist in carrying out the operation efficiently and to a professional standard of workmanship.

Joint mating faces and gaskets

Where a gasket is used between the mating faces of two components, ensure that it is renewed on reassembly, and fit it dry unless otherwise stated in the repair procedure. Make sure that the mating faces are clean and dry with all traces of old gasket removed. When cleaning a joint face, use a tool which is not likely to score or damage the face, and remove any burrs or nicks with an oilstone or fine file.

Make sure that tapped holes are cleaned with a pipe cleaner, and keep them free of jointing compound if this is being used unless specifically instructed otherwise.

Ensure that all orifices, channels or pipes are clear and blow through them, preferably using compressed air.

Oil seals

Whenever an oil seal is removed from its working location, either individually or as part of an assembly, it should be renewed.

The very fine sealing lip of the seal is easily damaged and will not seal if the surface it contacts is not completely clean and free from scratches, nicks or grooves. If the original sealing surface of the component cannot be restored, the component should be renewed.

Protect the lips of the seal from any surface which may damage them in the course of fitting. Use tape or a conical sleeve where possible. Lubricate the seal lips with oil before fitting and, on dual lipped seals, fill the space between the lips with grease.

Unless otherwise stated, oil seals must be fitted with their sealing lips toward the lubricant to be sealed.

Use a tubular drift or block of wood of the appropriate size to install the seal and, if the seal housing is shouldered, drive the seal down to the shoulder. If the seal housing is unshouldered, the seal should be fitted with its face flush with the housing top face.

Screw threads and fastenings

Always ensure that a blind tapped hole is completely free from oil, grease, water or other fluid before installing the bolt or stud. Failure to do this could cause the housing to crack due to the hydraulic action of the bolt or stud as it is screwed in.

When tightening a castellated nut to accept a split pin, tighten the nut to the specified torque, where applicable, and then tighten further to the next split pin hole. Never slacken the nut to align a split pin hole unless stated in the repair procedure.

When checking or retightening a nut or bolt to a specified torque setting, slacken the nut or bolt by a quarter of a turn, and then retighten to the specified setting.

Locknuts, locktabs and washers

Any fastening which will rotate against a component or housing in the course of tightening should always have a washer between it and the relevant component or housing.

Spring or split washers should always be renewed when they are used to lock a critical component such as a big-end bearing retaining nut or bolt.

Locktabs which are folded over to retain a nut or bolt should always be renewed.

Self-locking nuts can be reused in non-critical areas, providing resistance can be felt when the locking portion passes over the bolt or stud thread.

Split pins must always be replaced with new ones of the correct size for the hole.

Special tools

Some repair procedures in this manual entail the use of special tools such as a press, two or three-legged pullers, spring compressors etc. Wherever possible, suitable readily available alternatives to the manufacturer's special tools are described, and are shown in use. In some instances, where no alternative is possible, it has been necessary to resort to the use of a manufacturer's tool and this has been done for reasons of safety as well as the efficient completion of the repair operation. Unless you are highly skilled and have a thorough understanding of the procedure described, never attempt to bypass the use of any special tool when the procedure described specifies its use. Not only is there a very great risk of personal injury, but expensive damage could be caused to the components involved.

Conversion factors

Length (distance)
Inches (in)	X	25.4	= Millimetres (mm)	X	0.0394	= Inches (in)
Feet (ft)	X	0.305	= Metres (m)	X	3.281	= Feet (ft)
Miles	X	1.609	= Kilometres (km)	X	0.621	= Miles

Volume (capacity)
Cubic inches (cu in; in³)	X	16.387	= Cubic centimetres (cc; cm³)	X	0.061	= Cubic inches (cu in; in³)
Imperial pints (Imp pt)	X	0.568	= Litres (l)	X	1.76	= Imperial pints (Imp pt)
Imperial quarts (Imp qt)	X	1.137	= Litres (l)	X	0.88	= Imperial quarts (Imp qt)
Imperial quarts (Imp qt)	X	1.201	= US quarts (US qt)	X	0.833	= Imperial quarts (Imp qt)
US quarts (US qt)	X	0.946	= Litres (l)	X	1.057	= US quarts (US qt)
Imperial gallons (Imp gal)	X	4.546	= Litres (l)	X	0.22	= Imperial gallons (Imp gal)
Imperial gallons (Imp gal)	X	1.201	= US gallons (US gal)	X	0.833	= Imperial gallons (Imp gal)
US gallons (US gal)	X	3.785	= Litres (l)	X	0.264	= US gallons (US gal)

Mass (weight)
Ounces (oz)	X	28.35	= Grams (g)	X	0.035	= Ounces (oz)
Pounds (lb)	X	0.454	= Kilograms (kg)	X	2.205	= Pounds (lb)

Force
Ounces-force (ozf; oz)	X	0.278	= Newtons (N)	X	3.6	= Ounces-force (ozf; oz)
Pounds-force (lbf; lb)	X	4.448	= Newtons (N)	X	0.225	= Pounds-force (lbf; lb)
Newtons (N)	X	0.1	= Kilograms-force (kgf; kg)	X	9.81	= Newtons (N)

Pressure
Pounds-force per square inch (psi; lbf/in²; lb/in²)	X	0.070	= Kilograms-force per square centimetre (kgf/cm²; kg/cm²)	X	14.223	= Pounds-force per square inch (psi; lbf/in²; lb/in²)
Pounds-force per square inch (psi; lbf/in²; lb/in²)	X	0.068	= Atmospheres (atm)	X	14.696	= Pounds-force per square inch (psi; lbf/in²; lb/in²)
Pounds-force per square inch (psi; lbf/in²; lb/in²)	X	0.069	= Bars	X	14.5	= Pounds-force per square inch (psi; lbf/in²; lb/in²)
Pounds-force per square inch (psi; lbf/in²; lb/in²)	X	6.895	= Kilopascals (kPa)	X	0.145	= Pounds-force per square inch (psi; lbf/in²; lb/in²)
Kilopascals (kPa)	X	0.01	= Kilograms-force per square centimetre (kgf/cm²; kg/cm²)	X	98.1	= Kilopascals (kPa)
Millibar (mbar)	X	100	= Pascals (Pa)	X	0.01	= Millibar (mbar)
Millibar (mbar)	X	0.0145	= Pounds-force per square inch (psi; lbf/in²; lb/in²)	X	68.947	= Millibar (mbar)
Millibar (mbar)	X	0.75	= Millimetres of mercury (mmHg)	X	1.333	= Millibar (mbar)
Millibar (mbar)	X	0.401	= Inches of water (inH₂O)	X	2.491	= Millibar (mbar)
Millimetres of mercury (mmHg)	X	0.535	= Inches of water (inH₂O)	X	1.868	= Millimetres of mercury (mmHg)
Inches of water (inH₂O)	X	0.036	= Pounds-force per square inch (psi; lbf/in²; lb/in²)	X	27.68	= Inches of water (inH₂O)

Torque (moment of force)
Pounds-force inches (lbf in; lb in)	X	1.152	= Kilograms-force centimetre (kgf cm; kg cm)	X	0.868	= Pounds-force inches (lbf in; lb in)
Pounds-force inches (lbf in; lb in)	X	0.113	= Newton metres (Nm)	X	8.85	= Pounds-force inches (lbf in; lb in)
Pounds-force inches (lbf in; lb in)	X	0.083	= Pounds-force feet (lbf ft; lb ft)	X	12	= Pounds-force inches (lbf in; lb in)
Pounds-force feet (lbf ft; lb ft)	X	0.138	= Kilograms-force metres (kgf m; kg m)	X	7.233	= Pounds-force feet (lbf ft; lb ft)
Pounds-force feet (lbf ft; lb ft)	X	1.356	= Newton metres (Nm)	X	0.738	= Pounds-force feet (lbf ft; lb ft)
Newton metres (Nm)	X	0.102	= Kilograms-force metres (kgf m; kg m)	X	9.804	= Newton metres (Nm)

Power
Horsepower (hp)	X	745.7	= Watts (W)	X	0.0013	= Horsepower (hp)

Velocity (speed)
Miles per hour (miles/hr; mph)	X	1.609	= Kilometres per hour (km/hr; kph)	X	0.621	= Miles per hour (miles/hr; mph)

Fuel consumption*
Miles per gallon, Imperial (mpg)	X	0.354	= Kilometres per litre (km/l)	X	2.825	= Miles per gallon, Imperial (mpg)
Miles per gallon, US (mpg)	X	0.425	= Kilometres per litre (km/l)	X	2.352	= Miles per gallon, US (mpg)

Temperature

Degrees Fahrenheit = (°C x 1.8) + 32

Degrees Celsius (Degrees Centigrade; °C) = (°F - 32) x 0.56

*It is common practice to convert from miles per gallon (mpg) to litres/100 kilometres (l/100km), where mpg (Imperial) x l/100 km = 282 and mpg (US) x l/100 km = 235

Safety first!

Professional motor mechanics are trained in safe working procedures. However enthusiastic you may be about getting on with the job in hand, do take the time to ensure that your safety is not put at risk. A moment's lack of attention can result in an accident, as can failure to observe certain elementary precautions.

There will always be new ways of having accidents, and the following points do not pretend to be a comprehensive list of all dangers; they are intended rather to make you aware of the risks and to encourage a safety-conscious approach to all work you carry out on your vehicle.

Essential DOs and DON'Ts

DON'T rely on a single jack when working underneath the vehicle. Always use reliable additional means of support, such as axle stands, securely placed under a part of the vehicle that you know will not give way.

DON'T attempt to loosen or tighten high-torque nuts (e.g. wheel hub nuts) while the vehicle is on a jack; it may be pulled off.

DON'T start the engine without first ascertaining that the transmission is in neutral (or 'Park' where applicable) and the parking brake applied.

DON'T suddenly remove the filler cap from a hot cooling system – cover it with a cloth and release the pressure gradually first, or you may get scalded by escaping coolant.

DON'T attempt to drain oil until you are sure it has cooled sufficiently to avoid scalding you.

DON'T grasp any part of the engine, exhaust or catalytic converter without first ascertaining that it is sufficiently cool to avoid burning you.

DON'T allow brake fluid or antifreeze to contact vehicle paintwork.

DON'T syphon toxic liquids such as fuel, brake fluid or antifreeze by mouth, or allow them to remain on your skin.

DON'T inhale dust – it may be injurious to health (see *Asbestos* below).

DON'T allow any spilt oil or grease to remain on the floor – wipe it up straight away, before someone slips on it.

DON'T use ill-fitting spanners or other tools which may slip and cause injury.

DON'T attempt to lift a heavy component which may be beyond your capability – get assistance.

DON'T rush to finish a job, or take unverified short cuts.

DON'T allow children or animals in or around an unattended vehicle.

DO wear eye protection when using power tools such as drill, sander, bench grinder etc, and when working under the vehicle.

DO use a barrier cream on your hands prior to undertaking dirty jobs – it will protect your skin from infection as well as making the dirt easier to remove afterwards; but make sure your hands aren't left slippery. Note that long-term contact with used engine oil can be a health hazard.

DO keep loose clothing (cuffs, tie etc) and long hair well out of the way of moving mechanical parts.

DO remove rings, wristwatch etc, before working on the vehicle – especially the electrical system.

DO ensure that any lifting tackle used has a safe working load rating adequate for the job.

DO keep your work area tidy – it is only too easy to fall over articles left lying around.

DO get someone to check periodically that all is well, when working alone on the vehicle.

DO carry out work in a logical sequence and check that everything is correctly assembled and tightened afterwards.

DO remember that your vehicle's safety affects that of yourself and others. If in doubt on any point, get specialist advice.

IF, in spite of following these precautions, you are unfortunate enough to injure yourself, seek medical attention as soon as possible.

Asbestos

Certain friction, insulating, sealing, and other products – such as brake linings, brake bands, clutch linings, torque converters, gaskets, etc – contain asbestos. *Extreme care must be taken to avoid inhalation of dust from such products since it is hazardous to health.* If in doubt, assume that they *do* contain asbestos.

Fire

Remember at all times that petrol (gasoline) is highly flammable. Never smoke, or have any kind of naked flame around, when working on the vehicle. But the risk does not end there – a spark caused by an electrical short-circuit, by two metal surfaces contacting each other, by careless use of tools, or even by static electricity built up in your body under certain conditions, can ignite petrol vapour, which in a confined space is highly explosive.

Always disconnect the battery earth (ground) terminal before working on any part of the fuel or electrical system, and never risk spilling fuel on to a hot engine or exhaust.

It is recommended that a fire extinguisher of a type suitable for fuel and electrical fires is kept handy in the garage or workplace at all times. Never try to extinguish a fuel or electrical fire with water.

Note: *Any reference to a 'torch' appearing in this manual should always be taken to mean a hand-held battery-operated electric lamp or flashlight. It does NOT mean a welding/gas torch or blowlamp.*

Fumes

Certain fumes are highly toxic and can quickly cause unconsciousness and even death if inhaled to any extent. Petrol (gasoline) vapour comes into this category, as do the vapours from certain solvents such as trichloroethylene. Any draining or pouring of such volatile fluids should be done in a well ventilated area.

When using cleaning fluids and solvents, read the instructions carefully. Never use materials from unmarked containers – they may give off poisonous vapours.

Never run the engine of a motor vehicle in an enclosed space such as a garage. Exhaust fumes contain carbon monoxide which is extremely poisonous; if you need to run the engine, always do so in the open air or at least have the rear of the vehicle outside the workplace.

If you are fortunate enough to have the use of an inspection pit, never drain or pour petrol, and never run the engine, while the vehicle is standing over it; the fumes, being heavier than air, will concentrate in the pit with possibly lethal results.

The battery

Never cause a spark, or allow a naked light, near the vehicle's battery. It will normally be giving off a certain amount of hydrogen gas, which is highly explosive.

Always disconnect the battery earth (ground) terminal before working on the fuel or electrical systems.

If possible, loosen the filler plugs or cover when charging the battery from an external source. Do not charge at an excessive rate or the battery may burst.

Take care when topping up and when carrying the battery. The acid electrolyte, even when diluted, is very corrosive and should not be allowed to contact the eyes or skin.

If you ever need to prepare electrolyte yourself, always add the acid slowly to the water, and never the other way round. Protect against splashes by wearing rubber gloves and goggles.

When jump starting a car using a booster battery, for negative earth (ground) vehicles, connect the jump leads in the following sequence: First connect one jump lead between the positive (+) terminals of the two batteries. Then connect the other jump lead first to the negative (–) terminal of the booster battery, and then to a good earthing (ground) point on the vehicle to be started, at least 18 in (45 cm) from the battery if possible. Ensure that hands and jump leads are clear of any moving parts, and that the two vehicles do not touch. Disconnect the leads in the reverse order.

Mains electricity and electrical equipment

When using an electric power tool, inspection light etc, always ensure that the appliance is correctly connected to its plug and that, where necessary, it is properly earthed (grounded). Do not use such appliances in damp conditions and, again, beware of creating a spark or applying excessive heat in the vicinity of fuel or fuel vapour. Also ensure that the appliances meet the relevant national safety standards.

Ignition HT voltage

A severe electric shock can result from touching certain parts of the ignition system, such as the HT leads, when the engine is running or being cranked, particularly if components are damp or the insulation is defective. Where an electronic ignition system is fitted, the HT voltage is much higher and could prove fatal.

Index